Ultimate Devotion

Approaches to Anthropological Archaeology

Series Editor: Thomas E. Levy, University of California, San Diego

Editorial Board:
Guillermo Algaze, University of California, San Diego
Geoffrey E. Braswell, University of California, San Diego
Paul S. Goldstein, University of California, San Diego
Joyce Marcus, University of Michigan

This series recognizes the fundamental role that anthropology now plays in archaeology and also integrates the strengths of various research paradigms that characterize archaeology on the world scene today. Some of these different approaches include 'New' or 'Processual' archaeology, 'Post-Processual,' evolutionist, cognitive, symbolic, Marxist, and historical archaeologies. Anthropological archaeology accomplishes its goals by taking into account the cultural and, when possible, historical context of the material remains being studied. This involves the development of models concerning the formative role of cognition, symbolism, and ideology in human societies to explain the more material and economic dimensions of human culture that are the natural purview of archaeological data. It also involves an understanding of the cultural ecology of the societies being studied, and of the limitations and opportunities that the environment (both natural and cultural) imposes on the evolution or devolution of human societies. Based on the assumption that cultures never develop in isolation, anthropological archaeology takes a regional approach to tackling fundamental issues concerning past cultural evolution anywhere in the world.

Published:

Archaeology, Anthropology and Cult: The Sanctuary at Gilat, Israel
Edited by Thomas E. Levy

Connectivity in Antiquity: Globalization as a Long Term Historical Process
Edited by Øystein LaBianca and Sandra Arnold Scham

Israel's Ethnogenesis: Settlement, Interaction, Expansion and Resistance
Avraham Faust

Axe Age: Acheulian Tool-making from Quarry to Discard
Edited by Naama Goren-Inbar and Gonen Sharon

New Approaches to Old Stones: Recent Studies of Ground Stone Artifacts
Edited by Yorke M. Rowan and Jennie R. Ebeling

Prehistoric Societies on the Northern Frontiers of China:
Archaeological Perspectives on Identity Formation and Economic Change during the First Millennium BCE
Gideon Shelach

Dawn of the Metal Age: Technology and Society during the Levantine Chalcolithic
Jonathan M. Golden

Metal, Nomads and Culture Contact: The Middle East and North Africa
Nils Anfinset

Animal Husbandry in Ancient Israel – A Zoo-archaeological Perspective:
Herd Management, Economic Strategies and Animal Exploitation
Aharon Sassoon

Forthcoming:

Structured Worlds: The Archaeology of Hunter-Gatherer Thought and Action
Edited by Aubrey Cannon

Desert Chiefdom: Dimensions of Subterranean Settlement and Society in Israel's Negev Desert (c. 4500 – 3600 BC) Based on New Data from Shiqmim
Edited by Thomas E. Levy, Yorke M. Rowan and Margie M. Burton

Early Bronze Age Goods Exchange in the Southern Levant: A Marxist Perspective
Ianir Milevski

Agency and Identity in the Ancient Near East: New Paths Forward
Edited by Sharon R. Steadman and Jennifer C. Ross

The Technology of Maya Civilization: Political Economy and Beyond in Lithic Studies
Edited by Zachary X. Hruby, Geoffrey E. Braswell and Oswaldo Chinchilla Mazariegos

Ultimate Devotion

The Historical Impact and Archaeological Expression of Intense Religious Movements

By Yoav Arbel

LONDON • OAKVILLE

Published by Equinox Publishing Ltd.

UK: Unit 6, The Village, 101 Amies St., London, SW11 2JW

USA: DBBC, 28 Main Street, Oakville, CT 06779

www.equinoxpub.com

First published 2009

© Yoav Arbel 2009

All rights reserved. No part of this publication may be reproduced or transmitted in any form or by any means, electronic or mechanical, including photocopying, recording or any information storage or retrieval system, without prior permission in writing from the publishers.

British Library Cataloguing-in-Publication Data

A catalogue record for this book is available from the British Library

ISBN 978 1 84553 226 0

BL
53.5
.A73
2009

Library of Congress Cataloging-in-Publication Data

Arbel, Yoav.
 Ultimate devotion : the historical impact and archaeological expression of intense religious movements / Yoav Arbel.
     p. cm. -- (Approaches to anthropological archaeology)
 Includes bibliographical references and index.
 ISBN 978-1-84553-226-0 (hb)
 1. Religious fanaticism--Political aspects--History. I. Title. BL53.5.A73 2009
  200.9--dc22
                           2008023966

Typeset by the David Brown Book Company, Oakville, CT, USA
www.dbbconline.com
Printed and bound in Great Britain by CPI Antony Rowe, Chippenham, Wiltshire

To my parents.

"It is a strange dialogue, where God,
with His infinite knowledge,
is being alerted by a mortal…"

Contents

Acknowledgments — ix
Abbreviations — x

Part I

1. Introduction – A Theory of Religious Intensification — 1
2. God and Country — 7
3. One God, One Way — 22
4. A Quest for Immediate Salvation — 41
5. Messianic Hopes Shattered — 52

Part II

6. Introduction – History, Archaeology and Religious Ideology — 63
7. Uprising in Judea — 70
8. Narrative of Crisis — 83
9. The Sacred Contract — 105
10. Unearthing Religious Intensity — 123
11. Conclusions – Between Rome and Jericho — 141

Notes — 151
References — 167
Index — 201

Acknowledgments

I wish to express here my gratitude to all who have been of assistance during the research for this book, while stressing that the responsibility for the ideas and opinions in the final text – and certainly for any imperfections – is entirely mine.
While working on the doctoral thesis upon which this book is based, Thomas Levy of the Department of Anthropology at the University of California, San Diego (UCSD), and David Goodblatt of the Judaic Studies Department at UCSD, co-chairs of my doctoral committee, offered indispensable guidance, information, and constructive criticism. I also want to thank other faculty members of both departments for their support and encouragement. I am grateful to the Gumpel Family Graduate Student Fellowship and other awards and grants from the Anthropology and Judaic Studies departments. Without them, time that was dedicated to research would have been spent on survival.
Several individuals kindly agreed to share with me the results of their work, practical data, photographs from their collections, or just original ideas. Danny Syon, senior archaeologist with the Israel Antiquities Authority and editor of the final report of the Gamla Excavations generously contributed invaluable expertise and photographed materials whenever asked – and he was asked a lot. Yehiel Zelinger (Israel Antiquities Authority), Hillel Geva (Israel Exploration Society), and Orit Tsuf (Haifa University) kindly permitted the use of materials from archaeological publications they are working on. Special thanks to Adolfo Muniz and Peter Kragh, two gentlemen whose skills with computers are only matched by their endurance in working with the likes of me, whose talents lay elsewhere. Other helpful and cooperative people were Donald Ariel, Gideon Avni, Peter Gendelman, Rachel Bar-Nathan, Natalya Katsnelson, and Hagit Torgë (all of the Israel Antiquities Authority), Joel Robbins, Guillermo Algaze, and the late David Noel Freedman (UCSD), Yoram Tsafrir, Gideon Foerster, and Benny Arubas (The Hebrew University of Jerusalem), Mordechai Aviam (University of Rochester), Malka Hershkowitz (Hebrew Union College), Anna De Vincenz (Albright Institute), Christopher Lightfoot (The Metropolitan Museum), Laura Mazow (East Carolina University), Mucahide Koçak (Fund for the City of New York), and David Parsons (The International Christian Embassy in Jerusalem).
In any long term project there are people whose contribution is difficult to define, but was certainly there. Oded Ron, Ute Bartelt, Nimrod Shinar, Angelica Marcello, Celia de Jong, Jon Bialecki, Kate Knorr, Stacie Wilson, Sarah Scott, and Jenny Dillon all fall into this category, as does Sonia Zawadski, who was always available for advice, encouragement and, well, sheer faith. I would finally like to thank Janet Joyce and Valerie Hall of Equinox Publishing, Ltd. in London for their professional assistance and just as much for their patience, and Susanne Wilhelm of the David Brown Book Company in Oakville, CT for her efforts in editing the manuscript.
Three scholars who have significantly influenced my work are no longer with us. Yizhar Hirschfeld of the Hebrew University belonged to the narrow group of professional archaeologists who still conduct scientific archaeological exploration with the spirit and enthusiasm of the founders of the discipline. Donald Tuzin of UCSD, an accomplished anthropologist and field researcher, was a professional, meticulous, yet always supportive academic advisor. Shmaryahu Gutman initiated and directed the Gamla Excavations Project, his last venture in a life dedicated to outstanding missions. Thank you all. I do appreciate it.

Yoav Arbel, Tel Aviv, January 2008

The publisher and author are grateful to the Judaic Studies Program of the University of California, San Diego, for a contribution of $2000 towards the editing of this book.

Abbreviations

AASOR	Annual of the American Schools of Oriental Research
AA	American Anthropologist
ADAJ	Annual of the Department of Antiquities of Jordan
BA	Biblical Archaeologist
BAR	Biblical Archaeology Review
BASOR	Bulletin of the American Schools of Oriental Research
CA	Current Anthropology
EI	Eretz Israel
ESI	Excavations and Surveys in Israel
HA	Hadashot Arkheologiyot
IEJ	Israel Exploration Journal
INJ	Israel Numismatic Journal
JAA	Journal of Anthropological Archaeology
JAS	Journal of Archaeological Science
JJS	Journal of Jewish Studies
JRA	Journal of Roman Archaeology
JSJ	Journal for the Study of Judaism
JSQ	Jewish Studies Quarterly
JRS	Journal of Roman Studies
LA	Liber Annuus
NEAEHL	New Encyclopedia of Archaeological Excavations in the Holy Land
PEQ	Palestine Exploration Quarterly
QDAP	Quarterly of the Department of Antiquities in Palestine
RB	Revue Biblique
SCI	Scripta Classica Israelica

1 Part I — Introduction
A Theory of Religious Intensification

> The ranks entered [Jerusalem] magnificently at the noonday hour on Friday, the day of the week when Christ redeemed the whole world on the cross. With trumpets sounding and with everything in an uproar, exclaiming: "Help God!" they vigorously pushed into the city, and straightaway raised the banner on top of the wall. All the heathen, completely terrified, changed their boldness to swift flight through the narrow streets of the quarters.
>
> (Fulcher of Chartres, *Chronicle of the First Crusade*)[1]

The landscape of history is marked with the unmistakable imprints of ideology and religion. Key historical events across the globe can be credited to or blamed on the influence of religious agents, who show no signs of relinquishing their power in the foreseen future. In an era of constant scientific innovation, relentless global capitalism, and instantaneous coverage by an extensive and cynical media, much of humanity still esteems and fears supernatural forces and dedicates time, efforts, and funds to placate them. Secular ideologies based on science, social justice, or nationalism emerge and later fossilize or dissipate. Religion, like the proverbial Phoenix, even where thrown into the fires of rational thought and secular zealotry, always rises from its ashes. Its versatility and adaptability deserve much of the acclaim for its admirable survival. Religion not only *has* something for everyone – it *is* something for everyone. It balances spiritual concerns and material needs, provides moral guidance, alleviates suffering and avenges grievances. Its agents fill complex and sometimes contradictory capacities. They are supposed to anticipate the future but also be able to change it. They are urged by some to preach toleration of other faiths, by others to stress theological exclusiveness. They are called to be exemplary figures, exalted from common human beings, yet are reminded that they are mortal and therefore imperfect. It is expected of them to heal where medicine fails, to relieve where psychology can not, to see where science is blind, to encourage where hope has been lost. They are, after all, the ambassadors of divinity.

Religion has prevailed despite only partially meeting these impossibly high demands. For better or worse, it remains everywhere, actively and passively. High Priests and kings may no longer sacrifice in front of thousands of reverend pilgrims packed into ritual compounds, but even in modern, democratic, and technologically-based nations the officials of religion still earn public attention, enjoy (or suffer) mass media exposure, and continue to sway the careers of leaders and the stability of political establishments. How can this be explained? Rational answers may sometimes be found in irrational psychology. Human beings need hope at all times, and religion is the ultimate supplier of hope. Science accepts that there are limits beyond which hope is futile. Religion needs and can not acknowledge limits of hope, because nothing is beyond the capacity of its all-powerful divinities. Its approach is therefore more optimistic than that of science, and it offers a stronger sense of control over life than science ever could. The agents of religion have always been aware of this, and, whether out of genuine devotion or personal ambitions, or both, most have never hesitated to exploit and manipulate this advantage.

Manipulating Faith

Most scholars agree that religious ideologies have impacted on political decision-making and played roles in historical developments (Miller and Tilley 1984; Conrad and Demarest 1984; Bintliff 1991; Bauer 1996; Earle 1997). Yet, their relative influence in specific events and broader processes of the past is not simple to assess. One of the obstructions is the overrepresentation of religion in surviving literary and material evidence. Many pre-modern rulers and governments worldwide have claimed some form of divine sponsorship of their authority. Some continue to do so at present, as attested by religious contents in modern national symbols. Hence the motto "In God We Trust," famously printed on American currency, and the dictum "God is Great" (الله اكبر) at the center of the flag of Iraq – a somewhat ironical resemblance, given the recent history between the two countries.

In pre-modern states the presumed association with divinity was more intimate. It often included the deification of rulers or the belief that they had been chosen by the gods and could personally interact with them. A common trait can be traced in traditions as distant as the Sumerian belief that "kingships descended from Heaven" (Sandars 1972: 14), the heavenly emperor of Japan (Benedict 1989: 32), the semi-divine Shilluk kings in Sudan (Evans-Pritchard 1948: 202), the proclaiming of the god Ptah as the First Principle of the Pharaonic capital of Memphis (Pritchard 1958: 1), and the depictions of Roman-Byzantine rulers receiving divine commission for their construction projects (Sutherland 1974: figs. 237, 360–61; Breglia 1968: 59–60, 80–81). These are but a few examples of many. The close affiliation between rulers and gods is widely represented in the literature, art, and architecture of ancient societies. How can we then see through this mass of biased material and better evaluate the proportional contribution of religion and of non-religious factors to historical developments? A first step should be an examination of the complex and multi-layered relationship between politics and religion in historical scenarios.

This relationship can be vague and passive on occasion. In his history of the Seychelles Islands, William McAteer (1991: 257) tells of a nineteenth-century British visitor who was not impressed by the quality of religious observance among the approximately 300 mostly French settlers: "[they] profess the Roman Catholic religion," the man complained, "but their conformity to this or any other faith is very lax." Catholic ritual is intricate, and in the absence of priests and schools the locals naturally drifted away from dogmatic worship. This spiritual elasticity mayhave been inconsistent with British Victorian education, but it was what could be expected in a remote colony that in most civil affairs was left to its own devices (McAteer 1991: 257–58). The Seychelles Islands were simply too distant, and French interests there too narrow, for Paris to invest in religious edification.

Yet, the broader historical view tells a different story. Organized religion has been one of the more common means of control used by governments. Rulers in nearly all state-level societies manipulated faith, propagated their divine sponsorship, and exploited it for the promotion of political programs. Nonetheless, the extent of utilization, the degree of its success, and the actual impact of this political-religious collaboration remain debatable. The subject is of a width, depth, and complexity that expose holistic approaches to a high risk of superficiality. Investigation would be more effective if it concentrated on narrower and more distinct aspects, the roles of which are more apparent and simpler to distill. Intense religious movements qualify as such.

Intensity and Extremism

Documents, chronicles, testimonies, popular traditions, and even myths tell of relatively brief but significant episodes, when alternative religious movements broke away from religious institutions and dogma and swept through entire societies. History owes some of its more dramatic affairs to these movements. Many of them espoused innovative theologies that dictated extreme modes of behavior, some of which were diametrically opposed to the standard personal and communal conduct of the outside world. A new intensity of faith, which the movements both demand and engineer, motivates disciples to follow these extreme theologies.

The terms "intense" and "extreme" are close but not symmetrical. Religious extremism carries a negative connotation that religious intensity does not necessarily deserve. The Random House Dictionary of the English Language (1987) defines intensity as "great energy, strength, concentration, vehemence, as of activity, thought or feeling...a high degree of emotional excitement." The faith of devout believers who regularly visit houses of worship and of monastic communities who commit their lives to their divinities is certainly intense, but most of them lead a subtle and peaceful existence, letting others pursue their own choices undisturbed. These people should not be branded as extremists, even if some radical atheists say they must, which serves to show that one does not need a god to be a zealot. Extreme religious movements are those that lure believers into irregularly aggressive, often violent, and sometimes lethal modes of action, inspired by the steadfast conviction that they, and they alone, understand God's will and have the sufficient faith and determination to execute it on earth.

Irony, it seems, is a frequent theme in the story of intense religious movements. Time and again we meet governments that, in recognition of the service religion can render, work blindly and irresponsibly to increase its influence on their subjects, until at some point regulation fails. Had they bothered to learn from the experience of others, they would have realized that the type of ideological storm they were helping to fan could turn against them at some stage and batter them with a destructive force they had never anticipated.

A "Phantom Alliance"

Communal suffering due to political failures or environmental afflictions on the one hand, and individual distress owed to personal circumstances and psychological stress on the other, provide the mortar that holds together the ideological bricks of the intense religious structure. When effectively managed, the construction work is fast and the structure is swiftly elevated. The problem with these "heaven-scrapers" is that they tend to exceed their engineering blueprints, and size comes at the expense of solidness. The ideological structures end up being as fragile as they are impressive, and tremors that established religion could easily withstand might bring down those faith anomalies. Until that happens, disciples live blissfully in the reassurance of their newly-established alliance with God. In return for their unlimited, unconditional, and unrestrained devotion, their problems will be over and their utmost desires will be readily available within a perfect society of which they only could have dreamed earlier in life. Sooner or later these circumstances are proven to be phantom alliances, but while they are believed, their influence can be tremendous.

Idyllic realities, even phantom ones, require some physical framework within which they can be manifested. Intense religious movements are not democracies. Disciples are promised tangible and immediate rewards the religious establishment never could offer, but to reach that end they must obey their leaders rather blindly and follow instructions with neither questions nor doubts. They are expected to live up to the solemn vow of the Israelites, as they stood by Mount Sinai: "All that the Lord has spoken we will do, and we will be obedient" (Exodus 24:7). The exact Hebrew text reads even stronger: "We shall do and we shall hear" (נעשה ונשמע), suggesting that following God's decrees should be so unconditional that any contemplation of its meaning must be avoided.[2] Not that the Israelites themselves ever came close to keeping their word, but these ancient imperfections are usually of no consequence to the visionaries and leaders of intense religious movements. Their point is that wishing and praying does not suffice to obtain God's ultimate blessing. One must also act, and since intense religious movements may call for rather extreme action, it is wise to reassure disciples with pious examples from the past. The idyllic alliance demands such examples, and these can be collected from the Scriptures selectively.

The Religious Logic of Irrational Choices

The intentional ambiguity in the messages of institutional religions helps to maintain the reliability of the belief system despite situations that seem inconsistent with basic notions of divine justice. Positive expectations are preconditioned by fatalistic reference to a vague and untraceable "God's Will." Retribution for conduct in life is postponed to after death. The harsh lot of people whose record is known to be spotless is explained as punishment for sins that only God is aware of or as a test of faith. If all that does not suffice, there is always the anticipation of an undetermined "end of days" when all wrongs will be righted. Non-monotheistic faiths may seek similar explanations of apparent injustice in witchcraft or the influence of evil spirits.

Intense religious movements are less concerned with such inconsistencies. Their generously spread promises are as attractive as they are improbable, but they come accompanied by specific stipulations. The excessive ritual and behavioral modes often included in those stipulations are unconditional. All members of the "sacred community" must follow them to the letter. Hesitation or refusal may carry severe sanctions from the leadership, as well as from the more complying members of the group, who will strike out at anyone whose choices might anger the divinity and jeopardize the fulfillment of the great prophecies.

Many intense religious movements contain such violent streaks. They are necessary for their short-term perseverance against institutional pressure and their long-term survival, which both depend on the recruitment of additional members and the ensuring of their total commitment. Alleged sinners, moral transgressors, and the weak of faith inside the movement must be tracked down and punished, infidels outside must be proselytized, and once the movement acquires sufficient strength, holy struggles have to be carried out against those who resist it. Such energies tend to leave a lasting historical imprint on affected societies. Repercussions are often felt and recognized within the lifetime of the people involved, and the historical experience shows that intense religious ventures rarely meet a happy conclusion.

Religious intensity is not a secondary stimulant of historical developments, with the real causes to be found in social, economic, or environmental circumstances. The simultaneous contributions of these factors are invariably at the background, but the extreme actions and irrational choices are the direct offspring of religious zeal. It is only such zeal that is capable of luring whole groups and communities into irresponsible adventures that defy logical evaluations of unlikely odds against probable failure – unless God's favorable interference upsets the equation.

A Model of Religious Intensity

This book investigates religious intensity and its implications through the observation and interpretation of various historical cases. Its basic theory follows four complementary suppositions:

1. Societies facing severe threats to their life modes and ideological codes may resist through violent or non-violent reactions, and usually through a combination of both.

2. Exceptionally fierce opposition can be expected if religious values and practices are being threatened. Resistance leaders may define absolute goals, and a limited crisis may assume momentous proportions.

3. There is a close correlation between monotheism and religious intensity. Direct or indirect monotheistic influence is standard in intense religious theologies, including nativist millenarianism, which commonly rises as a hostile reaction to missionary activity.

4. Mass action triggered by intense religious movements invariably fails to meet its main objectives and often ends in disaster. Related fundamental changes will affect institutions, hierar-

chies, and cultural and ideological understandings. Ramifications will be of both immediate and long-term varieties.

The first part of this book delineates the origins and main characteristics of religious intensity, discusses its attractions and risks, and identifies its human followers. The cross-cultural aspects of religious intensity are examined through consistencies and discrepancies between several extreme and moderate historical examples. The possibility of reciprocal influence or diffusion is eliminated by a choice of cases that occurred in distant locations, involving people who lived under various conditions and circumstances, shared no religious, cultural, or commercial contacts, and in all likelihood had never heard of one another. Aspects of modern Islamic fundamentalism are addressed from two perspectives. A comparative presentation confronts two conflicting views of the role of radical Islam in the motivation for violence and terrorism. In a later chapter, the Mahdi Revolt in nineteenth-century Sudan is used as one of the main case studies for semi-millenarianism.

The Archaeological Perspective

Ancient religion has been the focus of archaeological research since its infancy, but little attention has been devoted to the detection of ideological variations *within* religious systems. One such variation is religious intensity, which is expressed in increased ritual observance and the amplified utilization of cult-related vessels and structures, including new types, all of which can be detected in the archaeological record. This issue is discussed in the second part of the book through a detailed presentation of the ideological background of the First Jewish Revolt against Rome (66–70 CE), which is reflected in the marked increase of religious items and structures in first-century Jewish sites in Judea. With necessary adaptations, similar material evidence may be used to discover and investigate religious intensification in other locales.

Patterns of Ultimate Devotion

Popular action resulting from the intensification of religious faith is a relatively uncommon historical phenomenon, but its impact is strong and its repercussions are dramatic. Religious intensity thrives on emotions, behavior, reactions, and ambitions that otherwise may seem irrational, excessive, and unwarranted. When the number of affected people is small, the outcome is contained to their groups, with little effect on the larger community, and of more interest to psychologists and social scientists than to historians. Yet, if the intense religious movement captivates a wide enough following, its related shock waves and collateral damage can match or exceed episodes triggered by socioeconomic stress or political rivalries.

While there are various ways in which people choose to contend with turbulence, insecurity, and misery, the intensification of religious faith and practice seems to be one of the more frequent responses. Countless historical examples worldwide attest to this observation, involving a wide array of people born into diverse cultures and subject to different experiences. Religious intensity is not always about zealotry or madness. Its basic motives are often embedded in human ambition and anguish. Yet, people are often too restless and impatient, and sometimes too desperate, to simply pray hard and wait long. Many are ready to take action in order to persuade God to fulfill their expectations, provided someone will show the way. Some of these people end up among the most dangerous actors on the historical record, willing and even eager to pave the way to salvation with the skeletons of infidels, a term that sometimes includes almost everyone who is not part of the movement. So it is imperative for us to become familiar with the basic intricacies and attractions of religious intensity, as well as its historical record, a field to which this book attempts to contribute from an analytical perspective.

6 A THEORY OF RELIGIOUS INTENSIFICATION

I have no pretensions to offer innovative remedies to the religion-related tensions that have replaced the Cold War as the focus of friction and violence in the global arena. Hopefully, though, with the help of studies that illuminate the background to religious intensification, those voted or assigned to confront those tensions, as well as other interested individuals, will be in a better position to identify the patterns of ultimate devotion. They must be identified, and intelligent conclusions based upon them must be reached, for these are the patterns through which pious but peaceful religious commitment turns into self-destructive and homicidal ideological extremism.

2 God and Country

For nearly a century, the Tambaran cult had been the artery of life for Ilahita, a large village in northern Papua New Guinea. In 1984, everything suddenly changed. In the course of a dramatic iconoclastic spell, Ilahita's men violated a fundamental taboo of Tambaran by disclosing its secrets to the women and shattering its revered ritual paraphernalia. A belief system that had provided spiritual guidance and social solidarity for several generations had thus been contemptuously purged. Donald Tuzin (1997: 33), who spent several years studying Ilahita, observes that with the fall of Tambaran

> the traditional grounds of male solidarity and association were obliterated…without all of the ancillary topics and projects [that Tambaran] gave men to talk about, without the stimulating need to coordinate competitions and displays, without even the companionable sharing of betel nut and tobacco, male society quickly declined. Without the cover of secrecy, without the protection of the Tambaran's canopy, masculinity as the Ilahita had known it for a hundred years could not continue…so when it died, masculine identity, purpose, and agency died with it.

It seems remarkable that members of a community would ruthlessly dispose of their own sacrosanct spiritual symbols. Yet, the fate of Tambaran reflects the adaptability of religion to changing circumstances, a quality responsible to a large degree for its perseverance and vibrancy from pre-historic days to the present. The eradication of Tambaran was the *coup de grâce* to a ritual framework that had lost its substance and outlived its usefulness (Tuzin 1997: 42). Once removed, the vacant spiritual ground was filled with new and more functional beliefs and rites. The fury of Ilahita's iconoclasm, far from being an atheistic expression, was actually a striking manifestation of intense religious faith, and it left the village irreversibly changed.

Ilahita is an unusually large village in its own country, but it remains small enough for developments in its religious culture to affect virtually every member of society. Matters get more complicated in larger places, where spells of religious intensity sweep only some of the population. Rather than alter the social makeup as a whole, they crystallize into alternative religious movements that act at the margins of society but constantly strive to grow, spread, and increase their influence. As related in later chapters, it does happen on occasion that a radical cult, sect, or ideological faction conquers the main stage, but in most cases intense religious movements must either be locked in constant and costly conflict with the political and religious establishments or compromise and find common grounds for cooperation. This complex relationship between intense religious movements and states comprises the core of this chapter, following an overview of the origins and course of development of religious intensity.

Religious Intensification: Patterns of Emergence

Early religion probably consisted of little more than ceremonial exchanges between humans and gods, with prayers and sacrifices offered in return of some comfort, reassurance, and a sense of control over life and environment (Renfrew 1994: 48–49). Later, as communities grew larger and more circumscribed, tighter social control became essential, and regulations affecting personal and social conduct were forged under a religious canopy (Service 1962: 171; Wallace 1966: 261). Gifts of blood across altars and vocal supplications no longer sufficed to placate the heavenly forces, on whose good will all and everyone presumably depended. They now also dictated individual and communal morality.

Morals are culturally determined. What is accepted or desired by some may challenge the understandings of others, and such differences tend to be loaded with emotion. To many people the notion that their neighbors might not share their convictions can be a source of concern, frustration, and indignation. After all, the well-being of the community depends on divine favor, which will never be granted unless the infection of heresy is either healed through reason or seared with fire. Some may feel duty-bound to ensure that as many people as possible also

Figure 1 Pilgrims worshipping by the Stone of Anointment in the Church of the Holy Sepulcher, Jerusalem. Genuine devotion is at the base of the motivation for joining intense religious movements, but other factors must also be involved for full commitment to be made (photograph: M. Koçak).

see the light, if need be, by forcing their eyes open. The option that alternative opinions may hold some merit, or even their very right of existence, is categorically denied. Ideological tensions have a way of escalating through their own generated energies, with each rival side constantly burrowing deeper into its own convictions, while further de-legitimizing opposite views. The deeper they burrow, the more intense their faith becomes, as do its ritual manifestations and the commitment to its aggressive defense and promotion. Thus, some of the most basic human emotions and insecurities can be found behind ostensibly moral and intellectual facades. As we will see, this process is particularly dominant in periods of crisis, when divine assistance is needed the most.

Religious intensity may materialize as strict conservatism that rejects all ideological reforms and alternative interpretations, but it can also assume the opposite form: a radical reform movement that challenges dogma and ritual at their roots and struggles to rid belief systems of presumed ideological corruption. Extreme ideas, those with a "tendency to go to the poles of the ideological scale" (Lipset and Raab 1970: 4), may remain camouflaged for some time within more moderate religious ideologies. At some point, as conditions ripen, and often during a time of crisis, they are disclosed to the faithful as messages miraculously revealed to some chosen messenger. The worldwide similarities of this process are telling. All varieties of religious intensity are essentially branches of the same tree, carrying similarly attractive fruit, and hiding similarly sharp thorns.

Religious intensity crystallizes at the social margins, although individuals of all classes and backgrounds can be found in its ranks. Its innovative worldviews are promoted by resolute exponents, many of who are willing and even wishing to collide with political and religious establishments. Yet, the energy of zealous faith must be judiciously and competently administered if its goals are to be accomplished. Believers must be clearly instructed on what distinguishes them from infidels and convinced that these distinctions bring them closer to God. Spiritual teachings should also coincide with symbolic but meaningful physical measures, through which the understanding of good and evil, or sacred and profane, is methodically rearranged.

Fluctuations of 'Sacred' and 'Profane'

Religions tend to define some territories, animals, objects, and even people as ritually pure – 'sacred' – and others as impure, or 'profane.' While the delineation of spheres and the clarity of the distinctions may vary (Renfrew 1994: 51; Bell 1992: 123), such partitions are essential for the development of religious ideologies because they enfold all aspects of life within the religious sphere. Usually, the ambition of religious agents is satisfied at that. With the omnipotence of religion firmly established, they wisely allow daily pursuits to be followed mostly unhindered by unnecessary ritual restrictions. The radicalization of religion tends to upset this balance. The more distilled the convictions, the more eager their promoters become to expand their influence into the temporal sphere, and the less willing they are to retain the status quo (Bell 1992: 123; Rappaport 1999: 414ff.). A theocracy ay be established, with priests vested with absolute political power and official religious legislation touching all aspects of public and individual life.

Where the political and religious establishments do not succumb, zealous popular movements may rise, energized by waves of blind devotion. The ideological platforms of such movements generally dictate that if one has to fight wars, accumulate wealth, exchange trade, and mold cultural values, God must always be involved. These movements rarely last long on the historical stage, but they nonetheless tend to leave an altered social and religious landscape and affect long-established relationships. Neighbors may be estranged, foreign cultural influences curbed, doubts and transgressions ruthlessly suppressed. Life may be subjected to religious scrutiny based on radical but often inconsistent principles, as is characteristic of the early days of revolutions. The uncompromising implementation of extreme ad hoc ideological edicts may even jeopardize keen believers who dare to espouse independent views or object to the interference of the movement

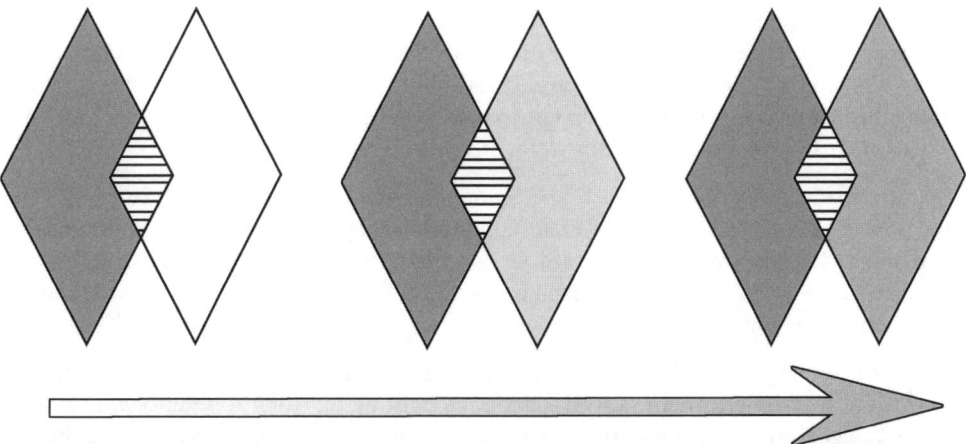

Figure 2   Renfrew's model modified: The image to the left represents the original model, showing the initial balance between the spiritual (grey) and the temporal (white) spheres. The smaller striped diamond at the center marks the strictly delineated territory of blending, such as public religious services, ceremonies, and festivals. The images at the center and right represent the intensification model suggested in this book, with religion gradually infiltrating and modifying the temporal sphere until there is hardly a distinction left between them.

in previously dogma-free matters. Intense religious movements simply cannot stay within the circumscribed "sacred spheres" of old and regularly shake off such restrictions. Thus, the healthy balance between the spiritual and temporal spheres, or, in Colin Renfrew's words (1985: 17), the "outer world experience" and the "world of temporal experience," which has oiled social mechanisms for generations, will be upset irreparably.

Even religious ideals, however, must make some concessions to reality and be integrated into the conditions in which people live. If exponents of intense religious ideologies are unable to guide new believers through the challenges of daily existence, they risk disillusion, popular relapse into the "old ways," and, as a natural consequence, the disintegration of the movement. To maintain long-term relevance, compromises are inescapable and some adaptation to the subjective circumstances of time and place has to occur.

Religious Intensity and Adaptation

Ideological adaptability is to be expected from institutional religions. Evolving over prolonged and gradual historical processes, compromises have to be made all along. However, most intense religious movements grow rapidly, partly as a reaction to unusual stress. The specific circumstances, exclusive promises, and innovative modes of worship tend to produce segregated communities, confident in their spiritual superiority and contemptuous of unbelievers – hardly places where the flexibility of adaptation may be expected (Castells 1997a; Wuthnow and Lawson 1994: 21). Yet, as adaptations must be made, ways are found to keep them on the more superficial levels, while the core tenets are preserved unscathed. Even religious-ideological movements on principle opposed to presiding governments and disdainful of common cultural values are known to abide to state laws and spread their message through legitimate channels. The transmitted image is that of a modern, open-minded, spiritual alternative, far from medieval fundamentalism. It supposedly lives and breathes the issues of the day, and permits – even encourages – the enjoyment of technological innovations and leisure activities. At the same time, a deeper inspection of the propagated material clarifies that none of the strict, core, ideological doctrines are compromised.

Founded in 1872 in Pittsburgh, Pennsylvania, by Charles Taze Russel, the Jehovah's Witnesses presently have congregations in over 200 countries. The Witnesses' sole and unequivocal allegiance is to Christ and His Kingdom as they perceive them. They equate national flags and hymns to idolatry, abstain from political voting, and resist military service regardless of the circumstances (Bergman 1995: 40). The roles of major Christian churches in the global political and military theater are under frontal attack in the movement's promotional literature:

> Century after century, the clergy of Christendom has meddled in politics and has supported the wars of their nations. They have even supported the opposing sides in wars within Christendom, such as the two world wars of [the twentieth] century. In those conflicts the clergy on each side prayed for victory, and members of one religion from one country were killing members of that same religion from another country.[1]

The ideological totality of the Jehovah's Witnesses is revealed in this simplistic perception of the Nazis and those who fought them as rival Christians fighting out their differences. Another inflection of this categorical worldview is the terrible fate allegedly awaiting unbelievers in the afterlife, as described in explicit detail in other Witnesses literature.[2] By any parameter, these are the rigid components of a non-adaptive and rather extreme religious ideology. That, however, is not the impression projected in the style, format, and contents of the Witnesses' extensive promotional publications, which display technological proficiency, graphic expertise, and up-to-date familiarity with subjects of general interest.[3] Furthermore, the Witnesses remain an integral part of American society despite their ideological resentment of much of what it represents. Even the unconditional refusal to bear arms can hardly be classified as seditious, as this same principle is followed by Witnesses on all rival sides. The Jehovah's Witnesses illustrate how intense religious movements may coexist grudgingly with the establishments they are ideologically opposed to, while utilizing the technological means of those establishments to dexterously attract potential recruits.

Richard Evans (1990: 40) argues that while elites codify rules, rituals, and morals that confirm their legitimacy and superiority, the masses must keep such boundaries fluid, flexible, and ready to respond to the insecurities of daily existence. This particularly applies to remote communities with minimal contacts to the establishment, whose members find some solace from their bleak material prospects in religion. The alternative churches of South Africa exemplify Evans' principle, and, despite the vast differences in place, conditions, ideology, and historical circumstances, they also agree with the Jehovah's Witnesses on the aspects at the heart of our present narrative. Under apartheid rule, many black South Africans, mostly from the underprivileged and impoverished periphery, became disillusioned with the Christian churches of European origin, which seemed indifferent to their plight and averse to their cultural traditions. Many were consequently drawn to innovative pseudo-Christian religious movements, founded by local charismatic preachers (Comaroff 1985: 168, 188–89, 176). These alternative churches offered lively and spontaneous services spiritually and rhythmically embedded in the local culture and extended sorely needed welfare assistance and health care. Simultaneously, they were committed to inexorable, non-violent campaigns against apartheid, defining it not only as humanly unjust but also as a religious abomination.

Zeal born out of anger tends to produce a reaction that impresses some with its dedication and self-sacrifice and amazes others as senselessly reckless. These frustrated and deeply religious people could be expected to employ all means of struggle against Pretoria, despite the risk of violent retaliation by its powerful security forces. Yet, rather than waste lives, funds, and motivation on heroic catastrophes, African church leaders chose to gradually but consistently forge a common identity and mutual solidarity among their believers and wisely channeled political resistance into a passive but influential detachment from the government, its agencies, symbols, and affiliated religious institutions. Disciples withdrew from official political involvement, ceased to take part in institutional religious services, and banned European cultural and material imports, including foodstuffs and medications, preferring local products and traditional healing instead. The use of food and medicines as a method of social control in religious ideological struggles has been observed cross-culturally (Harris 1985; Mauss 1990; Douglas 1973: 93, 98–99; Beattie 1960: 26; Waters 1963: 11; Turner 1967: 359ff.). Affecting all aspects of daily life and subjecting people to discomfort and hazard, it reflects the power and appeal of ideological movements. The fundamentally religious yet rational church leaders maintained their movements physically and ideologically intact through the risky struggle, while denying the government a pretext for military intervention that the dissidents could never hope to repel. Along with various other factors, this extreme but contained religious dissension contributed to the struggle that eventually was to change the political realities of South Africa.

The Jehovah's Witnesses and the alternative African churches share a high level of devotion among believers, an acute comprehension of cultural settings, and a proficiency in adaptation to the conditions and constraints of reality. Adaptation comes in various forms, and the South African approach contrasts that of the Jehovah's Witnesses. while the latter adopted the technological means and cultural expressions of the "adversary" to influence it from the inside, African churches challenged their opponents through spiritual, cultural, and material detachment. Both cases prove that religious intensity needs not compromise its tenets, nor contradict sane rationality, while furthering its goals in rather hostile environments.

The Uneasy Alliance between State and Temple

The wisdom of adaptation is not limited to the more rational leaders of alternative religious movements. It can also be found among political rulers, forming the basis of an uneasy but fertile cooperation between ideologically opposed organizations. The tradition of partnership between religion and state reaches back to the origins of complex societies. Religion, with its mandatory codes of conduct, class-assigned roles, and categorized privileges helped advance group consolidation and the establishment and maintenance of hierarchies (Wallace 1966: 74–75; Geertz 1968: 1–2; Johnson and Earle 1987: 246, 270; Joyce and Winter 1996: 35). This does not imply a constantly smooth and natural cooperation between temple and state. In fact, competition and enmity are omnipresent in the historical experience, from the genesis of states to the present day. To cite three examples among many, the Akkadian king Naram-Sin (ruled ca. 2255–2218 BCE) attempted to bypass the opinionated local priesthood by declaring himself a god (Pollock 1999: 193), and the Egyptian pharaoh Akhenathen (ruled 1350–1334 BCE) and the Roman emperor Julian (ruled 360–363 CE) both launched ultimately failed campaigns against dominant religious institutions (Aldred 1988; Kemp 1989: 229, 261ff.; Bowersock 1978). Yet, the awareness of mutual dependence and the prospects of political and material benefits often encouraged coordination between civil and religious authorities (White 1959: 301; Johnson and Earle 1987: 264; Blanton et al. 1996: 10). This coordination came in myriad shapes. The stele of Hammurabi (Pritchard 1973: 140) and the Hebrew Bible (Old Testament) attribute civic legislation to divine sanction and inspiration. Religious officials regulated Berber markets in Roman North Africa (Shaw 1979: 95–99). Late medieval feudal aristocrats in England erected crosses in public marketplaces (Johnson 2000: 220). Confucian and Protestant ethics partly inspired initiative, industry, scientific innovation, and reverence of authority in Japan and the United States, respectively (Weber 1958: 133; Bellah 1985: 14, 107–8; Castells 1997b: 5). To promote imperial consolidation, both Vijayanagara in southern India (14th–17th century CE) and the Inca of Peru relocated images of the gods of subjugated peoples to the imperial capital, where they were worshipped alongside the deities of the victors (Sinopoli and Morrison 1995: 87; Bauer 1998: 25, 56, 58; Canseco 1999: 51). These are but a few of a multitude of examples worldwide.

Could intense religious movements, which usually rise outside the establishment and often as an alternative to it, also be harnessed to promote the agendas of governments? The analysis of various historical cases shows that in certain conditions and under the influence of astute political and religious actors this unlikely scenario is quite possible. Early Christianity and Biblical Israel offer two very different but equally instructive examples.

Religious Intensity in the Service of the State: Constantine's Conversion

Centuries of persecution of Christians in the Roman Empire culminated under the iron rule of Diocletian (284–305 CE). However, in 313 CE, merely eight years after the emperor had stepped down and retired to his estate, the Edict of Milan officially allowed Christians, for the first time in Roman history, to practice their faith unmolested:

> We, Constantinus and Licinius the Emperors…are of the opinion that among the various things which we perceived would profit men, or which should be set in order first, was to be found the cultivation of religion; we should therefore give both to Christians and to all others free facility to follow the religion which each may desire, so that by this means whatever divinity is enthroned in heaven may be gracious and favorable to us and to all who have been placed under our authority.[4]

Later, as the sole ruler of the empire, Constantine not only endorsed Christianity himself but bestowed it a prime religious status in his empire. His new faith may have been sincere (Jones 1986: 81; Odahl 2004: 282–83), but Constantine was a rational, ambitious, and ruthless general and politician, and less pious ulterior motives probably played additional roles in his conversion (Grant 1993: 150). The emperor may have wished to create a new common ideological platform for the peoples of the empire, one that would strengthen the hierarchical order and enhance social solidarity, a task for which, at that stage, the pagan religions of the empire were ill-equipped. In the words Edward Gibbon (2000 [1776]: 173), "as long as [the pagans'] adoration was successively prostituted to a thousand deities, it was scarcely possible that their hearts could be susceptible of a very sincere or lively passion for any of them."

Passion was not lacking among the zealous followers of Christ. By that time, Christianity had followers throughout the empire but still maintained the characteristics of an intense religious movement. It was spreading fast outside the political and religious institutions, and it exhibited, through devotion and solidarity, remarkable resilience through generations of persecution and martyrdom. In her study of Satan's origins, Elaine Pagels (1995: xix) states that an important innovation of Christian tradition "is how the use of Satan to represent one's enemies lends to conflict a specific kind of moral and religious interpretation, in which 'we' are God's people and 'they' are God's enemies, and ours as well…Such moral interpretation of conflict has proven extraordinarily effective throughout western history in consolidating Christian groups." This stark differentiation between the realms of "us" - the sacred – and "them" - the profane - which is characteristic of intense religious movements worldwide, has always attracted new converts and must be credited with much of the success of many such movements, be it short or long-term, peaceful or violent. Under the encouragement, sponsorship, and regulation of the government, these remarkable energies could now be channeled to serve foreign and domestic imperial goals. Constantine's move proved to be a historical success. Christianity, with its ideological commitment and group solidarity now forged within solid and effective state institutions, significantly contributed to the perseverance of Roman civilization against countless challenges for another thousand years.

Religious Intensity in the Service of the State: Josiah's Reforms

King Josiah of Judah (ruled 639–609 BCE) ascended to the throne of Jerusalem during a fragile and perilous period for the kingdom, being wedged as it was between the major rival powers of Egypt and Babylon. Yet, Josiah was highly ambitious and aimed to restore Israelite unity while maximizing the potential benefits of political and military maneuvers between the regional antagonists. The restoration of the ancestral Israelite religion centered around the Temple of Jerusalem and himself as the legitimate heir of David was at the focus of his program (Finkelstein and Silberman 2001: 167). Josiah embarked on comprehensive religious reforms in full collaboration with the more zealous members of the Jerusalem priesthood. In the words of Israel Finkelstein and Neil Silberman (2001:122), "one God, worshipped in one Temple, located in the one and only capital, under one king of the Davidic dynasty were the keys to the salvation of Israel – both in David's time and in the time of the new David, King Josiah."

The biblical narrative is charged with the drama of the events. The ostensibly accidental discovery by the high priest Hilkiah of a "book of the law," possibly a version of Deuteronomy, while the Temple was undergoing repairs (Kings II, 22:8), triggered a ruthless iconoclastic campaign against all semblance of pagan ritual (Kings II, 23:4–20). This was followed by a Passover kept with a rigor not seen "since the days of the judges who judged Israel, even during all the days of the kings of Israel and of the kings of Judah" (Kings II, 23:22). The desecration of objects, altars, structures, and images revered for generations must have disturbed more than a few Israelites, but the official record tells of no objections.

As with Constantine nearly a thousand years later, there is no reason to doubt Josiah's religious earnestness, but calculated political considerations also must have been present. To reach his ambitious goals, he needed not only the willing collaboration of ideological priests, but also the support of a people stirred to renewed devotion to the common ancestral faith. This religious revival was no spontaneous frenzy, but rather a planned and forcefully executed ideology-based campaign. While carried out by state officials and their representatives, it still contained an almost millenarian fervor and enthusiasm. Josiah skillfully exploited the zealotry that may have always been embedded in distinguished circles among the Israelite society, fanned it to fiery determination, and allowed those circles a free hand to transform the religious, social, and political reality according to their core religious beliefs, as well as in keeping with the agendas devised at the royal court.

Sacred Projects and Sacred Leaders

The political use of religious intensification extends beyond ideological initiatives. Rulers and priests have successfully presented long-term projects to their people as the will of their deities, certain to earn the gods' appreciation if carried out and likely to invoke their wrath if neglected. Some of the more prominent engineering feats of antiquity may be credited at least partly to the efforts of masses of committed individuals, convinced by their political and religious leaders that they were doing God's work. For instance, let us take the monumental mounds in the American southeast. The exact historical circumstances behind their construction remain unknown. There is no evidence for coercion – quite the contrary: oral traditions preserved through generations imply willing and even enthusiastic public participation in the labor during annual festivals (Knight 1986). While these traditions cannot be proven, they make sense. The mounds were of no material benefit to individuals or the community and offered no military protection. In practical terms, these people would have done themselves better service by investing their time and energy in their own fields or workshops. Religious enthusiasm inspired and flared by charismatic figures, as stressed in the oral traditions, remains a strong and viable model. If so, it is easy to see how these projects would have contributed to group consolidation and the status of the elites, who would have cooperated with the priests and fulfilled central roles in the practical aspects of organization and funding.

A completely different facet of government-sponsored religious intensification relates to the actual deification of rulers.[5] Ruler deification in itself needs not be associated with particular religious devotion. It was essentially a theological expression of a political condition, an effective but rather standard means in the legitimization monarchs and dynasties (Krader 1968: 60; Sahlins 1985: 35; Johnson and Earle 1987: 208). Even the divine pharaohs of Egypt did not hold exactly the same exalted status as the actual gods or were ascribed identical powers (Baines and Yoffe 1998: 206). Yet, if radicalized, faith in the supernatural substance of leaders may elevate the basic loyalty of the common people to a blind and unquestionable commitment. Such zealous devotion can be channeled into the fulfillment of any political program, including extreme self-sacrifice on the leaders' behalf and in their wars. Medieval Islam produced the Ismaili Assassins, who, out of absolute religious dedication to their leaders, murdered prominent Muslim and Christian politicians, commanders, and clerics of whom those leaders disapproved. The killers had no plans to survive their missions (Lewis 1968: 48; Franzius 1969: 34–36; Bartlett 2001: 82). A similar uncompromising dedication to a deified leader led young Japanese pilots to crash their planes on American ships and thousands of Japanese soldiers to fight to the end in the jungles of the South Pacific during World War II (Iritani 1991: 160–61; Bix 2001: 314; Wetzler 1998: 197). Japanese soldiers who survived to become prisoners of war told their mystified American interviewers that "the Japanese Emperor is the symbol of the Japanese people, the center of their religious lives. He is a super-religious object" (Benedict 1989: 32).

A single but significant common denominator connects the otherwise vastly diverse iconoclasm of Josiah, the American mound-building festivals, and the suicidal determination of the

Islamic medieval *hashashin* and WWII Japanese *kamikaze*: the formidable potential of intensified religion to generate support and voluntary participation in projects that blend religious devotion and political goals.

Political Manipulation of Religious Intensity: When Things Go Wrong

While the utilization of religious intensity in the advancement of political goals has many benfits, it also carries substantial risks, and the potential ramifications to the very people who initiated the process and he aims they were trying to promote can be severe. Seventeenth-century Spanish history in North America provides an instructive example. Beginning with missionaries who joined armed exploratory expeditions or ventured alone into uncharted territories, the involvement of the Catholic Church along the North American frontier progressed into the establishment of flourishing mission centers (Sanderson 1974; Dunne 1968: 425–26; Weber 1992: 45–48, 242–43). Growing numbers of Native Americans from the pueblos along the Rio Grande were lured by the shelter, employment, and spiritual comfort offered at those compounds. However, the missions met strong opposition from traditional Pueblo circles, who considered them an arm of the Spanish colonial administration and a threat to local cultural identity (Barber 1932; Hacket and Shelby 1942a: 61). Pueblo activists engaged in a ruthless campaign to de-legitimize all Spanish colonial institutions, including the missions, by accusing them of endangering native communities by antagonizing the local gods. Preachers explained recurring disease, heavy droughts, and crop failures as the retribution of the neglected spirits (Preucel 2000: 64; Graziano 1999: 116; Knaut 1995: 59ff., 159–60), adding a new dimension to protests over more earthly grievances such as heavy Spanish taxation and other material exploitation.[6]

In 1680, the tensions between local Pueblo activists and Spanish farmers, clerics, and administrators escalated into a violent uprising. Native Americans targeted missions along with Spanish farms and administrative centers. Churches were destroyed, crosses and statues shattered, baptismal names abandoned, Christian marriages dissolved, and twenty-one Franciscan priests and missionaries were counted among the casualties. In the aftermath of the uprising, the Church was practically purged from the Pueblo domains. It took another twelve years and the internal disintegration of the Pueblo movement before Spanish control was reinstated and Catholicism was reestablished in the region (Hacket and Shelby 1942b: 247–48; Knaut 1995: 14, 175ff.; Graziano 1999: 118–19). The Pueblo Revolt marked the only serious setback Europeans were to suffer in the history of the colonization of the Americas.

By sponsoring missionary activity in the New World, the Spanish court was pursuing a religious duty but also an acute political program. Conversions blurred native cultural distinctions, weakened traditional leadership, and facilitated the expansion and consolidation of colonial rule. The deeper the missionaries embedded the Catholic faith into local consciousness, the faster the process of cultural assimilation would be, until Spain would no longer be viewed as an intruder that some may always want to repel. The missionaries could be trusted to possess enough ideological fervor to carry out this political plan, even if that was never their intention. This calculation was sound, but it had underestimated not only the local fidelity to ancestral traditions, age-old religions, and cultural values, but also the mounting frustration under brutal colonial exploitation, in which the missions were considered full accomplices. A century later, Robespierre reasoned that "no one likes armed missionaries," and this insight could certainly be applied along the Rio Grande. What the Spaniards had ignored was eventually to erupt in the rage of the rebellion. The court of Spain had hoped that the religious intensity of the converted would work on the behalf of colonial control, but the rebels retributed with an even fiercer reactionary zealotry. The prime Spanish tool in solidifying their rule along the Rio Grande ironically became the instrument of their own destruction.

The eradication of the missions cleared the way for the reinstatement of the original Pueblo belief systems, as well as a local political leadership and an affiliated priesthood. The renaissance of the ancient deities also gathered historically distinct groups into a joint league that could be directed against the alien oppressor. It should be noted that a pan-Pueblo ethno-religious identity was more a political and religious ideal than historical reality (Preucel 2000: 62). In many ways, it exemplifies Benedict Anderson's (1983) notion of "imagined communities." Thus, Pueblo religious intensity was just as infused with political considerations as was its Catholic counterpart, and, in the long run, this intricate blend proved to be similarly unsuccessful.

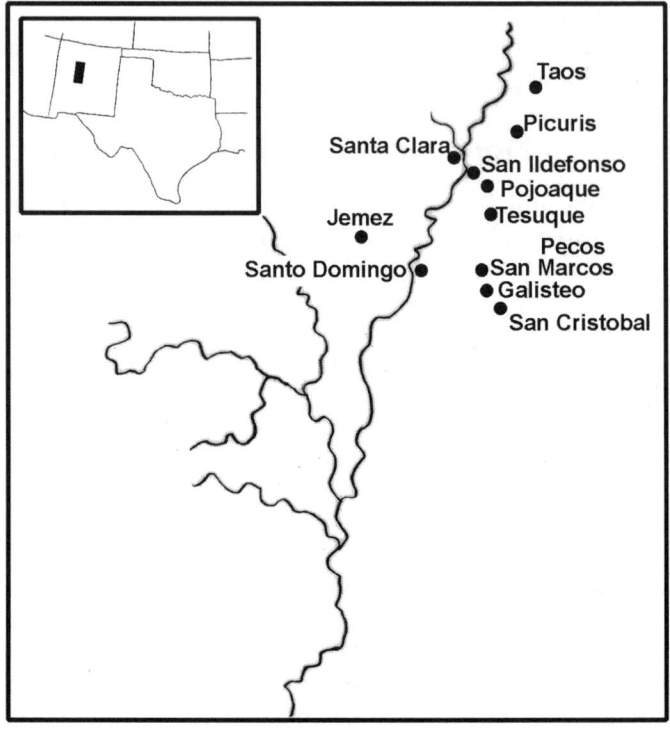

Figure 3 General region of the Pueblo Revolt and pueblos involved (after Knaut 1995).

The uprising that aimed to restore ancient local glories has left few tracks outside the history books. It is true that with the reinstatement of Spanish rule more attention was given to the needs of the native population and even missionary activity became less aggressive (Knaut 1995: 184–85). Yet, the revolt had depleted the already-dwindled energies of indigenous culture and religion, and through its ultimate disintegration it proved their inadequacy against the enduring power of the Church. Furthermore, the relative moderation of the post-uprising colonial administration actually facilitated Spanish religious and cultural penetration, which were now seen as less of a threat. Today, the ancient religions and cultures of the Rio Grande have almost disappeared, leaving only traces of tradition interwoven with the Christian ritual that dominates the region. Even in remote settlements, people attend services on Sundays and pray to Mary and Jesus – a Mary and Jesus first-century Galilean Jews would have found somewhat peculiar, but a Mary and Jesus nevertheless.

The ideology of the Pueblo Revolt contains some of the core attributes of religious intensity, such as its tendency to unite previously separate communities under a common religious banner, the use of comprehensive religious explanations for anything that affects the well-being of society, including environmental phenomena, and the heightened distinction between "sacred" (the intense religious community) and "profane" (the outside world). Since much of the same could be said about the missions, we see – once again – that the perspectives of the two antagonists mirror each other. This is not surprising: intense religious movements and episodes show striking cross-cultural and cross-temporal similarities, despite local variances.

The core aspects of religious intensity are not always distributed equally. The notion of an imagined community, it seems, was particularly accentuated in the Pueblo Revolt. In the brutal wars that plagued the Balkans during the last decade of the twentieth century, more emphasis was placed on the distinction between "sacred" and "profane." Religion was only one factor contributing to the toxic atmosphere out of which the war erupted, but it was nevertheless partly responsible for some of its viciousness, especially in its latest phase, with the province of Kosovo at the heart of the dispute. Of particular relevance to our present discussion is the fact that the war over Kosovo is another example of a failed attempt by a secular government to exploit religious intensity for the promotion of political goals.

Muslim occupation of Serbia was established in 1389 after the decisive Battle of Kosovo, in which Ottoman forces defeated the Christian Serbs under Prince Lazar. Serb tradition has laced the battle with memories of tragic heroism and mystical-religious connotations (Vucinich and Emmet 1991). Many Serbs were therefore revolted at the prospect of officially relinquishing control over this historic province to the Albanian-Muslim ethnic majority that had formed there during the subsequent centuries of Ottoman rule. The government of Slobodan Milošević skillfully harnessed these strong emotions to buttress public support for a Serb military offensive against the Albanians. He augmented it with particularly aggressive propaganda, interspersed with powerful religious codes where they would stir the most support. Thus, the semi-mythological ghosts of medieval Serbs who had honorably died protecting their homeland from Ottoman invaders were summoned to fill new roles in contemporary minds, hearts, and political ambitions. Albanians, as other Balkan Muslims, were depicted as a demographic, cultural, and moral threat (Mertus 1999: 7; Sells 2002: 58; Judah 1997: 121–22). There simply was no place for the co-religionists of the long-gone but never forgiven *profane* Muslim occupation in the *sacred* realm of Kosovo, soon to be Christian again.

The campaign failed not only owing to NATO interference, but also because the Serb populace was not committed enough to endure a prolonged war of attrition against the superior allied forces. Serbia is a European nation, which after decades of communist rule was now able to enjoy the liberty and opportunities of the West. As a modern *Christian* nation, it was also less susceptible to the influences of intense religious propaganda. Unlike modern Islam, present-day Christianity no longer inspires the sort of violent zealotry it did during medieval times.

To illustrate this point, let us turn briefly to the Christian Maronites of Lebanon. Isolated inside an increasingly hostile Muslim environment, they actually might have benefited from the resilience, courage, and solidarity religious intensity usually grants. Instead, their Christian identity is no more than a common denominator that allows them a hedonistic and secular European lifestyle, second in the modern Middle East only to what can be found in neighboring Israel. In his analysis of Israel's alliance with Lebanese Christian factions in the early 1980s, Thomas Friedman (1995: 136–37) explains that

> Because [Israeli Prime Minister Menachem Begin] saw Lebanon as basically a Christian country threatened by Muslims, he viewed the Maronites and other Christian sects as similar to the Jews. Begin was forever asking aloud why the Christians of the world never spoke out when their co-religionists were being "slaughtered" (*sic*) in Lebanon by the Muslims… [Lebanon's Christians] were not a group of hooded monks living in a besieged monastery but, rather, a corrupt, wealthy, venal collection of Mafia-like dons, who favored gold chains, strong cologne, and Mercedeses with armor plating. They were Christians like the Godfather was a Christian.

This is admittedly a polar example – a lot more than geography separates the Balkans from Lebanon, and Serbs and Maronites had to make their choices under completely unrelated circumstances. Still, both groups share with virtually every modern Christian nation the reluctance or downright refusal of the majorities to risk their lives for the Cross or, for that matter, for any other ideological symbol. Milošević thus overestimated the extent to which historical grievances and ethnic animosity might motivate his people to make ultimate sacrifices, even with strong reminders of ancient religious duties present. State-sponsored intensification of religious emotions did not work here. The political leader behind the plan lost it all and ended his life ignominiously in a Hague prison during his trial in an international court of law. Slobodan Milošević probably believed that he was serving his country and the heritage of his people, but, like many before him, he was to learn the hard way that the exploitation of religious intensity for political purposes may well turn out to be a double-edged sword.

Intense Dissension

The intense religious movements discussed so far operated on the outer fringes of political and religious establishments and maintained a flexible attitude toward them. Some found ways to cooperate with political authorities while others did not but still deferred to them at least to the extent of refraining from frontal attacks. Even the Jehovah's Witnesses and the South African alternative churches, which came closest to the outer limits of legitimacy, generally avoided crossing that line. Agents of adaptive intense religious ideologies are basically strict conservatives who strive to return to what they believe to be the original and untainted tenets of their faith that mainstream institutions have allegedly corrupted. Visionaries of nonconformist intense religious movements, on the other hand, who may believe to be doing the same thing, actually seek neither return nor reform, but radical innovation.

Nonconformist movements are attractive to many of their followers precisely because of this resistance to compromise and adaptation. Through their absolute reliance on pure and passionate faith, believers are exempt from the tedious and often disappointing search for wordly solutions to normal problems and exceptional crisis. It is easy to see why governments resent movements that disregard their mechanisms and ignore their agencies. Resentment grows as more people are drawn to those movements, drifting away from the institutional sphere of influence and its pool of human resources. In most cases, aggressive measures aimed to intercept the non-adaptive religious movement are unavoidable, and some conflicts may turn violent.

It is true that most intense religious movements remain mere episodes, drawing only a small following and leaving no discernible imprints. People tend to strive for stability, and established governments and religious institutions are best equipped to provide it. Governments, for their part, tend to be wise enough to infuse their major undertakings with religious content, thus satisfying citizens who need the reassurance that their leaders rule under divine inspiration and properly recognize its higher authority. To illustrate, let us take the extensive irrigation systems built under government sponsorship in Peru (Earle 1997: 184), India (Sinopoli and Morrison 1995: 91), Egypt (Butzer 1976), and Mesopotamia (Adams 1966: 68). Elman Service (1975: 80) supposes that the systems, which were essential for regional agriculture and benefited thousands of people, were endowed with religious meaning. Ritual ceremonies would have assured the people that the channeling projects were presumably being carried out with the blessing of the gods. Yet, if this message was inadequately communicated, the far-sighted vision of those who commissioned the projects would have been lost on the masses of enlisted common laborers actually sweating at the work sites.

As Barbara Price (1978: 171) dryly remarks, people do not engage in monumental construction "as a form of recreation." Peasants would have wanted to know why they were being compelled to leave their families and land behind to dig irrigation systems, when the shallow water ditches on their own farms served their plots perfectly. Their neighbors, who were conscripted to build a grandiose temple in the capital, may have wondered of what use it would be to them, when the communications they maintained with their gods in the modest sanctuary right outside their village were quite satisfactory. These people were not always given a choice in the matter, and historical experience shows that long-term coercion can be dangerous. On many occasions, oppressive rulers discovered that while religion can indeed be used as a means to encourage participation in their ambitious projects, it may also turn out to be the most effective tool against them, with its zealous agents inside and outside the establishment spearheading the opposition.

The Hebrew Bible (Old Testament) offers a famous example in the uprising against Rehoboam, King Solomon's son and heir, which led to the breakup of his kingdom with the secession of the northern tribes (Kings I, 12:1–19). Overbearing taxation and extensive forced labor under Solomon as well as his religious transgressions (Kings I, 11:5–8, 33) are marked in the biblical narrative as the two main reasons behind the fateful events. Rehoboam's own *hubris* sealed the fate of the United Monarchy. We may assume that the causes were interconnected. The crucial role of the prophet Ahijah in the biblical version indicates that non-institutional religious agents were probably among the leaders of the insurgence. Solomon's idolatry provided the ideological justification for a move made inevitable by the merciless and irresponsible exploitation of his people. Solomon's fabled wisdom may certainly be questioned in this context. Like other, less reputable rulers, he had mistaken religious symbols for religion and trusted that, with the lavish investment in temples, sacred objects, and public ceremonies, he had that angle covered. His son was to learn that faith is an awesome yet unstable and unpredictable energy that cannot be bottled in golden urns or locked within structures of cedar.

There are various similar historical cases, and others may be assumed based on circumstantial evidence. As an example, one of the more viable models regarding the enigmatic fall of the Mesoamerican Olmec culture (ca. 1500–500 BCE) suggests socio-religious domestic upheaval as the cause (Drucker et al. 1959: 126–27; Coe 1984: 71–75). Indications for this theory can be found in the iconoclastic rage that apparently swept through the Olmec domain during the latest stage of its existence, claiming as victims the giant head sculptures that stood in several Olmec centers (Coe 1984: 71). The fact that the statues were not only smashed, but also defaced and buried, strongly suggests ritual action. Made of stone blocks weighing between twenty and thirty tons that had been hauled across difficult jungle terrain, these figures of gods or semi-divine kings attest to a high degree of sophistication, planning, and control (Wicke 1971), but possibly also hint of social callousness. Jonathan Haas (1982: 188–89) observes that the monuments glorified the elites but were of no benefit to the general population, whose members undoubtedly were the ones who had toiled in their production and transportation. If this was part of a standard policy of forced public labor, Olmec civilization had been living on borrowed time. It seems that to the Olmec masses there was nothing sacrosanct about the statues. The official and exploitative elite cult the statues symbolized would have been no match for a simple faith in benevolent gods who cared for their people and shared their anger, as it was preached to a restive and attentive audience striving for immediate change.

Admittedly, the Olmec model is speculative, and the Israelite narrative may be telling us more about the agenda of its author than about documented facts (Finkelstein and Silberman 2001: 162–67; Finkelstein 2005: 35). Yet, regardless of historical accuracy, the two cases illustrate the role of non-adaptive religious intensity in socio-political dissension and represent a pattern with parallels in numerous empirical cases. Israelite kings maintained and supported religious institutions, and it can be assumed that Olmec rulers did the same, but nonconformist intense religions owe governments nothing. If the latter's policies violate the core religious convictions of the former, especially in cases where socioeconomic stress is also involved, major conflict is assured. Frustrated and desperate people with little to lose will welcome the radical messages and absolute guarantees of intense religious preachers. Discredited official religious institutions that collaborate with oppressive governments will not be able to intercept the rapidly growing impact of their non-institutional adversaries. It is an uneven contest: while official priests constantly explain, non-institutional preachers need only promise. Emotions that priests must contain, preachers will gladly ignite. Priests are committed to the bonds of reality; preachers relate to the bliss of Utopia.

Assuming the Olmec model represents what has really happened, can we draw parallels between the desecration of the massive Olmec figures and the similar fate of the imposing statues of tyrants like Benito Mussolini, Nicolae Ceaușescu and Saddam Hussein? Based on plain observation, the answer should be negative. There are simply too many distinctions between the ancient example, with its strong ritual connotations, and the modern ones, where more contemporary political and social motivations were behind the action. However, at the symbolic level, some significant resemblance can be found. In antiquity, all leaders ruled under canopies of religious legitimacy, and that also includes, no doubt, the Olmec princes. Modern thought made this connection optional, and all three tyrants mentioned above were essentially secular.[7] Yet, one can't have it both ways, and it is no more than poetic justice that those who demand semi-religious adulation while in power should be treated with semi-religious iconoclasm as they fall.

The Perfect Answers

Extreme religious intensity can bear no social, moral, or political adaptations, as they will shatter the notion of axiomatic and uncompromising faith. God commands all individual and communal destinies, and His will, only His will, and nothing but His will should be followed and done unquestionably. Mainstream believers must accommodate doctrines and rituals to cultural principles and shared understandings of their time and place. As religious intensity is an alternative to those principles and understandings, its disciples are exempt from such considerations. C. S. Lewis (1991) envisions Heaven as a place with "no sphere of usefulness…no scope for talents… no atmosphere of inquiry… the land not of questions but of answers." Extreme religious devotion strives to transport this place of bliss, with its perfect answers and lack of doubt, down to earth. In doing so, it dramatically narrows the range of human responsibility in daily conduct, but what is left is heavily accentuated. Doctrines are sharp and clear, and one is exactly instructed on what he or she is to do. Many concerns of people in the outside world, making daily decisions and moral judgments, need not trouble the disciples of extreme religious movements. On the other hand, commitment to the movement's doctrines must be absolute.

Instead of adaptation, intense religious movements engage in exploitation. As the logic goes, if the profane realm leaves its technological means and ideological latitude at the disposal of the sacred domain, then there is no reason they should not be put into good use. The electronic media and the Internet are utilized extensively by intense religious preachers of various religions, not only to spread their views and attract new followers, but often also to try and sway political developments. Some American evangelist organizations, for example, are deeply concerned with Middle Eastern politics and actively work to influence the US government on related issues. Several of them, for their own theological and ideological reasons, staunchly oppose any Israeli territorial concessions in the Promised Land and in the Holy City. TV broadcaster Pat Robertson of the Christian Broadcasting Network (CBN) warned his government that "He that touches Jerusalem touches the apple of God's eye…and if we decide we're going to wrest east Jerusalem away from the Jews and give it over to the Palestinians, we're risking the wrath of God on this nation…."[8] Pastor John Hagee, head of the Cornerstone Church of San Antonio, Texas, whose multimedia preaching events are broadcasted worldwide, concurs: "America must never pressure Israel to give up land. It must never pressure her to divide Jerusalem. Turning Jerusalem over to the Palestinians is tantamount to giving it to the Taliban."[9] Afghanistan's Islamic Taliban, incidentally, provide a rare example of religious fanaticism that treats high technology as an eminent threat. While in power, they attempted to shut down mass communication throughout the country (Roy 1998).

Let us move for a moment to another type of radical Islam, a branch of intense religious involvement in current affairs (thus, another form of regulated adaptation) that can be found among Islamic groups based in the West. Unlike Christian evangelists, whose emphasis, aggressive as it might be, is on winning new disciples for Christ, Islamic fundamentalism focuses on an uncompromising struggle against infidels wherever they may be found. Under the canopy of the freedom of expression, some Muslim clerics and activists in Europe spread venal oral and printed messages against the cultural, moral, and political fabrics of their host nations. Some material is of such vehemence that alarmed local authorities have been known to initiate legislative countermeasures (Rex 2002: 60, 66–70).[10] Ironically, these groups skillfully exploit democratic political freedom in order to undermine the liberal ideology behind this freedom. Both these examples, despite their elementary differences, prove that religious intensity does not have to depend on modern technological advances and ideological moderation for its existence, but that it certainly has found myriad ways in which to use them to its advantage.

Intensification, by definition, is not a pristine innovation but a mutation of something that was already there. As the next chapters show, the mutant gene in the vast majority of modern and pre-modern cases worldwide is monotheism. Monotheism, unlike polytheism, is inflexible in its ideological directives and intolerant of deviations from its fundamental tenets. To a polytheist, all monotheistic faiths seem inherently extreme. This is not an unreasonable assessment. A singular entity tends to encourage a singular worldview, even, and perhaps especially, if that entity is God Himself – one perfect being dictating one perfect direction leading to all perfect answers.

3 One God, One Way

Extreme religious intensity develops in monotheistic faiths and in those that have been notably influenced by them. Even militant nativistic religious movements ironically tend to "borrow" basic theological principles and ideas from Judeo-Christianity, against which they have originally emerged. The Pueblo Revolt's ideology, for example, contained themes such as belief in the resurrection of the dead (compare to Kings II 4:32–35; John 11:17–44; Acts 9:36–41), the nullification of marriages (Ezra 9–10), ritual cleansing in water (Matthew 3:5, 11),[1] and the destruction of enemy temples and ritual objects (see Kings I, 15:13; Kings II, 11:18, 18:4, 23:6–7). The Catholic Spaniards themselves may have been the unwitting instructors in the latter case, considering the annihilation of the temples and artifacts of New World religions by the earlier *conquistadores* (Todorov 1984: 200–201, 203–4). The readaptation of Judeo-Christian doctrinal themes is especially common in nativistic millenarianism, as seen in the North American Ghost Dances (La Barre 1970: 229; 232, Hittman 1997: 183–84; Coleman 2000: 5–7), the Cargo Cults of Melanesia and the Pacific (Brewster 1922: 240–41; Crocombe 1961; Williams 1978: 17, 26; Steinbauer 1979: 158) and the millenarian movements of South Africa (see chapter 4).

The connection between religious intensity and monotheism is the subject of this chapter. It focuses not on the deeper psychological and sociological levels but rather on the association between monotheism and intensification in the historical experience of Islam and Christianity.[2] Both sides will be represented by rather extreme examples. The Christian perspective will be illustrated by the frenzied pseudo-military campaign historically known as the People's Crusade of 1096 CE, while fundamentalist Islam will be represented by the recent wave of suicide terrorism. The choice of such obviously distinct cases is consistent with the paradigm that guides this book. It is not my intention to analyze specific historical episodes or circumstances but to trace patterns of human behavior at a wide spectrum, beyond singular conditions. Common denominators exist despite the vast differences between the two examples. Christian "terrorism" is rare, but the occasionally lethal attacks on abortion clinics and their personnel in the United States prove that the potential is there and some forms do exist. Medieval Islam may not have stimulated mass movements of the Crusader scale but did inspire zealous and ultra-violent groups such as the Assassins. Both Christianity and Islam thus share an ancient tendency for intensification as well as the potential for extreme violence in the name of religion. Polytheistic religions apparently do not. This distinction holds one of the keys for the understanding of religious intensity as a whole.

Challenging Polytheism

Polytheism can be attractive, as well as somewhat disturbing, because its deities so closely resemble humans, and its celestial settings, as noted by Emile Durkheim (1915), mirror those of human societies with all their imperfections. The similarity to the human world also implies a relationship that reflects the connection between human kings and their subjects. Certain rules must be respected and sacrifices offered on altars to placate the celestial authorities, just as laws must be obeyed and taxes paid to avoid unwanted attention from law enforcement and tax collectors. In return, both divine and human authorities are expected to provide the common person with basic security against human and natural threats. No king, however powerful, governs by himself. thus, it was only natural to project the monarchic court, with its many offices and functionaries, to the celestial sphere. Elaborate and colorful mythologies subsequently emerged worldwide. As gods and spiritual entities spread, places and objects of worship could be positioned at will, usually in convenient proximity to the place of residence. Ancient Israelites worshipped "on every high hill and under every green tree" (Kings I, 14:23; see also Kings I, 15:14; Kings II 12:4, 14:4, 15:4, 17:9–11; Ezekiel 5:3–4, 13; Hosea 4:13, 10:8; and by implication Jeremiah 2:20, 3:13, 13:27) as well as in the comfort of their homes (Judges 17:5; and see Holland 1977). East African groups also addressed spirits on prominent hills and by holy trees (Sutton 1998: 65). Celtic druids performed rituals in groves and by wells (Ross 1970: 136–37). Divine forces in Hawaii were presumed to dwell in boulders scattered throughout the landscape (Earle 1997: 177). This sensible approach inevitably permeated into monotheism.

Although Jews, Christians and Muslims may worship at any location, monotheistic authorities maintain a marked preference for the performance of public religious services in consecrated shrines. This preference is not a monotheistic innovation. Archaeological and ethnographic studies have proved that permanent shrines were established even while populations still led nomadic lifestyles (Howitt 1904; Canaan 1927: 7–10; Matthews 1975; Mann 1986: 47; Levy 2005). Yet later, official places of worship were given central roles in the monotheistic struggle against the lure of polytheism. Recognizing the Sisyphean nature of that struggle, some monotheistic establishments halfheartedly accepted compromises, allowing local traditions to prevail as long as the object of worship remained the One God. For example, the villagers of Milta in Mexico convene each New Year's Eve at a nearby consecrated site, supplicate a stone cross for their needs, and purchase miniature replicas of their material desires, paying with pebbles which they refer to as 'God's money' (Leslie 1960: 74–75). None of this corresponds to orthodox Catholic dogma, but this striking blend of Christianity with traditions that may have their roots in pre-contact days can be tolerated. After all, the object of reverence is a cross, and Jesus, not Tláloc, Quetzalcoatl, Huitzilopochtli, or their local equivalents, is addressed.

The Catholic Church has been dealing with such paradoxes since its earliest days, and its recent approach is far more lenient than has been the case historically. The Constitution on the Sacred Liturgy of 1964 states that "anything in the [believers'] way of life that is not indissolubly bound up with superstition and error [the Church] studies with sympathy, and if possible, preserves intact." (Cited from Johnson 1994: xvi). This pragmatic approach, which roughly resembles what Winston Churchill (1943: 128; after William James) named "The Religion of the Healthy-Mindedness," is based not only on the confidence that the Church no longer needs to fear native rituals but also on the realization that it cannot obliterate them completely. The influence of the lower clergy, who lives with the people in the land, can also be traced through the surprisingly moderate streaks found in some monotheistic religious establishments.

Priests did not start out as an elevated or privileged class. Ethnographers working in traditional societies witnessed shamans and priests leading common lifestyles when not officiating religious ceremonies or rituals. Among them were farmers (Wolf 1966: 101), hunters (Balikci 1970: 225), and soldiers (Fadiman 1997: 96). Lack of ritual specialization is also evident in the Hebrew Bible (Judges 17) and clearly disdained by later authors, who were educated in more hierarchical systems and considered it the result of anarchy. The monotheistic clergy is mostly specialized, but that does not necessarily prevent its members from understanding the basic mentality of their communities. Many professional clerics, especially among those living with the masses, realize that minor adaptations to polytheistic traditions that refuse to die out need not compromise the dominance of monotheism. Stiff dogma can be suspended, as long as the monotheistic tenets of morals, justice, and compassion continue to be stressed, and monotheistic spiritual guidance remains solid (Wolf 1966: 105). Not all religious establishments warmed up to these compromises, and some conflicts found their way into popular myth. The peculiar figure of Friar Tuck in the tale of Robin Hood epitomizes the rustic clergymen who defied religious and political establishments by actively siding with the peasantry, the very people Jesus had blessed. In doing so, they actually solidified the foundations of Christian monotheism in their societies. Social justice is a low priority in polytheistic religions, while all three monotheistic faiths present it as a primary divine expectation. It is an integral part of their overall concern with morals.[3]

Following Victor Turner (1967: 30), genuine devotion causes "norms and values [to] become saturated with emotion, while the gross and basic emotions become ennobled through contact with social values." This emotional emphasis on values and morals is a vital link to religious intensity. Morals are determined culturally and even individually, and once a version of morality is canonized, all other perspectives are branded as immoral and illegitimate. This absolute judgment of what God approves and abhors in human behavior characterizes religious extremism. The deeper one's commitment to an espoused version, the more one detests alternative views, disassociates from their representatives, and is willing to act aggressively against them when being called upon.

Passion for Justice, Zeal for God

Early Babylonians believed in rather impatient and ill-tempered gods who flooded the world and drowned almost all living beings because "the uproar of mankind is intolerable and sleep is no longer possible."[4] Nobody likes noisy neighbors, but drowning them all seems a somewhat disproportionate solution. On the other hand, in the biblical version of the Flood, God's wrath is invoked by His bitter disappointment at the thoroughly immoral conduct of His choice creations. Seeing "that the wickedness of humankind was great in the earth, and that every inclination of the thoughts of their hearts was only evil" (Genesis 6:5), He washes the earth with the killer rains. Again, this collective death sentence may sound rather harsh, but when God explains to Noah that "all flesh had corrupted its ways upon the earth" (6:12), He probably refers to more than just partying past curfew time and disturbing the neighbors. The biblical Flood essentially acts as a cleansing mechanism, meant to leave behind a wholesome environment where the few surviving humans are allowed a fresh start.

The biblical God cannot possibly be associated with the gods of Babylon or Greece, whose constant "malice and jealousy…trickeries and whims…disguises, deceits and treacheries" (Richards 1993: 10) distinguish them from humans solely in their supernatural powers and immortality, which they often exploit for endless plots and mischief. The biblical perception, about which all three monotheistic faiths are in complete agreement, is that God is an infallibly moral being, whose virtues are his essence. Yet there is more:

> [God] judges the world with righteousness; he judges the people with equity. The Lord is a stronghold for the oppressed, a stronghold in times of trouble." (Psalms 9:8–9)

> The Lord tests the righteous and the wicked, and his soul hates the lover of violence. On the wicked he will rain coals of fire and sulfur; a scorching wind shall be the portion of their cup. For the lord is righteous; he loves righteous deeds; the upright shall behold his face. (Psalms 11:5–7)

The psalmist depicts God as a supreme righteous judge who visits justice upon the land. Biblical injustice is entwined with immoral personal and social behavior, and the prophets leave little doubt as to the severity of such sins and the deserved retribution:

> Hear this, you that trample on the needy, and bring to ruin the poor of the land, saying, "[We shall] practice deceit with false balances, buying the poor for silver and the needy for a pair of sandals, and selling the sweepings of the wheat." The Lord has sworn by the pride of Jacob: Surely I will never forget any of their deeds. Shall not the land tremble on this account, and everyone mourn who lives in it, and all of it rise like the Nile, and be tossed about and sink again, like the Nile of Egypt? (Amos 8:4–8)

Alas for those who devise wickedness and evil deeds on their beds! When the morning dawns, they perform it, because it is in their power. They covet fields, and seize them; houses, and take them away; they oppress householder and house, people and their inheritance. Therefore thus says the Lord; Now, I am devising against this family an evil from which you cannot remove your necks; and you shall not walk haughtily, for it will be an evil time. (Micah 2:1–3)

Jeremiah takes the idea further when warning that those who "steal, murder, commit adultery, swear falsely, make offerings to Baal, and go after other gods" (Jeremiah 7:9) will not find shelter from God's justice even in the Temple of Jerusalem. Having been turned into "a den of robbers" (7:11), God's wrath will "be poured out on this place, on human beings and animals, on the trees of the field and the fruit of the ground; it will burn and not be quenched." (7:20). This extension of the meaning of sinful conduct cannot be overstated. Moral transgressions are placed in equal standing with idolatry, and God's determination to punish the guilty disregards even the most sacrosanct symbol of ceremonial ritual, which already has been defiled by those transgressions anyway. The prophet's zeal reveals a concept broader than anything previously found in the ancient world. It also introduces an extensive set of new principles by which divinity ostensibly judges human behavior, leaving it up to individuals to decide the degree to which they can or wish to follow the rules, thus proving their devotion. The range is vague and, in fact, limitless.

These biblical teachings laid the foundations for later Jewish thinking, and early Christianity followed in the same spirit. Jesus scolds the scribes and Pharisees who "tithe mint, dill, and cumin", but neglect "the weightier matters of the law: justice, mercy, and faith" (Matthew 23:23). Paul elaborates on the same ideas:

> For [God] will repay according to each one's deeds: to those who by patiently doing good seek for glory and honor and immortality, he will give eternal life; while for those who are self-seeking and who obey not the truth but wickedness, there will be wrath and fury. There will be anguish and distress for everyone who does evil, the Jew first and also the Greek, but glory and honor and peace for everyone who does good, the Jew first and also the Greek. For God shows no partiality. (Romans 2:6–11)

> Now the works of the flesh are obvious: fornication, impurity, licentiousness, idolatry, sorcery, enmities, strife, jealousy, anger, quarrels, dissentions, factions, envy, drunkenness, carousing, and things like these. I am warning you, as I warned you before: those who do such things will not inherit the kingdom of God. (Galatians 5:18–21)

In some of its earliest passages The Koran[5] addresses similar issues and instructs in similar ways:

> He is pious…who, for the love of God disburses his wealth to his kindred, and to the orphans, and the needy, and the wayfarer, and those who ask, and for ransoming; who observes prayer, and pays the legal alms, and who is of those who are faithful to their engagements…these are they who are just, and these are they who fear the Lord. (Sura 2.173)

> What think you of him who treats our religion as a lie? He it is who trusts away the orphan, and stirs not others up to feed the poor. Woe to those who pray, but in their prayer are careless; Who make a show of devotion, but refuse to help the needy. (Sura 107)

This inexorable stress on interpersonal morals as an essence of the monotheistic divinity makes the ideological gap between monotheism and polytheism virtually unbridgeable. The emphasis monotheistic faiths place on moral conduct equals and even exceeds the importance of ritual services, which define much of polytheistic practice. The basic behavioral taboos found in some polytheistic ideologies pale against the complexity of monotheistic definitions of what is good and evil in the eyes of the Lord and the array of corresponding theology. Passion for justice transliterates into zeal for God, the supreme champion and protector of justice, and resentment of villainy turns into a religious abhorrence of sin. Religious intensification is born out of the ways in which these definitions are understood and manifested.

Striving Higher

Father Paneloux, the priest in Albert Camus' novel *The Plague*, offers his frightened congregation the classic monotheistic explanation for the plague ravaging their town:

> The first time this scourge appeared in history, it was wielded to strike down the enemies of God. Pharaoh set himself up against the divine will, and the plague beat him to his knees. Thus from the dawn of recorded history the scourge of God has humbled the proud of heart and laid low those who hardened themselves against Him. Ponder this well, my friends, and all on your knees.[6]

Monotheistic explanations for times of trouble revolve around the concept of sin against God and humans, and are inspired by a wealth of biblical references. The Book of Judges has a recurring pattern. Displeased with the Israelites' sinful conduct, God submits them to some oppressive neighbor as punishment. The distraught Israelites cry out to God for rescue and He consents. A man of the people (in one case a woman, Deborah) is elected by God to lead successful military strikes against the enemy, after which the Israelites live in peace for a while. As the Israelites return to sin, a new cycle begins. The stories read more like educational legends than recounts of facts, but their historicity is immaterial to the fundamental message: sin leads to punishment and misery, repentance to redemption and joy. While in most cases the said sin is idolatry, we are also given examples of corruption and criminal violence, which are just as repugnant to the author, if not more. Chapters 19 and 20 of Judges tell the gruesome story of the abuse and murder of the Levite's concubine and its dire consequences, while Samuel I, 8:3 laments the corruption of the sons of Samuel, the last of the judges, who have "turned aside after gain; they took bribes and perverted justice." The establishment of the monarchy comes as a measure against moral and ritual anarchy. The Israelites demand a king "so that we also may be like other nations, and that our king may govern us and go out before us and fight our battles." (Samuel I, 8:20). The prophet Samuel reluctantly consents, but adds a stern warning: "Only fear the Lord, and serve him faithfully with all your heart; for consider what great things he has done for you. But if you still do wickedly, you shall be swept away, both you and your king." (Samuel I, 12:24–25). The king thus emerges as an advanced and official version of the *ad hoc* judges. More importantly, the formula of curse and blessing is fully preserved, and so it will remain throughout the Old Testament historical narrative.

Without the constant struggle against sin, monotheism is hollow. The gods of pagan pantheons need not be perfect, for, as in a human royal court, the characters are complementary. The strengths of one make up for the faults of another, and upon this balance the whole structure stands. Yet what would be the point of the existence of one Supreme Being, if that being were anything less than perfect? Such perfection cannot endure transgressions on earth passively. The All-Powerful must also be All-Moral, and the crucial test of individuals and societies lies in the degree to which they are able to match their conduct to His standards and expectations. The test lasts for as long as an individual lives and a society exists. The possibilities of refinements are endless, and there is no set limit to the proximity one may reach to God. One must strive always higher. In normal times, few are willing or capable to follow this hard and exhausting quest , but situations of crisis create an immediate and powerful new incentive.

Seeking God in Times of Trouble

Archaeologists excavating Norse settlements in Greenland noticed a marked increase in the construction of new churches during the "Little Ice Age" of the fourteenth century (McGovern 1991: 81,94; Amorosi et al. 1997: 494–95). The final abandonment of the sites probably resulted of this climatic change. In retrospect, we may wonder at the folly of spending dwindling funds and energy on building new shrines, rather than seeking practical ways to adapt to the deteriorating conditions. Survival might have been possible, had the settlers adopted some of the native peoples' technical methods of coping, refined during countless generations of existence in this extreme climate. Yet, ethnographic studies show that Inuit peoples developed their own complex religious frameworks, which were as adapted to life in the Arctic as was their technology, and which played a major role in their survival. In his classical study of the Netsilik groups, who live by Baffin Bay in Northeastern Canada, Asen Balikci (1970) makes some interesting observations about the local religion:

> Clearly, evil spirits and supernatural beings of uncertain intentions vastly outnumbered the good souls; even the two major deities were inimical to mankind. The Netsilik thus lived in perpetual fear of sudden attacks by malevolent spirits (1970: 208).

> To the Netsilik, life was dangerous. This is the basic assumption underlying the way the Netsilik saw the physical world around him and the supernatural forces behind it…Skill in hunting, perseverance on the chase, and continuous endurance were qualities that helped to overcome the dangerous environment, but there were supernatural spirits behind the natural world which had to be contended with as well. It is a perilous visible world controlled by unreliable supernatural beings that is most characteristic of the Netsilik world view, a world of double danger (1970: 212).

This approach, however disconcerting, has helped the Netsilik and possibly also the Inuit peoples in ancient Greenland to persevere in their unforgiving environment. Constant fear sharpens instincts, encourages countermeasures, and if efforts still fail, as they occasionally must, some fatalism eases acceptance of personal loss and tragedy. Yet, the notions of omnipresent and erratic evil, of random and indiscriminate disasters, and of cruel whims of nature that cannot be explained through the workings of divine justice are diametrically opposed to the fundamental dogmas of Christianity. If the survival package of the Inuit of Greenland resembled that of the Netsilik, it included technology, diet, but also ideology. The Norse settlers may have been capable of using new tools and eating more meat, but it would have been harder to dismiss their fundamental religious beliefs. Rather than change into a new faith, they intensified the one they grew up with, and, like the distressed biblical Israelites in their formative period, they responded to crisis through shows of devotion and appeals to the Lord. In the context of local cultural understandings this would have been a perfectly sensible course of action.

This behavioral mode is not exclusive to monotheistic societies. To mention one other example, outstanding new temples were built by the Maya during the late eight century CE, as their state experienced increasing foreign threats and marked general decline (Sabloff 1990: 173). People of all creeds tend to turn to whatever divinity they believe in for relief in times of distress. What generally distinguishes monotheistic faiths is the focus on inter-personal morals, along with theological themes, such as idolatry, in the explanation of crisis. The more severe the crisis, the harsher the questions asked, the deeper the fear experienced, the stronger the incentive to seek God, and the more widespread the willingness to act upon that incentive, be the nature of the acts what they may.

The Inuit feared whimsical spirits who could strike down anyone, at anytime, in anyplace, with no just reason. Early Babylonians were taught that the gods might annihilate masses of innocent people at the slightest provocation. Greek warriors familiar with the *Iliad* knew that their fate in battle might be decided by skirmishes between the eccentric Olympians, regardless of virtues, courage, and piety. Margaret Mead (1963: 13) observes the terror the Mountain Arapesh of New Guinea felt of sorcerers, who needed little incentive to curse individuals and cause them great harm. According to Tacitus,[7] early Germans inspected tree boughs, the flight of birds, and the snorting of horses to predict fortune or disaster – not their individual or communal behavior. Southeast Asian Hmong immigrants in the United States blamed the random work of spirits for epileptic seizures, and similar explanations were provided for illness in general (Fadiman 1997: 21). In none of these polytheistic cases immoral conduct is responsible for the afflictions. The spirits and gods injure human beings at will. The good and the bad, the virtuous and the sinful, the devout and the indifferent, each and all are subjected to the same risks and face the same odds. Basically, the only thing a polytheist can do to improve those odds is to make an offering at the altar of one of his moody and capricious gods. Yet, for all the supplicant knows, the deity might well just chew the roast, sip the wine, savor the incense, and then move on, having done nothing at all to mark its satisfaction.

The monotheistic God, on the other hand, has taken upon Himself a sacred obligation: be decent to me and to each other, and I will be decent to you. This simple condition offers each person the key to his or her destiny. Poverty and misery are considered as "the result more of a lack of justice than of a lack of resources" (Hamel 1989: 141). If so, the problem would be solved if justice were restored. The same applies for troubles with health and war, which are also understood as the measured and systematic retribution for moral-religious offenses. Punishment, like surgery, is a healing mechanism that involves some inevitable destruction, but is visited by a wise and sympathetic Master, always with a firm hand and constructive intentions. True repentance starts the process at the end of which all afflictions will disappear. However, the mere recognition of sin and remorse over it will not solve an immediate and severe crisis, no matter how bad one feels about misbehaving and how loud one cries out to the Lord. Corrective action is also needed and, within it, proof of faith must be embedded.

Religious intensification takes this already desperate search for God to a new level. Since the results of this passionate search are believed to decide both individual and communal destiny, no proof of faith will suffice unless it is an *ultimate* proof of *perfect* faith. The determination of that proof and its manifestation become the rivet of collective attention. As the following segments show, in some historical circumstances and cultural settings this rather drastic state of mind, combined with the external factors responsible for crisis, produced extremely aggressive outlooks and action.

A Case Study of Christian Zealotry: The People's Crusade, 1096 CE

In July of 1099, the knights and troops of Christian Europe captured Jerusalem and the Church of the Holy Sepulcher from the Muslim Fatimids of Egypt at the conclusion of what is historically known as the First Crusade. Yet despite its title, a failed crusading campaign of a rather different nature preceded this successful military expedition. The People's Crusade, or Paupers Crusade, gathered as a largely spontaneous response to the appeal of Pope Urban II on November 27, 1095, at the Council of Clermont to free the Holy City from Muslim domination:

> ...I, with suppliant prayer – not I but the Lord - exhort you, heralds of Christ, to persuade all of whatever class, both knights and footmen, both rich and poor, in numerous edicts, to strive to help expel that wicked race from our Christian lands before it is too late. I speak to those present, I send word to those not here; Moreover, Christ commands it. Remission of sins will be granted for those going thither, if they end a shackled life either on land or in crossing the sea, or in struggling against the heathen. I, being vested with that gift from God, grant this to those who go.[8]

The religious incentive was boosted by the lure of spoils of war, free land, and a fresh start in the East, while conditions in Europe were becoming increasingly difficult. Floods, droughts, and widespread disease struck the continent during the late eleventh century, bringing large numbers of peasants, impoverished town dwellers, and some knights and nobles to the brink of disaster (Runciman 1954: 114, 121; Bridge 1980: 46; Riley-Smith 1986: 44). In both spiritual and material terms, Urban's message gave hope where hope was sorely needed.

The Pope had envisioned an orderly army led by aristocrats and knights, but his earliest recruits were masses of exuberant peasants, urban poor, brigands, and adventurers, along with opportunist merchants going after easy profits, and dispossessed gentry. Among their captains were some reputable nobles, but also rogue knights, bandit chiefs and charismatic preachers

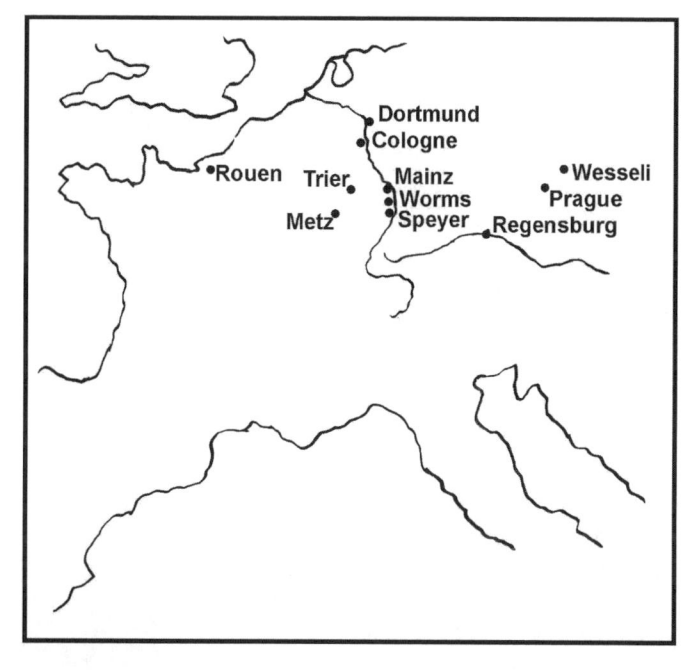

Figure 4 European centers where Jewish communities were massacred during the People's Crusade.

(Stephenson and Lyon 1951: 257; Cohn 1970: 48–51, 62; Foss 1997: 57; Riley-Smith 1984: 54–56). The most prominent among the latter, Peter the Hermit (originally known as Pierre d'Achéry, or Pierre d'Amiens), was described as a man whose physically unimpressive appearance was shadowed by a sharp mind, eloquent speech, and commanding presence (Peters 1998: 108). This combination of uninspiring exterior and alluring charisma is characteristic of European medieval messianic figures (Cohn 1970: 39). The makeshift regiments soon marched southeast towards Anatolia, ravaging and pillaging entire regions throughout Christian central Europe and the western Byzantine provinces. The alarmed Byzantine emperor Alexius I Comnenus wisely closed the gates of Constantinople and urged these unruly soldiers of Christ to march on to the hinterland and battle the Muslims there. The adventure ended ignominiously near Nicaea, in western Anatolia, with nearly all of the hapless campaigners slaughtered or captured by the Seljuk armies.

Economic hardships and material ambitions certainly encouraged the People's Crusade. As noted by John France (1997: 17), the Crusades "offered something for everyone – salvation, cash, land, status." Yet most participants were essentially religious people who would have been truly upset over the alleged humiliation of the Holy Sepulcher by the Muslims and who believed that salvation may be earned by fighting for its redemption (Cohn 1970: 63-4). A common, deep-seated Catholic heritage bonded the diverse groups into a religious community – short-lived, unstable, and rapacious, but a religious community nevertheless. The distant Muslims were not its first ideological target. Eastern Christians, whose rescue was ironically an important additional goal in the Pope's original message, suffered considerable loss of life and property from the crusading mobs. The western peasants must have had difficulties in identifying with these alien followers of Christ, whose shrines and religious customs were so different tfrom the ones they were accustomed to at their Catholic homes. Jewish communities living in central Europe since Roman imperial days fared even worse, as they were decimated by a sequence of unprecedented massacres (Cohn 1970: 68–70; Riley-Smith 1984; 1986: 50; Chazan 1996,; Foss 1997: 58–62). Greed, ignorance, and sheer vandalism were certainly involved, but the fact that Jews who accepted baptism were usually spared indicates that Catholic zealotry played a major role in the violence.

Many may have seen the slaughter of infidels as the kind of display of devotion that would speed the advent of Jesus. Marking the passing of a millennium since the crucifixion, the eleventh century spurred a wave of pilgrimage to Jerusalem, despite the many dangers of the journey. The Pope's dramatic description of the real or imagined hardships of the captive tomb of Christ were bound to receive a strong response in the unusually potent religious atmosphere (Runciman 1954: 115). Indications of millenarianism may also be detected in the violations of hierarchical boundaries that were common practice during the People's Crusade. On several occasions, attacks on Jews defied the explicit orders of aristocrats and priests who under other circumstances would have been almost blindly obeyed (Riley-Smith 1984: 53, 58–59, 62; Foss 1997: 60–61; Peters 1998: 110, 118–25). Rogue survivors from the rout in Anatolia were particularly blunt in their disregard for hierarchies. Having regrouped and joined the later First Crusade, they still deferred to none but their own captains. The knights and nobles who officially commanded the campaign did not dare to challenge them.

Figure 5 Crosses and graffiti incised by generations of pilgrims on a column by the entrance of the Church of the Holy Sepulcher, Jerusalem, attest to the powerful religious sentiments generated by this site. The earliest datable graffiti dates to 1384, a century after the final expulsion of the Crusaders from the Holy City (photograph: M. Koçak).

These highly irregular displays of defiance may have been inspired by the millenarian notion that in God's kingdom, the apocalyptic reality designed in the spirit of the gospels, the old feudal distinctions would be null and void, and the sinful aristocrats and corrupt clerics would be brought low as the meek inherited the earth (Matthew 5:5).[9]

Still, it would be inaccurate to describe the People's Crusade as a millenarian movement. Conflicts between medieval establishments and popular religious movements, which emerged from time to time, were not uncommon in the period. Remission of sins through piety and salvation through self-sacrifice are both elementary concepts in Christianity. Furthermore, the Pope never promised an apocalypse, or even hinted at it. The enthusiastic promises of some of the numerous self-declared prophets, preachers, and commanders may have gone that far, but the idea never consolidated into a cohesive doctrine. Finally, medieval Christian mobs did not need eschatological pretexts to attack their Jewish neighbors. Jesus' imminent return was not a precondition for punishing his "killers," and the opportunity to loot Jewish property must have been an additional incentive. Still, other motivations notwithstanding, the People's Crusade remains a fundamentally *intense religious* campaign. All other motives combined could not have stirred a movement of its proportions. Even more than the later Crusades, on which the political power play in European Christendom had considerable influence, the People's Crusade demonstrates the lure of spontaneous and distilled religious intensification, its potentially virulent manifestations, and the severe risks to those under its influence and to others they come in contact with.

This chaotic crusade met its demise a long way from Jerusalem, and its only conspicuous memories seem to be turmoil and bloodshed. Yet, a broader perspective exposes a deeper and more lasting effect on medieval Christian and Muslim relations. The background to the popular motivation for the Crusade resembles that of numerous other medieval intense religious movements (Cohn 1970; Dickson 2000: 7–8; Runciman 1954: 114; Riley-Smith 1986: 44; Brown 1971: 85). All show the volatile frustration caused by a combination of feudal exploitation, environmental afflictions, and devout Christianity. The People's Crusade represents one of the climaxes of a phenomenon whose effect continued over an extended period of time, manifested itself in accordance with the circumstances of each case, and distinctly influenced political realities. It probably also had a more immediate outcome. The conduct of the unlikely warriors for Christ was certainly savage and irresponsible, but as true warriors for Christ they had left their homes, families, and fields, and fought valiantly, many to their death. Their example could hardly be ignored by the European gentry. They probably would have set on their own Crusades anyway, but the People's Crusade must have added some incentive and probably helped recruit new troops to their armies among the peasants who had earlier stayed behind, and who would now want to avenge their neighbours while proving their own dedication to God.

It should be remembered that several intense religious movements predated the Crusades; some emerged independently while the Crusades were being fought, and a few continued to challenge European political and religious institutions long after August 14, 1291, when Château Pèlerins,[10] the last fort of the Knights Templar in the Holy Land, was abandoned. At least fifty millenarian movements emerged in Europe between 975–1537 (Dickson 2000: 7–8). The establishments in their respective countries of origin did all they could to curb them. Charismatic preachers were severely persecuted; some were tortured and executed, several were declared insane or accused of moral and sexual perversion,[11] and others were simply ignored in the hope that they would exhaust their appeal and be forgotten (Cohn 1970: 39, 42–50, 267, 280). All of those measures failed to eliminate the phenomenon. Intense religious movements offered a short-term, dangerous, yet vital and attractive alternative to people in genuine need of hope. The psychological dimensions at which they aimed were evidently beyond the reach, and possibly the very comprehension, of the official functionaries of the Church. Thus, as long as environmental hazards, feudal exploitation, and clergy corruption afflicted the peasantry and urban poor of medieval Europe, and as long as less talented or less fortunate gentry and clergy were left destitute and embittered, holy men and innovative doctrines were bound to emerge, gather momentum, and defy religious and political institutions. Divine messages of ultimate justice as stressed in the sacred literature of both Judaism and Christianity provided perfect incentives. Message and incentive, as well as the seed of extreme dedication to their fulfillment by any and all possible means, were effectively communicated to their youngest sibling faith – Islam.

A Case Study of Violent Islamic Zealotry: Terrorist Campaigns

An Arab-American imam, Shaikh Abdallah Adhami, marks the differentiation between the earthly and divine domains as a basic principle in Islam, with important consequences to the daily existence of both Muslims and non-Muslims living inside an Islamic state:

> Within the Islamic state, what minorities – religious or otherwise – did in their private lives was left to their own discretion, even if it may have been technically termed as "deviant" or against Islamic teachings. Shari'a, like all religious law, governs rights of worship and codes of

Figure 6 Muslim women at prayer, the Dome of the Rock, Jerusalem. The compatibility between the ideology of Muslim terrorists and the actual tenets of their religion remains the subject of an unresolved and multi-faceted debate (photograph: M. Koçak).

> individual and communal conduct and ethics. Contrary to stereotypical notions of religion, the earthly realm within shari'a is in fact pragmatically understood to be essentially secular…
> No prophet was ever given the license to pass judgment over the faith of a human being – as the Koran repeatedly reiterates, judgment is ultimately with God alone. Hence, constructive service of our sacred traditions lies in showing their relevance as a vehicle of infinite creativity, not in demoting them to preoccupation with judgment of contemporary culture.[12]

Modern Islam is torn between such moderate views, which merit an honorable seat in any intellectual, academic, or theological exchange, and the teachings of renowned Islamic teachers who advocate the promotion of the goals of that religion, as they see it, by all available means. Extreme violence is only the most conspicuous facet of the radical wing. Another, subtler in action but potent in impact, is blatant disinformation, much of which is absurd enough to contrast a plethora of indisputable evidence, yet likely to convince those driven by religious faith alone. There is no need to refer here to Al Qaida or Hamas propaganda. It should suffice to cite Ikrema Sabri, the Mufti of Jerusalem. Sabri, a formal and legitimate high-ranking religious official recognized by the Israeli authorities, openly declared to an Israeli newspaper that "there was never a Jewish temple on Al-Aksa…The [Western] wall…is just the western wall of the mosque...It is not the Temple Mount, you must say Al-Aksa…It was always only a mosque – all 144 dunams, the entire area."[13] The context of this interview was the upcoming peace negotiation between Israel and the Palestinians at Annapolis, with the status of Jerusalem as one of the most problematic subjects of debate. Yet, to many Muslims who are either uneducated in the array of historical and archaeological evidence for the antiquity of Jewish presence in Jerusalem or choose to deny it, the Jewish claims over the city's holy sites would be a *casus belli*, and all means are justifiable in a war for God.

Religious platforms reinforce the ideological motivation of groups or movements by crediting the cause to God himself, the highest moral authority. Those who fight for God need not doubt the merit of the cause and the methods employed, nor should they be concerned with the personal identity of the victims. They will also be more willing to risk and often sacrifice their own future during the mission. These problematic qualities are especially suitable for violent campaigns against established enemy societies possessing superior military forces, and are most infamously expressed in the relatively recent but fast spreading worldwide spell of terrorist suicide bombings.[14]

Jerusalem is only one of numerous causes over which Muslim *mojahedin* sacrifice their own lives while killing others. It should also be noted that contrary to popular impression, suicide bombing is not an exclusively Islamic phenomenon. In fact, the Hindu Tamil Tigers of Sri Lanka are responsible for a substantial percentage of suicide attacks in recent years worldwide (Pape 2006: 4). Even some Arab suicide attackers were actually Christians or had been born Muslims, but were ideologically distant from religious fanaticism (2006: 205). Islamic suicide terrorists owe their notoriety to several factors:

1. Targeting of civilian population in the hearts of Western cities, as happened in New York, London, Paris and Madrid.
2. Targeting of local and Western institutions or civilians in Muslim or largely Muslim countries whose governments are considered allies of the West, such as Saudi Arabia, Kenya and Tanzania.
3. Targeting of Western military and civilian personnel in countries under partial Western occupation, such as Iraq and Afghanistan, and sensational large-scale killing of Muslim troops, police, and civilians in those countries.
4. Targeting of countries of particular political importance to Western governments or disproportionate interest to the Western media and public, such as Russia and Israel.
5. Targeting of international tourist sites, as happened in Egypt and Indonesia.
6. The sheer volume, horrifying outcome, and vast media coverage of the attacks.

A more detailed analysis of each of these factors exceeds the aims of this basic survey, as would the introduction of historical-psychological aspects, such as the effect of centuries of complex and often violent relations between Christianity and Islam.[15] Of more interest to this study is the actual contribution of Muslim religious intensification to the acts of terrorism carried out in the name of that faith.

All dissident groups and irregular militant factions claim just and honorable causes, and many sum up their aspirations in the names of their organizations. The gap between the worthy ideal expressed in the title and the brutal methods espoused by the members is sealed with cynicism. To cite one example in many, the Rwandan civil war of 1994 featured factions bearing unarguably respectable names, such as *Mouvement Démocratique Républicain, Coalition pour la Défense de la République, Mouvement Révolutionnaire National pour le Développement et la Démocratie*, and even *Parti Ecologiste*. These groups, according to foreign observers, committed some of the worst atrocities since World War II (Prunier 1995). Likewise, several Islamic groups that accept responsibility for murderous terrorist acts (although referring to them in other terms) emphasize religious ideological motivation in their documents, emblems, and names. Examples are Hezbollah in Lebanon, Islamic Jihad and the Hamas[16] in the Palestinian Territories, Jamaah Islamyia in Southeast Asia, and many more.

Figure 7 The legacy of Islamic suicide terrorism: two sites of attacks along Tel Aviv's beachfront, Israel[17] (photographs: Y. Arbel).
Above: On April 30, 2003, a Muslim British citizen, Asif Muhammad Hanif, blew himself up at this popular bar, killing 3 and wounding over 50 others. The explosive belt of a second British Muslim attacker, Omar Khan Sharif, failed to detonate. Sharif escaped the scene, but his body was washed ashore twelve days later. Below: Parking lot of a now derelict dance club at the old Dolphinarium Compound, north of Jaffa. 21 Israelis, mostly teenagers, were murdered while queuing by the entrance on June 1, 2001, by Hamas suicide bomber Saeed Hotari. 120 other youngsters were wounded.

The professed religious core of their ideological motivation is the common denominator between these otherwise distinct organizations, and between them and Al Qaeda (literally: The Base), the movement most identified with contemporary anti-Western terrorism. Amidst vehement objections from moderate Muslim clerics, academics, and politicians, Al Qaeda's leader Osama Bin Laden incessantly correlates his struggle with the true spirit of Islam:

> to push the enemy – the greatest Kufr [infidel] – out of the country is a prime duty…[Our] youths…have no intention except to enter paradise by killing you…they stand up tall to defend the religion…It is a duty on every tribe in the Arab Peninsula to fight, Jihad, in the cause of Allah and to cleanse the land from those occupiers.[18]

Ayman el-Zawahiri, his chief deputy, describes the measures that must be taken to ensure the "victory for the Islamic movements against the Crusader alliance," stressing that no limits on time and sacrifices must be placed in pursuing the sacred goal of "the restoration of the caliphate and dismissal of the invaders from the land of Islam."[19] While the messages are political and strategic, the aggressive lingo is patently religious and relies on Koranic passages that preach for Islamic world domination. Sura 8:40, for example, calls believers to "Fight then against [the infidels] till strife be at an end, and the religion be all of it God's." The Koran leaves no doubt regarding Allah's attitude towards the believers on the one hand and the opponents of Islam on the other:

> Let not prosperity in the land on the part of those who believe not, deceive thee. It is but a brief enjoyment. Then shall Hell be their abode; and wretched the bed. But as to those who fear their Lord – for them are the gardens beneath which the rivers flow…Such their reception from God – and that is which is with God is best for the righteous (Sura 3:197–98).

This is only one in numerous such passages (see below). It is hardly surprising that many Muslims, for various personal and cultural reasons, wish to expedite the reception of their divine reward by personally sending the infidels to their gloomy but well deserved destiny. It should be noted that the Koran also warns against a Muslim taking his own life:

> O believers! Devour not each other's substance in mutual frivolities; unless there be a trafficking among you by your own consent: and do not commit suicide: - of a truth God is merciful to you. And whoever shall do this maliciously and wrongfully, We will in the end cast him into the Fire; for this is easy with God (Sura 4:33–34).

Yet, a prospect suicide attacker could rely on the clause that seems to limit the prohibition only to suicide that is committed "maliciously and wrongfully." One who does that for the Faith, it could be argued, is not a transgressor but a martyr. Indeed, instances of extreme violence inspired by Muslim zealotry against perceived foreign and domestic enemies of Islam can be traced back to the Middle Ages. The familiar scene on the media of the parents of a young Palestinian suicide bomber celebrating the success of the holy mission, rather than mourning their loss, has parallels in medieval testimonies concerning the Ismaili Assassins sect (Franzius 1969: 45–46). Yet, is modern Islamic violence truly based on religious convictions, or is religion merely a supporting factor in a struggle that is motivated by ethnic, political, and socio-economic grievances? The countless explicit religious references in the written and oral communications of Islamic terrorist groups and individuals do not preclude a broad debate over this question. The following paragraphs briefly relay some of the numerous different opinions.

In his critical study of religion, Sam Harris (2005) directly associates lethal violence, as manifested in modern suicide terrorism, with the basic teachings of Islam:

> It is not merely that we are at war with an otherwise peaceful religion that has been "hijacked" by extremists. We are at war with precisely the vision of life that is prescribed to all Muslims

in the Koran…A future in which Islam and the West do not stand on the brink of mutual annihilation is a future in which most Muslims have learned to ignore most of their canon, just as most Christians have learned to do. Such a transformation is by no means guaranteed to occur, however, given the tenets of Islam (2005: 109–10).

The world, from the point of view of Islam, is divided into the "House of Islam" and the "House of War," and this later designation should indicate how many Muslims believe their differences with those who do not share their faith will be ultimately resolved. While there are undoubtedly some "moderate" Muslims who have decided to overlook the irrescindable militancy of their religion, Islam is undeniably a religion of conquest (2005: 110).

While Muslims are quick to observe that there is an inner (or "greater") jihad, which involves waging war against one's own sinfulness, no amount of casuistry can disguise the fact that the outer (or "lesser") jihad – war against infidels and apostates – is a central feature of the faith. Armed conflict in "defense of Islam" is a religious obligation for every Muslim man (2005: 111).

Muslim religious tradition allows truces with unbelievers if it is estimated that Muslim military power is insufficient to subdue them, but the truces are understood to be temporary, until the disadvantage is remedied. At that time, the struggle must resume until the complete conversion or subjugation of the infidels is secured (Lewis 2003: 32). Harris' main point is forthright. Those who dismiss or reduce the dominant religious aspect in Muslim militant motivation overlook the simple but vital fact that many Muslims believe their sacred scriptures literally and are committed to the explicit commands that are conveyed (2005: 250, footnote 2). To support his point, Harris dedicates no less than five pages (2005: 118–22) to nothing but dozens of relevant quotations from the Koran, many of which, such as the ones cited above, are explicitly hostile to non-believers. In addition, he offers recent statistical surveys that demonstrate widespread popular support for suicide bombing in defense of Islam in many ostensibly moderate Muslim nations (2005: 125–26). Harris refutes the common perception of suicide bombers as impoverished and angry individuals with nothing to lose and much to avenge (2005: 133) and dismisses apologetic arguments that brand Al Qaeda's terrorists as merely insane and irresponsible fanatics (2005: 130). The conclusion is hence inescapable: "If you believe anything like what the Koran says you must believe in order to escape the fires of hell, you will, at the very least, be sympathetic with the actions of Osama bin Laden" (2005: 117). Harris' thesis is eloquent, forceful, and outspoken, and it needs to be, as it confronts a wide assortment of other views that attempt to look behind the explicit religious statements and search for more complex components in the motivation of terrorists in the name of religion, in particular those who claim to kill for Islam.

One point in common between Harris and his opponents is the refutation of the popular theory that explains extreme religious tendencies as an effect of poverty and hopelessness. Osama bin Laden is a very wealthy man, Aiman al-Zawahiri is the son of a university dean and a surgeon himself (Burgat 2003: xv, note 7), and the leadership of Hamas includes individuals with college degrees (Harris 2005: 133). The profiles of many of their followers are likewise distant from their popular image. Based on the demographic analysis of terrorists from various organizations who carried out suicide missions, Robert Pape (2006: 216) concludes that

> suicide attackers are not mainly poor, uneducated, immature religious zealots or social losers. Instead, suicide attackers are normally well-educated workers from both religious and secular backgrounds. Especially given their education, they resemble the kind of politically conscious individuals who might join a grassroots movement more than they do wayward adolescents or religious fanatics.

Far from being social or psychological misfits, they are "typically mentally normal, with good prospects for employment or other advancement in their society" (2006: 218). Mohammed Atta, leader of the attacks of September 11, 2001, personifies these statistics (Robins and Post 1997: 78-79). Atta was hardly one who had nothing to lose by dying in the prime of life. He was the son of an attorney, grew up in material comfort, held a bachelor's degree from a Cairo university, and did well in a graduate program in urban studies in Hamburg. There is no evidence at all that hints to personal depression or any other irregular mental condition, which might have driven him to spectacular self-destruction.

Kenneth Pollack[20] suggests that the phenomenon of Islamic suicide terrorism has its roots in the frustration of Middle Eastern Muslims with the stagnation of their own societies compared with the glaring success of the Judeo-Christian West. Other authors stress a more ideological economic incentive. In his study of the Iranian Islamic movement, Ervand Abrahamian (1989) refers to the *Mojahedin* ("holy warriors") group, whose fury is aroused by the social and political effects of capitalism. In their struggle against capitalism, these religious extremists sought allies in some unexpected places:

> In our view, there is only one major enemy: capitalism and its local collaborators…in the present situation there is an organic unity between revolutionary Muslims and revolutionary Marxists…Islam and Marxism teach the same lesson, for both fight against injustice. Islam and Marxism contain the same message, for they both inspire martyrdom, struggle and self-sacrifice. Who is closer to Islam? The Vietnamese who fight American imperialism or the Shah who collaborates with imperialism and Zionism?[21]

Hence a striking example of the "politically conscious individuals" who Pape suggests may be found in ostensibly Islamic radical groups. Francois Burgat (2003) urges for the recognition of cultural and political aims behind the motivation of anti-Western Muslim groups, rather than religious extremism. His perspective is diametrically opposed to that of Harris, but voiced in similarly blatant style:

> The Quran (*sic*) can 'explain' Osama Bin Laden no more than the Bible can 'explain' the IRA… The ideologisation of terror reinforces perceptions of the Islamic resurgence as a purely religious phenomenon, when it evidently serves as a vehicle for broader cultural demands, in addition to political ones…By confining itself to this misleading perspective, the West is depriving itself of understanding that at least a part of the demands voiced by this generation of Islamists is no more illegitimate than those expressed by their nationalistic fathers in their time (2003: xv–xvi).

In his worldwide analysis of militant organizations that use suicide terrorism, Pape (2003; 2006) detects a strategic program to coerce democratic states to withdraw their military forces from the territory which the terrorist group claims as the historical realm of its society. Based on statistical and comparative research, he points out that many attacks cannot be explained in terms of religious fanaticism. Neither the statements of the groups, nor the identities of the individuals who carry out the attacks show a fixed pattern of predominantly religious incentive. Religious ideological terms and justifications may be used, but the declared goals are firmly political, and attacks decrease if not stop altogether once the concessions demanded by the terrorist groups are made (2006: 57, 67–73). As mentioned above, the perpetrators themselves adhere to different religions, many are far from fanaticism, and some are not religious at all. His conclusions are unambiguous: "The data shows that there is little connection between suicide terrorism and Islamic fundamentalism, or any one of the world's religions." (2006: 4).

In fact, according to Pape (2006: 197–98), suicide missions are carried out, ironically, by altruistic individuals who are willing to sacrifice their own lives for their communities, the benefit of which, they believe, is ensured if the cause they kill and die for is achieved. This point is clearly plain in the speeches of Hezbollah and Hamas leaders, as well as in the martyr video testimonials of the perpetrators themselves (2006: 188–93). Publications and declarations issued by Sri Lanka's Liberation Tigers of Tamil Eelam (LTTE), and dedicated to its "Black Tigers" suicide bombers, convey a similar message, as they eulogize the gallantry of those willing to die to liberate the Tamil homeland and people from Sinhalese occupation (2006: 193–95). Even Osama Bin Laden's own statements stress the eviction of American military presence from Saudi Arabia, land of the holy cities of Islam, as a chief purpose of his followers' sacrifice (2006: 195–97). The message implies that once America stops prying into Islamic countries and their affairs, it will be left alone. Communiqués corresponded by Hamas add interesting evidence against the notion of a wholesale Islamic offensive to impose Islam worldwide (Rashad 1993: 37). The organization condemns acts of violence against Christian institutions and their personnel in Palestine, and regards Palestinian Christians as partners in the struggle against Israel.[22]

Finally, Pape (2006: 105ff.) uses detailed statistical analysis to show that Islamic suicide terrorism cannot be viably associated with any specific fundamentalist doctrine, either Sunni or Shi'a, and that the common denominator between the various schools that embrace this form of action should be traced back to their antagonism to foreign military involvement. His theory could be summed up in that "foreign occupation by a democratic state, national resistance, and religious difference are the main causal factors leading to the rise of suicide terrorist campaigns" (2006: 108). Religion is purposely placed third and last in his list of chief causes.

Religion vs. Strategy

Time, culture, religion, historical background, dimensions, and practical manifestations are only some of the aspects that make the People's Crusade and the modern suicide bombing campaigns so obviously distinct cases. Yet, closer analysis reveals several important comparative parameters. These parameters are common not only to those two cases but to most historical episodes of aggressive religious intensity, in particular, if not exclusively, in cases featuring monotheistic religious frameworks.

Religious Affiliations

Unlike the obvious affiliation of the Crusades with Christianity, modern suicide bombing campaigns are launched by members of more than one religion. Yet, the LTTE is the only significant non-Muslim example against an array of Islamic organizations worldwide, which engage in this form of violent struggle. Political, strategic, and mainly cultural reasons unique to Sri Lanka need to be examined to explain why the phenomenon took hold there, and not in non-Muslim terrorist and guerrilla campaigns elsewhere, such as in Northern Ireland, Japan, West Germany, and several South American and African countries. The statistical fact remains that suicide terrorism is chiefly endorsed by Islamic groups and widely supported by Muslim populations. Even non-Muslims or non-practicing Muslims carrying out such attacks for reasons other than religion usually (though not always) do so under the auspices of Islamic organizations. The association between suicide terrorism and Islam is very complex and should be studied with caution, but it must not be ignored or sidestepped.

Popular Participation and Support

As unpleasant as this insight might be to many, religious intensity and its extreme manifestations are not at all limited to the bizarre margins of predominantly moderate and benevolent religions. The People's Crusade was a popular movement of the masses. Within that cultural and historical context it is both conceivable and likely that many participants would have taken quite literally the papal promises of sins being expunged and salvation ensured, regardless of the additional earthly benefits. Relatively few Muslims are registered members of extreme groups that engage in suicide attacks and much fewer actually carry them out, but the massive popular support for them in their societies cannot be denied. The relatives and inner communal circles of suicide bombers who fulfilled their missions may be comforted by simple, yet powerful excerpts from the Koran, such as Sura 2:149: "And say not of those who are slain on God's path that they are dead; nay, they are living.…" Naturally, the colorful traditions regarding the delights of paradise and the proverbial seventy virgins don't hurt either.

The Notion of Violence

The murderous violence associated with the Crusades and suicide bombings speaks for itself. Homicidal brutality was and is an integral part of the campaigns. Still, in both cases the killing of infidels is not the actual purpose but a means to reach a broader goal, namely, freeing sites and territories deemed sacred to the perpetrators from the political and military domination of members of a rival religion. Even though the goal is also political, the tight religious connection heavily contributes to the violent nature of the struggle, not only through the sanctification of the killing of "enemies of God," but also by assuaging the fear of death during the missions with promises of extravagant posthumous rewards in Paradise.

The Altruistic Effect

In pre-modern societies, social responsibility evolved side-by-side with religious awareness in both peace and war. Those who fell in battle for the Cross believed that they would be joining the long and distinguished list of Christian martyrs, to the pride and honor of their families. Similar considerations encourage suicide bombers to join the ranks of the martyrs for Islam. The particular theology that defines an individual martyr and the specific menu of heavenly pleasures the martyr can expect is of little consequence to this study. Besides, the scientific appliances that would allow us a glimpse into what happens to the souls of martyrs once they depart their carnal host are yet to be devised. There is, however, ample data to prove their conviction that they would be posthumously awarded the status of heroes. Their satisfaction with the contribution of their imminent self-sacrifice to the welfare of their loved ones and community has also been widely recorded. These are the materials a martyr's altruism is constructed of.

The Equivalent Enemy

Pape (2006: 101) comments that "religious difference has accounted for much of the variance in the pattern of when nationalist rebellions against occupation by a democratic state evolve into suicide terrorist campaigns." Regardless of theological nuances, the concept of Jihad in Islam has always been implemented in battle against infidels, whether of other religions, apostates of Islam, or the allegedly misguided within the Faith. The European crusades occasionally targeted Eastern Christians, but violent attention focused on those outside the Church altogether, namely, Muslims and Jews. Extreme religious movements –*any* extreme religious movements –are defined by their infidel rivals and depend on them for their ideological perseverance.

Probably the most important denominator common to the People's Crusade, suicide bombing campaigns, and other violent manifestations of religious intensity is the monotheistic basis of the religious structure within which they have all formed. While not conditional for the emergence of intense religious violence, monotheism is found in most of the related cases. Its tight association with the notions of social and moral responsibility corresponds to the situations of crisis in which religious intensity finds its most fertile grounds, as well as to the version of altruism that characterizes those willing to die while killing for their faith. The progression of the eternal monotheistic struggle against sin into a relentless war against the sinful is only to be expected.

For an intense religious movement to grow, spread and have an impact on history, it must fuse a substantial core of devout supporters. Yet, extreme religious ideologies, appealing as they might be in times of crisis, usually attract only a fraction of a courted population. Even in rare cases where they ensure the support of a majority, there will always remain substantial numbers of unaffected dissenters. Understanding the background and common traits of the men and women who are swept by radical religious movements and are driven to offer any sacrifice, even their own lives, on the virtual altar of their uncompromising new god is one of the keys for the unfolding of religious intensity in general and of millenarianism, its most visible phenomenon, in particular.

4 A Quest for Immediate Salvation

Millenarianism is one of the more striking and identifiable manifestations of religious intensity. In its radical forms, it rarely allows any kind of adaptation to extant political and social realities and demands from its disciples a degree of commitment unmatched by any other ideological framework. It is precisely this potential extremism that can help to isolate and crystallize the causes and motives behind the tendency of people to make religion the focus of their lives and, in some cases, sacrifice themselves for its sake. The two following chapters comprise a general survey and the analysis of specific cases. Since the religious phenomenon and the case studies are well known and extensively researched, my intention is not to introduce new data or innovative models, but to examine them within the broader context of religious intensity, perceive similarities and differences, and sharpen the distinctions between millenarian and non-millenarian intense religious movements.

The Judeo-Christian Origins of Millenarianism

The term "Millennium" originally referred to the intermediate period of a thousand years between the Second Coming of Jesus and the Final Judgment, as relayed in Revelation 20:4–6:

> Then I saw thrones, and those seated on them were given authority to judge. I also saw the souls of those who had been beheaded for their testimony to Jesus' and for the word of God. They had not worshipped the beast or its image and had not received its mark on their foreheads or their hands. They came to life and reigned with Christ a thousand years. The rest of the dead did not come to life until the thousand years were ended. This is the first resurrection. Blessed and holy are those who share in the first resurrection. Over such the second death has no power, but they shall be priests of God and of Christ and they will reign with him a thousand years.

This apocalyptic Christian imagery is based on the theological notion of the universal rule of God, formulated in Israelite monarchic days and promoted by post-exilic prophets[1] (See Isaiah 40–66, esp. 44:5–9, 45:18–22, 51:5, 54:5, 56:7, 60:9–12, 66:18–24. For pre-exilic references, see Kings II 5:15; Isaiah 2:1–22; Jeremiah 2:10–11, 10:2–16, 11:9–13; Hosea 2:4–15, 13:1–4; Amos 5:8, 9:5–8; Micah 4:1–4; Habakkuk 2:14). By the early Roman period, the universal rule of God became a fundamental concept of the Judaic belief system, providing sensible explanations of world events and their impact on the Jewish people (Cohn 1962: 32; 1970:19–20). Foreign kings and emperors were envisaged as God's unwitting lieutenants who, for the better or worse, carried out His plans and verdicts for the human race in general, and the Jews in particular.[2] This did not imply that fortunes must be accepted passively and unconditionally. Many Jews who resisted the Hellenistic and the Roman occupations of the Holy Land also did so based on religious grounds. Determined armed resistance to a superior military foe and resilience against the hardships of war would have been considered as ultimate tests of faith (see following chapters). God's assistance in the ejection of the foreign occupiers would have been anticipated. Some may have expected it to assume biblical proportions, perhaps a miraculous decimation of enemy forces, as happened to Pharaoh's armies in the Red Sea and to the Assyrians of Sennacherib by the walls of Jerusalem. Others may have simply hoped that God would grant the rebels victories in the battlefield despite their military disadvantage. Either way,

Figure 8 The Nailing to the Cross, depicted in the Catholic part of the Chapel of the Golgotha in the Church of the Holy Sepulcher, Jerusalem. Nascent Christianity's greatest crisis was later to develop into its theological keystone (photograph: M. Koçak).

He would reward their dedication. Once the idolatrous invaders were annihilated, along with their Jewish traitors and collaborators, the avenged Faithful would enjoy liberty, peace, and prosperity.³

Most early Christians opposed the notion of armed resistance and stressed other originally Jewish concepts, such as rigorous faith, communal piety, and unconditional rejection of idolatry, as the proper ways to fulfill divine expectations. Yet, at least in its early decades, Christianity was still close enough to its parent religion to include dissenting militant views. A passage from Luke (24:18–21) indicates that some of the earliest followers of Jesus believed that he would liberate the Jews from Roman occupation:

> Then one of them, whose name was Cleopas, answered him, "Are you the only stranger in Jerusalem who does not know the things that have taken place there in these days?" He asked them, "What things?" They replied, "The things about Jesus of Nazareth, who was a prophet mighty in deed and word before God and all the people, and how our chief priests and leaders handed him over to be condemned to death and crucified him. But we had hoped that he was the one to redeem Israel.

Apparently, these hopes died hard. Before the final Ascension, the apostles questioned Jesus whether he would now "restore the kingdom to Israel" (Acts 1:6), an inquiry which may well be interpreted in political-military terms. The presence of a 'Simon the Zealot' among the Twelve (Luke 6:15; Acts 1:13) may also hint at militant aspirations, although the exact meaning and connotation of the term are not sufficiently clear in this case (Hengel 1989: 60–70; Stegemann and Stegemann

1999: 212). Still, Jesus never came close to promise immediate political redemption, miraculous or otherwise. His main concern was with the corruption of religious values and the pervasive social immorality among his fellow Jews. Nothing in his sermons encouraged armed struggle. His famous recommendation to the Pharisees to "give to Caesar what is Caesar's" (Matthew 22:15–22; Mark 12:13–17) illustrates his lack of interest in military resistance. An even stronger signal is his warning to Peter, as the latter had violently resisted Jesus' capture, that "all who take the sword will perish by the sword" (Matthew 26:52). That did not help to abate the suspicions of the Roman authorities and Jewish elites towards him. As numerous other popular preachers of the time, Jesus was arrested, endured torture and humiliation, and died on the cross.

As Jesus was dying on the cross, his Roman executioners mockingly dared him to save himself, and a similar sarcastic and stinging appeal was made by one of the two convicts crucified by his side (Luke 23:36–39). The fact that these challenges were never met must have stunned his disciples. How could their spiritual leader, who spoke and acted in the name of divinity, suffer such grisly demise, with God doing nothing to prevent it? Jesus' remaining steadfast believers had to resolve the disappointment and disorientation, make theological sense of the distressing turn of events, and divorce Jesus from the numerous would-be saviors who acted during the same period and met a similar end. The ignoble conclusion of his life was presented as the very purpose and summit of his terrestrial ministry. Jesus came to the world to atone for the sins of all humanity through his own suffering, and with his duties fulfilled, he temporarily left the earth until the time would come for him to return and gloriously rule over an eternal and universal kingdom. A period of a thousand years was to pass between the initial signs of the apocalypse and its final advent. Then the faithful – *only* the faithful and *all* the faithful – would live in bliss, peace, and joy. The promise was made to all humanity, as Pauline Christianity divorced the notion of a 'Chosen People' from the Jews and offered salvation to true believers in Christ of all ethnicities (Pagels 1996: 35ff.). In Paul's own words,

> …for in Christ Jesus you are all children of God through faith. As many of you as were baptized into Christ have clothed yourself with Christ. There is no longer Jew or Greek, there is no longer slave or free, there is no longer male and female; for all of you are one in Christ Jesus. And if you belong to Christ, then you are Abraham's offspring, heirs according to the promise (Galatians 3:25–29).

Peter follows the same direction: "God shows no partiality, but in every nation anyone who fears him and does what is right is acceptable to him" (Acts 10:35). In essence, they embraced the Jewish concept of the universal rule of God while dismissing the ethnocentric Jewish perspective (Paul somewhat more enthusiastically than Peter). This inclusive approach ensured Christianity's independence from Judaism and won new converts throughout the Roman domains. In his capacity as the governor of Bithynia in northwest Asia Minor, a concerned Pliny the Younger informed his emperor of "numerous persons of every age and every class, both genders, [who] are being brought to trial, and this is likely to continue. It is not only in the towns but villages and countryside as well which are infected through contact with this perverse superstition" (*Epistles* 10.96.9). The fast dissemination of Christianity through the diverse peoples and cultures of the empire, however, exposed the young religion to ideological schism, as is evident in the writings of Church Fathers and the sensational discovery of a corpus of otherwise unknown Christian scriptures at Nag Hammadi in Upper Egypt in 1945 (Robinson 1977; Pagels 1979). The official Church successfully suppressed these early independent theological outcrops, but was unable to obliterate the inevitable tendency towards ideological variance. Christianity just grew too fast, engulfed too many cultures, and was exposed to too many ideas for any monolithic ideology to be established.

Millenarianism is the offspring of three of the main features of early Christianity: the commitment of early Christians, their conviction that theirs is the true and only way to God, and the inherent sectarian variance. The promised apocalypse is remarkably attractive, not only as a wishful future goal, but also as a basis for daily existence. It is a release from suffocating earthly constraints and the ultimate tool with which to break the bonds of oppressive realities. It is also versatile and may be readily modeled after local cultures, customs, beliefs, and yearnings. Its theological axioms derive from Judeo-Christian theology, but their appeal is cross-cultural. Ironically, after some adaptation they even have been absorbed by those resisting Judeo-Christian domination. Yet the apocalypse is also rather terrifying. While ultimate salvation is in store for some, all others are doomed to perdition, and the exact criteria were never made crystal clear. Christianity has always searched for answers to this crucial but complex question; millenarianism claims to have found them. It is a claim that many would find audacious, pointless, and irresponsible, but it is the source of the millenarian appeal.

The Millenarian Distinction

The millenarian realm is an alternative reality in which everything and everyone are changed. Believers are subjected to revolutionary sets of theological and behavioral principles, and the only division that counts is the one that sets apart the blessed from the cursed and the saved from the doomed. Millenarian ideologies respond to local customs, culture, and conditions, but also show some basic common components. Millenarian disciples worldwide see the millennium as certain and imminent, expect it to be experienced collectively, and believe that while its launch and exact manifestation must be left to the divinity, humans must be properly prepared, and their conduct may accelerate or postpone the Advent (Cohn 1970: 13). Their personal and communal behavior tends to be severely at odds with conventional understandings.

Millenarian movements are often rebellious, sometimes nihilistic, highly unstable, and bitterly antagonistic to extant political and religious institutions. The feeling is mutual. Only the uncompromising zealotry of believers allows millenarian movements to survive the pressure of hostile establishments. To forge and solidify this crucial commitment, many movements work to uproot their disciples from their former daily lives, sever as thoroughly as possible their dependence on official administrations, and change their fundamental shared understandings. Because the strictly faith-based millenarian ideology demands full social integration, personal markers such as social status, accumulated property, professional achievements, even kin relations, are annulled, and codes based on ethnic and cultural upbringing are dismissed (Worsley 1968: 227–37). Formerly independent-minded individuals with established positions in their communities become what Victor Turner calls "liminal entities," people who "are neither here nor there…betwixt and between the positions assigned and arrayed by law, custom, convention, and ceremonial" (1969: 95). People consent to this process, often enthusiastically, because their initial attraction to the alternative ideology derives from profound dissatisfaction with the former direction of their lives and a subsequent eagerness for change. Thus, while outsiders may be appalled by the apparently careless dismissal of a lifetime of efforts and achievements, to the new believers this feels like no sacrifice at all.

While personal anguish, disillusion, and confusion draw individuals to millenarian ideologies, the maturation into mass movements often depends on communal crisis resulting of political turbulence, social disintegration, and environmental afflictions (Burridge 1969: 34; Turner 1969: 112). If the usual means of subsistence and personal security are at jeopardy, and as established institutions have proven themselves incapable of ensuring sorely needed relief, alternative movements quickly step up to fill the vacuum. Even in their precarious state, many people will dismiss promises of the apocalypse, but others will grasp at them as the sole remaining source of hope and gladly join the assault on traditional establishments and their sacrosanct values. The assault is absolute, as classical millenarianism does not aim to influence or reform traditional institutions, but to replace them altogether.

The Prophets of the Apocalypse

Millenarian movements must secure a broad and solid enough support base among target populations to fend off suppressive measures by hostile religious and political establishments. The odds of success depend to a large degree on the personality, ingenuity, and resilience of their leaders, men and women who in various places, times, and historical circumstances have risen from obscurity to announce the imminent apocalypse and its tremendous repercussions. Some of those individuals identified themselves as merely messengers. Others claimed to be divinely charged with leading roles in the preparations for the Advent and promised extraordinary signs to prove the authenticity of their mission. Many preachers progressed to self-declared prophets, onwards to miracle-workers, and all the way to full-fledged messiahs.

Eric Hoffer's (1951) study of mass movements is not focused on millenarian cases. Rather, National Socialism and communism were on his mind. Still, the principles and patterns he delineates apply quite as much for religious and millenarian movements, including the profiles of both disciples and popular leaders. Hoffer's model leaders of mass movements are defiant, brazen, iron-willed but also nihilistic individuals, confident in themselves, their mission, and their destiny, and capable of spotting and exploiting opportunities. They can eloquently present their cause, in both speech and writing, as worthy of struggle and sacrifice. In establishing themselves as the most suited person to lead the way, they are aided by substantial personal charisma.

According to Max Weber (1947: 358–59) truly charismatic leaders inspire such reverence that it is not the logic in what they say that draws people, but the fact that *they* are the ones who say it. Intense religious movements exacerbate the effect, as the leaders are understood to be God's chosen. In his narrative of the twelfth-century radical Ismaili leader Hasan i-Sabah, founder of the Assassins sect, Enno Franzius (1969: 36) stresses the impact of this highly charismatic religious figure on his believers: "Impressed by his intellect, conviction, and asceticism, fired by his fervor, overcome by his magnetism, many broke completely with their previous existence and abandoned wives, children, and homes to follow him. Thereafter they devoted their life to him. Indeed, belonged to him." Differences in time, culture, and specific creed are of little consequence under the combined effect of electrifying personal charisma and religious intensity. The following excerpt is taken from Charles Lindholm's (2002: 369) depiction of Bhagwan Shree Rajneesh, the exceptionally charismatic leader of a cult active in the United States mainly during the 1970s and early 1980s:

> Hypnosis is used again and again by disciples and nonbelievers alike to describe the way Rajneesh affected those around him. Whether Rajneesh was consciously trying to mesmerize his audience, it is clear that he had an amazing theatrical capacity for enchantment. His performances were expressive improvisations that moved, without pause or doubt, from highly abstract philosophical reflections to obscene jokes and racist remarks that were designed to shock his audience, who were caught up in the exhilaration of his rapidly changing moods, his intonations and dramatic pauses, his potent rhetoric…As he caressed the audience with his voice, shifted emotions and rhetoric with fluidity, and used his expressive hands to counterpoint his remarks, Bhagwan gave the faithful a sense of being carried onto a higher level of existence, both immediate and transcendent. For the devotees, being close to Bhagwan was ineffable.

This is an awesome power to possess, perhaps disturbingly so. Sigmund Freud (1959: 55) warns that charismatic leaders tend to be exploitative narcissists who care for the cause that they champion only as long as it serves their personal and egoistic interests. Not all charismatic leaders are necessarily so cynical, but genuine ideological sincerity may be just as dangerous, if not more so. On April 19th, 1993, seventy-four members of the Branch Davidians sect, including many children, perished when federal agents stormed their compound in Waco, Texas. James Tabor (1998: 420) notes that their charismatic leader Vernon Howell, a.k.a. David Koresh, who also perished in the catastrophe, truly believed that he alone possessed the true code to all divine revelations.

The effects of charisma are not without limits and would not suffice for the longer-term consolidation and perseverance of movements. To reach this purpose, certain adjustments must be made and a degree of compliance with standard behavioral norms and moral values is inevitable. Leaders must also prove some practical skills at actually carrying out their programs without snapping the delicate thread on which hangs the tolerance of the constantly vilified establishment (Hoffer 1951: 130; Lindholm 2002: 370; Worsley 1968: xii–xiii). Having to promote compromises on what they originally presented as no less than God's Will is a major leadership test to the self-proclaimed prophets. At the same time, far-reaching compromises would undermine their credibility and empty the movement of its ideological substance and distinctiveness. The future of the movement depends on finding a golden path that will maintain it in the extant environment but also allow the introduction of revolutionary visions. Nonetheless, millenarianism and compromises of any kind are not a common match. Millenarian leaders tenaciously tend to dismiss the quest for the golden path, and some, such as Koresh at Waco and James Warren ("Jim") Jones in Jonestown, Guyana, paid the price through their own destruction, along with their disciples and movements.

The Millenarian Disciples

Members of mass movements, secular or religious, are never a homogenous group, and where intense ideological action is concerned, no discernible demographic lines can be drawn at either the leadership or follower levels.[4] The characterization of millenarian disciples therefore demands the detection of common motivators across ethnic and socioeconomic origins. Some of those common motivators are discussed in the following survey.

Sense of Deprivation

Persons and groups feeling illegitimately deprived of status, wealth, or freedom tend to distance themselves from the establishments they hold responsible for the perceived injustice. Religious institutions viewed as collaborators with political governments may be abandoned in favor of spiritual alternatives, including extreme millenarian movements (Aberle 1962: 209; Berger 1969: 1). Millenarian theologies, however, seldom offer practical relief. Some even idealize material and other deprivation, alleging that suffering and endurance bestow the purer spiritual state that is conditional for joining God's sacred community (Turner 1969: 99, 111). Frustrating predicaments are thus brilliantly turned into sources of pride and confidence, virtually freeing the movements from the responsibility to resolve the problems that originally led many of their followers into their ranks.

Group Solidarity

The strong sense of group solidarity within intense religious movements lures individuals experiencing loneliness, insecurity, disappointment, and depression, regardless of social status. Members surrender their individuality, personal judgment, and independent thinking in return for the "security against the torture of doubt" (Fromm 1943: 134). According to James Lewis (1998: 35), "[intense religious] communities…provide participants with a ready-made fellowship, a stable worldview and clear ethical guidelines that sharply contrast with the ambivalence and ambiguity of life in a contemporary mass society." Opponents of intense religious movements consider the promise of relief from personal responsibility in exchange for total commitment as illusive and constituent of illegitimate brainwashing (Shupe and Bromley 1995: 411–16; Lewis 1998: 17–20). Many people, however, would welcome the bargain.

The "Alternative Family"

Alarmed medieval women in Europe are reported to have hidden their sons and husbands from the messengers of St Bernard of Clairvaux (1090–1153), least they were tempted to abandon their families and join the Second Crusade (Adams 1943: 142). Bernard's indifference to the potentially disastrous domestic repercussions of the holy mission he vigorously promoted is hardly surprising. Intense religious ideologies, such as those that inspired the Crusades, are typically unconcerned with traditional social institutions. The more radical movements adopt an outright nihilistic approach, based on the notion that the apocalyptic future cannot be built on the foundations of the present but must *replace* it and all of its works. A covenant with the sacred community therefore invalidates all previous commitments, including those to kin and family.

This phenomenon was already ancient in St Bernard's days. A form of alternative family solidarity bonded Christian communities since the genesis of this faith. Paul, in his epistles, addressed his fellow believers as "brothers" and "sisters" (Romans 10:1, 15:30, 16:17; Corinthians I 3:1, 16:12, 15; II 13:11; Galatians 3:15, 5:13; Philippians 1:14; Colossians 1:2, 4:15; Thessalonians I 4:1; II 1:3, 3:14). This influential apostle was probably inspired by Jesus himself, to whom, as the following extracts from the gospel of Matthew imply, the only family that mattered was that of the faithful:

> Someone told [Jesus], "Your mother and your brothers are standing outside, wanting to speak to you." He replied, "Who is my mother and who are my brothers?" Pointing to his disciples, he said, "Here are my mother and my brothers. For whoever does the will of my Father in heaven is my brother and sister and mother" (12:47–50).

> For I have come to turn a man against his father, a daughter against her mother, a daughter-in-law against her mother-in-law, one's enemies will be members of his own households (10: 35–36).

> Another man, one of his disciples, said to him, "Lord, first let me go and bury my father." But Jesus told him, "Follow me, and let the dead bury their own dead (8:21–22).

A similar idea is expressed in Sura 9 of the Koran:

> They who have believed, and fled their homes, and striven with their substance and with their persons on the path of God, shall be of the highest grade with God: and these are they who shall be happy (9:20).

> O believers! Make not friends of your fathers or your brethren if they love unbelief above faith: and who so of you shall make them his friends, will be wrong doers (9:23).

> If your fathers, and your sons, and your brethren, and your wives, and your kindred…be dearer to you than God and His Apostle and efforts on His path, then wait until God shall Himself enter on His work: and God guides not the impious (9:24).

> It is not for the Prophet or the faithful to pray for the forgiveness of those, even though they be of kin, who associate other beings with God, after it hath been made clear to them that they are to be inmates of Hell. For neither Abraham ask forgiveness for his father…when it was shown him that he was an enemy to God, he declared himself clear of him (9:114–15).

The concept of the alternative family spread to numerous millenarian movements and in many variations. Some evolved into eccentric ideological frameworks that consciously challenge elemental cultural understandings and violate social and religious taboos. Recent examples can be found in American millenarian groups active in the 1980s and 1990s. Members of a cult founded by David Brandt Berg actually referred to themselves as "the Family," and colonies were addressed to as "homes," At the same time, the cult's ideology dictated promiscuous sexual relations between the 'brothers and sisters' (Van Zandt 1995: 127–32; Lewis 1998: 86-7). David Koresh claimed his numerous female disciples as his spiritual wives. This spiritual designation nevertheless granted Koresh exclusive sexual access to the women and girls, purportedly to produce a generation of princes under God. Male followers, meanwhile, including the original husbands, were generously promised female consorts in Heaven (Tabor 1998: 424; Bromley and Silver 1995: 154–56; Lewis 1998: 75). The above mentioned Bhagwan Shree Rajneesh dismissed pre-cult marriages, discouraged ties between family members, including parents and children, and promoted abortions and the sterilization of disciples, so that children would not distract the attention of their parents from the leader. Similarly to Berg and Koresh, Rajneesh strictly regulated sexual relations between group members, although unlike the former two "prophets," he restricted his own involvement to watching the procedures (Lindholm 2002: 367, 372).

It is likely that some of the millenarian leaders who challenged traditional family relationships cynically manipulated their disciples to their own advantage and gratification. In other cases, however, this aggressive aspect of millenarianism may have been genuinely rooted in ideological matter. The revocation of religious or civil marriages, and their replacement with behavior rendered immoral or even bizarre by the outside world, also worked as a statement of defiance towards the political and religious establishments. Moreover, the brutal annulling of these most vital and intimate earlier commitments symbolized the spiritual re-birth of the disciples into the alternative religious family. The willing submission to these demands can only be explained by the spellbinding effect of charismatic leaders over their followers.

Shifting Blame

The more intense a religious movement, the sharper its delineations of good and evil, and the more simplistic its responses to complex situations. Thus, intense religious movements enjoy a substantial advantage over official institutions, because the latter's most realistic appraisals and applicable measures can never match the absolute and immediate solutions that God could provide, if only He would. To merit His favor, one might try to improve one's own conduct, but it is easier and infinitely more satisfying to pick on others, to charge them with provoking God's wrath, and to hold them accountable for everything that goes wrong, from individual misfortune to environmental disasters. Targeting "heretics," whatever their identity or background, also enhances inner cohesion of the movement. The conviction that members of the movement alone represent righteousness and decency in an evil and decadent world is likely to upgrade the devotion and commitment of disciples and steel their resolve against punitive measures by hostile institutions.

This is a dangerous route to pursue. Infusing ancient grievances with intense religious meaning can spur destructive confrontation between enticed groups and their rivals (Hobsbawm 1985: 65), antagonists that until then were held back by more rational mutual fear. Some radical religious agents will welcome such lethal outbreaks of violent emotions, either out of cynical calculation or the zealous conviction of the need to purify by fire. Millenarian movements led by such individuals naturally attract much attention and intrigue popular imagination to the point that all millenarian ideologies are collectively perceived as radical and nihilistic theological variations. Millenarian disciples, accordingly, are seen by many as wide-and-wild-eyed fanatics, staring at the skies every waking moment for obscure apocalyptic signs, and likely to kill themselves and others if their hallucinating leader proclaims that this is their ticket to Paradise – or at least to an alien spaceship headed that way. Some millenarian disciples actually fit this mold, but, as with all generalizations, reality is far more intricate.

Moderate Millenarianism

Historical experience understandably designates irrational zealous devotion as the more familiar trait of millenarianism. Still, not all members of intense religious movements are devout idealists. Some may join for rather prosaic reasons, such as to appease family or friends who are members, to stimulate their social life, to find a spouse, to satisfy their need for attention, or simply out of boredom (Hart 1999: 209, 264; Kalyvas 2001: 110). In certain circumstances, even trivial interests may inspire some courage and dedication (Grossman 1995: 89–90), but egotistic and non-ideological motivation tends to be short-lived, unstable, and unpredictable. Intense religious movements have survived major setbacks, including the inglorious demise of their founders, because enough believers maintained their fidelity to the fundamental ideological message (see below), while non-ideological members might scatter at the first sign of trouble. Yet, even steadfast millenarian convictions may have more moderate manifestations, just as non-millenarian religious faith can stir unyielding devotion.

Some extreme millenarian groups actually set specific dates for the Advent, often close enough in time to make believers abandon normal activities, dismiss daily duties, and wait, usually together as a group, for signs from Heaven (Festinger 1957: 13–23). These more captivating manifestations of millenarianism tend to overshadow subtler and more pragmatic millenarian expressions that actually comply with day-to-day existence. 'Everyday millenarians' (Robbins 2001) are no less confident of and committed to the imminent Millennium than their less patient counterparts, but, anxiety notwithstanding, they pursue their regular occupations, schedules, and behavior until definite signs are directly observed or convincingly reported.

This phenomenon is not limited to specific ethnic groups in narrow geographical locations. Joel Robbins (2001) shows that people as culturally distant as fundamentalist Protestants in the U.S. and the Urapmin people of Papua New Guinea employ intriguingly similar means in order to live under the shadow of an impending apocalypse, the exact arrival of which nevertheless remains obscure. In both cases, normal occupations correlate with religious preparedness. Robbins (2001: 532) reports that during his twenty-five months of fieldwork among the Urapmin, "scarcely a week went by without someone announcing that they had heard that somewhere in the world a sign had appeared announcing the Advent of the last days." The news would excite conversation, encourage soul-searching, and inspire personal vows, but simultaneously daily chores were fulfilled, fields cultivated, even soccer games played. The ethnographer did witness several occasions at which millenarian anticipation noticeably intensified, involving larger church attendance, higher concern over personal fortunes, and some neglect of regular duties. But within two or three weeks life gradually returned to normal, and the villagers were left strikingly unperturbed by the experience:

> People realized that during these times everyone was talking more than usual about the last days, but no one seemed to think anything qualitatively new had begun, and when things died down no one thought anything special had ended or failed. Furthermore, it was not as if the topic of the apocalypse vanished once this movement-like behavior died down. The never ending discourse of speculation on Jesus' return simply settled back into the flow of daily life (Robbins 2001: 533).

Dispensational American millenarianism[5] also avoids consigning the Millennium to specific calendar dates. Believers are very conscious of the Millennium, and its clues are regularly searched for in dramatic political and environmental events, but in the meantime they pursue their earthly goals as usual. In fact, they even strive to excel financially. The approach, as noted in Manuel Castells' study on fundamentalism (1997a: 24), is that "God will help the good Christian in his business life; after all he has to provide for the family." At the same time, ideological awareness dictates minimal interaction with 'outsiders,' allowing only what is necessary and beneficial to individual and communal well-being. Modern technology and infrastructure are readily utilized and commerce with the outside world is carried on, but undesirable ideals and ethics are screened out. Means of control include a strictly traditional family life, as well as alternative religious services, education, media, and social activities (Castells 1997a: 23). An ideal moral 'order' against the surrounding decadent 'chaos' is maintained (Wuthnow and Lawson 1994: 21), and the interests of the religious community are efficiently served and satisfied with no need for outside interference. Thus, the pursuit of daily occupations does not disturb the cognitive expectation of the Millennium, nor does it compromise the ensuring of moral preparedness for the event.

The line that separates millenarian and non-millenarian religious manifestations thins out in 'everyday millenarianism,' but it exists nonetheless. An illustration of this fine line can be found in the notices commonly pegged by the entrance of conservative churches in the United States, in which forthcoming local events are dutifully stipulated with the addendum 'God Willing' (Bruce 1996: 76). Robbins (2001: 529) contextualizes these notes within 'everyday millenarianism:' no one necessarily expects the Second Coming of Jesus to interrupt the seasonal charity fair or the meetings of the local Christmas decoration committee, but true faith demands recognition that it might, and one should be ready in case it does. Nevertheless, the attribution of millenarian connotations to this little ritual seems to overplay its meaning. It is also customary for religious Jews to head written materials, be they billboards announcing new construction, administrative directives, or personal letters, with the acronym for the idiom "by God's consent" in Hebrew (*be'ezrat ha-shem* – בע"ה) or Aramaic (*besi'ata de-shamaya* – ד"בס).[6] The Koran has a similar notion. Sura 18:23 instructs: "Say not thou of a thing, 'I will surely do it to-morrow,' without, 'If God will.'" Appropriately, the expression *Bism'Illah*, meaning literally 'In the name of God,' or in its full form *Bism'Illah el-Rahman el-Rahim* (بسم الله الرحمن الرحيم) – 'In the name of God the Compassionate, the Merciful' – not only opens each sura of the Koran but also commonly heads Muslim official statements.[7] These customs carry no millenarian implications; they merely proclaim faith in the involvement of God in all paths of life, and the recognition that all human pursuits depend on His will. The church notes should be seen as keen but simple statements of faith, bare of millenarian inferences.

Semi-Millenarianism

The distinction between millenarian and non-millenarian religious intensity can be found not so much in the theological concepts about the Millennium than in the roles that people are expected to play prior to its Advent, at the level of here and now. The Second Coming of Christ is indispensable in the belief system of all devout Christians. Yet, most of them surmise that since humans lack the right and the means to interfere with the divine schedule, their duty should be to sanctify God's name and prove fidelity to Him through the daily performance of the ritual duties and moral teachings of the Scriptures (Ammerman 1991: 5). The Millennium constitutes an expectation and an aspiration, but its impact on immediate daily concerns remains minimal. This distinction is certainly viable in Western Christian settings, but the issue finds intriguing equivalents in nativistic intense religious movements that were acutely influenced by monotheism. Several examples will be discussed in the following chapter, but for an introductory case let us return for a few moments to the Pueblo Revolt along the Rio Grande. Was the uprising a millenarian phenomenon, or does it merely illustrate the degree of religious intensity that non-millenarian religion is also capable of?

Popé, the most prominent leader of the revolt, behaved as a millenarian prophet when he claimed to be inspired by supernatural forces and promised in their name immediate rewards to those who re-embraced the allegedly corruption-free native faith and customs (Knaut 1995: 168; Graziano 1999: 117–18). In retrospect, his ambition to abolish the Spanish-Catholic cultural and religious influences and to restore the untainted pre-contact life modes seems unrealistic. Yet, it was true to the principles of intense millenarianism, which has no interest in religious reforms, disparages political compromises, and seeks absolute alterations after its own visions. At the same time, clear traces of strategic thinking can also be found – those that contrast with the irrational dismissal of objective conditions so characteristic of extreme millenarian action. It was no coincidence that the revolt erupted in the period preceding the arrival of the triennial supply convoy. During that time, the Spanish community and military units were short on provisions and therefore more vulnerable (Knaut 1995: 169). It should also be noted that promises of supernatural military intervention on the side of the rebels, as typical in millenarian cases, were never made. The expectation was evidently only for standard divine assistance on the battlefield, something that most religions assure deserving believers of in times of war.

Whether millenarian or not, there was a dominant intense religious element in the basic motivation for the uprising. The subjects of the Pueblos were all touched to varying degrees by the tentacles of the Spanish colonial system and the Catholic missions. The fervor shown by the Pueblo masses in ejecting them and reviving what they understood to be pre-contact religious culture seems to have been keen and genuine, regardless of whatever ulterior motives their leaders may have had. Close analysis shows that the Pueblo Revolt never evolved into full millenarianism, but that it retained enough millenarian aspects of ideology and action to merit a semi-millenarian definition.[8]

Semi-millenarianism differs from everyday millenarianism in being the product of upheaval, an outcome of action no less than a generator of it. It is also closer to extreme millenarianism, but the distinctions must not be blurred. Extreme millenarianism does share some elements with "everyday" and "semi-" millenarian varieties, but in reality it exists as an isolated religious farm, with no ideological next-door neighbors. It is by far the most visible and dramatic expression of religious intensity, at odds with the most fundamental established codes of behavior and social understandings. The new cultural landscape that extreme millenarianism has in mind demands nothing less than the complete obliteration of the extant. It is dedicated to the preparations for and, indeed, the hastening of an ultimate apocalypse. Various and complex reasons drive people to become extreme millenarian leaders, disciples, and sometimes martyrs, but the tracks of the truly dedicated among them begin with an irresistible striving for change. From that point on, charisma, ambition, psychology, and circumstances decide their individual roles. All of them, regardless of status inside or outside the movement, will work to appease their version of God, often in rather unconventional ways, and thus speed the advent of the day of ultimate change. Change they will achieve – radical behavior usually does – but as far as historical experience goes, the new reality never corresponds to that for which they struggle.

5 Messianic Hopes Shattered

The temptations of millenarianism are matched by its risks and the hopes it inspires by the disappointments it incurs. Facing the failure of their apocalyptic promises, members of intense religious movements will see hope, joy, and pride turn into despondency and depression, as well as confusion. Having lost all confidence in traditional institutions, they invested mental, spiritual and material assets in an alternative that, incredibly, has let them down. Repercussions on both the individual and communal level are severe.

This outline can be traced in the careers of the two intense religious movements with which this chapter is concerned. Both emerged in Africa during the nineteenth century, but the people involved shared no historical, cultural, or religious background, and it is highly unlikely that many among them, if any, were even aware of the other's existence. The Cattle Killing cult of South Africa is a classic millenarian case. The Mahdi Revolt of Sudan epitomizes semi-millenarianism. These examples demonstrate clear cross-cultural patterns in the emergence, growth, action, and fall of mass intense religious movements, as well as their unmistakable historical imprint. They also indicate that while the immediate causes of religious intensification may be political and economic, those affected do not primarily seek communal freedom or material relief, nor retribution against those who deny them these essentials. More than anything they are after hope, and having faced the dehydration of other sources, they spare no means to appease the one Entity left that is able to provide it.

Extreme Millenarianism – The Cattle Killing, South Africa, 1856–57

Like many other millenarian movements, the Cattle Killing cult had modest beginnings. In April of 1856, Nongqawuse, an orphaned teenage girl from a Xhosa homestead in Cape Colony, experienced visions while watering her herd by the Gxara River. Ancestral spirits, she later told, revealed to her that they would soon return to life en masse, drive out the white soldiers and settlers, and bestow prosperity and happiness upon the Xhosa people in their justly regained lands. Yet, as proof of faith the spirits ordered the Xhosa to kill their cattle, a vital element of Xhosa subsistence, consume or destroy all their vegetable food, and dispose of their property. All of these losses, it was promised, would be replaced sevenfold with wealth bequeathed from heaven (Millin 1954: 43–44; Meintjes 1971: 241–43). Nongqawuse was ridiculed at first, but she found a persuasive disciple in her uncle Mhlakaza, who had his own past experiences with prophetic visions. Mhlakaza engaged in a vigorous and effective campaign to convince chiefs and common people that his niece's testimony was truthful, and that it was not only their duty but also to their great benefit to fulfill the demands of the spirits.

The slaughter of cattle began hesitantly, but its pace increased with the conversion of prominent chiefs. During that same period, parts of Xhosaland suffered from crop failure and spells of a lethal cattle lung disease, and the most enthusiastic response to Nongqawuse's message came from the regions worst afflicted (Peires 1989: 97). Nongqawuse went as far as pinpointing two specific dates for the apocalypse (August 16, 1856; February 16 or 17, 1857), but even as her prophecies failed to materialize, believers remained undeterred. Each disappointment was explained by insufficient devotion on the part of the Xhosa, who obviously failed to appease the ancestral spirits. As a consequence, rather than saving what was left of the herds, the killing intensified (Meintjes 1971:2

MESSIANIC HOPES SHATTERED 53

43, 255; Hodgson 1982: 27). Rumors that ancestral spirits had been sighted somewhere in the land encouraged believers elsewhere, and the coincidental illnesses suffered by some leading skeptics were interpreted as divine punishment for their lack of faith. Only when nothing happened on a third and final appointed date (April 17, 1857) did people realize the calamity they had allowed themselves to be led into. By then it was too late. Despite emergency assistance from the British authorities, starvation, disease, and exhaustion were to claim tens of thousands of victims.[1]

The ensuing despair is vividly portrayed in the records of the period. One of the more dramatic documents describes the Xhosa King Sarhili, once proud and self-assured but now defeated and broken-spirited, pleading to the hated British colonial administration for his life and the lives of his people:

> I, this day, in the presence of my brothers and councilors, ask the forgiveness of the Governor for what I have done. I have fallen. I and my family are starving. I ask help from the Governor to save me from dying. I this day place myself in the hands of the Governor. I am willing to come to any terms the Governor may think fit to dictate to me – I wish to be the subject of the Governor... (cited in Peires 1989: 280).

A report by a British agent, written in late 1857, confirms the total collapse of Xhosa resistance, asserting that the "whole country [can be taken] with of a force of 100 men – for [it] is nearly desolate. 100 cows would buy all their guns – they even offer [gun]powder for corn. You can dictate any terms..." (cited in Peires 1989: 282). The Cattle Killing devastated Xhosaland, eliminated all hopes of halting European expansion, and placed the very existence of Xhosa society at jeopardy. It remains to this day an embodiment of catastrophic millenarianism. Three main factors contributed to the context within it developed. One was the combined effect of environmental afflictions and government policies; the second was the dominant place of visions and magic in Xhosa religious culture; the third was Christian influence.

During the nineteenth century, much of Xhosa's pasture and agricultural land was being lost to British confiscations and to the rapidly growing farms of industrious white settlers. Xhosa resources were further depleted by taxation and recurring cattle epidemics,[2] while prolonged spells of drought exacerbated the crisis. A relatively frequent ordeal in the region, droughts had influenced another Xhosa millenarian movement several years before (1850–53). The prophet in that case, Mlanjeni, had limited his demands to the eradication of witchcraft (probably under Christian influence), as had Nxele, a still earlier millenarian leader active between 1818–19 (Millin 1954: 42–43, Hodgson 1982: 26). Millenarian tendencies and some ideological principles similar to those of the Cattle Killing were thus rooted in Xhosa tradition. The failures of earlier movements may have in fact indirectly inspired the unprecedented excesses of the Cattle Killing doctrine. Believers might have reasoned that the relatively moderate ritual measures dictated by earlier prophets had been insufficient incentives for the intervention of the ancestral spirits. Sacrificing all cattle, on the other hand, would have been more proportional to the predicaments of the period and to the quality of the supernatural assistance sorely needed.

Yet, the assemblage of an apocalyptic platform demanded an amalgamation of these nativistic traditions with Christianity. Such fusion is already evident in the case of Nxele. Educated by missionaries in his youth, Nxele came to see himself as the younger brother of Jesus, claimed to possess a similar miraculous power of healing, and emphasized the theme of resurrection in his teachings. Mhlakaza, Nongqawuse's first and most ardent disciple, grew up under Anglican influence, approached Christianity, and even adopted the somewhat peculiar name Wilhelm Goliath until the Europeans' ridicule of his visions distanced him from their faith (Peires 1989: 33–36). Judeo-Christian themes were nonetheless woven into the Cattle Killing prophecies, probably under Mhlakaza's influence (1989: 98). The resurrection of ancestral spirits is an obvious example. Another is the prediction that the Europeans would be cast into the sea, which was probably inspired by the fate of Pharaoh's army (Exodus 14:19–30). Ideological, ritual, and symbolic motifs all reflect the cultural-religious synthesis that made possible the Cattle Killing. In that, the cult resembles other nativistic millenarian movements. The magnitude of failure, however, is a more distinct aspect of this particular case.

The Cattle Killing illustrates how a grave crisis can deteriorate under religious intensity into an utter disaster. This tragic millenarian movement led the Xhosa nation into a fateful historical crossroads. Its traumatic outcome invalidated some of the spiritual axioms that guided the Xhosa through crisis since time immemorial. Painful psychological and ideological readjustments were needed at its aftermath to accommodate the ceding of Xhosa aspirations for freedom in their land. One option was to simply join the victors; following the catastrophe, Christian missionaries intensified their efforts among the Xhosa and urged the stricken survivors to forsake their ancestral faiths and recognize the greater power of Jesus (Hodgson 1982: 27).

The subsequent capitulation to white rule and, partially, to Christianity did not obliterate Xhosa ethno-cultural identity but called into question some of their basic values. Recuperation demanded a reevaluation of the Xhosa past, including the pivotal Cattle Killing disaster, which for many Xhosa of later generations became an embarrassment. The voluntary embarking of their ancestors on a trek to self-destruction following the hallucinatory visions of a feeble-minded girl and the fantasies of her eccentric uncle was hard to owe up to. Alternative explanations had to be found, such that would at least partly clear the forefathers of the responsibility for the calamitous folly. Popular conspiracy theories placed the Cattle Killing at the core of an intricate plot devised by various enemies to destroy Xhosa power (Peires 1989: 218ff.). These theories have no historical foundations: the Cattle Killing spread as vigorously as it had because all traditional and rational responses had failed to contend with an increasingly grim objective situation. Miracles seemed the only solution, and miracles were precisely what Nongqawuse had promised. The attraction and appeal of the movement were overwhelming, with only few non-believers among the Xhosa daring to openly resist the frenzy. "Believers obeyed the spirits," comments Sarah Millin (1954: 44), "unbelievers obeyed their chiefs." The cult was a communal human reaction to hopelessness, fear, and frustration, a desperate last measure to curb personal and social degradation – but one that was rooted in Xhosa cultural grounds. There were no enemy conspiracies. The Cattle Killing was initiated by Xhosa, aimed at Xhosa, captivated Xhosa, and Xhosa were its victims.

Non-Millenarian Intensity – The Mahdi Revolt, Sudan, 1881–98

Sudan was among the least appealing lands in Africa of the nineteenth century, and Victorian visitors spared no superlatives in their descriptions of its misery.[3] Humans and livestock there endured relentless heat, prolonged droughts, swarms of insects, waves of locusts, and an array of gruesome diseases. Yet, between the years 1881–1898 this inhospitable territory became the theater of a remarkable historical drama, featuring one of the more vigorous religiously motivated political movements in the annals of Islam.

The founder of the movement, Mohammed Ahmed, was born on November 10, 1845, in central Sudan, to a modest family that nevertheless claimed the bloodline of the Prophet Mohammed. Mohammed Ahmed received a strict religious education and excelled in his studies but, following a discord with his teachers, abandoned the school and eventually withdrew to an ascetic existence, soon to become a reputable holy man, admired in the region and beyond. In 1881, Mohammed Ahmed officially declared himself the expected *Mahdi,* a divinely appointed savior under whose leadership pious Muslims were to enforce justice and equity in the world (Holt 1961: 78–80). As a primary objective, he openly preached for ridding Sudan of the corrupt and unpopular Egyptian administration, which ruled the country under a British political and military canopy. Violent resistance was presented as a religious duty and a means to spiritual salvation (Farwell 1967: 8).

MESSIANIC HOPES SHATTERED

Anticipating punitive military measures, Mohammed Ahmed departed with his followers on a *hijra*[4] to Jebel Gedir, a remote mountain in the southern Kordofan, where they were joined by large numbers of religious extremists, runaway slaves, outlaws, and other malcontents.

On December 9, 1881 and June 6, 1882 the Mahdi's forces overwhelmed two military expeditions dispatched by the government. Many Sudanese regarded the triumph of Mahdist clubs and spears over Egyptian firearms in miraculous terms. A comet became known as "the Star of the Mahdi," and myths circulated over the alleged invulnerability of the leader and his warriors to enemy bullets (Holt 1961: 80; Farwell 1967: 17, 191). As support for him surged and scattered insurrections erupted in various parts of the country, the Mahdi declared holy war – *jihad* – against all who refused to acknowledge him. Symbolically following in the political footsteps of the Prophet, he nominated four caliphs and launched a campaign to capture the country. On December 5, 1883, at Shaykan in the Kordofan, the Mahdi's army annihilated a force of 10,000 mostly Egyptian troops under the British Colonel William Hicks, a veteran commander, and several European officers. It was said that the Mahdi had promised that 40,000 angels would fight with his men against Hicks, and many of his ecstatic troops swore to have actually seen them. The preparations to advance on the capital Khartoum could now count on devoted following through most of Sudan (with the exception of a few central tribes and the non-Muslim south) and on widespread faith in the Mahdi's divine mission.

Amid mounting public pressure, British Prime Minister William Gladstone assigned to the defense of Khartoum Charles George Gordon, an eccentric but renowned officer with a proven record as governor and commander in China and in Sudan itself. Nonetheless, on January 26, 1885 the Mahdi's armies broke through the fortifications of the besieged capital, subjecting the population of the city, including several prominent Europeans, to an indiscriminate massacre. Gordon himself was killed on the steps to the governmental palace (Farwell 1967: 94–96). Omdurman, across the Nile from the devastated Khartoum, replaced it as capital under the new Mahdist regime. Sudan was now free from foreign occupation, but the Mahdi himself, whose health steadily deteriorated, died less than five months later (June 22, 1885). He was succeeded by Caliph Abdullah Ibn Sayed Mohammad at-Taaisha, a cattle herder in his youth and one of the Mahdi's early and most devoted disciples.

Caliph Abdullah maintained the Mahdist rule in Sudan for another thirteen years. Determined, ruthless, and cunning, he stood firm against Anglo-Egyptian pressure at his northern border, defeated the Christian Abyssinian kingdom in the south (March 1889), endured calamitous episodes of famine and locusts (1889–1890), and survived frequent domestic unrest and several assassination attempts (Holt 1961: 97–101; Farwell 1967: 185–89, 205–7; Ibrahim 2004:7). His faith in Mahdism never faltered. In 1887, the Caliph went as far as dispatching letters to Ottoman Sultan Abdul Hamid II, the Egyptian Khedive Mohammed Tawfiq, and even Queen Victoria, advising them to accept Mahdist Islam or suffer the consequences.

Domestically, however, the Mahdist state was a stringent but functioning theocracy, founded on the axiom that supreme power was assigned to the Mahdi and the Caliph by Allah Himself. Books and theological texts that were not directly related to Mahdist doctrines were destroyed. Much of the legal code devised by the Mahdi consisted of puritan regulations based on the leader's understanding of the true spirit of Islam. Vices, luxuries, gluttony, smoking, and drinking were to be strictly avoided, as were jewelry, music, dancing, feasting, cursing, and the purchase of brides. Followers were urged to uphold humility, meekness of spirit, and endurance, and were expected to always perform the five daily prayers and visit the tombs of saints. The Mahdi glorified poverty and simplicity and established a code dress for his people, consisting of the *jibba*, a long white dress with colored patches, and sandals or bare feet instead of shoes (Farwell 1967: 8, 18–19, 23–24). These regulations were strictly enforced both by the Mahdi and Caliph Abdullah, and violators were incarcerated or publicly executed.[5]

Yet in the longer term, the aggressive but isolated Mahdist state could not sustain the combined pressure of its African and European foes. In July 1889, a reformed Egyptian army under British command crushed a daring but disorganized Sudanese invasion. In December 1893, an Italian force routed the Caliph's troops in Eritrea. During the following year, Belgian and French colonial troops stepped up their operations in southern Sudan. Finally, on September 2, 1898, a joint British-Egyptian expedition under General Horatio Herbert Kitchener destroyed the army of the Caliph near Omdurman. Abdullah escaped but was found and killed by British soldiers in the following year (Holt 1961: 98, 104–8; Farwell 1967: 181–82, 297ff.).

To better understand nineteenth-century Islamic intensification in Sudan and the subsequent rise of the Mahdi, we must look into the country's broader political and religious context. The eighteenth and nineteenth centuries saw much debate and contemplation among Muslim thinkers and leaders on how to impede the gradual political and economic decline in the realm of Islam, while Christian Europe grew constantly stronger and more successful. Two opposing directions were suggested. Rational Muslim leaders such as Mohammed Ali (1805–48) in Egypt and Sultan Mahmud II (1801–39) in Istanbul considered ideological and technological stagnation as the heart of the problem and worked diligently to reform their societies and armies after European models (Brockelmann 1980: 348–50; Lewis 1993: 183–84; Hourani 1991: 272–73). Opposite them stood conservative clerics and religious activists who believed the solution to be a return to what they considered the original and immaculate values of Islam, purified from corrupting European influence. The latter approach in its more radical manifestations, including Wahhabi[6] schools, dominated the Sudanese ideological landscape (Ibrahim 2004: 1). Thus, far from being a temporary aberration in time of crisis, Mahdism was an extreme feature of Islamic fundamentalist doctrines that already fermented the religious culture of Sudan.

There can be no doubt that mounting resentment towards the corruption, exploitation, and incompetence of the Egyptian government in Sudan contributed handsomely to the popularity of the Mahdi. Gordon himself underlined social injustice and individual suffering as being responsible for the Mahdi phenomenon, a feeling echoed by other Europeans familiar with the country (Farwell 1967: 4, 37, 78). Yet, it would be positively wrong to downplay the role of intense Islamic faith in Sudan to a mere consequence of political and economic duress. European observers were well aware of the independent power of religion in many parts of their expanding imperial domains. Winston Churchill (1943: 129) commented that a common "climate of opinion" among the British in the late nineteenth century was that "too much religion of any kind…was a bad thing. Among natives especially, fanaticism was highly dangerous and roused them to murder, mutiny or rebellion." Hence, the Mahdi movement should primarily be perceived as an aggressive and uncompromising crop of religious intensity, which absorbed toxic moisture from the hardships of Anglo-Egyptian occupation, but whose seeds drew their cultural minerals from the peculiar ideological soil of Sudan.

Sudanese Mahdism was never a true millenarian phenomenon, even though it did show some millenarian features. Islam adopted the idea of the redeemer, or Mahdi, of which there is no mention in the Koran, from Christianity and Judaism (Ibrahim 2004: 2–3).[7] Despite the trust of his fanatical followers in his superhuman qualities, Mohammed Ahmed, as a Sunni Muslim, apparently considered himself a divinely inspired leader and teacher, whose mission was nevertheless worldly and immediate. That outlook differs from the Shi'a fundamental faith in the Twelfth Imam, who is to lead the righteous believers to ultimate victory over the forces of heresy and evil near the final Day of Judgment (Rippin 2001: 118–19). The Mahdi of Sudan wished to return Islamic faith to the pristine form practiced by the Prophet and his Companions, restore the hegemony of religion in the realm of Islam, and broaden that realm by all available means (Farwell 1967: 8; Ibrahim 2004: 4). Those ambitious yet rational goals were expressed in his own acts and policies, as well as in those of his successor Caliph Abdullah. Ottoman and Egyptian laws were substituted with a legal code derived from Islamic religious law (*shari'a*). Shari'a law is inspired by and based on religion, but it was formulated for an earthly, not heavenly, society. A new administration was established, with judges appointed, coins struck, taxes imposed, and a central treasury built in Omdurman (Holt 1961: 89–91; Farwell 1967: 25) – institutions that are likely to lose their relevance in any Final Apocalypse. Mahdist Sudan certainly was religiously zealous, but, similar to the original Muslim society of the Prophet's day, it was foremost a physical political entity, one which left eschatological expectations to an unspecified future date.

The perseverance of Mahdism merits consideration. Mahdist puritanical law denied the Sudanese the few pleasures available in their otherwise harsh existence. Warfare, rife with casualties, was frequent. Crippling environmental afflictions did not concur with the notion of divine favor that the Mahdist government claimed to enjoy. Yet, Mahdist Sudan prevailed for thirteen years, succumbing not to domestic dissent but to massive pressure from superior foreign armies. It has been claimed that the absolute doctrinal definitions of good and evil, or of faithful and heretic, denied the movement crucial ideological maneuvering space and thwarted the long-term consolidation of its initial success (Ibrahim 2004: 5). Yet, ideological rigidity was imperative for Mahdism. Islam in its more radical, mystic, and populist forms was the only power in Sudan capable of gathering enough support and determination to sustain the adversities, suffering, and risks involved in the campaign against Anglo-Egyptian domination.

The idea and ideal of the Mahdi outlived the state he had founded, as proven by the stubborn allegiance of many Sudanese to Mahdism even after the Anglo-Egyptian re-conquest, and despite relentless efforts by the occupiers to uproot all semblances of the movement (Ibrahim 2004: 8). During the two decades that followed the fall of Abdullah, there was a surge of self-acclaimed prophets who claimed divine powers, gathered supporters, and tried in vain to reproduce Mohammed Ahmed's original accomplishments (Holt 1961: 31ff.). Furthermore, while the ideological structure built by the Mahdi and the Caliph as a whole may have proven too rigid to withstand contemporaneous domestic and foreign pressures, some of its principles were of sufficient appeal to the authentic necessities of Sudanese culture and society to serve more flexible future political frameworks. Mahdist ideas in modified form featured in the long political struggle led, among others, by the Mahdi's own son, a struggle that ended with the Sudanese declaration of independence on January 19, 1955.

Contending with Disappointment

In a memorable episode of Charles Dickens' *The Chimes*, Will Fern ends his appeal to a surprised group of gentry with a warning. His fellow laborers had been brought to utter despair by the oppression of the ruling classes, and are at the brink of secession from the common social bond of England. The laborer's spirit must be won back "afore the day comes when even his Bible changes in his altered mind, and the words seem to him to read…'Whither thou goest, I can Not go; where you lodgest, I do Not lodge; thy people are Not my people; Nor thy God my God!'."[8]

Dickens was concerned with social issues, not religious ones, but Will Fern's choice of analogy epitomizes the common principle. A spirit that needs to be won back must have once been in the right place. Disappointment, and disillusion with those behind it, might distance it. Disillusion is one of the more intense human conditions and often among the more volatile. It can be found in the core of rebellions as well as in processes of social disintegration, which may be less dynamic but potentially destructive in their own right. The long-term fate of intense religious movements, both millenarian and non-millenarian, depends on the factor of perseverance, in the ability of leaders to explain and disciples to endure the failure of acute and vital promises. Since no apocalypse has ever materialized, all intense religious movements to date have faced this critical test. Cognitive dissonance (Festinger 1957: 3), a variance of the psychological tendency to reduce to insignificance the gap between wish and reality, can go a long way in abating the crisis. Imaginative variations of it are frequently found among flustered members of failed intense religious movements, especially among disoriented millenarian disciples. In one of its curious but not infrequent forms, cognitive dissonance may actually bolster support for the beleaguered movement. This supposedly irrational attitude makes more sense when considering what admission of failure actually means to the devout. In his analysis of Xhosa insistence to continue the slaughter of their cattle, even as Nongqawuse's promises repeatedly failed to materialize, Jeffrey Peires (1989: 151) rationalizes:

> The possibility that the prophecies might be at fault was simply too horrific to consider and since the believers had no way back, they were compelled to go forward, stifling their doubts. Thus it was that the more the evidence mounted that they should give up hope the more the believers clutched at every straw, and the more that logic demanded that they slacken their pace the more they redoubled the effort to slaughter every last beast that walked and to eliminate the small band of unbelievers who had refused to share their hopes and their tribulations.

The American mid-nineteenth-century Millerite movement shared neither the multitude of followers nor the calamitous outcome of the Cattle Killing, but this testimony of shock, despair, and disorientation expressed by a disheartened Millerite disciple in all likelihood echoes the feelings of the distraught Xhosa:

> Our fondest hopes and expectations were blasted…weeping came over us as I never experienced before…we wept and wept till the day dawn. I mused in my own heart saying, my Advent experience has been the richest and brightest of all my Christian experience. If this had proved a failure, what was the rest of my Christian experience worth?…Is there no reality to our fondest hope and expectation of those things? (cited in Nichol 1944: 247–48).

This is hardly the kind of mood that produces a healthy mind in a healthy body, and studies in the United States have indeed revealed that nightmares, amnesia, hallucinations, violent outbursts, and self-destructive tendencies are commonly experienced by former millenarian disciples (Lewis 1998: 20–23). Numerous people are drawn to millenarian movements due to frustrations and dissatisfactions in the outside world, which they feel no longer apt to brave. To many of those, the prospects of dealing again with these bad old situations would seem out of the question, having had so much hope, efforts, and resources invested in the alternative bliss (Festinger et al. 1956: 26–28). Likewise hard to surrender would be the solidarity, companionship, and mutual support within the movement that replaced the loneliness outside, the conviction of moral superiority that substituted that of crippling inadequacy, and the exhilarating certainty of intimacy with divinity itself among those who formerly felt cared about by no one at all. The pain, frustration, and confusion in a hopeless existence does not distinguish between an urban middle-class American unable to cope with the stresses of modernity and a Xhosa herder feeling powerless against the British. Members of both societies have found strikingly similar solace and hope in the intoxicating tenets of millenarian movements, and the resistance of many in each group to the excruciating sobering process is fittingly parallel. Under this same light we have to examine the suicidal determination of Sudanese warriors against Kitchener's vastly superior firepower during the final Battle of Omdurman. Winston Churchill (1943: 198, 200, 202), fighting as a young officer in Kitchener's forces, vividly described these fearless, yet futile assaults:

> They are advancing and they are advancing fast. A tide is coming in. But what is this sound which we hear: a deadened roar coming up to us in waves? They are cheering for God, his Prophet and his holy Khalifa…I saw the full blast of Death strike this human wall. Down went their standards by dozens and their men by hundreds. Wide gaps and shapeless heaps appeared in their array. One saw them jumping and tumbling under the shrapnel bursts; but none turned back…However, discipline and machinery triumphed over the most desperate valour…

Figure 9 The theological glorification of the execution of Jesus finds exuberant expression in the ecclesiastical art of Orthodox denominations. The Chapel of the Golgotha in the Church of the Holy Sepulcher, Jerusalem (photograph: M. Koçak).

British war correspondent G.W. Steevens was similarly impressed: "our men were perfect, but the [Caliph's warriors] were superb – beyond perfection. It was their largest, best and bravest army that ever fought against us for Mahdism, and it died worthily of the huge empire Mahdism won and kept so long" (Cited in Farwell 1967: 309). When considering the thirteen years of fervent faith in the cause, the immeasurable sacrifices made on its behalf, and the joy that came with the self-perceptive as the only Muslims truly close to Allah and his two holy Messengers, it becomes easier to comprehend this implausible resolve.

Still, severe setbacks cannot be just ignored, and the desire to preserve a failed movement, keen as it might be, must be supported with some imaginative and convincing explanations, including a revision of the theological framework (Tabor 1998: 419). The eagerness of believers to retain their faith may ensure a smoother ideological adaptation. If, for example, an apocalyptic advent fails to occur at a promised date, the leader can explain that believers are not yet found to be worthy of it, or that it did take place in Heaven and that its manifestation on earth demands additional faith and devotion (Festinger et al. 1956: 26–28). In 1947, an old "cargo prophetess" (see below) in the Cook Islands promised her people a spirit ship loaded with splendid commodities if they were baptized in the name of Satan (Crocombe 1961). When the miracle ship failed to materialize, she conveniently blamed it on the single man who resisted conversion. This historical anecdote is in itself harmless, but it contains some of the same basic components that can be found in the Cattle Killing and numerous other movements, and it also exemplifies the innumerable ways through which the non-confirmation of millenarian promises can be negotiated.

Even the personal demise of prophets need not cause the disintegration of intense religious movements, since the ideological passion of disciples may surpass the commitment to any one individual, authoritarian and charismatic as he or she may be (Gager 1975: 47; 1998: 41). Paradoxically, if the death of the leader is successfully formulated into an ideological doctrine, it can actually *add* to the popularity the movement and help its expansion. We need not search exotic past cults for an illustration. No believing Christian, regardless of denomination, would think of the crucifixion of Jesus in terms of failure; the gruesome conclusion of his earthly life is celebrated as his ultimate glory, a fulfillment of the preconceived divine plan. The event, which, as we have seen before, might have destroyed Christianity while still in its infancy, thus became its most solid spiritual foundation.

This fundamental Christian precept was later oversimplified and distorted by myriad millenarian leaders and disciples while maneuvering their movements through crisis. The otherwise inconceivable decease of prophets received imaginative interpretations that allowed those who wished to maintain their faith to do so. In some cases, the dead prophets were presented as the mere precursors of the real divine redeemer; in others, the actual event of death was disbelieved, and the disappearance of prophets was rationalized as a necessary temporary departure before their glorious final return to complete their holy mission. In his *Historia Francorum,* St. Gregory of Tours tells of a sixth-century self-proclaimed messiah from Bruges, who was hacked to pieces by the troops of a local bishop. This inconvenience, however, did not prevent his disciples from maintaining their faith in him through the remainder of their lives. Nxele, previously mentioned here as one of the millenarian prophets that preceded the Cattle Killing cult, was imprisoned by the British on Robben Island and drowned during an attempt to escape. Decades later, and only a few years before Nongqawuse experienced her fateful visions, Nxele's son Mjuza announced that his father was returning to fight the British at the head of a spectral army of ancestors, and many Xhosa believed him (Peires 1989: 72). Ndungumoi (active 1882–85), leader of the Tuka revival in Fiji, was banished by the British to another island, married locally, led a quiet life for years, and passed away while peacefully sailing back to his native land. Neither his prolonged and content retirement, nor his unobtrusive death deflected the adoration of his disciples or their confidence that he would someday lead them again. Some even claimed to have received letters from him, allegedly written well after the reported date of his demise (Brewster 1922: 278).

An interesting analogy emerges between millenarian leaders and some popular bandit chiefs. Having made a career out of robbing and harassing members of institutional elites, these men earned the admiration of oppressed peasants. In some cases, the latter refused to believe reports of the violent deaths of their idols. Eric Hobsbawm (1985: 51) explains that this peculiar phenomenon "expresses the wish that the people's champion cannot be defeated...but will come back one day to restore justice." Much separates popular bandits from founders of intense religious movements, but identical methods have been employed by the supporters of charismatic leaders of both classes when contending with their untimely demise – and with the possible disintegration of the groups they led and the hopes they represented.

Siren's Song: The Universal Lure of Religious Intensity

Intense religious behavior is essentially an irregular manifestation of the original religious exchange. Prayer, piety, and sacrifice in return for divine assistance are taken to the extreme by social confusion, political oppression, material loss, or simply psychological and emotional stress. As conventional means of coping fail, intense religious movements become attractive alternatives. Spiritual relief and faith-based directives to immediate action cannot solve complex earthly situations, but they provide temporary relief and comfort, even if based on fantasy. Variations notwithstanding, this principle applies to all the movements discussed in this book. Medieval Europeans also were escaping feudal duress when setting off to battle Muslims for a distant shrine. Pueblo Indians, made desperate by exploitative colonial authorities, finally rose to eject Spain along with its Church. South African Xhosa, feeling deprived and marginalized, engaged in self-destruction to evoke ancestral spirits. Oppressed Sudanese offered minds, hearts, and weapons to a prospected redeemer. Alternative religious ideologies respond to genuine despair and, even if mostly innovative, they have sufficient roots in local cultural traditions to relate to target populations. Their call is as tempting and elusive as a Siren's song, and the consequences to those lured by it are often equally disastrous.

In the struggle for self-preservation, the sensible and educated may seek the shelter of religious intensity along with the superstitious and ignorant, and the rich will share that same refuge with the poor. Alternative ideological orders tend to challenge the taboos, divisions, and understandings of the outside world. Like the authors of the American Declaration of Independence, the prophets of such orders also hold their truths to be self-evident, although in their case all men are *re*-created equal and rather than being "endowed by the Creator with certain unalienable rights," as stated in this great historical document. Disciples are charged with specific undeniable duties. The appeal of intense religion is so deep that if the original stress remains unresolved, new movements are likely to replace failed ones, despite the suffering caused by the previous experience. This unfortunate cycle may cause immense material and psychological collateral damage before it is finally exhausted. In its aftermath, the reinstatement of the old order becomes impossible, even if the futility of the intense religious choice is fully acknowledged. After a period of distress and disarray, the community will have to forge new shared understandings affecting social organization, relations with the outside world, and religious ideological codes and precepts.

This pattern defies particular cultural backgrounds and time frames. Pueblo Indians, Xhosa, and Sudanese were all aggravated by roughly similar types of stress, all turned to extreme religious action for relief, all met ultimate failure, and all were subsequently subjected to profound cultural, ideological, and social readjustments. The People's Crusade was not a movement of liberation, but it follows the pattern of communal and individual stress, religious incentive to action, and failure followed by consequential historical repercussions. The same pattern can be found in numerous other examples worldwide. Several of them, like the Cattle Killing and the Mahdi Revolt, emerged out of the political and ideological turbulences of the nineteenth or the early twentieth century.

The Ghost Dance movements of North America's Plains Indians were effectively a desperate response to the loss of vital hunting grounds and tribal lands to white American farmers, soldiers, and entrepreneurs, and to the subsequent economic, cultural, and social crisis. With the suppression of the last significant Ghost Dance revival (1888-1890) by the American government, Plains Indians found themselves facing an ambiguous future that would inevitably dictate profound alterations in their ways of life (La Barre 1970: 229; Burridge 1969: 81). Their perplexity and frustration are candidly expressed in the testimony of Benjamin Black Elk, a former Oglala Ghost Dance disciple:

> …before the white man came we were better off. We didn't know what the dollar was. We didn't know what whiskey was…. We believe that the Great Spirit has created us and all of the nature. The things that we see are part of the Great Spirit. That's what we believe. We were intact, but the white man came and broke that nation's hoop, and today, now, today, we Indians don't know what we are – whether we are going or coming back or what. We're a confused people (cited in Coleman 2000: xiii).

Roughly during the same period, but an ocean away, South Pacific peoples were likewise pitched in a losing confrontation with European and Australian physical impact and ideological influence. Local intense religious response involved an array of "Cargo Cults," so named after the standard promise made by local millenarian prophets that the imminent apocalypse would include a miraculous delivery of shiploads of highly desired European commodities (Brewster 1922: 240–41; Crocombe 1961; Williams 1978:14–15).[9] Some varieties of Pacific millenarianism, especially in Papua New Guinea, are also outstanding in the contempt and aversion with which their prophets treated local ancestral beliefs and ritual customs. Their spite of indigenous religious traditions inspired ecstatic spells of iconoclastic aggression. The obliteration of Ilahita's Tambaran cult, which opens the first chapter of this book, is merely a relatively recent illustration of a much older phenomenon. A shocked European witness described almost incomprehensible cultural self-destruction in the aftermath of the 1919 New Guinean revival known as the Vailala Madness:

> It is with the utmost disappointment that one finds in village after village the devastation which this movement has caused; with disgust also, and something like incredulity, that one hears on all hands the condemnation of the old customs. It seems nothing less than preposterous that old men, who have been brought up among the ceremonies, and who have taught their sons that their prime moral duty is to carry on the ceremonies, should of their own accord come to despise and abandon them. Yet no old man has the initiative to speak a word of defense of his dishonored tribal customs… the Vailala Madness has been the principal direct agent in the destruction of the Gulf culture (Williams 1978: 37, 39).

This attitude diametrically contradicts typical nativistic millenarian practice elsewhere, which works to revive the original religions on the expense of Christianity. This is undoubtedly an outcome of the influence of Christian missionaries – ironically so, given the blatant anti-European vein in typical Cargo Cult ideology.

The zealous streak in Muslim and Christian alternative religious movements, as well as in pseudo-Christian millenarianism, derives from Judaism, the parent monotheistic faith. Jesus himself, his twelve disciples as well as Paul, the formative figures of early Christianity, were Jews living and acting during a turbulent period of intensifying conflict between Jewish militant factions on one side and the local Roman administration in Judea and its local non-Jewish civilian allies on the other. Various socioeconomic and political factors contributed to the escalation of tensions and bursts of violence. Yet, to the Jews, the ejection of the foreign occupiers and their infidel supporters was foremost an ideological mission and religious obligation. Bloody skirmishes, violent riots, and guerrilla warfare eventually matured into two major uprisings, the first of which is at the focus of the following chapters.

6 Part II — Introduction
History, Archaeology and Religious Ideology

For the structure that we raise,
Time is with materials filled;
Our todays and yesterdays
Are the blocks with which we build.

(Henry Wadsworth Longfellow, *The Builders*)

The First Jewish Revolt against Rome (66–70 CE)[1] is among the earliest religiously-inspired large-scale confrontations of which extensive documentation survives. Convictions of exclusive intimacy with divinity, adherence to strict ritual demands, contempt for extant political restrictions, confidence in moral superiority, and assuredness of success against all reasonable odds were all characteristic traits of the Jewish rebel factions. Variations of these same traits can be found in the ideological teachings of later radical offshoots of Christianity and Islam. An assessment of the ideological motivation that led the Jews to challenge the formidable armies of Rome is therefore indispensable for the analysis not only of this particular historical case, but of monotheistic religious intensity in general. The uprising and the period during which it occurred illustrate the workings, impact, and outcome of mass religious intensity through a wealth of textual and archaeological materials. The same body of evidence is also of considerable value for the history of warfare and for the research of ethnic and cultural identities.

History and Archaeology – Sisters and Rivals

The coordination between history and archaeology, upon which stands the model introduced in the following chapters, should not be taken for granted. Although one would expect such coordination between sister disciplines in the study of the past, scholarship reflects no small amount of thinly veiled rivalry. Some writers maintain a professional stance, offering objective assessments of the subjects that might be better addressed by one field or the other. It has been claimed that archaeology is only effective, or at least most effective, in the study of prehistory (Arnold 1986: 32). It has also been suggested that archaeology should focus on technology and subsistence, while historians are better equipped to investigate societies, politics, and ideology (Hawkes 1954: 161–62). Other historians are more aggressive. Jean Bottéro (1992: 28) states that while documents provide a "knowledge of the past that is precise, detailed, and analytical," archaeologists offer no more than a "hazy and uncertain outline." There are also those who go as far as ridiculing the work of archaeologists and practically dismissing its scholarly value.[2]

From their part, the advocates of archaeology hold that the materials retrieved from ancient grounds "are historical documents in their own right, not mere illustrations to written texts"

(Childe 1956: 9). They warn against the 'tyranny of the text' (Champion 1990: 91; Dever 1996: 19; Papadopoulus 1999)[3] and highlight the objectivity of archaeological data against inevitable prejudices in historical records (Vermeule 1996: 10). Regarding the question of whether archaeologists should be studying ideology, where religion is central, Joyce Marcus and Kent Flannery (1994: 55) offer an adamantly positive answer. Following them, the "realm of the mind" must not be left exclusively to humanists, who "for the most part, do not have the ecological and evolutionary perspective of the anthropological archaeologists." The heated exchanges and occasionally acidic rivalry are based (at least on the academic level) on critical views on the sources each discipline uses for analysis. Yet in fact, as the following summary shows, both history and archaeology must contend with significant problems of source availability, reliability, and interpretation.

Personal Agendas in Literary Records

Ancient historiographies were composed by authors who had experienced the events themselves or had lived near enough the relevant period to enjoy access to archives, eye witnesses, and even original actors. There is no reason to doubt that most of them took their profession seriously and would probably identify with Thucydides, who stated that his chronicle of the Peloponnesian War was aimed for posterity. Yet, ancient historians tended to be more concerned with literary grace than with accuracy and impartiality. Some of the best among them occasionally slid into exaggerated superlatives.[4] Furthermore, most authors worked under the protection and sponsorship of powerful political figures and many were of aristocratic stock themselves. These privileged positions granted them admission to archives and the cooperation of witnesses but inescapably undermined their objectivity.[5] Potential distortions also include the overemphasizing of military victories to the expense of less dramatic peaceful periods (Postgate 1992: 241), the misrepresentation of the vanquished in records written by the winners (Paynter 1990: 59), limited critical research (Gruen 2002: 34–35), and disregard of cultural and ideological undercurrents (Postgate 1992: 241).

Particular caution should be engaged when studying ancient testimonies of religion. As members of their communities, authors probably believed in local religions, participated in rituals and regarded them as an integral part of their culture and identity (Renfrew 1994: 48). At the same time, they were exposed to misconceptions over the religions of other peoples and cultures and to the vilification of those practiced by the enemies of their societies.[6] Subsequently, religion sustained broader misunderstandings, livelier propaganda, and harsher prejudices than most, if not all, other subjects with which ancient authors were concerned.

Much of our information about ancient polytheism comes from the writings of hostile and contemptuous monotheistic authors or editors.[7] Equally tainted narratives obscure the testimonies of mainstream Jewish and Christian authors relating to splinter ideological factions within their religions. Josephus makes no effort to disguise his admiration for the Essenes and his spite for the Zealots and the Sicarii. Early Christian writers described Gnostic groups as religious abominations, threats to the unity and integrity of the Church, or at least as worthless theological aberrations (Pagels 1995: 149ff.).[8] Most of our understanding of this fascinating facet in the development of Judaism and Christianity would have to be based on such critically tilted perspectives, had not been for chance discoveries like the Dead Sea Scrolls and the Nag Hammadi texts. Similar aspects of religious diversity in antiquity, such as religious intensity and millenarianism, are consistently compromised by the natural desire of authors to offer their perspectives and interpretations.[9]

That is not to say that the misrepresentations of ideologies hold no interest in themselves. The embedded bias and the emotions that can be traced in the narratives unveil some of the debates, tensions, and rivalries that stirred the ideological and intellectual scenes of the period, undoubtedly affecting its spiritual texture as well as its religious, social, and political institutions. Besides, detecting that bias is not always difficult, and once isolated, it loses much of its distorting potential. The problem is that there are many other cases where prejudice is too deeply implanted to be effectively weeded out and it radiates into real information and corrupts it. Nonetheless, compromised impartiality has always accompanied historical writing and will continue to challenge scholars of history for as long as the discipline is practiced.

The Limited Scope of Material Culture

Archaeological identification of the cognitive and spiritual spheres of antiquity is never a simple task. In this brief survey, let us concentrate on religious ideology, the aspect closest to the subject of this book.

Artistic representations of faith are very ancient. A figurine from Berekhat Ram in northern Israel hints to some kind of symbolic thought as early as the Lower Paleolithic (Goren-Inbar 1986), and images with possible ritual meaning can be seen in Upper Paleolithic European parietal art (Mithen 1996: 176). Still, how can we be sure of the religious connotation of these prehistoric representations? Actually, we cannot, and the same problem remains relevant in much later periods. "On what grounds," wonders Colin Renfrew (1985: 2), "is one pit, with animal bones and a few artifacts, dismissed as domestic refuse, while another is seen as a ritual deposit with evidence of sacrifice? In what circumstances shall we regard small terracotta representations of animals and men as figurines, intended as offerings to the deity, and when shall we view them as mere toys for the amusement of children?" Renfrew (1985: 13–14, 19–20; 1994: 51–53) suggests that recurring elements in structures, objects, and art may infer religious meaning. We will not, however, always be able to detect and exclude from the shortlist objects made after aesthetic tastes or periodical fashions. Louis Binford (1972: 23–25) proposes a classification based on technological-practical utilization, social performance, or symbolic significance. This classification is only partially viable, because many artifacts could fit into two or all of those categories. Thus, a domestic flint knife found at a Bronze Age rural site could have also been used for ceremonial sacrifices or butchering during communal festivals. Archaeologists are likely to miss this domestic-ideological interchange and "bag and tag" the knife as just another utilitarian tool. On the other hand, they may assign mysterious symbolic meaning to an unusual looking scraper, which, in its day, was merely the imitation by a creative boy of nothing more spiritual than his father's goat skin scraper. A few such interpretations later, the unassuming Bronze Age rustic community would be credited with ideological complexity to make the ghosts of its peasant shamans proud.

Similar problems affect religious locales. Ritual was not always or everywhere confined to designated and invested structures. In fact, 'sacred' and 'profane' often intersected and worship also took place in improvised units or otherwise domestic buildings. Textual and archaeological evidence indicates that biblical Israelites worshipped in rough stone enclosures (Zevit 2001: 256ff., and see Judges 6:25–26), as well as in dwellings, caves, and possibly even tombs (Kenyon 1974: 139–43; Zevit 2001: 241–47). Early Christians convened in private homes (Corinthians I, 16:19; Colossians 4:15). Muslim nomads traditionally demarcated open-air perimeters for common prayer (Tapper 1984: 249–60).[10] This 'transparent ritual' will rarely be identified by archaeologists, unless inscriptions or objects specifically related to cult are found near or inside the improvised worship locales.

Even when religious function is recognized, its ideological contents may remain obscure, as may the actual standing of the faith in that society. Traces of early ideology within the theologies of later and more familiar religions can be difficult to segregate, even if in its own period the earlier religious framework was dominant and widespread. (Marcus and Flannery 1994: 56). Conversely, the obvious remains of imperious religious structures do not always reflect a comparable influence or popularity of the religion they are dedicated to. As an example, Graeco-Roman paganism boasted countless temples during the first centuries of the Common Era while material evidence of the secretive but vigorous spread of Christianity, which was destined to soon inherit its place, is scarce. Finally, architectural resemblance does not necessarily imply ideological affinity. Solomon's Temple was apparently built after the architectural traditions of Canaan and Phoenicia (Mazar 1990: 377–78). Even if its remains are ever unearthed, only the biblical testimony would attest to its ideological distinction. Of other cases about which textual evidence is sparse or non-existent we will know little, if anything at all.

The Shared Problem of Anachronism

In his characteristically blunt yet elegant style, eighteenth-century historian Edward Gibbon (2000 [1776]: 75) criticizes the custom of deifying emperors in classical Rome:

> We should disgrace the virtues of the Antonines, by comparing them with the vices of Hercules or Jupiter. Even the characters of Caesar or Augustus were far superior to those of the popular deities. But it was the misfortune of the former to live in an enlightened age, and their actions were too faithfully recorded to admit such a mixture of fable and mystery, as the devotion of the vulgar requires. As soon as their divinity was established by law, it sunk into oblivion, without contributing either to their own fame, or to the dignity of succeeding princes.

Gibbon's indignation is uncalled for. After all, if the age was indeed enlightened and the emperors so upright and wise, more attention should perhaps be invested, rather than condemnation poured, on the political advantages of ruler deification. Gibbon also seems to be taking the matter too personally. Researchers need to maintain a professional relationship with the past, not an emotional one. Modern historians attempt to be more impartial, but a truly objective reconstruction of history is just as unlikely now as it has been in antiquity or in Gibbon's day. As historian Anthony Saldarini (2002: 221–22, 232) candidly observes:

> Even though we stress data, analysis, argument, and a self-conscious interpretive perspective (often named "objective"), we interpret strongly when we write history…the questions we ask as historians, the data we choose to address, and the methods we develop in our work all serve to further diverse research goals…[which] motivate each of us differently and move us in various directions governed by our politics, social policies, religious views and philosophies of life.

The tendency to anachronistic interpretation of bygone realities along contemporary ideals also affects archaeologists. Following Michael Shanks and Christopher Tilley (1987: 19), the narrative that modern historians and archaeologists produce "is not restricted (and cannot be) to the perspective within which the people of the past viewed themselves." Ian Hodder (1999: 62) goes further to argue that the interpretation of the past is not only affected by the present but sometimes aims to shape it: "Different arguments will hold sway at different historical moments [thus] our assessment of an adequate explanation will change because of wider political factors". In plain terms, our historical and archaeological conclusions may be slanted by what we watch and hear on CNN, Fox, Sky, or the BBC World Service. Yet, if at times the present has an impact on the interpretation of the past, in other cases the past is used to impact on the present, with ruins, artifacts, and texts given meanings that promote modern political, national, religious, and ideological agendas, but such which the ancients could never have fathomed.

Some scholars actually advocate the utilization of the past in order to mend contemporary social injustice. Opinions along these lines can be found in the writings of historians Theodore Adorno (cited in Rose 1978: 51) and Herbert Marcuse (1968: 24), as well as in the conclusions of some archaeologists.[11] In conflict regions such as Kosovo (Volkan 2002) and the Middle East (Ben-Yehuda 1995; Yahya 2005: 68) the past and its sciences are frequently employed by the antagonists to reinforce their national causes, both in the domestic and international arenas. History and archaeology may also be recruited for less belligerent purposes. In places as diverse as Egypt,

Iraq, Iran, Denmark, Poland, Japan, as well as in England, at least in its Victorian age,[12] they have been used to bolster collective self-image, encourage social cohesion, and invoke national pride (Trigger 1989: 148, 179–80, 183, 205–6; Jones 1997: 6–8, 136–37). Many Indonesians, including local archaeologists, reacted enthusiastically to the recent discovery of a previously unknown prehistoric human species on the Indonesian island of Flores. According to reports from the site, the discovery "has inspired national pride," and one of the Indonesian scientists described the 15,000–17,000-year-old fossils as "very important for Indonesian society."[13] Sadly, the past has also been enlisted into the service of some rather unpleasant agendas. An infamous example is the work of Gustaf Kossinna (1858–1931), who used archaeological data as evidence of German racial and cultural superiority. Kossinna's conclusions were later enlisted to bolster the ideological platforms of National Socialism (Trigger 1989: 165–66).

Despite the problematic facets of ideological exchanges between past and present we should not rule out history and archaeology's potential contributions to contemporary debates. Scientific work does not take place in limbo and should be exposed to some public treatment beyond the confines of pure academy. Moreover, researchers are part of the societies they live in, and it is only natural that they should refer to the historical experience they are familiar with when discussing current affairs. In fact, some rather critical global miscalculations could have been avoided had their political and military engineers been better acquainted with the lessons of the past.

This interchange needs not come at the cost of scientific impartiality. Educational projections from the past into the present must not undermine the quality and credibility of the investigation, and the border between science and populism has to be clearly delineated (Hodder 1999: 63–64; Moreland 2001: 105, 116).[14] This can certainly be achieved. Archaeologists and historians, like surgeons, may be capable of professional performance even on subjects with which they feel personally involved. Medical doctors are usually precluded from such procedures, but researchers of antiquity are not in the business of saving lives and may be allowed some controlled latitude. Of course, models must still relate to science rather than science fiction, theories ought to be imaginative, not imaginary, and conclusions should incorporate evidence but never replace it. If these lines are observed, if caution is exercised and scrutiny rigorously practiced, there might be no harm, and possibly even some merit, in the occasional relocation of history and archaeology to more central spots of public interest, attention, and involvement.

The Interdisciplinary Advantage

An interdisciplinary coordination between history and archaeology could overcome some of their individual and shared deficiencies, extend the boundaries of interpretation beyond the maximal point each could reach separately, and help control ideological anachronism. Biblical scholar Baruch Halpern proposes an optimal balance:

> The textual scholar can escape the inability to test hypotheses precisely by crossing the lines dividing the fields, and grounding hypotheses in archaeological correlates. The archaeologist can escape the potential atomization of units – larger kinship groups, nations with variation in local cultures- through appeal to the texts (1997: 313).
>
> One can…privilege [archaeology and text], as appropriate, not one or the other programmatically…What occupies the higher ground is intelligent analysis of both together (2005: 436).

Collaboration demands less investment than what used to be expected of each discipline by some of its own people. No dramatic change of emphasis is asked from historians, as was the case with the *Annales* scholars.[15] Neither is archaeology compelled to incorporate new methods of analysis, as advocated by the New Archaeology promoters.[16] Actually, the product of cooperation between excavators and textual analysts may be invaluable for the investigation of ancient religious ideology and its intense offshoots, among other issues of interest. In order to evaluate ideological variation, its relative social and cultural substance and its historical impact, historians must read between the lines of documents, compare various testimonies of single events, and test the contents of texts against what is known about the personal circumstances and ideological agendas of its authors. To answer similar questions, archaeologists need to search behind the façades of official temples and look into domestic assemblages for evidence of the depth and character of daily religious practice. The methods differ, but the goal is the same. Coordination between historians and archaeologists can not only fill in some blanks but also expose contradicting evidence, which must be investigated, comprehended, and judged. In the process, it may also expose and mend analytical flaws on both sides, assuming that personal egos can be put aside or at least assuaged to a degree that allows recognition of the problems and reassessment of vital points.

No purely empirical or flawless reconstruction of the past is possible, and the scenes emerging from surviving textual and material materials are never complete. The idiosyncrasies of each case study need to be identified and tended to, and it would be practically irresponsible for a researcher to ignore data, methods, and modes of thinking of neighboring disciplines, and thus neglect information that can only be gathered there. The interdisciplinary approach is also essential for input and ideas to be tested for cross-cultural and cross-temporal application, even in case of lessons learned from seemingly unique case studies. This is the primary aim of this book.

An Interdisciplinary Research of the First Revolt

The First Revolt has been the subject of numerous studies from various historical perspectives, and archaeologists have discovered and uncovered several key sites of the war. Yet, the information available to both fields regarding the causes of the conflict and the motivations of the rebels remains inconclusive.

The writings of the Jewish first-century historian Josephus remain the base for any historical analysis of the Second Temple period, which ended with the First Revolt. Yet Josephus' reliability is compromised by his personal circumstances. Having originally served as a rebel commander, Josephus was captured by the Romans, pardoned, and re-settled in Rome under the auspices of the Flavian Caesars. He owed his life, freedom, comfort, as well as the prospect of earning his fame as a historian to the emperors Vespasian and Titus, who, in their previous capacities as generals, devastated Judea, killed thousands of Jews, destroyed Josephus' home city Jerusalem, and sacked and burnt down the magnificent temple, which his priestly family had served for generations. They were nonetheless the author's sponsors, and their images as projected in his writings are exceedingly flattering. On the other hand, his treatment of his antagonists among the rebel chiefs is merciless. Their religious ideological arguments are presented to an extent but denied any sincerity, and they are repeatedly charged with insatiable ambition, irrepressible greed, deplorable moral degradation, and total disregard for their Jewish brethren's suffering, for which they are held largely responsible. This invaluable but highly biased author is the key resource available to historians researching the First Revolt.

Archaeology fares no better. Several sites from the first century CE contain rich remains of the uprising, projecting dramatic images of its violence and destruction but leaving the ideological background obscure. Architectural and artifactual finds have clear religious connotations, but on their own they communicate nothing more than a fundamentally observant way of life, as common in many pre-modern cultures.

Yet, viable models concerning the role extreme religious ideologies played in the instigation of the uprising can be assembled even in this difficult environment. In the following chapters extensive historical and archaeological evidence will be analyzed and tested in conjunction. I believe that this combined body of evidence suffices to assert that the exceptionally strict religious interpretations that dominated the cultural-ideological scene in first-century Judea were the key factor in leading the rebels to their daring yet hopeless endeavour and encouraged their extraordinary perseverance against mounting disasters. The allocation of text, buildings, and artifacts within a single theoretical framework demonstrates the advantages of the interdisciplinary approach through the lens of a specific, well-documented historical case. It also offers an important illustration of the historical impact of religious intensity and its long-term ramifications, in addition and in remarkable resemblance to the intense religious cases discussed thus far.

7   Uprising in Judea

Various political and economic causes can be found at the background of the First Jewish Revolt against Rome, but the persistence, determination, and resilience of the rebels should be credited, to a large degree, to the intensification of religious beliefs and practice in Judea[1] between the later part of the first century BCE and the first century CE. Rigorous religious faith and ritual observation, affecting virtually every aspect of life, supported the notion that God would not stand by while an armed struggle raged to rid the Holy Land from foreign oppression and religious sacrilege. The strength of this conviction helped the rebels overcome immeasurable afflictions and sustain hope to the extent that thousands fought on even after the destruction of Jerusalem and annihilation of the bulk of the Jewish force.
Several considerations make this case invaluable for the research of religious intensity and its historical impact and justify its detailed treatment in this study:

Timeline

The First Revolt took place during the mid-first century CE, nearly a thousand years earlier than the People's Crusade, sixteen centuries prior to the Pueblo Revolt, and nineteen hundred years before the Xhosa began killing their cattle and the first battle was fought under the Mahdi's banner. This timeline shows religious intensity to be no more tethered to the circumstances of specific historical periods than it is bonded to particular cultural scenes.

Jewish Identity

So far, all intense religious movements discussed here were Muslim, Christian, or nativistic reactions to Christianity. The First Jewish Revolt thus complements the tight association of the phenomenon with all three main branches of monotheism.

Determination against Failure

A strong testimony to the intensity of faith in a religious movement is the reaction of disciples as the said movement fails to deliver its promises (Festinger et al. 1956; Burridge 1969: 168). The Jewish response to the disastrous outcome of the revolt not only reflects the substance of faith in the motivation of the rebels but also resembles the pattern of disciples' reactions in other historical cases. Jewish post-revolt conduct thus contributes to the delineation of a pan-human behavioral model.

First-Hand Testimony

The Jewish revolt is related by Josephus, a historian who served in the rebel leadership during the early part of the war. While his character and personal circumstances demand rigorous screening of his testimony, we are still offered a rare look into the inner workings of politically-oriented intense religious movements.

The Jewish revolt has an additional dimension that distinguishes it from the other cases discussed in this book: the wealth of related archaeological testimony from sites across Israel, Jordan, and the Palestinian Authority. This evidence can be divided into two main categories. The first includes the material testimony to the actual fighting, such as fortifications, destruction layers, weapons, and securely associated mortuary remains. The second category addresses the form and character of religious ideological thought in Judea during that period. Naturally, this class of evidence depends on considerable interpretation. Nevertheless, it stands on the solid fact that specific classes of religiously related objects, structures, and artistic styles are common in Jewish archaeological assemblages dating between the first century BCE and the time of the revolt itself but are absent in previous periods and change or completely disappear in post-war sites and strata. In principle, similar methods could be applied for the detection of intense religious motivation in other cases in antiquity. Such cross-cultural and cross-temporal analysis would extend the range of interpretative data available to archaeologists, historians, as well as anthropologists interested in sociopolitical implications of religion.

Historical Background

During the sixth century BCE, several waves of Jewish immigrants returned from the Babylonian exile to Judea and established an autonomous agrarian theocracy under the auspices of the Persian Empire. Administration centered in Jerusalem, where a new temple was erected over the ruins of the Solomonic structure razed early that century by Nebuchadnezzar. The minute Jewish province prevailed despite the hostility of its neighbors (Ezra 4; Nehemiah 2:10ff), consolidated and grew in population and territory, but it was to develop into a rather different entity than the fallen monarchies. Among the many distinctions was the rejection of the flexible religious synchronization of pre-exilic times (Propp 1999: 549, 552; Zevit 2001: 690), replacing it with strictly monotheistic ritual.

In 332 BCE, Alexander of Macedon annexed Judea into his empire. Following Alexander's death in 323 BCE, his generals shared his vast domains and Judea came under the Ptolemaic rulers of Egypt until 198 BCE, when it was annexed by the Seleucids of Syria. Aggressive attempts by the Seleucid king Antiochus IV Epiphanes to impose Hellenistic rituals and life modes on the Jews triggered a Jewish uprising in 167 BCE.[2] The Hasmonean family from Modi'in in the northwestern Judean foothills led the struggle with considerable military skill and political ingenuity. By 142 BCE they had won religious freedom and political independence for the Jews, concluding four and a half centuries of foreign occupation. Their heirs formed a dynamic royal dynasty whose princes carried out a costly but generally successful policy of territorial expansion.[3] Judea gradually grew to become a powerful state in the region, supported by a firm economy based on agriculture and international trade. It was nevertheless crippled by constant domestic discord between political and priestly factions, as well as between the cosmopolitan aristocracy and the more conservative Jewish masses. Under the assertive rule of Alexander Jannaeus (103–76 BCE), conflicting interests and social grievances deteriorated into bloody civil disturbances. These internal divisions would eventually facilitate the loss of independence to Rome.

Relations between Jews and Romans had a positive genesis, including formal political alliances between the early Hasmoneans and the Senate of the Roman republic (Maccabees II,4:11; *Antiquities* 12.414–19, 13.163).[4] The situation changed with the disintegration of the Hellenistic kingdoms and the Roman expansion eastwards, eventually leading to Pompey's violent annexation of Judea to the empire in 63 BCE. The last Hasmonean princes challenged the Romans in a sequence of popular revolts, all of which were ruthlessly crushed. The degree of severity that Jewish religious observance had reached by that time is illustrated by the abstention of the defenders of Jerusalem from interrupting Roman siege works on Sabbath days, thus facilitating the fall of the city (*Antiquities* 14.63–4). In 37 BCE the Romans enthroned Herod, the son of a prominent Roman collaborator, as king of the Jews. Effective taxation and profits from trade and customs provided Herod with substantial funds, much of which he invested in the construction of temples, ports, and civic centers in Judea and throughout the Roman imperial East. One of his most ambitious projects was the replacement of the old Jerusalem Temple with a lavish acropolis complex. The Jews appreciated the formidable structure yet detested the king who built it as a usurper and Roman lackey who assassinated Hasmonean princes and ruthlessly persecuted popular dissidents.

Herod's death (4 BCE) left a power vacuum that his less proficient sons and heirs proved unable to fill. In addition, with the elimination of the higher echelons of the Hasmonean dynasty the traditional and experienced elite was lost, among them most of the people who in time might have found ways to satisfy Jewish political and religious sensitivities while avoiding Roman suspicions (Goodman 1987: 38). Roman governors were eventually appointed over the land. Some ruled fairly, but the terms of others were marred by corruption, repression, and a pattern of bias against the Jews during the frequent and occasionally violent conflicts with the Helleno-Roman populations of the large urban centers scattered throughout the land.[5] As the authority of the political and religious establishment constantly eroded, the popularity of militant dissident movements spread unchecked. So did the influence of self-appointed prophets and would-be saviors who openly challenged the religious legitimacy of submission to Rome and promised miraculous deliverance (Josephus, *War* 2.258–63). The Romans spared no measures in curbing Jewish dissension, but to no lasting avail.

The Jewish Revolt (66–70 CE)

Neither the prolonged governmental crisis of Nero's final years nor the ensuing civil war compromised the fundamental solidity of the Roman imperial system, with its skillful administration, strong economy, and effective armies. Judea, on the other hand, remained a small province with few natural resources and an increasingly polarized population. Jewish insurgence nevertheless gathered momentum, and two chaotic years under Governor Gessius Florus finally triggered a large-scale uprising (late summer of 66 CE). In a symbolic act of defiance the daily sacrifice in honor of the emperor at the Jerusalem Temple was cancelled. Violence followed symbolism, as government buildings and tax archives in Jerusalem were burned and Roman troops overpowered and killed. An expedition against the Jews under Cestius Gallus, the Roman legate in Antioch, ended with the Twelfth Legion (*Fulminata*) and strong auxiliary forces routed and nearly annihilated by Jewish irregulars (*War* 2.540–555; Tacitus, *Histories* 5:10; Suetonius, *Lives* 8.1,4). The success stimulated popular support for the rebels, whose ranks now swelled with new recruits. Members of the aristocracy and upper priesthood of Jerusalem, realizing that a full confrontation was inevitable, formed a provisional government and appointed regional commanders in preparation for the forthcoming Roman onslaught.

The severity of the situation in Judea was soon recognized in Rome, and Nero wisely appointed Vespasian, an experienced veteran of wars in Germany and Britain, to the command of the Roman offensive in Judea. Approximately 60,000 troops, comprised of four legions,[6] reinforcements from other legions, and twenty-two auxiliary cohorts were allotted to the expedition. Vespasian, joined by his son Titus, began his campaign in the Galilee. The rebels resisted with stamina from the walls of fortified towns, but the Roman army was well versed in siege warfare, and by the autumn of 67 CE Vespasian had subdued the region. Joseph ben Mattathias, the Jerusalem-appointed Galilean commander, was captured alive in the aftermath of the siege of Yodfat (*War* 3.141ff). He then cunningly talked his way into the confidence of Vespasian and Titus, became their advisor for the duration of the rest of the war, and took much abuse from the rebels as he advocated surrender in front of city walls. He was later to win lasting fame as the historian Flavius Josephus.

Roman forces then moved on against rebel strongholds elsewhere in Judea and Transjordan, and by the summer of 69 CE only Jerusalem and three desert forts were still in rebel hands. Vespasian was back in Rome, where he had ascended to the imperial throne following the suicide of Nero and the subsequent civil war.

Titus completed the conquest of Jerusalem in August of 70 CE after a long and costly siege that was nonetheless facilitated by the chronic fratricidal violence between Jewish factions within the

Table 7.1 Major disturbances in Judea between Herod's death and the First Revolt.

Authority	Cause and circumstances	Outcome	Reference
Archelaus (4 BCE–6 CE)	Popular demands for alleviation of economic pressure caused by Herod's policies	Military suppression, massacre	W 2.5–13; A 17.204–18
Archelaus (4 BCE–6 CE)	Widespread violence in various parts of the land aimed at Archelaus and Roman unit	Uprising suppressed by Varus, Roman governor of Syria	W 2.39–79; A 17.286–98
Coponius (6–9 CE)	Uprising of Judas the Galilean against Roman census and demands for divine kingship. Circumstances unclear	Possible non-violent dissipation.	W 2.118; A 18.2; Acts 5:37
Pontius Pilate (26–36 CE)	Introduction of military banners carrying cultic images into Jerusalem	Resolved peacefully with the withdrawal of the banners	W 2.169–74; A 18.55–59, Philo, *Legatio ad Gaium* 209–306
Pontius Pilate (26–36 CE)	Appropriation of Temple's treasury for the construction of new aqueduct	Military suppression	W 2.175–77; A 18.60–62
Marullus (37–41 CE)	Caligula's order to place his statue in the Temple court in Jerusalem	Resolved peacefully with Caligula's assassination	W 2.184–203; A 18.261–309; Philo, *Legatio ad Gaium* 190ff.; Tacitus, *Histories* 5.9
Cumanus (48–52 CE)	Provocation by Roman soldier in the Temple courts	Military intervention, mass panic, multiple casualties	W 2.223–27; A 20.105–12
Cumanus (48–52 CE)	Provocation by Roman soldier during raid at Beth Horon	Resolved peacefully with soldier's execution	W 2.228–30; A 20.113–17
Cumanus (48–52 CE)	Violence between Jews and Samaritans over the murder of a Jewish pilgrim in Samaria	Military suppression	W 2.232ff.
Festus (60–62 CE)	Construction of a wall commanding the Temple court	Resolved peacefully with removal of the wall	A 20.194–95
Florus (64–66 CE)	Disturbances in Caesarea and Jerusalem between Jews and Helleno-Romans	Military suppression, massacres, revolt	W 2.289–307

city. He then returned to Rome and joined his father in a grandiose triumphal parade, depicted on the famous Arch of Titus still standing in the forum. The task of overpowering the last remaining rebel strongholds was entrusted to the new Roman governors. Lucilius Bassus captured Herodium (71 CE) and Machaerus (72 CE). The fall the formidable Dead Sea fortress of Masada to Flavius Silva in 73 (or 74) CE concluded the revolt.

Some scholars downplay the substance of the revolt within the general context of Roman imperial realities. Gruen (2002: 38) believes that the Romans were less concerned than outraged that such a "puny and insignificant" people would have the audacity to challenge Rome. Overman (2002) credits the substantial revolt-related Roman propaganda to efforts by Titus to emphasize his military career in compensation for his non-aristocratic origins.[7] Yet, other facts indicate that the Jewish War was a significant event also from the Roman perspective:

Figure 10 The hill of Machaerus, a fortified Transjordanian town overlooking the Dead Sea and site of one of the last battles of the revolt. Smaller image (below right): The ramp erected by the Romans during the siege of Machaerus in 72 CE (photographs: Y. Arbel).

- Even before its conclusion, the successful campaign in Judea placed Vespasian in an excellent strategic position from which he could interfere in the civil war in Rome and resolve it to his personal advantage (Rajak 2002: 164).

- The Flavian emperors certainly went to great lengths to ensure that their victory over the Jews was glorified throughout the empire. Celebrations attended by Titus himself were held in several eastern Helleno-Roman cities (*War* 7.23–24, 37–40). Triumphal parades marched in Rome (*War* 7.121ff.). The Arch of Titus was erected.[8] It was made public that the construction of the Temple of Jupiter Optimus Maximus and the Temple of Peace was funded with spoils from Judea. A large volume of gold, silver, and bronze currency boasting the achievement was minted by all three Flavian emperors, including Domitian who did not take part in the fighting (Rappaport 1983: 135–37; Meshorer 1997: 161). All of this would not have been done merely to bandage Titus' insecurities.

- The Flavian triumphal festivities deviated from standard Roman tradition in that they commemorated not a new conquest or the routing of a foreign invader but a victory over rebels in an established province that had been under Roman control for over 130 years (Millar 1993: 79).

- Josephus would not have risked his credibility with his educated Greek and Roman readers through utterly preposterous declarations.
- The tenacious Jewish insurgency was an anomaly within the generally submissive scene of the Romanized East (Mendels 1992: 355).
- Although political developments in Rome prevented maximal military pressure on the Jews during most of the year 69 CE, the intensity of Jewish resistance was the chief reason for the long duration of the war (Goodman 1987: 3). The siege of Jerusalem alone stranded nearly one seventh of the total military force of the Roman Empire (Millar 1993: 76).
- The Roman success came at a high cost. The routing of Gallus' complete legion and auxiliary forces and the humiliating loss of an Eagle standard had no precedent in established provinces (Millar 1993: 71). The initial defeat at Gamla must have been rather traumatic for the Romans, as it had taken place *after* the Romans had already broken through the town's fortifications, a highly unusual event in Roman military experience.
- The triumph over the Jews and the devastation of the famed city of Jerusalem sent a warning to the other peoples of the East as well as to the Parthians. It directly contributed to the consolidation of Roman control in its Eastern provinces, even as Rome itself was immersed in a chaotic period of interregnum.

Be the relative place of the Jewish revolt in Roman imperial history what it may, there can be no doubt that it completely changed the political, religious, and cultural realities in which the Jews lived. This aspect and the motives that may have driven the Jews into their hazardous adventure will be discussed in the following chapters.

Figure 11 Part of the southern wall of Jerusalem, recently discovered on the steep slope of Mount Zion. The wall was built under Hasmonean rule while Judea was still independent, hence the investment in both solidity and aesthetic appearance (photograph: Y. Arbel).

The Archaeology of the Revolt: A General Survey

Excavations at several first-century sites in Israel and Jordan yielded several types of material remains related to actual events in the revolt. While in most cases the evidence is fragmentary and circumstantial, at a small number of sites substantial and unequivocally war-related layers have also been exposed. The following survey discusses each of the major classes of data.

Fortifications

Defensive construction associated with the revolt was unearthed at sites in both the central hill country and the Galilee. In some cases the remains coincide with the list of Galilean sites Josephus claims to have fortified as a preparation for the Roman onslaught. Remains consist mostly of fragmentary sections of defensive walls, associated with the uprising through diagnostic first-century pottery and coins and, in some cases, through clear signs of destruction and burning. As should be expected, preservation is best at sites that remained abandoned or were not widely settled after their destruction.

Jerusalem was fortified since Hasmonean times, but in many cases fortifications related to the First Revolt were haphazardly improvised (Bar-Kochva 1974; Aviam 2004: 103–4). This concurs with Josephus' record of his harried construction of defenses in nineteen Galilean settlements, which prior to the revolt were unfortified and relied on their topographic advantage for security (*Life* 187–88). The wall surrounding Mt. Tabor, for example, is reported to have been built in only forty days (*War* 4:56). In several towns the defenders simply sealed gaps between peripheral buildings, thickened their façades, heightened walls, and filled in rooms with stones and soil. Such scenes are particularly evident at Gamla and Yodfat but were probably repeated elsewhere. Other defense measures included underground systems, used both as hideouts and as base of guerrilla operations.[9] Working under time pressure before the arrival of the legions and faced with the indifference, suspicion, and hostility of many Galileans, little more could have been accomplished.

Figure 12 Above: The hastily erected wall of Gamla (courtesy of D. Syon/Gamla excavations). Below: General view of the site, the 1985 archaeological expedition camp at the front (photograph: B. Schön).

Table 7.2 Sites containing fortifications related to the revolt.

Site	Reference in Josephus (not including repetition)	Archaeological references
Jerusalem (The "Third Wall")	*War* 5.155	Sukenik and Mayer 1931; Ben-Arieh and Netzer 1974
Gamla	*Life of Joseph* 186	Gutman 1994: 83–87; Syon 2002: 136–41; Syon and Yavor 2002:2
Yodfat	*Life* 188	Meyers et al. 1978: 5–6; Adan-Bayewitz and Aviam 1997; Aviam 2002: 122–23; Aviam 2002: 126–27; 2004: 112–15
Khirbet el-Hamam/*Narbata**	*War* 2.509	Zertal 1981; 1983: 40; 1984: 52
Mt Tabor	*War* 4.56	Zaharoni 1982; Aviam 2004: 98–99
Meroth	*War* 2.573-4	Ilan and Damati 1987
Arbel	*War* 2.573	Ilan and Izdarechet 1988: 63–67; Aviam 2004: 98–100
Selame	*Life* 188	Aviam 2004: 96
Gischala	*Life* 188	Aviam 2004: 106–9
Beersheba in Galilee	*Life* 188	Tal et al. 2000; Aviam 2004: 95
Masada	*War* 7.286-7	Yadin 1966; Foerster 1995

* The site of Narbata was identified by Adam Zertal (1981) as Khirbet el-Hammam in northwestern Samaria. Josephus describes a brutal punitive expedition sent by Cestius Gallus to the region but does not mention a siege. The fortifications and Roman siege works dating to the First Revolt at the site may be associated with a second Roman effort under Vespasian that Josephus also fails to mention, as it is possible that Narbata, like Jaffa and Jerusalem, recovered from Gallus' attack to challenge the Romans again.

Sieges and Destruction

Josephus reports a field battle on the banks of the Jordan River (*War* 4.433–35) and clashes near Bethennabris and Machaerus, both in Transjordan (*War* 4.420–27, 7.210–15).[10] Other recorded confrontations were mostly sieges that invariably ended with the surrender or destruction of towns or forts. Corresponding archaeological testimony was detected at several sites, including, in some cases, impressive scenes of 'moments frozen in time.'

Destruction related to the First Revolt was also evident at smaller sites of which there is no specific mention by Josephus as having been theaters of violence, such as Hebron (Ofer 1986: 93; 1993a: 609), 'Aroer (Hershkovitz 1987a), and Horvat 'Ethri, in the Judean lowlands (Zissu 2001: 169–70; Zissu and Ganor 2001: 102; 2002: 21; *War* 4.552).[11]

Excavations at the First Revolt key sites of Yodfat and Gamla yielded important assemblages of military related finds. Approximately 1,600 iron-cast bow arrowheads and 100 catapult projectiles of various types were detected at Gamla, along with nearly 2,000 ballista stones (Syon 2002: 141, 144–45). Artifacts retrieved at Gamla that probably belonged to Roman military personnel include part of a silver-coated helmet, the tip of a gold-coated bronze scabbard, a spearhead, several fragments of scale armor, part of a shield, soldiers' identification tags, and numerous buttons and decorative fittings of army gear and battle horses (Gutman 1994: 65–67, 70–71, 73–75, 93–98; Syon and Yavor 2001: 31; Syon 2002: 145). Over 70 bow arrowheads and 15 catapult projectiles were found at Yodfat, along with 35 ballista missiles (Aviam 2002: 128–29; 2004: 116–17). Military finds in Yodfat also include a dagger, the rear point of a spear, and fragments of bronze and silver plates, all probably part of Roman equipment, as well as iron nails commonly used in Roman military footwear (Aviam 2004: 116–17). Small assemblages of projectiles, ballista stones, and other weapons were found at Masada (Yadin 1966: 55, 57; Holley 1994), Jerusalem (Avigad 1983: 135), Machaerus (Vardaman 1969: 20–21), Qumran/Ein Feshkha (Humbert and Chambon 1994; Hirschfeld 2004; Magness 2002: 188), Narbata/Khirbet el-Hammam (Zertal 1984: 52), and Aro'er (Hershkovitz 1987a).

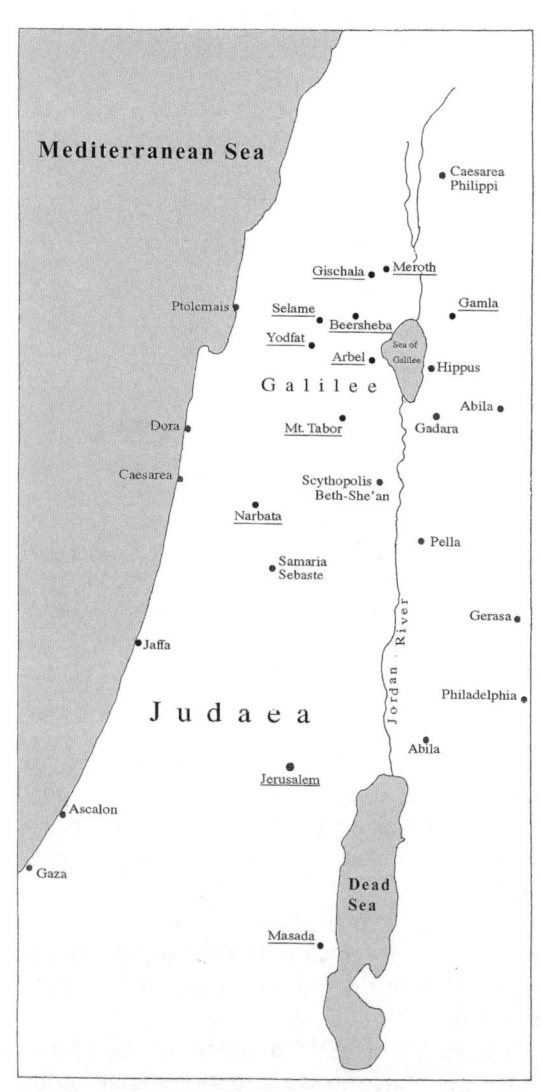

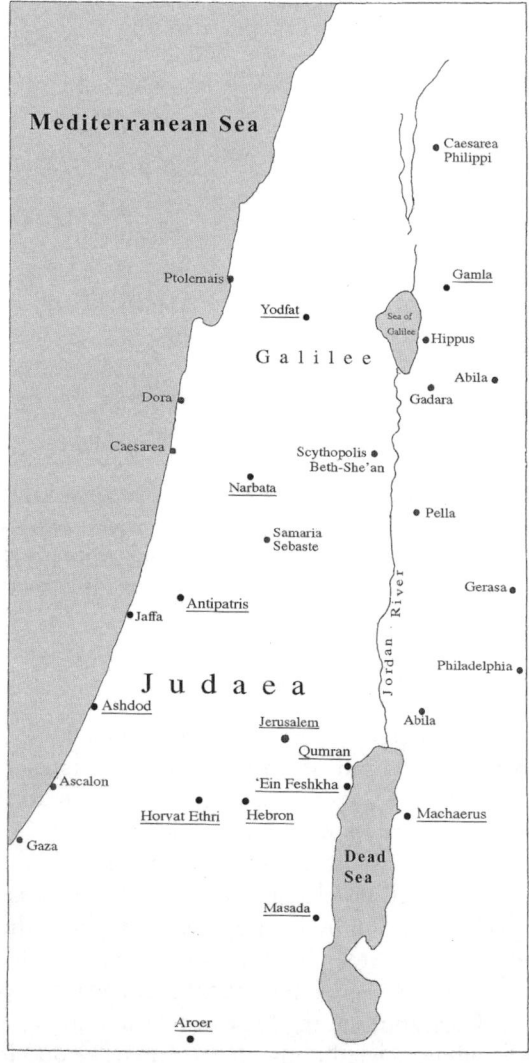

Figure 13 Sites containing fortifications related to the Jewish Revolt (underlined).

Figure 14 Sites containing battle artifacts or destruction remains related to the First Jewish Revolt (underlined).

Mortuary Evidence

Human remains that can be securely associated with First Revolt violence are rare. While Roman military gear is occasionally found, the custom of cremating soldiers killed in action and burying them in unmarked mass graves makes the discovery of Roman casualties unlikely (Hope 2003: 87).[12] Multiple Jewish casualties from single battles or siege events were in all likelihood deposited in common graves by their compatriots living in the same region. At least 23 individuals – men, women and children – were deposited within cisterns at Yodfat, with more bones discovered in the weight pit of an oil press hewn into the floor of a cave (Adan-Bayewitz and Aviam 1997; Aviam 2002: 130–31; and see *War* 3.336). Some of the remains were burnt or showed obvious marks of violence.[13] Complete skeletons or skeletal remains of 28 individuals were found at Masada, most of them in a single cave, but their classification as Jewish rebels is debatable (Yadin 1966: 54–56, 196–98; Zias 1998; Zias et al. 1994; see *War* 7.393–97). The fate of the defenders of Jerusalem and Gamla is symbolically represented by the skeletal remains of a young woman's arm found in a burnt residence at the affluent Upper City quarter of the former (Avigad 1983: 123, 135, 137; *War* 6.404–5), and by a facial bone unearthed near a destroyed public structure at the western urban section of the latter (Syon 2002: 151; *War* 4.80).

Regional Impact

Settlements and even whole regions may be abandoned due to plagues, prolonged droughts, shift of trade or industry to other areas, and even ambitious government-devised reforms. Yet when

Figure 15 Archaeological testimonies of First Revolt warfare. Above right: Mass of fallen blocks from the Temple Mount over a broken contemporaneous stone pavement. The Western Wall, Jerusalem (photograph: Y. Arbel). Right: Debris of the synagogue at Gamla (courtesy of D. Syon/Gamla excavations).

Figure 16 Arrowheads (left) and catapult projectiles (right) from Gamla (courtesy of D. Syon/Gamla excavations).

correlated with evidence for warfare, abrupt abandonment on a regional scale is likely to result of the anticipation of violence or as its outcome. Archaeological surveys and excavations reveal regional abandonment or significant reductions in Jewish rural settlement contemporaneous with the First Revolt. Affected regions include the heartland of Judea (Ofer 1993b; Eisenberg and Nagorski 2002), the central foothills (Zissu 2001), and parts of the Galilee and the Golan (Aviam 1993; Ma'oz 1987: 62–63; *contra*: Hartal 1987: 75). It should be noted that Josephus reports brutal unprovoked Roman assaults on the town of Lydda (Lod) (*War* 2.515–16) and the large Jewish villages of Betaris (Beth Govrin) and Caphartobas (Kfar Tov), where inhabitants were killed, enslaved, or evicted, and units were left behind to harass the neighboring countryside (*War* 4.447–48). As the dilapidation of the rural population of Judea would have denied the Romans considerable tax revenue, settlements that abstained from the revolt were usually spared. It seems, therefore, that even though Josephus does not report previous disturbances in these places, the Romans had reason to mistrust certain Jewish semi-urban or rural settlements and fear that their inhabitants intend to attack the Roman rear as the legions advanced towards Jerusalem. Whatever the causes of this violence, news over the unprovoked massacres would have terrified other residents in the region enough to make them flee their homes to the relative security of distant areas, fortified towns, or the capital.

It should be stressed that even though the Jewish rural population in Galilee and central Judea experienced severe harm and partial depletion during the uprising it was not completely eradicated. Archaeological evidence indicates that some villages in the Judean hill country were indeed destroyed or abandoned (Gershuny 2006: 176), but others had evidently survived the war (Kloner 2003: 49). Recent large-scale salvage excavations in the Modi'in region confirmed the existence of a relatively dense Jewish rural occupation dating between the end of the First Revolt

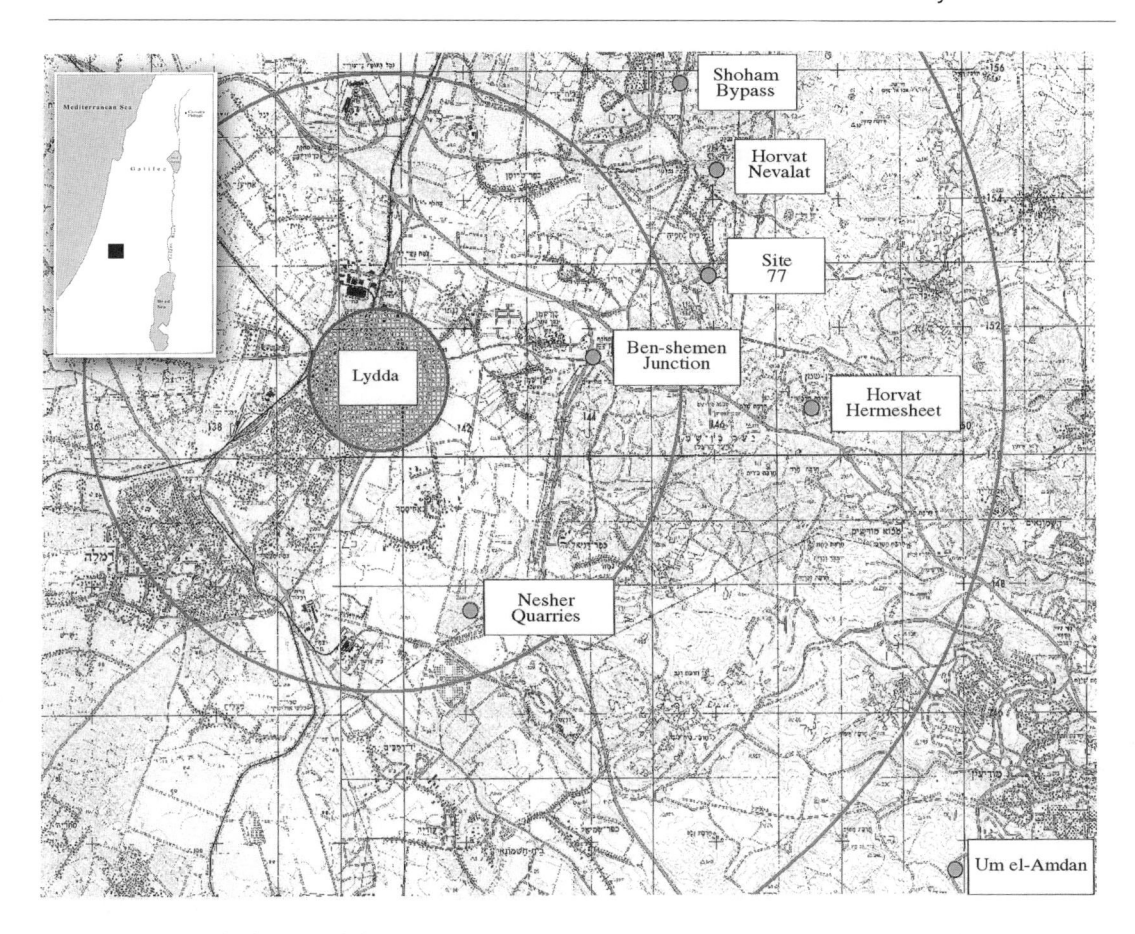

Figure 17 Newly discovered first-century-CE rural Jewish settlements in the Lydda (Lod) vicinity (courtesy of Y. Zelinger, Israel Antiquities Authority).

and the Bar Kochba uprising, during or following which the area was finally abandoned (Golani and Zbenovich 2001; Yekutieli et al. 1998; 2001; Zelinger 2004; Torgë 2002).

Summary

Despite occasional discrepancies, archaeological evidence related to the First Revolt generally substantiates the narrative of Josephus. Between 66 and 73 CE large numbers among the Jewish population in Judea committed themselves to an ambitious, highly dangerous, and ultimately disastrous military effort to liberate the Jewish homeland from Roman occupation. Archaeological excavations at sites such as Gamla and Yodfat, which were never rebuilt after their destruction, revealed vivid illustrations of the preparations for war, the siege, battle and final demise, as well as of the strict religious observance of the inhabitants. Valuable evidence to the siege emerged also at the sites of Narbata, Machaerus, and Masada, while excavations in the Upper City of Jerusalem (modern Jewish Quarter) brought to light both the residences of Judea's wealthy and impressive testimony to their violent demise as the Romans finally broke into the city in the summer of 70 CE. The archaeology of the Jewish Revolt thus supplies important data not only to the history of this specific event but also to wider subjects related to Roman warfare, weaponry, siege tactics, and military architecture and technology.

Yet the Jewish revolt was only one among numerous military attempts throughout the empire to regain freedom from Rome and certainly not the largest in scale and scope. What makes this uprising unique is the dominant religious-ideological element, which explains the otherwise senseless confidence of first-century Judean Jews in the feasibility of attaining liberty from Rome through military means. To the character, substance, and impact of this element the next chapters are dedicated.

8 Narrative of Crisis

The Jews were certainly not the only people under Roman rule to endure economic and administrative pressure. Like all other peoples under the Caesars they also faced inevitable adaptations due to the dynamic cultural exchanges in the vast imperial domains. Similar situations elsewhere prompted numerous uprisings, and some provinces remained restive for generations (see below). Yet conflicts generally took the form of pulses of violence and destruction, often during the early period of the occupation or near remote provincial frontiers. They seldom evolved into prolonged wars throughout a country that compromised entire legions for several years and reduced the local administrative and economic systems to chaos, as did the First Jewish Revolt. The reasons for this distinction must be uncovered in the peculiar motivation of the rebels in Judea.

Inter-class tensions, increasing economic stress, heavy taxation, ethnic antagonism, and oppressive Roman governors could all be found in first-century Judea. These hardships undoubtedly contributed significantly to the rising tensions that climaxed with the general revolt. Yet, could such factors, however stressful, have provoked an uprising of such scale and nurtured the perseverance of the rebels through years of suffering and against severe losses and increasing certainty of failure? This chapter examines various non-ideological aspects of the political, social, and material stress and the potential influence of each in the decision and determination of Judean Jews to fight Rome. An analysis based on both historical and archaeological data of their relative impact against that of the intense religious ideologies which prevailed in Judea at that time occupies the final chapters of this study.

Socioeconomic Stress

Contesting a socioeconomic explanation for the First Revolt, Jonathan Price (1992: 47–48) writes that the "collection of rebel groups was too diverse, the involvement of the Jewish aristocracy too heavy, Jewish society too fragmented on all levels, to support the notion of double uprising instigated by lower-class factions, against both the Roman provincial government and the upper-class Jews it supported." Jewish society in the first century CE was highly polarized, and it cannot be doubted that endemic social tensions sped up the erosion of public order and contributed to its final collapse. Still, any categorization of the support for the revolt along clear-cut socioeconomic lines would be simplistic and inaccurate.

As an aristocrat himself, Josephus had an obvious interest in minimizing the roles of members of his own class in the revolt and conveniently emphasizes the militant roles of popular leaders. His fortification of Sepphoris and Tiberias, the two largest Jewish towns in Galilee, could not have been carried out without the support that the war parties enjoyed from the local lower classes (*Life* 32, 38–40). Conversely, the eventual peaceful capitulation of both towns to the Romans was also made possible by the influence of local elites, which had supposedly opposed the uprising from its onset (Meyers 2002: 116–17; Horsley 2002: 92–93). Incidents throughout Judea during the early months of the revolt attest to popular fury against the allegedly pro-Roman exploitative upper classes. Estates were pillaged, their owners murdered, Herodian palaces ruined, debt archives burnt, and slaves freed (*War* 2.264–65, 2.426–27, 4.507). These events may be seen as the inevitable eruption of a crisis that had been fermenting for a long time.

The wealth and power of the elites (approximately 1% of the population) was based on the ownership of land.[1] Much of this type of wealth was accumulated at the expense of small farmers, who were compelled to sell their plots and become landless tenants or day laborers at the extensive estates that had annexed their patrimony.[2] Many of them, sons of respected families and members of established social networks, were reduced to poverty and lived on the brink of starvation (Fiensy 1991: 156, 159; Stegemann and Stegemann 1999: 127–35; Freyne 2002: 51; Applebaum 1975: 125; Hamel 1989: 156–58). Such situations were not unusual in peasant societies (Wolf 1966: 73–77), but cultural factors exacerbated their impact on the Jews. High birth rates, taboos against abortion, and charity networks that maximized infant survival resulted in a faster population growth than the Judean economy could sustain (Goodman 1987: 61). Roman taxation, confiscation of farmland on behalf of Helleno-Roman cities, and pressure by Jewish landlords aggravated the situation (Schürer 1961: 192; Hengel 1989: 335; Horsley 1987: 39; 1995: 51).[3] As emergency measures, some Herodian and Adiabene princes (a Mesopotamian dynasty that converted to Judaism) imported food for distribution and sponsored public works designed for the unemployed, but these efforts provided only localized and temporary relief (*Antiquities* 15.305–10, 20.101, 219–22). Even social systems aimed at countering the effects of relatively common environmental hazards such as droughts (*Antiquities* 15.299–308, 20.101) could no longer be effectively activated. It is thus easy to see how the indifference of the aristocracy to the plight of the masses – a plight which they themselves had a significant part in creating – could have generated much of the anger that made the revolt inevitable.[4]

Yet the politics of Judea were more complex than Josephus would have us believe. Following Goodblatt (2006: 84–8), the priesthood had a central role in the establishment of a Jewish national identity. Without such ideological awareness it is hard to see how the two major revolts against Rome would have been possible. Some leading aristocrats took active part in the rebellion, at least in its early stages, and for sound ideological convictions (Goodman 1987: 46–49; 1990: 43; Horsley 1995: 73; 2002: 105; Price 1992: 27ff.; McLaren 2003: 151). The inadequacy of a monolithic socioeconomic explanation for the revolt is also evident from the perspective of the common Jewish rebels.

Many of the latter began as desperate peasants who took to the mountains and deserts and regrouped to harass Roman forces and raid Jewish estates (Price 1992: 48–49; Schäfer 1995: 101). Josephus refers to the attackers as brigands, a sentiment that would probably also have been shared by the Romans.[5] Yet many of those "brigands," even if driven to the margins by economic stress, were far from common highway robbers. Richard Horsley (1979: 60; 2002: 100) compares Judean "brigands" to the "bandits" of Hobsbawm's (1985) model, popular champions who share the moral and religious values of the peasants and fight for justice against the oppressive establishment and exploitative gentry. Yet, remarking that "very seldom does social banditry lead to more serious popular rebellion," Horsley (1987: 39) suggests a simultaneous spread of millenarian ideas supportive of the uprising. Indeed, first-century Jewish brigandage cannot be fully understood if detached from ideological undercurrents.

One of the more celebrated "bandits," Eleazar ben Dineus, roamed the Galilee for twenty years before he could be arrested (*War* 2.232–46, 253; *Antiquities* 20.121, 161). Eleazar must have enjoyed considerable popular support to have dodged captivity for that long (Goodman 1987: 63). Among their feats, he and his men ravaged Samaritan villages at the instigation of the local leaders in Galilee in revenge for the murder of Galilean pilgrims in Samaria. In the eyes of his own people, Eleazar would have been more a hero than a criminal.

Within the context of the Samaritan affair, Josephus reports that the Galilean followers of Eleazar ben Dineus "persuaded the multitude of the Jews to betake themselves to arms, and to regain their liberty, saying that slavery was in itself a bitter thing but that when it was joined with direct injustices, it was perfectly intolerable" (*Antiquities* 20.120). In a later development, the Romans executed a man by the name of Dortus and his four associates for having "persuaded the multitude to a revolt from the Romans" (*Antiquities* 20.130). Another "brigand," Athronges, a

NARRATIVE OF CRISIS

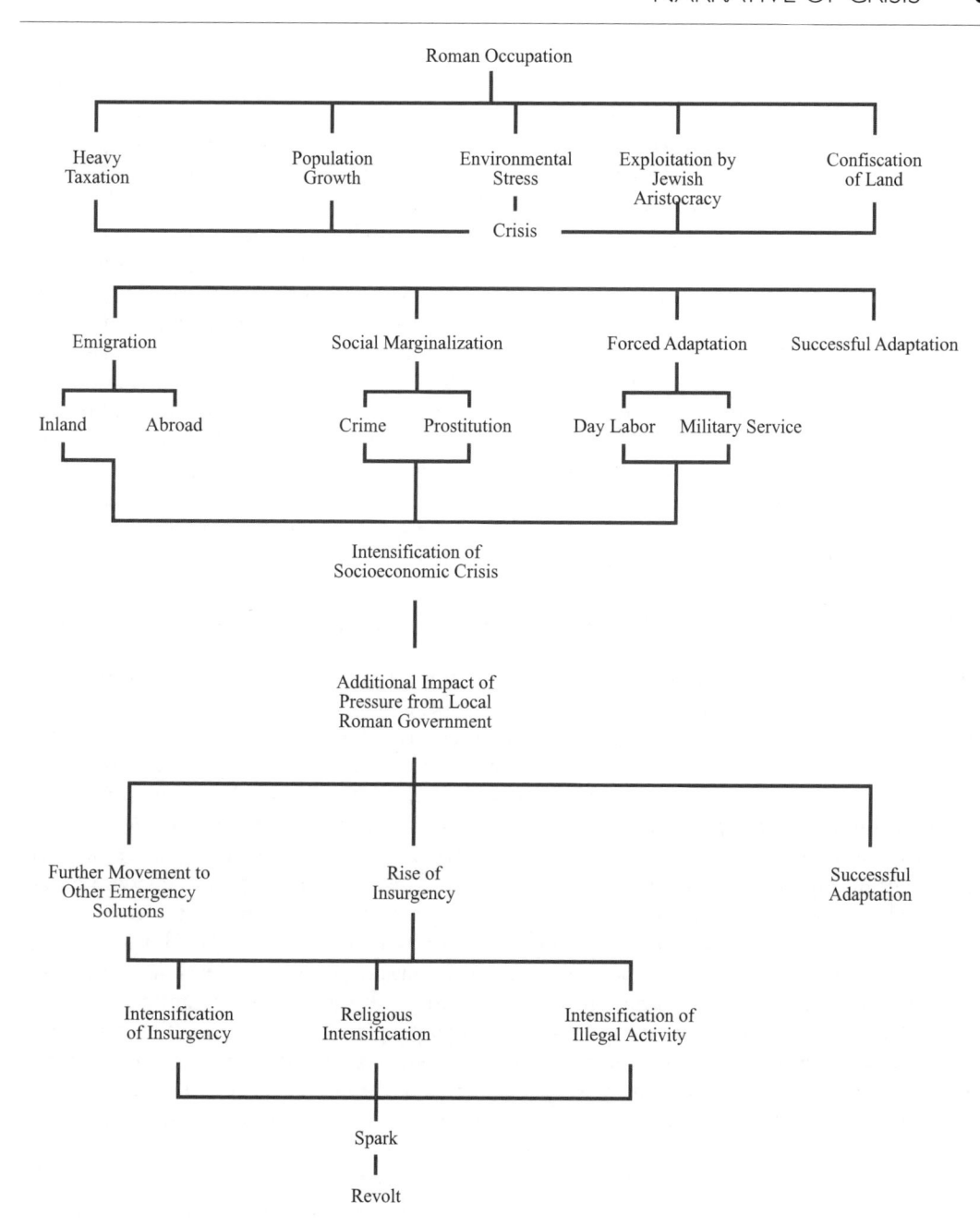

Figure 18 Socio-economic crisis model.

shepherd with ambitions to the crown, justified his attacks on Herodian troops as punishment for their "licentious conduct" (*Antiquities* 17.281). With issues like morality and liberty as incentives for "brigandage," at least some of Josephus' outlaws seem in fact to have been ideological rebels with purposes other than material profit. The considerable military efforts the Romans invested in subduing the large hosts that some of the outlaws managed to gather confirm the popular appeal of their cause (*Antiquities* 14.159, 17.271–85; *War* 1.204, 2.56–65; *Histories* 5:9).

Additional arguments can be made against the socioeconomic model of explanation for the revolt. Had socioeconomic improvement been so crucial to the Jews, they could have emulated their prosperous Helleno-Roman urban neighbors who remained unyieldingly loyal to the empire. Instead, the Jews chose to repeatedly defy Rome at huge risk and cost. The secondary importance of the material aspect is also indicated by the fact that palaces and estates were ravaged rather than occupied, and no systematic redistribution of lands among the peasantry is known to have been attempted. Although Josephus accuses rebel chief Simon bar Giora of hoarding and hiding away plundered treasures, he ends the very same sentence reporting the commander's preparation for an assault on Jerusalem (*War* 4.512–13). If money and assets were what Simon had wanted, as a leader during the early months of the revolt he now would have had them. Why bother with a dangerous and costly attack on the capital? Simon's immediate concern was evidently not personal enrichment or social justice, but raising funds for future military campaigns. Moreover, plain economic want does not furnish the endurance needed to sustain catastrophic and consecutive failures over several years. Ideological devotion does – and first-century Judea teemed with charismatic preachers propagating the formula of ultimate salvation for ultimate devotion. Many Jews did surrender to the Romans in order to save what was left, but tens of thousands throughout Judea did not. Socioeconomic grievances may have kindled their anger, but ideological motivation is the only viable explanation of their otherwise pointless determination to fight to the end.

Policy and Conduct of the Roman Governors of Judea

While the earlier and more competent Roman governors[6] appointed to Judea maintained a generally reasonable relationship with their Jewish subjects, the insensitive and corrupt administration of later appointees stirred incessant trouble. The long term of Pontius Pilate (26–36 CE), one of the least attentive governors to Jewish religious sensitivities,[7] exemplifies the nature of the clashes. Maliciousness, ignorance, carelessness, bad advice, or a combination of all set him several times against serious unrest. Pilate's intention to use temple funds for the construction of a new aqueduct to the capital sparked the worst confrontation. Thousands lost their lives during the military suppression of furious crowds in the sacrosanct temple courtyard (*War* 2.175–77). The Jewish outrage may seem an overreaction: the aqueduct was necessary and the bountiful temple resources had financed construction projects for public benefit before (Brandon 1967: 72–77; Horsley 1987: 99–108; Gabba 1990: 167–68). Nonetheless, given the religious atmosphere of the time it could have been anticipated that any appropriation of consecrated funds by Gentiles, regardless of purpose, would be considered as sufficiently offensive for enough people to rise up against the sacrilege.

Pilate was eventually replaced and exiled to Gaul, but most of the later governors who ruled Judea in the two decades prior to the revolt[8] contributed to the escalation of tensions. The Roman historian Tacitus, himself no friend of the Jews, testifies that the governor Felix "thought he might be guilty of all sorts of wickedness with impunity…by the use of unseasonable remedies [Felix] blew up the coal of sedition to a flame."[9] Tacitus adds that the governor Cumanus behaved in similar ways, both governors bringing the province to the brink of war. Josephus had worse things to say of the last two governors prior to the revolt. Concerning Albinus (62–64), there was no

> sort of wickedness that could be named but he had no hand in it. Accordingly, he did not only, in his political capacity, steal and plunder every one's substance, nor did he only burden the whole nation with taxes, but he permitted the relations of such as were in prison for robbery… to redeem them for money; and nobody remained in prison as a malefactor but he who gave him nothing (*War* 2.272–73).

The full context of Josephus' testimony reveals that many of these "robbers" were actually rebels, which clarifies his exaggerated comment that during the term of Albinus "those seeds were sown which brought [Jerusalem] to destruction" (*War* 2. 276). Yet Josephus thought even Albinus "a most excellent person" (2.277) when compared with Gessius Florus, the last pre-revolt governor. Florus' two years in office saw widespread extortion, corruption, and bribery, taxes raised to unbearable levels and flourishing brigandage, with the governor sharing the profits. The governor actively undermined the efforts of Jewish dignitaries to restrain the militant factions and terrorized them by sending troops to plunder their homes and crucify some of them as common criminals (*War* 2.305–8). Josephus believed that Florus intentionally instigated war to divert the attention of the imperial court from his crimes (2.282–83). Once war finally erupted, Cestius Gallus, the Roman governor of Syria and Florus' immediate superior, reported the latter's misdeeds to Rome (*War* 2.558). To Florus himself this may no longer have mattered. According to Suetonius, he had already been killed by the rebels by that time (*Lives* 8.1,4).

Several scholars (Brandon 1967: 128; Bilde 1979; Kasher 1983a: 80; Goodman 1990: 39) have raised the possibility that Josephus embellished the misconduct of the later governors in order to shift the blame for the revolt to them, thus exonerating the traditional Jewish leadership and the Roman court. It is improbable, however, that Josephus would have invented all of his accusations, as by the time of his writing many eyewitnesses were still alive and records were available in Roman archives. Furthermore, the testimony of Tacitus and the occasional Roman measures to amend the situation confirm awareness in Rome itself of the problematic conduct of some of the appointed governors (Goodman 1987: 7).

It should be noted that unwise and exploitative Roman governors were not sent exclusively to Judea. Quinctilius Varus, governor in Germany under Augustus, was partly responsible for a revolt during which the Seventeenth, Eighteenth, and Nineteenth Legions were wiped out and he himself killed in an ambush in the Teutoburg Forest in 9 CE (Harnecker 2004). Varus' chief sin was impatience. He considered the Germans too slow in adapting to the Roman modes of life, and his insensitive pressure for faster transition sparked violent counteraction (Millar 1967: 294). At least some of the revolts in Gaul during the first century BCE and the first century CE can be blamed on irresponsible taxation and administrative abuse by short-sighted provincial Roman administrations (Dyson 1975: 154). Similar causes were at the background of revolts in Sardinia (228–225 BCE), Spain (22 BCE), and Britain of the first and early second centuries CE (Dyson 1975: 145, 151, 167–68).

All of these provinces were eventually pacified, mostly as a result of local administrations more attentive to the cultural settings and practical needs of the population. Restraint and temperance were in fact more characteristic of Roman provincial governments than the despotic folly of individual officials. During the years following Boudicca's revolt in 60 CE, for example, the even-handed moderation of the Roman government in Britain allowed the recovery of the province and the reconstruction of Roman urban centers (Frere 1978: 109). The principle of moderation was also generally employed in Judea, and Roman base policy demonstrated notable patience with the peculiar demands of the Jewish religion. Why then did the experienced provincial system fail to pacify the Jews of Judea for much of the first two hundred years of occupation? The most viable explanation lies in the combination of foolhardy, greedy, and incompetent governors who had neither the will nor the talent – and least of all the understanding – to deal with an uncompromising religious ideology strictly averse to any Gentile rule, benevolent or otherwise, over sacrosanct Jewish land.

Jewish-Gentile Enmity

A History of Inter-communal Tensions

Hostility between Jews and non-Jews in Judea dates to the earliest days of the Second Temple period, when non-Jewish populations opposed the reconstruction of Jerusalem by returnees from the Babylonian exile (Nehemiah 4:7–17). Violent clashes between Jews and Gentiles took place during

88 NARRATIVE OF CRISIS

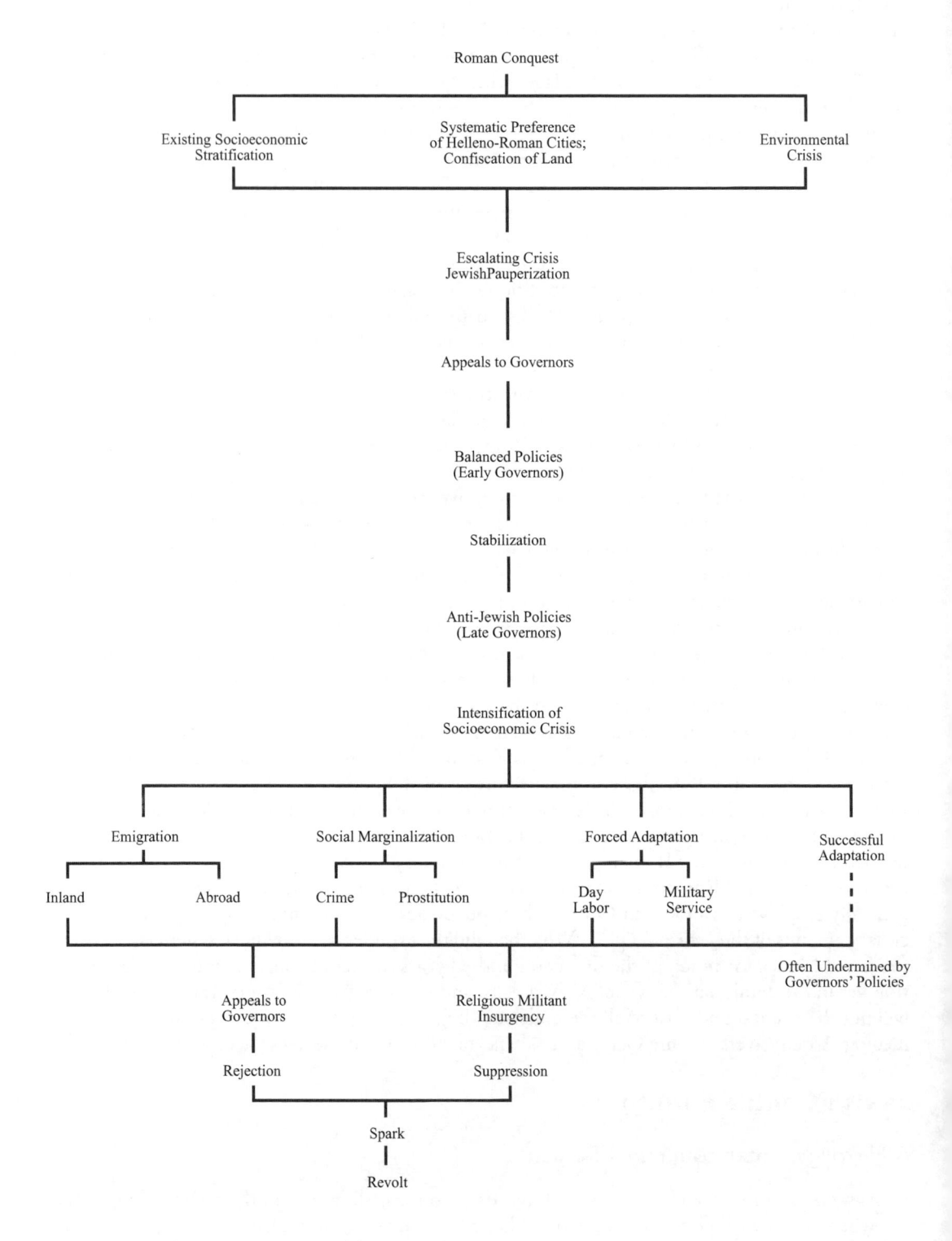

```
                              Roman Conquest
          ┌──────────────────────┬──────────────────────┐
  Existing Socioeconomic   Systematic Preference    Environmental
     Stratification        of Helleno-Roman Cities;      Crisis
                           Confiscation of Land

                           Escalating Crisis
                           JewishPauperization

                           Appeals to Governors

                           Balanced Policies
                           (Early Governors)

                              Stabilization

                           Anti-Jewish Policies
                            (Late Governors)

                           Intensification of
                           Socioeconomic Crisis
   ┌──────────────┬───────────────────┬───────────────────────┐
  Emigration   Social Marginalization   Forced Adaptation   Successful
                                                             Adaptation
  ┌──────┐      ┌──────┐        ┌──────┐
 Inland Abroad Crime Prostitution Day    Military
                               Labor    Service
  └──────┴────────┬──────┴────────┴─────────┘
           Appeals to      Religious Militant      Often Undermined by
           Governors          Insurgency            Governors' Policies
              │                   │
           Rejection          Suppression
              └────────┬──────────┘
                     Spark
                       │
                     Revolt
```

Figure 19   Roman Governors Model.

the Maccabean revolt against the Seleucids (Maccabees 1, 5:1–2, 37–55; Maccabees 2, 12:1–15). In order to rid the Holy Land of idolatry (and also to solidify their rule), successive Hasmonean princes systematically destroyed pagan temples throughout the land and forced non-Jewish populations to choose between conversion and deportation (*Antiquities* 13.254–58, 318, 397). Fortunes changed following the conquest of Judea by the Romans, who favored the friendlier and more culturally akin Gentile population. Josephus credits Gabinius, the Roman governor of Syria, with the founding of various Helleno-Roman cities throughout the land (*Antiquities* 14.87–88). These populous cities became the backbone of Roman administration in Judea and Transjordan, boasting colonnaded market streets, temples, theaters, baths, and sophisticated water conduits. Roman policy did not intentionally prejudice the Jews, who were allowed to practice their religious, civil, and communal affairs virtually unperturbed (Goodman 1987: 14). Nevertheless, the establishment and expansion of Helleno-Roman urban centers required the confiscation of valuable and sorely needed farmland, some of it from hapless Jewish owners.[10]

Most inhabitants of the cities were Greek-speaking descendants of indigenous non-Jewish populations and of Graeco-Roman officials, soldiers, and immigrants. They were fully assimilated into the Helleno-Roman cultural and social realm, and many of them joined the locally recruited Roman garrisons (*Antiquities* 19.365; *War* 2.268). Clashes between these local troops and Jewish civilians occurred immediately after the untimely death of King Agrippa I (*Antiquities* 19.357) and during the term of the governor Cumanus (*Antiquities* 20.105–17; *War* 2.223–31).[11] This deep-seated animosity led Josephus to accuse the locally recruited military units of partial responsibility for the instigation of the Jewish revolt (*Antiquities* 19.365). Hostilities between Jews and Helleno-Roman populations soared during the early stages of the war, and bloody confrontations raged in Judea, Transjordan, and Syria (*War* 2.457–82). Josephus graphically describes the gruesome outcome:

> It was then common to see cities filled with dead bodies, still lying unburied, and those of old men, mixed with infants, all dead, and scattered about together; women also lay amongst them, without any covering for their nakedness. You might then see the whole province full of inex-

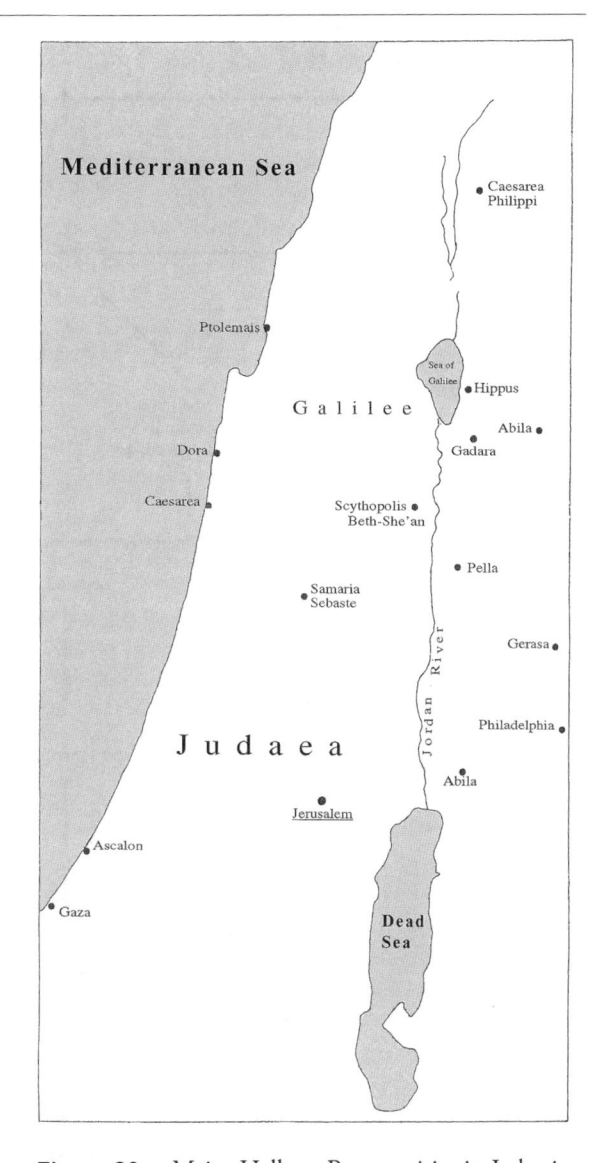

Figure 20 Major Helleno-Roman cities in Judea in the first century CE (Jerusalem not included).

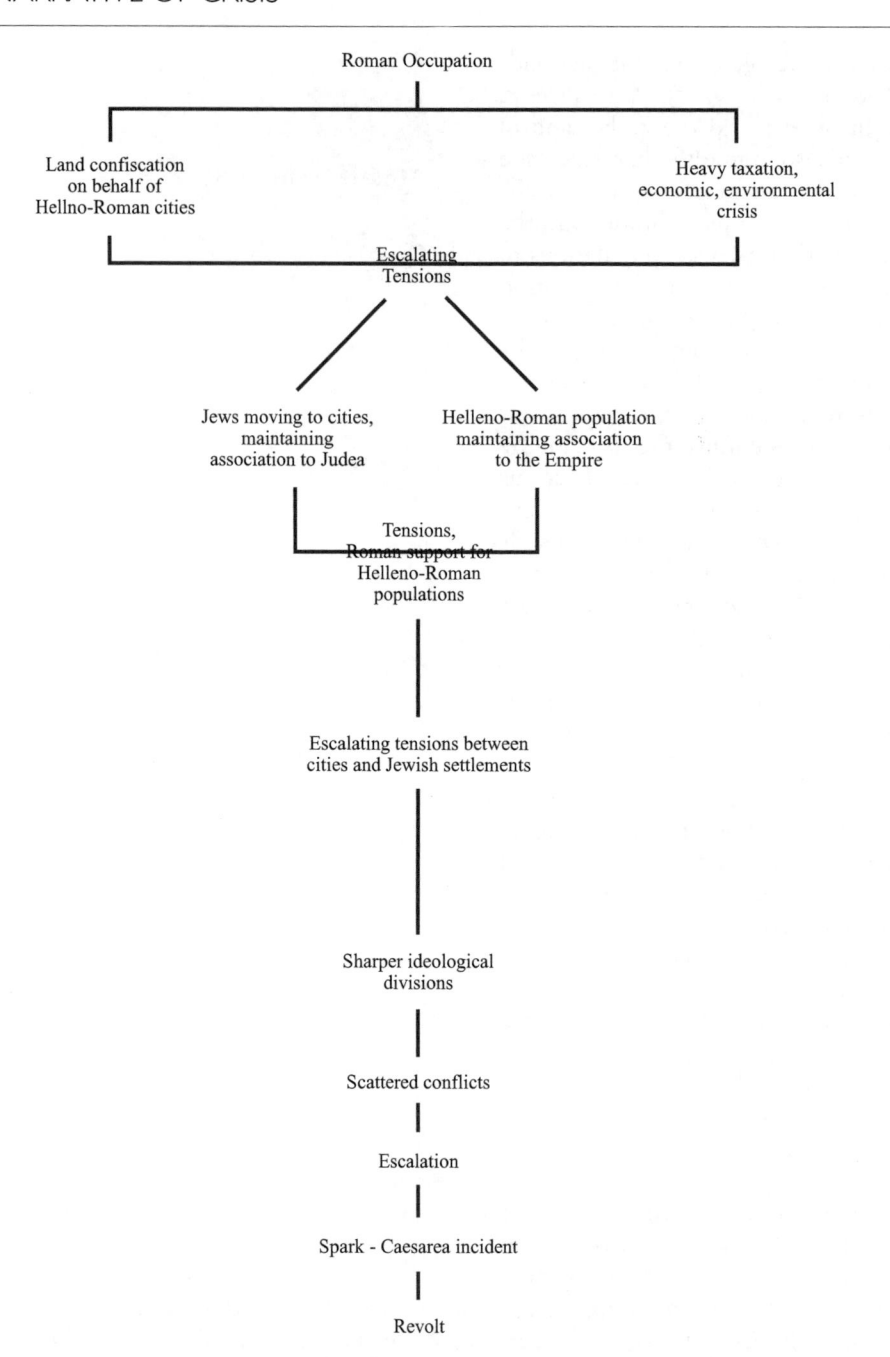

```
                        Roman Occupation
                               |
        ┌──────────────────────┴──────────────────────┐
   Land confiscation                            Heavy taxation,
     on behalf of                            economic, environmental
  Hellno-Roman cities                                crisis
        └──────────────────────┬──────────────────────┘
                          Escalating
                           Tensions
                          /        \
                         /          \
            Jews moving to cities,    Helleno-Roman population
                maintaining              maintaining association
             association to Judea            to the Empire
                     └──────────┬──────────┘
                            Tensions,
                        Roman support for
                        Helleno-Roman
                          populations
                               |
                               |
                   Escalating tensions between
                   cities and Jewish settlements
                               |
                               |
                      Sharper ideological
                           divisions
                               |
                       Scattered conflicts
                               |
                           Escalation
                               |
                    Spark - Caesarea incident
                               |
                             Revolt
```

Figure 21 Ethnic Tensions model.

pressible calamities, while the dread of still more barbarous practices which were threatened, was everywhere greater than had been already perpetrated (*War* 2.465).

Relations between Jews, Samaritans, and Arabs fared no better. The rejection of Jesus at a Samaritan village and the parable of the Good Samaritan (Luke 9:51–52, 11:30–37) reflect centuries of Jewish-Samaritan acrimony that fueled sporadic violence between the two communities, such as the mentioned episode featuring Eleazar ben Dineus.[12] When Vespasian's army marched into Judea, it was joined by units of Arab fighters. Tacitus offhandedly explains this with the "accustomed hatred" that is "usual in nations that are neighbors to one another" (*Histories* 5:1). Yet the hostility between Jews and their neighbors had more complex reasons than common neighborly disputes.

Mutual Bias Between Jews, Romans, and Helleno-Roman Populations

With the return of the Jews from the Babylonian exile in the late sixth and early fifth centuries BCE, the Jewish leadership enforced strict ethnic isolation upon the reestablished community as a means of cultural consolidation and religious preservation (Rappaport 1984: 25–29). By the early Roman period, many Jews in Judea lived up to the Hebrew Bible (Old Testament) idea of "a people dwelling alone and not reckoning itself among the nations" (Numbers 23:9). Ethno-cultural Jewish isolationism significantly exacerbated the resentment against Roman occupation and its impact on Judea. Shadows of that attitude can be traced in rabbinical sources from the late Roman and Byzantine periods. A passage states that "if a man tells you both are ruined – do not believe. Both live in peace – do not believe. Caesarea is ruined and Jerusalem lives – believe. Jerusalem is ruined and Caesarea lives – believe" (*Megilah* 6.61). In a discussion between sages, an indignant Rabbi Simon bar Yochai snaps at Rabbi Judah, who complimented the Romans for developing the land, "All they have built only for themselves did they build; built markets to place there prostitutes, built baths for their own pleasure, built bridges to tax travelers" (*Shabbath* 33a–b).[13] The degree to which these attitudes represent first-century thinking cannot be solidly evaluated, but as significant Jewish militancy had ceased centuries prior to the time when the passages were written it is likely that the expressions reflect historical memories of fierce antagonism to Rome. Even Josephus never advocates Roman occupation as such (Stern 1982). The historian, as other members of the peace party, perceived submission to the Romans as obligatory for national self-preservation.

Approaching the subject from the opposite side, scholars have traced different perspectives in Roman and Greek literature concerning the Jews and Judaism (Yavetz 1993: 14–18; Bohak 2003: 40–41; Gruen 2002). Some early Graeco-Roman authors were sympathetic to the Jewish religion (Gager 1975: 136–38; Isaac 1996: 102–3). On the other hand, some prominent Romans shared the flagrant anti-Jewish views of Helleno-Roman populations in Judea and Egypt (see Josephus, *Against Apion;* Philo, *Legatio ad Gaium*). It is probable that not only Jewish militancy against Roman occupation but also the relatively frequent conversions of Romans to Judaism during the first century, which alarmed many in Rome (Stern 1979), stimulated antagonism towards the Jews. Narratives unflattering to the Jews can be found in the works of Pliny the Elder (*Natural History* 7.46), Cicero (*In Defense of Flaccus* 67), and especially Tacitus, who thought the Jews to be ideologically disparate to all that Rome represents:

> all things are with them profane which with us are sacred...[and such] practices are allowed among them which are by us esteemed most abominable...among themselves there is an unalterable fidelity and kindness always ready at hand, but bitter enmity towards all others.... The proselytes to their religion...are taught nothing sooner than to despise the gods, to renounce their country and to have their parents, children and brethren in the utmost contempt (*Histories* 5:4–5).

Yet highlighting this endemic mutual dislike between Rome and Jerusalem as the main element that led to the revolt would neglect the complex and multi-leveled nature of Jewish-Gentile relations during that period as a whole. Some elementary misunderstandings of Judaism in Graeco-Roman sources led some scholars to detect more ignorance than actual spite at the base of the negative views of the Jews and their religion (Schäfer 1996; Goodman 1987: 236–37; Gruen 2002: 37; Rokeah 1990: 267; Bar-Kochva 2000; Bohak 2003; Modrzejewski 2003: 114–15, 117–18). The philosopher Martin Buber (1967: 116) perceptibly pointed out that "The idea of God as the sole owner of all land, incomprehensible to a Greek, is the cornerstone of the Jewish social concept." Indeed, the Jewish rejection of syncretism, which elegantly accommodated the vast array of religions in the empire, perplexed and annoyed the Roman mind. The actual impressions that some highly educated Greeks and Romans held about the Jewish religion itself were often based on folklore. Augustus, for example, thought that the Jews fasted each and every Sabbath (Suetonius, *Lives* 2.76). Tacitus explained the day of rest in terms of laziness (*Histories* 5:4), while Strabo, who compliments Judaism elsewhere (*Geography* 16.2.35ff.), believed that the Jews also circumcised females (*Geography* 16.4.9).

Furthermore, it should be remembered that the Jews were by no means the only 'barbarian' people whom Greek and Roman writers defamed and culturally misunderstood. Cicero's criticism of the Jews was no worse than the insults he heaped on other foreign peoples while assembling judicial arguments to refute their charges against Roman officials in his capacity as a solicitor (Stern 1991: 466). Graeco-Roman terminology, stereotypes, and bias regarding the Egyptians and their religion were as vicious as those used against the Jews, or worse (Goodman 1998: 4–5; Gruen 2002: 33; Bohak 2003: 32ff.). Judaism suffered some spells of repression in Rome, but so did the Egyptian cult of Isis and the Persian cult of Mithras (Witt 1971: 138; Clauss 2000; Beard et al. 1998: 231).

Another point that must be considered when weighing the impact of Jewish-Gentile relations on the atmosphere that led to the war is the existence, despite occasional frictions, of peaceful daily interaction and cultural exchange between Jews and non-Jews in the province. Rabbinical concerns over such influences refer mainly to later periods, when militant opposition to Rome was no longer relevant,[14] although some evidence for the penetration of Helleno-Roman cultural elements into first-century Judaism also exists. Theaters of probable first-century origins were discovered in the large Jewish town of Sepphoris (Strange 1992; Weiss 1998; Meyers 1998: 351–52).[15] Josephus mentions a theater and an amphitheater standing even in Jerusalem (*Antiquities* 15.268ff.). Their location, if they truly ever existed, remains unknown, although stone seats (Reich and Billig 2000; 2001) and bone and ivory discs tentatively interpreted as entry tickets (Avigad 1983: 193–94) have been discovered. Jewish sages of the later Roman period debated over how to relate to statues of gods, persons, and animals gracing colonnaded market streets, fountains, and public bathhouses, the attraction of which was not lost on the Jews[16] (Dvorjetski 1999; Schwartz 1998: 213–15; Friedheim 2002; Eliav 2002: 414–15, 421; Schäfer 2002: 346; Sperber 1998: 58–72; Porath 1998: 43; Mazor and Bar-Nathan 1998: 10). Such problems would also have been relevant in the realities of the first century.

Moreover, there is evidence of a strong sense of local patriotism among the Jews living in Helleno-Roman urban centers in Egypt (Philo, *Im Flaccum* 45–46) and Judea. The Jews of Caesarea went as far as demanding the city for themselves, evoking the Jewish descent of King Herod, the city's founder (*War* 2.266). This is an interesting illustration of the versatility of human thoughts and feelings, considering the public Jewish sentiments towards Herod during his lifetime. In the early months of the First Revolt, the Jews of Scythopolis actually joined their non-Jewish neighbors in repelling the rebels' attack, although this show of loyalty did not save them from the lethal treachery of their neighbors (*War* 2.466–68). The depth of Jewish roots in the Helleno-Roman cities is evident in the post-war recuperation of the Jewish communities in Caesarea, Scythopolis, and other cities, where they thrived well into the Late Roman and Byzantine periods (Fuks 1982; Foerster and Tsafrir 1986: 58; Holum 1998: 163–68). The impact of the Helleno-Roman urban centers and their culture on the Jews is also apparent in the architecture and art popular in the predominantly Jewish towns of Tiberias and Sepphoris (Weiss 1996a; 1998: 219; Netzer and Weiss 1994; Hirschfeld 1995a; Weiss 1998: 220–21; Meyers 1998: 351–52; Parapetti 1983/84). Such influence is also reflected in the architectural terminology (Hirschfeld 1995b: 292) of rabbinical literature.

Moderation in Jewish attitudes towards certain aspects of Helleno-Roman culture should not imply religious assimilation. What was accepted emphasizes the rejection of that which was not. Even pro-Roman Sepphoris, which called itself 'Eirenopolis-Neronias-Sepphoris' on a coin minted locally in 68 CE, avoided depictions of Nero on the currency (Seyrig 1950; Meyers 2002: 116). Still, violent episodes between Jews and Gentiles prior to the First Jewish Revolt were brief and sporadic, while peaceful interaction existed simultaneously, with material styles and intellectual ideas flowing both ways. Conflicting economic interests and mutual cultural misconceptions generated frictions, but a comprehensive and uncompromising religious-ideological framework was necessary to match sporadic, if bloody, local frictions with the overall Jewish case against Rome and generate major destructive violence.

Personal Agency

Unlike the second Jewish revolt against Rome, which is known after its assertive and undisputed leader Simon ben Kosiba ("Bar Kochba"), there was never an effective and unified leadership presiding over the first major uprising. The Jerusalem aristocracy and priesthood established a provisional government that was nominally in charge during the first two years (*War* 2.562–63) but, as shown by the problems of Josephus, the officially appointed but much challenged commander of Galilee, the scope of its authority was very narrow. The meager powers it did have eroded to insignificance as the bleak reports of fallen towns and mounting casualties throughout the country reached the capital. Following a bloody coup in the winter of 68/69 CE, authority shifted to rival warlords. John of Gischala and Simon bar Giora, the two most prominent among them, are the only viable non-prophetic candidates in an agency-based model.[17]

John of Gischala

Prior to the war, John ben Levy of the town of Gischala in northern Galilee had been a prosperous olive farmer and oil trader. He must have obtained a realistic appraisal of the political and military might of Rome through his commercial contacts and travel, and he had a lot to lose from the inevitable damages of war. It is thus not surprising that he opposed the revolt in its initial stages, until a destructive attack on his hometown by Syrian raiders under Roman sanction radically modified his views (*Life* 43–45). With no Jewish towns safe from catastrophe, John may have rationalized that Jewish survival depended on resistance (Rappaport 1982: 488–90). He soon metamorphosed into an influential and outspoken rebel leader, established his own militia, and worked vigorously to undermine the authority of the moderate Josephus in Galilee.

While John had evidently never entertained apocalyptic visions over the war, there is no reason to suspect the sincerity of his religious faith, and he probably did believe in, or at least hoped for, God's ultimate intervention on behalf of the rebels. However, his religious confidence coincided with a pragmatic and rational approach. John understood the necessity of fortifying Gischala[18] and financed the project himself by selling ritually pure oil to Jewish communities in Syria (*Life* 74; *War* 2.591–92). When it became obvious that holding out against the Roman siege would be impossible, John tricked Titus into allowing him to flee with his supporters to Jerusalem. To the Jews he sensibly explained that resistance in the vulnerable smaller towns would be futile and that fighters and resources should be spared for the defense of the capital (*War* 4.123). In the spring of 68 CE, John violently captured the prestigious and strategic court of the Temple from the rival Zealot faction, having taken advantage of the pious but naïve decision of the Zealot commander Eleazar ben Simon to allow access to Passover pilgrims (*War* 5.99–105). Once there, John did not hesitate to use the Temple's treasury to fund his forces, rationalizing that "such whose warfare is for the Temple, should live of the Temple" (*War* 5.564). He led his faction through the vicious civil war

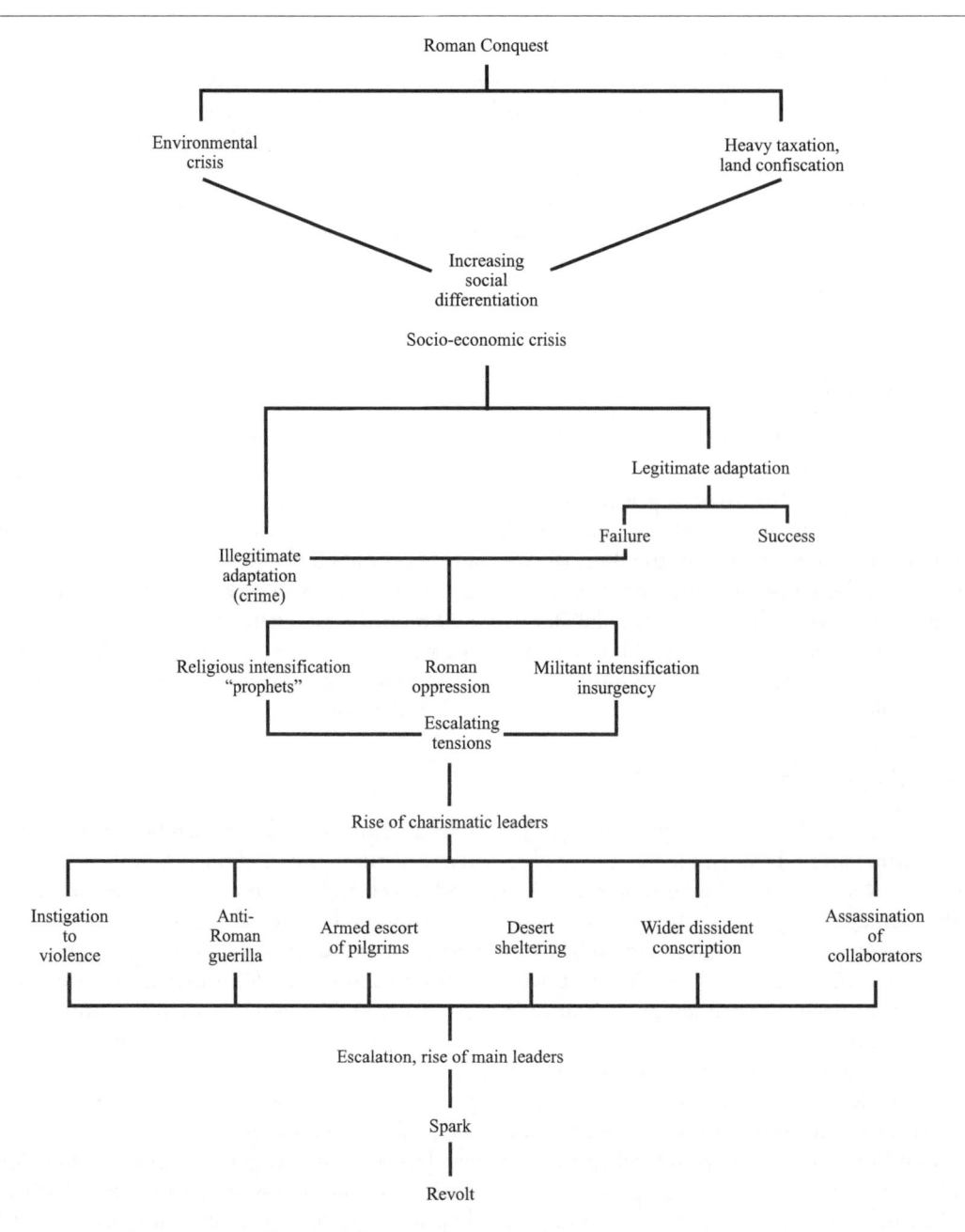

```
                        Roman Conquest
                              │
              ┌───────────────┴───────────────┐
      Environmental                      Heavy taxation,
         crisis                          land confiscation
              └───────────────┬───────────────┘
                        Increasing
                         social
                      differentiation
                    Socio-economic crisis
                              │
              ┌───────────────┴───────────────┐
                                       Legitimate adaptation
                                       ┌───────┴───────┐
                                    Failure        Success
         Illegitimate   ────────────┘
          adaptation
           (crime)
    ┌─────────┼─────────┐
Religious            Roman         Militant
intensification   oppression    intensification
 "prophets"                       insurgency
    └─────────┬─────────┘
           Escalating
            tensions
              │
     Rise of charismatic leaders
              │
┌──────┬──────┬──────┬──────┬──────┐
Instigation Anti-  Armed escort Desert   Wider dissident  Assassination
   to     Roman   of pilgrims shelter-   conscription         of
 violence guerilla            ing                        collaborators
└──────┴──────┴──────┴──────┴──────┘
              │
   Escalation, rise of main leaders
              │
            Spark
              │
            Revolt
```

Figure 22 Charismatic Leaders Model.

against Simon bar Giora, fought valiantly against the besieging Roman legions, and ended the war being captured alive and sentenced to spend the rest of his life in a Roman prison (*War* 6.434).

Some scholars accept Josephus' perspective and regard John as a ruthless extremist (Smallwood 1976: 304), an opportunistic ex-bandit (Horsley 1979: 59; 2002: 95), and a man motivated by personal ambition rather than ideological commitment (Rappaport 1982: 480–82). Yet, even if Josephus' predisposed narrative is to be believed, much could also be said in John's defense. The Galilean command was crucial and Josephus possessed neither sufficient military skills nor true ideological commitment. John's actions in Galilee were part of the overall violence that broke out throughout the province with the collapse of central government, and, as previously mentioned, "bandits" were often the only protectors many Jews could rely on. In either case, and of more relevance to our discussion, Josephus' testimony of John's early anti-war inclinations is to be trusted. John of Gischala rose to prominence only *after* the war had begun. He played no part in its instigation.

Simon bar Giora

Judging by Simon bar Giora's surname, his father may have been a convert (Schürer 1961: 262; Fuks 1989: 107).[19] As such, Simon may have absorbed the religious zealotry of the newly-converted at home, and with it a staunch anti-Roman ideology. Early in the war Simon raided estates, murdered landlords, and liberated slaves (*War* 4.508, 652). Some believe that his concern for social justice was genuine (Roth 1960; Rajak 1983: 136; Hengel 1989: 336), while others hold that it was politically motivated (Fuks 1989: 113–15). Either way, the humiliation of the exploitative gentry made him a hero among the lower classes (Malina 1981: 82–85; Goodman 1987: 60). With many Jews enthusiastically joining his forces and fueled by the resources obtained from the raided estates, Simon soon became a powerful figure among the rebels and a dangerous rival of the provisional government. He and his group nonetheless avoided direct confrontation with the forces sent against them from Jerusalem and found shelter at Masada with the Sicarii[20] until the fall of the regime.

Having failed to convince the Sicarii to join him and "undertake greater things" (*War* 4.507), Simon and his followers left Masada for Jerusalem, where they soon engaged the combined forces of John of Gischala and the Zealot faction of Eleazar ben Simon in a bloody civil war. Later he joined with John against Titus and his legions in a futile and desperate final resistance. In the end, like John, Simon did not possess the determination to fulfill his oath of no surrender. He was captured alive and publicly executed in Rome, after marching in bonds in the Flavian triumph as the paramount Jewish leader (*War* 6.434, 7.36, 154; Cassius Dio 66,71). It was thus ironically left to the Romans to bestow upon Simon bar Giora the recognition he had struggled for throughout the war. Vespasian and Titus were probably aware of Simon's exploits against the Gallus expedition (*War* 2.521), as well as of his courageous conduct during the siege of Jerusalem. Besides, the young and physically imposing Simon (*War* 4.503–4) must have cut a formidable figure for public display. It is also conceivable that Josephus prompted the Roman recognition of the preeminence of Simon, with whom he had no personal feuds, as a final stab at John, his old nemesis from Galilee.

There is no information about Simon prior to the revolt, and the question of his role as an instigator must be assessed through his actions, including the option of messianic ambitions on his part. Simon's early career is strikingly similar to that of David (Horsley 1987: 57). Like the revered ancient king of whom the Savior must descend, Simon began as a leader of fugitives, harassing the arrogant rural gentry and chased by the official authorities. The redemption of prisoners also carries biblical-messianic connotations (Isaiah 61:1). Still, numerous rebels in many times and places began their career as renegade outlaws, and the liberation of slaves earned Simon both manpower and popular support, which is sufficient incentive regardless of its religious meaning. Some scholars (Roth 1960; 1962; Kanael 1953) propose messianic notions in the replacement of 'freedom' with the more apocalyptic 'redemption' on Year Four bronze coins that may be attributed to Simon, but the interpretation has attracted the strong criticism of others (Hengel 1989: 117–18; Goodblatt 2001: 4; Fuks 1989: 119). There is also no reason to link messianic pretensions to Simon's final emergence from Jerusalem's underground refuges into the Temple's ruins cloaked in royal garments (*War* 7.29–30). It was probably merely a desperate and imaginative, if somewhat bizarre, attempt to escape capture (Fuks 1989: 117; Rajak 2002: 180), and Josephus himself shows no indication to have understood it in any other way. The messianic model is thus shaky in Simon's case, as in the case of the First Revolt as a whole. Without it we are left with no real motive for Simon, otherwise a ruthless yet calculating warlord, to instigate a practically hopeless confrontation.

It is highly unlikely that John and Simon cynically promoted rebellion only to further their personal ambitions. The consecutive defeats would have made the odds of failure clear. There was no conceivable way that further resistance could have served their material and political interests, as nothing short of divine assistance could have prevented Roman victory and Jewish demise during the last desperate months. John and Simon must have realized that. The only feasible explanation for their resilience is that they too may have believed that such assistance would be forthcoming, though probably not in the form of miracles as in the days of Moses and Hezekiah, but in Maccabean-style divinely inspired military victories. Rational conduct and profound religious faith did not necessarily contrast in first-century Judea. Thus, even a sensible man of the world such as John of Gischala could reassure his people that "those Romans, although they should take to themselves wings, could never fly over the wall of Jerusalem" (*War* 4.127). He simply refused to believe that God would let his own city be defiled by the enemy (Goodblatt 2001: 25).[21] As for Simon, if the Year Four coins were indeed struck under his administration, the stated messages of liberation, in whatever terminology, must have represented an ideology he truly believed in, as he had been willing to sacrifice so much for its manifestation.

Yet even if their religious belief and faith in divine intervention were sincere, the charge of instigation prior to the revolt would be inconsistent with the personalities of both John of Gischala and Simon bar Giora, as well as with the course of their careers. The two had sufficient charisma, faith, ruthlessness, and determination to reach prominence in the uprising when it was already in motion, but there is little to indicate that they were influential enough to initiate it themselves, or to suggest they ever tried. There is actually no reason to assume that we would have been familiar with their names had the conflict been avoided. Rather than place the responsibility for the war in the acts and influence of its principal agents, we should search for its roots in a broader ideological motivation, one which these agents shared with the mostly anonymous Jewish masses who followed their lead.

Impact of the Imperial Crisis

The latter part of the First Revolt was fought while Rome was in confusion, its armies over-stretched, and its government destabilized. In the words of Josephus, "…all was in disorder after the death of Nero" (*War* 1.5). Power struggles in the imperial capital deteriorated into civil war, serious uprisings rocked European and North African provinces, and the situation along the Parthian frontier remained volatile. Thus, rather than a spontaneous, religiously or economically motivated popular outbreak, the Jewish revolt could be considered an attempt by a cunning leadership versed in the world politics of its time to take advantage of a strategic opportunity to regain freedom.

Speeches to the rebels credited by Josephus to Agrippa II (*War* 2.358–87), Titus (6.331–32), and himself (5.366) survey various peoples that surpass the Jews of Judea in numbers, military valor, and in the resources of their countries, but acknowledge the superiority of Rome, sustain her occupation, and dare not challenge her rule. Mention is also made of the futility of Jewish hopes for assistance from their brethren abroad and for possible alliances with other enemies of Rome. In these literary historical speeches, Josephus intentionally underplays the crisis Rome was immersed in during that period.

Roman provincial policies facilitated administrative control, maximized tax revenue, and pronounced Roman supremacy but also fractured social, political, and economic contracts between native groups based on time-honored cultural understandings often consolidated by religious bonds. In these conditions, revolts become nearly inevitable, and in the late seventies of the first century several erupted, taking advantage of the governmental crisis during the later part of Nero's rule and the civil war that followed his suicide (June 68–December 69 CE). The situation along the eastern frontier was also delicate following a series of military confrontations with Parthia over Armenia. The following review briefly summarizes developments in various parts of the Roman Empire during the mid-first century CE. Their possible impact on the Jewish decision to rise against Rome will then be addressed. All title extracts come from Agrippa's speech.

Gallia

> "If great advantages might provoke any people to revolt the Gauls might do it best of all…[yet] these bear to be tributary to the Romans." (War 2.371–72)

Roman rule in Gaul (roughly corresponding to modern France) was far from stable in 68–69 CE. Roman governor Julius Vindex joined forces with local chiefs to oust Nero and revive the Republic but was defeated by the Rhine legions (Rudich 1993: 209–13; Woolf 1998: 21; Foss 1990: 69–71). Julius Classicus and Julius Tutor, Gallic leaders despite their Latin names, formed alliances with German and Dacian groups against Rome in order to establish an *Imperium Galliarum*. They failed, but only after having defeated several Roman contingents (Grant 1974: 206–8; King 1990: 165). In a separate development, druidic predictions of the fall of Rome inspired a local prophet named Mariccus and some eight thousand supporters to launch an offensive against rival Gallic tribes and Roman units (Millar 1967: 154; Dyson 1975: 159). Mariccus' forces were dispersed and a Roman executioner denied their leader's claim for immortality. Violent harassment of Romanized settlements by "brigand" attacks continued simultaneously throughout the country.

Dacia

> "Are not the Illyrians…governed by barely two legions, by which [the Romans] also put a stop to the incursions of the Dacians?" (War 2.369)

Stubborn resistance in Dacia (modern Romania) engaged the Danube legions throughout the first century CE (Millar 1967: 266, 271–72). Its seventh decade saw large Dacian forces forming anti-Roman leagues with German groups aimed at the reestablishment of full Dacian independence, while insurgents harassed Roman units and their local allies throughout the land. Anti-Roman action increased during the Roman civil war of 69 CE (Grant 1974: 206–8). The Dacians remained a tough opponent later in the century, forcing the emperor Domitian into several costly confrontations. An entire Roman legion (the Fifth Legion *Alaude*) under Cornelius Fuscus, commander of the Praetorian Guard, was decimated and its eagle standard lost during a Roman incursion into Transylvania in 86 CE (Amit 2003: 427). No earlier than the second century and only through the extensive military efforts of consecutive emperors (chiefly Trajan) was Rome able to suppress Dacian resistance.

Germania

> "These Germans, who dwell in an immense country, who have minds greater than their bodies, and a soul that despises death, are tamed by eight Roman legions." (War 2.377)

There was, in fact, hardly a time in Roman history when the term 'tamed' could be applied to Germany and its innumerable warlike tribes, and the first century was no exception. Between 68–70 CE, German leagues repeatedly challenged the legions. In one of the more serious incidents, a local client ruler named Julius Civilis formed a coalition of Germans, Dacians, and Gauls and rose against the empire, planning to incorporate large German territories into a unified independent entity. Roman military and organizational superiority allowed Vespasian to restore order (Millar

1967: 152, 271, 302; King 1990: 165; Grant 1974: 206–8), but the Germans remained a constant military threat to the empire for centuries, until successive German invasions put an end to the western part of the empire during the fifth century CE.

Britannia

> "Consider what a wall the Britons had, for the Romans sailed away to them and subdued them while they were encompassed by the ocean…and four legions are a sufficient guard to so large an island." (*War* 2.378)

Bloody revolts rocked various parts of Britain during the century that followed the Claudian conquest of 43 CE (Salway 1981: 90; Dyson 1971; 1975: 169–70). An extremely violent uprising erupted in 60 CE in the south of the island under Queen Boudicca, reducing to rubble several newly established Roman centers. Seventy thousand Roman soldiers, traders, and local inhabitants were reported to have been killed (Tacitus, *Annals* 14:32–33). Even if this particular figure is exaggerated, the cost in human lives must have been substantial. Archaeological traces of burning and destruction related to Boudicca's revolt were found at Colchester (Roman Camulodunum, the province capital), St Albans (Verulamium), and London (Londinium; Webster 1993: 113–24; Crummy 1997). As in Judea, Roman troubles in Britain did not end then. A second-century source (*De Bello Parthico* II.22) reports a "great number of Roman soldiers killed" in both provinces during the reign of Hadrian (117–138 CE). The Judean reference is to the Bar-Kochba war, while a conflict in northern England in 118 (Salway 1981: 173; Todd 1999: 116) and various disturbances during the early 130s (Frere 1978: 130) have been suggested for the British context.

During the reign of Domitian (81–96 CE), several Roman advances towards Scotland were attempted, but despite military successes against Caledonian coalitions (83–84 CE), the Romans could never establish their rule there. Faithful to his general policy of narrowing the imperial domain into more defendable borders, Hadrian decided to detach from Scotland and fortify a new borderline along the rivers Tyne and Solway (Birley 1998: 123ff.; Shotter 1996: 55ff). Hoards of Roman silver coins found in Scottish sites (Hunter 2002) indicate that relative stability along the frontier was also reassured through commerce, while appropriate gifts placated Scottish chieftains.

Hispania

> "The Romans have extended their arms beyond the Pillars of Hercules…upon the Pyrenean mountains…and one legion is sufficient guard for [the peoples of Spain]." (*War* 2.378)

By the time of Agrippa's speech, Spain had a history of numerous outbursts of resistance to Roman domination spanning over two hundred years (Dyson 1975: 146–52). Its warlike population, spread out in the mountains of the Iberian Peninsula, had never been easy to govern. The rugged landscape offered ample opportunities for local militants to harass the imperial forces and undermine Roman efforts to stabilize the province. Roman military assertiveness under Augustus pacified the country for a while, but the fragile calm gave way to violent spells during the rule of Nero. Direct references to actual fighting are rare (Millar 1967: 161), but a significant Roman military presence in the country was apparently required in order to counter widespread brigandage and guerilla-style militancy.

Africa

> "And as for the third part of the habitable earth, whose nations are so many that it is not easy to number them…these have the Romans subdued entirely." (*War* 2.382)

By the late first century CE, Roman occupation in North Africa was over two centuries old and large Roman settlements flourished mainly along the coast. Nevertheless, incessant raids and aggressive incursions along the frontiers remained a severe concern. Nomads outside the imperial borders and ethnically affiliated people within Roman territory repeatedly joined efforts against Roman troops and dependent settlements. Locally stationed Roman commanders took sides in the political upheaval during the Roman civil war or acted independently of Rome on their own behalf (Millar 1967: 172; Foss 1990: 69–72). In 70 CE, local tribesmen interfered in a dispute between the Roman cities of Lepcis and Oea, and Roman punitive action was demanded to repel them. Cassius Dio (67 4, 6–7) informs us that a later rebellion was crushed by Domitian's army (85 or 86 CE). These examples represent an on-going volatile situation, with the local Roman administration constantly occupied with the preservation of fragile military balances. It was a far cry from the pacified conditions that Josephus points out.

Imperial Crisis and the Jewish Revolt

Contrary to the narratives of Josephus, the political and military situation in the Roman Empire at the time of the First Jewish Revolt was neither peaceful nor stable, and serious challenges to Roman rule frequently materialized in many provinces. Awareness of Roman troubles elsewhere might have encouraged Jewish factions to open another front against Nero. Regardless of religious-ideological stimulation, it might have seemed to them that the time was right to lift the Roman yoke that had encumbered Judea for two centuries. Nevertheless, several countering factors must also be considered:

1. Most of the uprisings, or at least their major phases, took place during the final months of Nero's government and the civil war of 68–69 CE. The Jewish revolt began two years earlier, in the summer of 66. Consciousness of on-going foreign uprisings (*War* 6.341) may have encouraged Jewish perseverance while their own revolt was in progress but could have had no impact on their original decision to take up arms.

2. Any hopes the Jews might have entertained for Roman systemic disintegration due to Nero's erratic follies should have been extinguished with the sober appointment of Vespasian and the efficiency with which he gathered his army. Thus, as early as the first year of the uprising it must have become obvious that the imperial administration remained firm, functional, and effective, regardless of its eccentric head of state and the unstable situation in certain provinces.

3. The surveys of allegedly pacified lands in the speeches of Agrippa, Titus, and Josephus himself may have impressed the latter's educated Graeco-Roman audience but would have made little difference to the Jewish masses. It is unlikely that many among the rebels of Judea would have been versed enough in the histories of those distant European and African peoples and the natural conditions of their homelands to draw conclusions concerning their own chances in fighting Rome. On the other hand, with the exception of Armenia, the eastern provinces, with whom more Jews would have been familiar, remained generally peaceful in that period.

4. European rebellions often involved political and military alliances, but there is no trace in the available historical records for communication with the distant Jews.

5. The vast majority of first-century Jewish communities were situated in the Roman eastern Mediterranean, Rome itself, and within Parthian territory. Far fewer Jews lived in the provinces where the major disturbances took place, and they would have been in no position to influence the events or to establish military communications with Judea.

100 NARRATIVE OF CRISIS

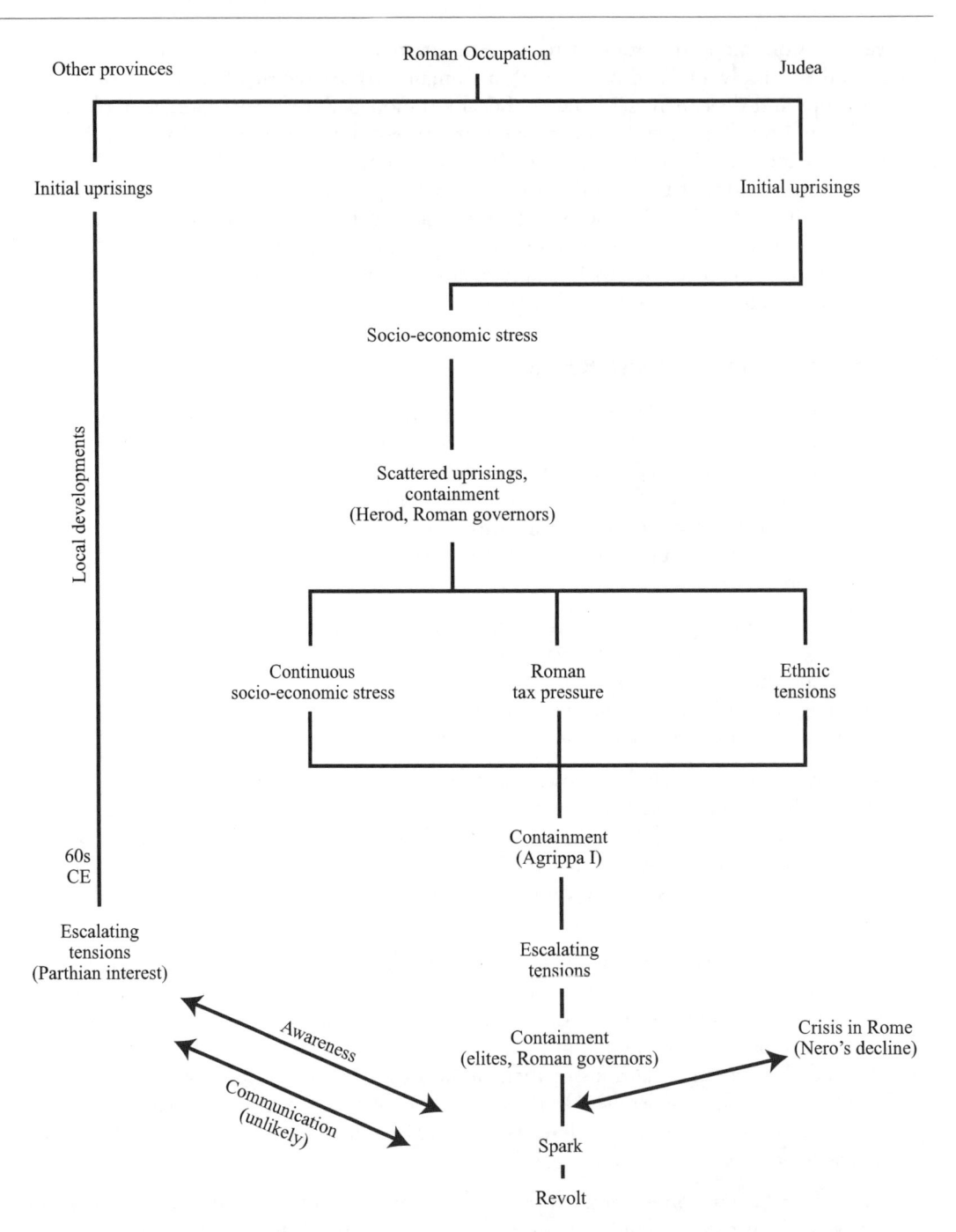

```
                          Roman Occupation
         Other provinces         |              Judea
              ┌──────────────────┴──────────────────┐
              |                                     |
         Initial uprisings                    Initial uprisings
              |                                     |
              |                          Socio-economic stress
              |                                     |
              |                          Scattered uprisings,
              |                              containment
              |                          (Herod, Roman governors)
              |                    ┌────────────┼────────────┐
              |               Continuous      Roman        Ethnic
              |          socio-economic stress tax pressure tensions
              |                    └────────────┼────────────┘
    60s                                         |
    CE                                    Containment
                                          (Agrippa I)
         Escalating                             |
         tensions                          Escalating
    (Parthian interest)                     tensions
                    ←——— Awareness ———             |                 Crisis in Rome
                    ←—— Communication ——      Containment     ——→    (Nero's decline)
                         (unlikely)        (elites, Roman governors)
                                                  |
                                                Spark
                                                  |
                                                Revolt
```

(Local developments label on left axis)

Figure 23 Imperial Crisis Model.

In conclusion, the historical timing was advantageous for the Jewish revolt, but there is no evidence whatsoever to indicate that the general turbulence throughout the empire was a factor in the original decision of the Jews to challenge Rome, or in their determination to fight to the end. It may well be that some western rebels had heard of the contemporaneous Jewish uprising and vice versa. If so, they all would have probably wished each other luck, but their wars, apparently, were carried out separately.

The Option of Parthian Intervention

> "For it is [the Parthian] concern to maintain the truce that is between them and the Romans."
> (*War* 2.389)

Josephus' offhand dismissal of the Jewish hope for assistance from their Babylonian brethren under Parthian sanction (*War* 1.5, 2.388–89, 6.343) should not mislead us. The Parthians were Rome's most formidable rival during that period, and the Jewish revolt could have been instrumental to a Parthian strike at a time when the empire was vulnerable. Judea could have offered a base of operations halfway to Europe and on the threshold of Egypt. Jewish success with Parthian support also might have encouraged client kings throughout the east to join an anti-Roman coalition. From the Jewish perspective, a substantial influx of fighters and funds from the large Mesopotamian Jewish communities might have improved the odds of success.

Parthian-Jewish pacts had presented problems to Rome in the past. In 40 BCE, an alliance between the last Hasmonean king Mattathias Antigonus and the Parthian ruler Pacorus I had ejected the Romans and their client king Herod from Judea for three years (*Antiquities* 14.330–69; *War* I, 248–73). Samuel Brandon (1967: 85) suggests that in his pro-Jewish stance during the crisis over Caligula's statue (39–40 CE), the Roman governor Petronius was also concerned over a possible Parthian offensive in Syria while the Romans were preoccupied with a major uprising in Judea. A Parthian anti-Roman league was probably on the mind of Domitius Marsus, a later governor of Syria, when Agrippa I (41–44 CE) initiated the construction of a massive new wall in Jerusalem and invited several vassal kings to a conference in Tiberias (*Antiquities* 19.338–42).

Figure 24 Remains of Agrippa's wall in East Jerusalem (photograph: Y. Arbel).

Still, while the Parthians presumably followed the events in Judea with interest, Josephus is probably correct in asserting that they did not seriously contemplate interference. The domestic chaos among the rebels and the antagonism between them and other peoples in the region would have made them unreliable partners in an already dangerous enterprise such as war with Rome. Furthermore, the impression of recent events in Armenia was still fresh. Between 51–63 CE, Parthians and Romans wrestled several times over supremacy in the kingdom, which was situated on the border between the two empires (Cary 1962: 545–48; Sinnigen and Boak 1977: 293–94). The struggle ended in a compromise, but as a symbol of Roman supremacy Tiridates, originally a Parthian appointee over Armenia and a brother of the Parthian king, had to travel to Rome and be officially crowned by Nero. It is improbable that the Parthians would have risked another conflict with Rome only three years after this embarrassment, either through direct military interference or by allowing large reinforcements of Parthian Jews to set for Judea (*War* 2.389).[22] Parthia could wait for better opportunities to challenge Rome in the future – and so it did.

Appendix: The Druids – Another Example of Ideological Insurgence?

Graham Webster (1993: 86–87) notes that in both Judea and Britain the Romans uncharacteristically found themselves immersed in bitter and costly conflicts against local religions. Indeed, other than the Jewish revolts, druidism in Britain is the only example where religion was a dominant motivator for intensive and prolonged objection to Roman rule. The fierceness of druid-inspired antagonism to the Roman conquest crystallizes in Tacitus' vivid description of the disconcerting scene faced by the troops of Suetonius Paulinus as they prepared to disembark in 61 CE on the island of Mona, present-day Anglesey in northern Wales:

> On the shore stood the opposing army with its dense array of armed warriors, while between the ranks dashed women in black attire like the Furies, with hair disheveled, waving brands. All around the druids, lifting up their hands to heaven and pouring forth dreadful imprecations, scared our soldiers by the unfamiliar sight so that, as if their limbs were paralyzed, they stood motionless and exposed to wounds (*Annals* 14:30).

The savage impression of such Roman descriptions distorts the true image of druidism. While best known for their mystic religious functions, druids were also trained in astronomy, natural sciences, history, as well as genealogy, philosophy and law, all acquired during a 20-year apprenticeship (Ross 1970: 37, 135; Ellis 1990: 17, 68, 125). Their religious and scholarly prestige earned them high social ranking. As it was standard Roman practice to establish the provincial administration around indigenous elites, the druids could be expected to take advantage of the occupation. Some did. During Julius Caesar's conquest of Gaul, two brothers, both druids, found themselves on opposing sides. Divitiacus collaborated with the Romans, while Dumnorix fought them tenaciously (Ellis 1990: 127, 130, 134). This equal balance was atypical; druidism more commonly proved a formidable rival to Rome and its provincial policies.

Druid hostility toward Rome needs to be understood within its cultural context. In his description of the declining fortunes of Native American leaders amidst the rapid expansion of English settlers in New England during the seventeenth century, Nathaniel Philbrick (2006: 192) comments that "…Christianity was a tremendously destabilizing influence that threatened the very underpinnings of [the] tribe's traditions and [the leader's] own power and prosperity." Christianity was to shake the foundations of traditional hierarchies throughout the globe, but as the druid experience proves, in many ways Romanization preceded it, and at least within the Roman domains probably facilitated its later progress. Religious, social, and personal aspects intersected to exacerbate the apprehension of these ancient cultural leaders. Cooperative local elites were expected to partake in the process of Romanization. Druids could not do that and remain druids, because the fundamental changes that the process invoked meant the undermining of the original religious and cultural traditions, of which they were the prime representatives and also the chief beneficiaries (Piggot 1975: 120–21). Their plight reverberated among their people, who resented the humiliation of the druids as offensive to the gods upon whom individual and communal fortunes depended. Violent resistance was inevitable.

Warfare was an embedded value in many cultures in pre-Roman Europe, with prowess in battle and the high quality of a man's weapons offering the fastest routes to social prominence (Ellis 1994: 26–27; Ross 1970: 55–56,164–65). Julius Caesar noted that religious symbolism and beliefs determined by the druids contributed to the bellicose motivation of local peoples (*The Gallic War* VI,16). As an example, widespread faith in a form of reincarnation lessened the fear of death and encouraged exceptional performance on the battlefield (Piggot 1975: 133; Ellis 1990: 17). Coincidentally, Tacitus makes a similar observation about the Jews: "They also look on the souls of those who die in battle, or are put to death for their crimes (i.e., insurgency) as eternal. Hence comes their love of posterity and contempt of death" (*Histories* 5.5). This is not the only similarity between the two cases. Like the Jews, the druids and their supporters fought to protect fundamental life modes and religious traditions. Religious-ideological aversion to Romanization, the central role of priests in the resistance, even the fact that there were also dissenting priests who believed that collaboration with Rome could be accommodated with their faith, are all common motifs in the histories of druidic and Jewish resistance.

Figure 25 Druids depicted by Charles Knight, 1845. In these solemn and dignified figures the Victorian artist attempted to project the stature of druids in their societies as priests and spiritual leaders, as well as scholars.

Nevertheless, there are also some important ideological distinctions. The firm bond between warfare, religion, and social prestige is absent from the Jewish culture of the time. Celts commonly adorned their weapons with votive motifs (Ross 1970: 150–51). This phenomenon is unknown in contemporaneous Jewish contexts where, on the other hand, the volume and variety of non-martial religious vessels, artifacts, art, and structures has no Celtic equivalent. For the Jews, warfare was a course of action taken to defend their ideology, while for the Celts it was part of ideology itself. The ambiguous Jewish notion of eternal life, which still entailed an irreversible departure from this world, probably generated higher anxiety and less reassurance than the Celtic faith in reincarnation. At least on the psychological level the Jews were taking a greater risk for their cause.

Consecutive defeats in clashes with the Roman legions set the two cultures on different tracks. In time the druidic religions, intense as they had been, faded to insignificance against the spread of Romanization and later of Christianity. Judaism prevailed against both, but it had to make substantial adjustments. Primarily, the Jews had to mollify the unprecedented religious intensity that climaxed during the first century CE, generating such antagonism towards Roman occupation that revolt was only a question of time and trigger. Manifold in its contents of thought, defiant in its political attitudes, and unbending in its ritual observance, this intense religious ideology positioned the Jews of Judea against the prime of Roman power in a sequence of confrontations they could never win.

9 The Sacred Contract

Jewish religious ideological resentment towards the Roman occupation of Judea reached its peak during the first century CE. Messianic figures, miracle makers, prophetic hermits, and charismatic preachers abounded throughout the province, along with revolutionary moral teachers and socio-religious reformers. Their promises of redemption from Rome and just retribution for the sinful elite were bound to draw large followings, and in many cases they did. At a difficult time, when the religious establishment seemed unable to provide answers, hope, or comfort, the charismatic preacher represented an attractive alternative, which neither the efforts of the moderate Jewish leadership nor brutal Roman suppression could quell. Religious zeal buttressed with historical memories and popular myths and intensified by political, economic, and social strain hazed the concrete reality of insurmountable Roman military advantage. This chapter summarizes the central factors that influenced first-century Jewish ideology and contributed to the intensification of zeal. These elements or their variations can later be found at the core of sentiment and commitment in both major Jewish uprisings against Rome, and these wars were fought in and over the ideological landscape they created.

The Hasmonean Legacy

The imperfections of the Hasmonean dynasty and the tumultuous reigns of some of its kings were a distant memory to first-century Jews. The successful revolt against the Seleucids, the ensuing regional conquests, the economic prosperity, and the demographic growth under Hasmonean rule made more compelling recollections. This sense of nostalgia was common among both masses and elites. Josephus, himself an aristocrat and a proud Hasmonean descendant (*Life* 1–2), describes Judas Maccabaeus, the leader of the original Hasmonean revolt against the Seleucids, as "a man of valor and a great warrior…[who] left behind him a glorious reputation and memorial, by gaining freedom for his nation, and delivering them from slavery…"(*Antiquities* 12.433–34). The same author praises the Hasmonean ruler John Hyrcanus as "esteemed by God worthy of the three privileges – the government of his nation, the dignity of the high priesthood and prophecy; for God was with him…" (*Antiquities* 13.299–300) and recalls Hyrcanus' daughter-in-law, Queen Shlomzion (Salome), as a woman "wise to the greatest degree in her ambition of governing" (*Antiquities* 13.430). Josephus diplomatically dedicates far fewer compliments to the later Hasmoneans who had tenaciously opposed the Romans and their client Herod. Yet, comments he inserts in the speeches of Agrippa II (*War* 2.356-7) and Titus (*War* 6.329) about the Hasmonean-era "ancestors and their kings, who were in much better circumstances…both as to money, and strong bodies, and [valiant] souls" (*War* 2.357) show that although their struggle had failed, they were still remembered and celebrated.

Under oppressive Roman occupation and locked in dilapidating cycles of violence with their Gentile neighbors, such longing for the days of the Hasmoneans on the part of the Jews is understandable. During the relatively brief historical term of the dynasty, its princes had restored the power and success of the biblical kingdoms. John Hyrcanus (135–104 BCE), Judas Aristobolus I (104–103 BCE), and Alexander (Jonathan) Jannaeus (103–76 BCE) extended the Judean borders into the northern Negev, the Galilee, the Golan, and parts of Transjordan. Local populations were forced to choose between conversion and expulsion. The Idumeans in the south and the Itureans of northern Galilee were thus absorbed into the Jewish people (*Antiquities* 13.257–8,318). This development may have been facilitated by ancient cultural affiliations (Rappaport 1984: 126; Kasher 1988). No such affiliations existed with the populations of the large urban centers, whose extensive political, social, and religious ties with the outer Hellenistic world emerge from both literary sources and archaeological remains (Clairmont 1954/55; Weinberg 1970; 1971; Foerster 1976: 971–72; Kloner et al. 1996; Kloner and Arbel 1996). The extent to which they were subjected to a forced conversion policy remains uncertain (Schwartz 2000: 69), but destruction layers associated with Hasmonean conquests were found in the cities of Samaria (Barag 1992–93), Scythopolis (Mazor and Bar-Nathan 1998: 33–34), Marissa (Kloner, personal communication, 1992)[1], as well as Pella in Transjordan (McNicoll 1992: 103–18). Aggressive measures were also taken against the Samaritans, long-time rivals of the Jews, whose sacred precinct at Mount Gerizim was destroyed during that period (*Antiquities* 13.254–57; and see Magen 1993: 109–22).

The Hasmoneans established dominant Jewish majorities in most parts of the land, including the Galilee, where a large influx of Hasmonean coins in the latest strata of formerly Hellenistic settlements reflects the transition (Rapapport 1984: 147–49; Hanson 1980; Aviam 2002: 130; 2004: 46). Absolute Jewish demographic advantage there and in the Golan is probably the reason for the absence of Helleno-Roman cities and the scarcity of Roman roads in these regions (Hartal 1987: 71; Aviam 2004: 137). The common people of Judea, who under the Hasmoneans enjoyed economic stability and personal security akin to the better days of the pre-exilic Israelite kingdoms, would have cared little about the political skirmishes in the capital that marred the rule of their kings. Hence the extensive popular support for the military campaigns of Judas Aristobulos II and his sons Alexander and Antigonus, the last princes of the dynasty, against the Romans and their Herodian subordinates (63–37 BCE). In all likelihood, Jews under Roman rule transmitted stories and myths based on those more glorious times across generations – thus nurturing the spiritual longing and earthly ambition for a renaissance of Jewish freedom, power, and prosperity.

The connection between the Hasmonean legacy and the first-century Jewish rebels receives wide scholarly support (Farmer 1958: 179–83; Kasher 1983a: 11–12; 1983b: 7–8; Ilan 1987; Price 1992: 86; Williams 1995). As John Gager (1998: 45) notes, "if *they* did – so the thinking must have run – so can we." Over-simplification should of course be avoided. Martin Hengel (1989: 172–73) advises caution when comparing religious motives between two cases relatively distant in time and circumstances, such as the Hasmonean uprising and the First Revolt. David Goodblatt (1998; 2006: 138) suggests that the Hasmonean preference for variations of the term "Judea" (*hever ha-yehudim*) on their coins, in contrast to the word "Israel" that appears on coins and documents from both Jewish revolts against Rome, terminologically may reflect some ideological discrepancies between these governments; the same holds true, following Goodblatt, for the use of other meaningful terms, such as "Jerusalem," "freedom," and "redemption" on the coins of the two revolts, that are absent from Hasmonean coinage. Still, even if such distinctions existed, they are unlikely to have preoccupied the Jewish masses, who would have strived for the military prowess of the Hasmoneans and the apparent divine blessing they seemed to have enjoyed. The fact that the initial Maccabean victory was commemorated as a *religious* festival implies that it was credited to divine assistance to those fighting in God's name. The revolt against Rome would have been seen in the same ideological light, and the results could be expected to be similar.

The Ideal of Zealotry

The biblical priest Phineas, a son of Moses' nephew, was the Jewish prototype for unyielding religious zeal. He earned this reputation through a ruthless act of devotion:

> ...one of the Israelites came and brought a Midianite woman into his family, in the sight of Moses and in the sight of the whole congregation of the Israelites.... When Phineas son of Eleazar, son of Aaron the priest, saw it, he got up and left the congregation. Taking a spear in his hand, he went after the Israelite into the tent and pierced the two of them, the Israelite and the woman.... So the plague was stopped among the people of Israel.... The Lord spoke to Moses, saying: Phineas son of Eleazar, son of Aaron the priest, has turned back my wrath from the Israelites by manifesting such zeal among them on my behalf that in my jealousy I did not consume the Israelites.... I hereby grant him my covenant of peace. It shall be for him and for his descendants after him a covenant of perpetual priesthood, because he was zealous for his God, and made atonement for the Israelites (Numbers 25:6–13).

Later biblical heroes like the prophet Elijah and the king Jehu are also credited with extreme acts of zeal for God (Kings I, 18:17–40; Kings II, 10:18–26). The Hasmonean patriarch and priest Mattathias, chronologically and culturally closer to the generation of the First Revolt, fought Seleucid occupation and also killed Jews who deviated from the Law (Maccabees I 2:23–24). His acts embody the two complementary duties of the zealot: fighting Israel's enemies (in Phineas' case the Midianites, symbolized by the stricken bride) and ensuring the loyalty of all Israelites to God, by force if necessary (Brandon 1967: 44–45). Members of the first-century Zealot faction would have seen themselves as followers of the same honored tradition, battling both Romans and rival Jews whom they considered traitors to God's cause (Goodblatt 2006: 100). The sarcasm and anger in Josephus' treatment of that faction (*War* 7.268–70) and his forceful attempt to disengage it from the exemplary Phineas and later biblical role models (Hengel 1989: 155; Goodblatt 1996: 243; 2006: 100–101) indicate that the ideal of zealotry was revered in most, if not all, segments of Jewish society.

Could this ideal have been a substantial motivator for revolt against Rome? Horsley (1987: 127–29) disagrees. In his opinion, the ideological focus of zeal was aimed at strict observance of the Law and against Jews who had broken it but would not have had a substantial impact on the decision of uprising against Roman occupation. Still, we must differentiate between the religious elites, who were mainly concerned not only with the minutiae of theological interpretation but also with the political implications, and the Jewish masses, which were probably less so. Furthermore, if Goodblatt (2006: 100ff.) is correct, the ideology of zeal had its origins within priestly circles themselves, which would render the efforts of those exercising caution and moderation all the more challenging. Revolt instigators, including priestly servants at the Temple court, could link objective circumstances across time to portray the Romans as the heirs of the reviled foreigners whom Phineas and Mattathias had smitten. Likewise, they might compare the Jewish collaborators of their day with the Israelite sinners who had also been felled by the hands of the two priests and with those killed by Elijah and Jehu. Moreover, God had rewarded Phineas and Mattathias and their descendants for their acts, the former with the priesthood, the latter with precisely what the Jews had eventually fought the Romans for – ultimate freedom. According to Farmer (1958: 176–77), confidence in divine reward for zealous devotion was the main ideological link between anti-Seleucid and anti-Roman Jewish rebels:

> Jewish resistance to foreign rule in the days of the Maccabees and the Zealots cannot be separated from their confidence that God would fulfill his promises concerning the inheritance of the land, and political sovereignty for his covenant people.... The Maccabees and the Zealots were Jews who so believed in these promises that they were willing to risk their lives and the lives of their wives and children in life-and-death struggles for religious freedom and political independence against overwhelming odds.

Hengel (1989: 172) follows a similar venue, suggesting that the occupation may have been regarded as God's punishment for the sins of Israel, which could only be atoned through supreme religious dedication proven by personal and communal sacrifice. The desperate attempts of Josephus to refute this fundamental, Bible-based reasoning suggest that it must have been widespread in Judea. "It is impossible," he pleads through Agrippa, "that so vast an empire should be settled without God's providence" (*War* 2.390). In other words, the Jews must not look for individual explanations of the Roman occupation, because the whole known world has been subjected to that same fate. Less cosmopolitan and more conservative Jews than Josephus and Agrippa, certainly also found among the influential priesthood, would have rejected this pragmatic logic, which contradicts the notion of an intimate and exclusive relationship between the Jews and their God. From their perspective, Judea was not like Gaul, Syria, or Greece and could not be treated as just another game piece on the global board. Regardless of the comparable fate of others, the reasons for Judea's subjugation to Rome must be unique and so should be the solution. Revered biblical prophets had blamed the sufferings of Israel on sins committed, and the ancient lesson had been learned: a sincere demonstration of zeal for God would earn His forgiveness and support, as it always had in centuries past. Phineas had shown the way, the Judges and better kings of Israel followed suit, as did the Maccabees. Their enemies had all been routed, regardless of objective military odds. Enough charismatic preachers roamed through Judea guaranteeing a similar fate to the Romans, if the Jews only dared undertaking the divine challenge.

The Influence of Charismatic Prophets

As tensions mounted in Judea, self-appointed prophets of various backgrounds drew widespread support with promises of redemption from Roman oppression. While styles and details varied, the common theme was that liberation was within grasp, if only people placed their trust in God, followed the prophets as His agents – and acted accordingly. Disciples came mostly from the lower classes in Judea (Gray 1993: 134–35). Having abandoned hope for practical solutions to their predicament, the now yearned-for miraculous remedies and miracles were exactly what the prophets promised, often according to famous biblical precedents. The Romans identified a potential for serious trouble in these movements, and their reaction was assertive and unforgiving.

The Jewish religious elites shared the Roman disdain for the charismatic prophets. Josephus, himself of distinguished priestly descent, did not mince words in trying to convince his readers that substantial blame for the revolt should be placed upon militant leaders and false prophets, rather than on the Jewish people as a whole:

> [The "prophets"] were such men as deceived and deluded the people under pretense of divine inspiration, but were for procuring innovations and changes of the government...[they] prevailed with the multitude to act like madmen, and went before them into the wilderness, as pretending that God would there show them the signals of liberty (*War* 2.259).

Yet, neither Roman sanctions nor criticism by the Jewish establishment could suppress the attraction of these movements. As shown in Table 9.1, the outcome was often tragic, with the preachers losing their lives along with many of their followers.

It should be noted that this is basically a shortlist, representing a far broader phenomenon. Some of the prophets may have been the opportunistic charlatans Josephus describes them as, but others must have earnestly believed in their divine mission, considering the high personal risk in their activities. Along with their hapless believers they were victims of historical circumstances as well as of their own illusions. The prophets were apparently answering to an authentic call, whatever their true intentions. In a period when heroes were desperately needed but few could be found, they invoked comforting memories of the exemplary figures and glorious events of the past. Their promises of deliverance as reward for faith and repentance reminded of popular biblical traditions familiar to any Jewish household (Gray 1993: 123, 132). The choice of the desert as

Table 9.1 Jewish prophetic figures, mid-first century CE to the decade after the revolt.

Prophet	Area of Activity	Time of Activity	Outcome	References
Theudas	Jordan River	Term of Fadus, 44–46 CE	Executed by Romans	*Antiquities* 20.97–99; Acts 5:36
Anonymous (various)	Jerusalem, Jordan River	Term of Felix, 52–60 CE	Killed by Romans	*War* 2.258-60; *Antiquities* 20.167–68
"The Egyptian"	Jerusalem, Jordan River	Term of Felix, 52–60 CE	Escaped, followers massacred	*War* 2.261–63; *Antiquities* 20.169–72; Acts 21:38
Anonymous	Judean Desert	Term of Festus, 60–62 CE	Killed by Romans	*War* 20.188
Jesus ben Ananias	Jerusalem	Term of Albinus, 62–64 CE, (also active during the revolt)	Killed during the siege of Jerusalem	*War* 6.300-9
Anonymous	Jerusalem	70 CE	Killed during Temple battle	*War* 6.283–87
Jonathan the Sicarius	Cyrene, North Africa	After 70 CE	Executed by Romans	*War* 7.437–50; *Life* 424–25

a place of shelter and gathering appealed to historical memories from the infancy of the nation, when the relations with God were less complex and obscure. Like a classic paternal figure, He punishes severely for evildoing and sin, but His forgiveness, love, and support are always readily available. Direct access to God, such as the charismatic prophets offered, meant hope, direction, and – foremost – a renewed control over one's destiny.

It must be stressed that most first-century prophets known to us presented themselves as mere agents of God and showed no messianic or royal pretensions (*contra* Gager 1998: 41). Their perception of the post-deliverance reality is unclear, but allusions to the desert and to the conquests of Joshua imply the restoration of a better past, rather than the creation of an innovative future. Many prophets may have had nothing more ambitious in mind than the introduction of religious reforms and the preaching for virtuous individual and social conduct, which would render the people worthy of a new alliance with God. They may well have considered their own role as merely spreading the message that deliverance was at hand and stirring the people through signs and miracles to strive for the appropriate degree of repentance and piety. As Rome had replaced Egypt in the role of enslaver, the prophets would substitute Moses and, with God's active guidance, lead the people to the reestablishment of a free and devout – yet earthly – Judea, purified from paganism. In the circumstances of the time, the appeal of such a message is self-evident.

Trust in Divine Intervention

Heroic epics like the Greek *Iliad* and the Hindu *Bhagavad-Gita* tell of gods physically fighting on the battlefield on the side of their favorites. The God of the Hebrew Bible does not wear armor or drives a chariot, but his intervention on the behalf of His favorites is comparably explicit. A remarkable instance is recorded in Kings II, 18:13–19:36: Besieged in Jerusalem by the Assyrians, pious King Hezekiah pleads for God's assistance. During the following night, "the angel of the Lord went forth and slew a hundred and eighty-five thousand in the camp of the Assyrians; and when men arose early in the morning behold these were all dead bodies" (Kings II, 19:35).[2] This is probably the most dramatic illustration of a fundamental element in biblical historiography: divine assistance in battle is granted to those who prove their full devotion to God and his commandments (see also Deuteronomy 28:1, 7, 15, 25–26; Joshua 24:1–19; Isaiah 41:12–13, 42:13). The same element recurs in early Hasmonean tradition. Facing a vastly superior Seleucid force, Judas Maccabeus makes a forceful appeal for God's aid:

> All praise to you, the Savior of Israel, who broke the attack of the giant by your servant David [and] delivered the army of the Philistines into the power of Saul's son, Jonathan, and of his armor-bearer. In like manner put this army into the power of your people Israel. Humble their pride in their forces and their mounted men. Strike them with panic, turn their insolent strength to water, make them reel under a crushing defeat. Overthrow them by the sword of those who love you, and let all who know your name praise you with songs of thanksgiving (Maccabees I, 4; 30–33).

The ensuing victory, as all ancient Jewish victories, was credited to divine intervention on behalf of the faithful (Gager 1998: 45–46; Van Henten 2003: 71). The point is vital for the understanding of the ideological foundations of the First Revolt. There is no explicit indication that the rebels expected any form of eschatological deliverance. Instead, they probably hoped for a Maccabean-style victory against a militarily superior enemy, rather than having the entire Roman expedition suddenly drop dead as the Assyrians had conveniently done in the days of the righteous Hezekiah. Based on later rabbinical statements, Tessa Rajak (2002: 181) holds that for salvation to be obtained, humans were prompted to prove personal piety, not necessarily such that involves military daring. Yet, theological perspectives during the earlier period of Roman occupation were more militant. One's willingness to risk property, family, and life itself fighting in God's War, for causes which He had presumably espoused, would certainly have been considered a most appropriate expression of religious piety, one meriting divine assistance.

This "sacred contract" bonded the Jews into an irreversible commitment to the war. After the costly confrontations with Helleno-Roman centers during the early months of the revolt and the crushing of the Gallus expedition, some members of the moderate Jerusalem leadership may have hoped that the rebels could be brought to reason. Frustrations had been vented, Jewish strength and determination had been proven, and, on the other hand, the bloody price of war was now also plain. Perhaps a compromise could be reached, through which paramount control over Judea would be peacefully relinquished to Rome, and a more respectful and favorable relationship with the Jews would be established. Still, the victory over Gallus was probably seen by many as proof of God's approval of the war, while defeats elsewhere would have been considered tests of faith. Renewed submission to Rome, regardless of conditions, would have meant a betrayal of the sacred contract, and God's retribution could be sevenfold harsher than that of Caesar. Ironically, many Jews may have considered war with Rome to be the *least* dangerous course to pursue.

Based on the testimony of Josephus and the desertion of Rabbi Yohanan ben Zakkai,[3] Doron Mendels (1992: 369–70) assumes that the consecutive defeats gradually eroded the rebels' confidence in God's ultimate aid. In his opinion, "the more the Roman side succeeded...more and more Jews believed that God had left the Jewish people and that the Romans were God's instrument for punishing the wayward Jews." Nevertheless, strong circumstantial evidence suggests that despite the disasters many rebels stuck to their faith in God's intervention to the end and perhaps thought of their many tribulations as God's way of examining whether they truly merited deliverance.

One type of evidence is a probably meaningful alteration in the slogans on rebel coins.[4] Several scholars (Kanael 1953: 19; Roth 1962: 43; Meshorer 1982: 122–23; 1986: 227; 1997: 114) explain the replacement of the term "freedom of Zion" *(heruth Zion)* with "redemption of Zion" *(ge'ulat Zion)* on issues of the forth year with a change of approach that was necessary in light of the desperate situation of the rebels. Freedom can be achieved through human agency, but redemption is in the hands of God. As more battles were being lost and the crucial hour for Jerusalem drew near, the leaders were presumably trying to reassure the defenders that God would never let His city fall. As previously mentioned, this was something that even John of Gischala, otherwise one of the more rational Jewish leaders, seems to have believed (*War* 4.127, 6.98).

The Jewish determination to sustain an otherwise clearly hopeless confrontation is in itself testimony to the endurance of religious hope. From its onset it was a war that the Jews could not win. Judea's geo-political position in the heart of the Roman East and on the land route to Egypt meant that unlike dwellers of remote and marginal zones, such as the Nabateans (until 106 CE), Berbers, and Scots, the Jews could not be allowed to remain outside the imperial borders. Furthermore, any compromise with them would have signaled weakness, something that Rome could not afford during this highly unstable period. The Roman army of the first century CE numbered nearly 30 highly trained legions, as well as numerous specialized auxiliary units (Webster 1969: 113; Saddington 1982). Even if by some strike of fortune Vespasian's expedition would have been overwhelmed, this formidable army was powerful, massive, and yet flexible enough to strike back decisively. For the Jews, on the other hand, each defeat meant irreplaceable loss of human and material resources. Bearing in mind the fall of most of the country and the slaughter or enslavement of dozens of thousands, only intense and unbending religious faith could explain the resolve of the remaining rebels not to surrender. Some so desperately held to that faith that even the fall of the capital did not crack their resolve. Resistance in three desert forts outlived the destruction of the Temple, refugees tried to stir rebellion in Jewish communities abroad with which they found shelter (*War* 7.410, 438), and decades later full-fledged Jewish revolts erupted in various provinces (117–119 CE) and again in Judea between 132–135 CE. Rebellion remained an option regardless of previous disappointments, as long as enough Jews believed in the principles of the sacred contract and revered its symbols.

The Temple Effect

One of the more dramatic narratives on the First Revolt appears in Cassius Dio 66.6–23, where the author records the outstandingly vigorous fight the Jews put up in protection of their Temple, even as the Romans had finally breached the walls and no viable chance remained to save the building. As the attackers had finally overcome that furious last Jewish effort, numerous among the defenders committed suicide, preferring to perish with the Temple rather than survive without it. This remarkable behavior can be better comprehended in light of the Jew's special attachment to the Temple of Jerusalem.

The Herodian Temple destroyed by Titus had replaced an ancient and humbler building inaugurated by the returnees from Babylon nearly six centuries earlier (516 BCE). The main phase of construction lasted from 19 to 11 BCE, but work was only concluded two or three years prior to the revolt. The new temple complex, with its adjacent network of commercial streets, was one of Herod's most ambitious projects and employed over 18,000 workers even during its latest phase of construction (*Antiquities* 20.219). At completion, it was one of the largest and most invested sanctuary compounds in the Roman Empire, capable of hosting over 200,000 people, as it did during the principal pilgrimages (Foerster 1976: 977–78; Ben-Dov 1982: 77–88).[5] Although the spectacular complex failed to grant Herod the legitimacy had always desired from his people, Jews recalled it with awe and pride for centuries after its demise (see Babylonian Talmud, *Sukkoth* 51b).

There can be no doubt that several disturbing developments directly related to the Temple contributed to the antagonism of the Jewish masses towards Roman rule and its supportive secular and priestly aristocracy. The first and worst insult was sustained immediately after the original Roman siege of Jerusalem had been successfully concluded in 63 BCE, when the Roman commander Pompey entered the innermost Temple sanctuary, the "Holy of Holiness," into which only the High Priest was permitted (*Antiquities* 14.71–72; Tacitus, *Histories* 5:9). Pompey's later permission to restore the building and renew its services did not compensate for the desecration. Roman abuse of the revered office of the High Priest augmented Jewish frustration. Following the failure of a Hasmonean attempt to restore Jewish independence (57 BCE), the Roman officer Gabinius reinstated the more compliant Hasmonean prince John Hyrcanus II as high priest despite the unpopularity of the latter (*Antiquities* 14.91). The Herodians adopted the precedence, imposing and deposing high priests at will. Thus, nomination into the most prestigious religious post in Jewry, the venerable link between God and the people, became dependent not on virtue, piety, and appropriate genealogy but on the political interests of pagan occupiers and their local collaborators.

Corrupt and avaricious appointees squandered whatever prestige the post still enjoyed, as the reputation of the associated priestly elites ebbed ever shallower (Goodman 1987: 110).[6] Once the rebels took control of Jerusalem, they executed Ananus, the presiding high priest and nominated a provincial candidate, Phineas ben Samuel, by casting lots. Deploring the act, Josephus charges them with "a cunning contrivance to seize upon the government, derived from those that presumed to appoint governors as they themselves pleased." (*War* 4.154). This, however, seems to have been precisely how many contemporaneous Jews viewed the way high priests were appointed under the Romans and their Herodian allies.

To appreciate the extent of the trauma that this pattern of sacrilege must have caused, the special place that the Temple of Jerusalem occupied in the minds and hearts of the Jews should be highlighted. The Temple was more than a place of ritual gathering, unlike the numerous pagan temples scattered throughout the Roman world. Jews revered the Temple as a unique monument to their special relationship with God and as a symbol of their devotion to Him (Alon 1980b: 49). It also epitomized the unity of the Jewish people, as Jews from Judea and the Diaspora gathered on the pilgrimage roads and worshipped together in the sacred courts (Philo, *in Flaccum* 45–46). Following Ze'ev Safrai (1975: 336–37),

> [the Temple] represented above all the dwelling place of the Lord God…the unrivaled center for the service of God through the offering of sacrifices in the name of all the people. But even for the individual and his personal religious experience, the Temple service was of paramount importance. The offering of sacrifices purified him and atoned for his sins, and served as a medium for his spiritual elevation and refinement…. That the Temple had in fact existed for so long, and had been rebuilt in even greater splendor than before, merely served to strengthen the belief in its eternality. Hence the people's great devotion to the Temple in time of peace, the strength of its resistance when the enemy breached its wall, and the utter despair and desolation of the soul as the Temple was reduced to rubble and ashes.

It should be noted that this unreserved veneration was not in full consensus. Biblical prophets had warned against a concentration on ritual aspects at the expense of righteous conduct and sincere adherence to the Law (Samuel I, 15:22; Hosea 6:6). A development of this outlook basically linked the welfare of the Temple not to its own sanctity but to the moral behavior of the people. This principle is manifested in Jewish commentaries that hold Israel's sins responsible for the desecration of the Temple by Antiochus IV and Pompey (Stone 1981: 197). Readapted, the same principle corresponds to the theological foundations of early Christianity, as reflected in the acts and words of Jesus (Matthew 21:12–13; Mark 11:15–17), and in the speech that cost Stephen, the first Christian martyr, his life (Acts 7:48–53).

However, it is highly unlikely that this theological complexity found many adherents in the Judea of the first century. Narratives in Josephus, other Jewish and Roman sources, and the New Testament all clearly illustrate the scale and depth of Jewish veneration of the Temple per se. Any semblance of abuse of the building by the Romans and their allies was treated with gravity. The act of Pompey and the deterioration of the high priesthood's status are the more obvious examples, but even necessary construction projects for the benefit of the city were forcefully opposed, if they were to be financed with Temple funds (*War* 2.175).

Mendels (1992: 280–81) suggests that Herod intended to preserve the Temple mainly as a religious center, while deflecting political substance to Caesarea and other Helleno-Roman cities in which he had also generously invested. If so, this would only reflect Herod's limited understanding of the people he governed. To the Jews, the Temple was also the palace of the supreme King, with all that corresponded to a king's position and responsibilities. The circumscription of the Temple to ritual activities implied to deny God's paramount authority over *all* aspects of life, an unacceptable idea in first-century Judea. It was thus ironic, yet only to be expected, that the temple courts erected with so much vigor by Rome's greatest ally became the hub of anti-Roman disturbances during the first two centuries of their rule in Judea.

Freedom as a Religious Concept

Some of the worst pre-revolt confrontations between Jews and Romans happened at the Temple compound during the annual pilgrimages. The Passover festival created the most volatile situations. Nearly three thousand pilgrims died during the Passover celebrations of 4 BCE, when Herod's son and successor, Archelaus, launched his troops to capture prospective rebels in the crowded Temple courts (*Antiquities* 17.213–18). During the term of governor Ventidius Cumanus (48–52 CE), thousands of Passover pilgrims were killed at the same place in riots triggered by a vulgar gesture of a Roman guard overlooking the ceremony, despite Cumanus' genuine efforts to calm down the multitudes (*Antiquities* 20.108–12). This hazardous condition explains the caution reportedly employed by the Jewish leaders two decades earlier, when they refrained from seizing Jesus during the Passover feast, "least there be uproar among the people" (Matthew 26:3–5).

The fact that those events all took place during Passover is not a coincidence. Freedom is the very focus of Passover, a festival also called *Heruth* (חרות), Hebrew for liberty. Submission to Rome contradicted the spirit of this festival. "The freedom celebrated was necessarily in *fantasy* form, there being no actual freedom," writes Horsley (1987: 34, emphasis original), and there were always enough individuals among the Jews quite ready to fight to turn this fantasy into actuality. To the agitated pilgrims amassed in the Temple courts the very presence of the Roman soldiers in plain view on the surrounding walls and galleries would have been a frustrating manifestation of slavery in the midst of the celebration of the liberty that God had awarded their ancestors. The prominence of freedom as an ultimate goal, as well as a religious concept, emerges from several incidents that took place during the First Revolt:

- In the early days of the war, the crowds in the Temple courts lynched Menahem, a son of Judas the Galilean who had claimed the Jewish kingship, because "it was not proper when they revolted from the Romans, out of desire for liberty, to betray that liberty to any of their own people" (*War* 2.443). In other words, the kingship of no human, either Roman or Jewish, was to be recognized.

- Hiding from the Romans in a cave and about to commit group suicide, the forty survivors of the siege of Galilean Yodfat admonisheed the frightened Josephus over his willingness to "see the light in a state of slavery" (*War* 3.356–57).

114   THE SACRED CONTRACT

- In his appeal to the people of Jerusalem, High Priest Ananus depicted the desire for freedom as "that most honorable and most natural of our passions "(*War* 4.175).

- Facing the frustrated Idumean warriors locked outside Jerusalem's walls during a stormy night as a precaution, former High Priest Joshua ben Gamala desperately tried to reassure them that he and the moderate leadership did not intend to betray "that most desirable thing, liberty" (*War* 4.246).

- Furious and unconvinced, Idumean commander Simon ben Cathlas bitterly criticized those who "speak to the Idumeans from their own towers, and enjoin them to throw down their arms which they have taken up for the preservation of [Jerusalem's] liberty" (*War* 4.273).

- Urging his followers at Masada to choose suicide over slavery, Eleazar ben Yair reminded them that "we, long ago…resolved never to be servants to the Romans, nor to any other than to God Himself" (*War* 7.323).

Josephus' literary flair should be credited for the eloquence of the statements, but the spirit and reasoning are probably genuine. It would serve Josephus no purpose to fabricate the very same ideological desire in persons whom he resented, such as Simon and Eleazar, and in those he identified with, such as Ananus and Joshua.

The tenacious Jewish resistance to Roman rule owes much of its vigor and temper to the ideological link between religion and freedom, which the Romans were hard pressed to comprehend. In his speech to the defenders of Jerusalem, Titus complains that the Jewish rebellion cannot be justified, because the Romans have always respected the Jewish religion and never interfered with its practice (*War* 6.333–34).[7] This was mostly the case (Gruen 2002: 29–30), but it was a gesture wasted on the many Jews who considered the very submission to any ruler other than God intolerable (*Antiquities* 18.23). Even the pragmatic elites, whose members realized that freedom was unattainable under the prevalent circumstances and had led comfortable lives under Roman occupation, maintained the hope of regaining liberty, should an opportunity present itself at a more appropriate time (Horsley 1987: 82–83; Price 1992: 26–27).[8]

The violent antagonism towards Roman occupation is inconsistent with the relative compliance of the Jews to three and a half centuries of temperate Persian, Ptolemaic, and early Seleucid rule (539–175 BCE).[9] It may be that the bitter Jewish experience with Antiochus IV, which ended the period of mutual tolerance, influenced the change in the Jewish approach. As elucidated by the episode of Caligula's statue (see below), one could never tell when the Romans, whose cultural and religious background roughly resembled that of the Seleucids and who occasionally crowned rather eccentric Caesars, might alter their policy of tolerance towards the Jewish religion. As a consequence, freedom from Rome would have been perceived not merely in light of its economic and other practical advantages, nor primarily as a matter of national pride;[10] it would have been seen as first and foremost condition for religious survival, without which there could be no survival at all.

The Emperor Cult

Despite the general Roman policy of tolerance towards the manifold idiosyncrasies of the Jewish religion, there were several occasions during the first century in which Jews and Romans came to the brink of conflict over Roman violations, in the Jewish understanding, of religious taboos. The main threat to the delicate balance was the Roman emphasis on the "peace of the gods" (*Pax Deorum*) and the emperor cult. The former related to the belief that as the empire's well-being depended on the favor of the gods, they must be constantly placated by the appropriate rituals, conducted not only by the Romans themselves but also by their subjects. Yet the Jews were generally exempt from pagan services, and friction over this issue was usually prevented. Similar Roman moderation was most times applied regarding the emperor cult. In Rome, the religious rituals honoring living and dead emperors were considered to be a statement of allegiance to the Caesars and a means of showing appreciation for the benefits they granted to everyone. The concept of ruler deification had to be artificially introduced into western provinces like Gaul and Britain, where it was alien to local cultures (Fishwick 2004: 218–9). In the East, on the other hand, principally in Egypt, the deification of monarchs reached back several millennia, and it had been natural to shift the rituals towards the much greater rulers of Rome (Millar 1967: 100–101: Mendels 1992: 278). A somewhat reluctant Augustus was the first emperor to be honored this way (Suetonius, *Lives* 2.52).[11] By the time of his death, temples dedicated to him and his family stood in towns and cities of many provinces, with local aristocrats competing for the honor of sponsoring additional structures (Zanker 1988: 316–17). One of the most active builders of Augustan temples in the East was King Herod of Judea, who had them erected in Caesarea, Sebastia, and Caesarea Philippi (Paneas) (*War* 1.413–14; *Antiquitues* 15.218, 339, 363; Philo, *Legatio ad Gaium* 305). It can be safely assumed that his Jewish subjects did not share his enthusiasm, but they tolerated these initiatives as long as they were limited to the Helleno-Roman regions.

By the first century CE, the emperor cult had spread throughout the East, except in Judea (Schnapp 1994: 41; Geiger 2004: 5). The Romans may have found the Jewish abstention eccentric, but as far as they were concerned the daily sacrifice in Jerusalem in honor of the emperor signaled their allegiance (Gruen 2002: 31). A grave incident that took place in 39 CE, and whose impression survives in both Jewish and Roman sources (*Antiquities* 18.261–309; *War* 2.184–203; Philo, *Legatio ad Gaium* 199ff.; Tacitus, *Histories* 5:9), proved just how precarious this arrangement was. The unsound Gaius Caligula, who was very particular in his demand to be honored as a god throughout the empire (Suetonius, *Lives*, 4.22), ordered Publius Petronius, the Roman governor in Syria, to place a large statue of Jupiter with the emperor's features at the Temple court in Jerusalem. Such order could have never been carried out without a major confrontation with the Jews, who considered it an absolutely unbearable affront against God (Brandon 1967: 84–85). A large Jewish crowd congregated at the northern port city of Ptolemais (Acre), where Petronius awaited the completion of the statue, and vowed to prevent this religious abomination by all means (*Antiquities* 18.266–68). Petronius, apparently touched by the Jewish devotion and desperate to avert a violent uprising, risked his own life by writing to the mad emperor, urging him to reconsider his order. An infuriated Caligula stood fast by his decision that the statue should be erected in the heart of Jerusalem regardless of the repercussions and directed Petronius to commit suicide for his vacillation. Fortunately, the ship carrying the orders was held back by a storm and reached Ptolemais only after Caligula's assassination became known. The Jews attributed this favorable outcome to God's intervention and, according to Josephus, so did Petronius himself (*Antiquities* 18.309). Later this gallant official harshly reproached the Gentiles of the coastal city of Dora for forcing a statue of Caligula's successor Claudius into a local synagogue on their own unsolicited initiative (*Antiquities* 19.300–11).

Despite the fortunate conclusion of both episodes, the rejection of the emperor cult put the Jews in a delicate position and increased their vulnerability to hostile propaganda. The Alexandrian rhetorician Apion, for example, accused the Jews of "neglecting the honors that belonged to Caesar" and emphasized that "these Jews alone thought it a dishonorable thing for them to erect statues in honor of him, as well as to swear by his name" (*Antiquities* 18.257–58). The response of Josephus is assertive though somewhat apologetic: "Our lawgiver has forbidden us to make images, not by way of denunciation beforehand that the Roman authority was not to be honored, but as despising a thing that was neither necessary nor useful for either God or man" (*Against Apion* 2.75). Yet Josephus knew that as a problem the emperor cult exceeded scholarly debates. Along with his efforts to stress the passive nature of the Jewish demonstration in Ptolemais, Josephus candidly admits that at least some of the Jews "were very ready to revolt about the statue, and that they seemed resolved to threaten war against the Romans" (*Antiquities* 18.302).

This was not the only occasion in which the Jews challenged Roman sacred symbols. Shortly before Herod's death, two distinguished Jewish teachers, Judas ben Saripheus and Matthias ben Margalothus, along with some of their students, pulled down a golden eagle erected by the king at the gate to the Temple court and were burnt on the stake for their zeal (*Antiquities* 17.149–67; *War* 1.648–654). Three decades later, Pontius Pilate attempted to set up a few gilded shields in honor of the emperor Tiberius in front of Herod's old palace in Jerusalem, then serving as the governor's residence. While the exact reasons remain unclear, the shields were considered a serious enough offense to justify the sending of a protest delegation headed by four Herodian princes to Pilate, as well as a letter to Tiberius himself, who ordered the problematic shields removed (Philo, *Legatio ad Gaium* 299–305). In 37 CE, the Roman governor of Syria, Vitellius, honored a Jewish appeal to change the route of his military expedition against the Nabateans in order to prevent Roman military standards with their pagan contents from crossing Jewish territory (*Antiquities* 18.120–23).

Only the first of these episodes claimed Jewish lives, and it was Herod, not the Romans, who had ordered the killings. Behind the remarkable Roman tolerance toward Jewish religious sensitivities was the pragmatic perception that flexibility in these matters served the paramount Roman interest of maintaining peace in Judea (Hengel 1989: 105). Yet, Roman compromises could at most slow down the pattern of destabilization. Moreover, the more zealous Jews may have interpreted them as signs of weakness (Brandon 1967: 83). If so, they would have been encouraged to seek further concessions in order to gradually undermine Roman authority and eventually dispose of it altogether. Even moderate Jews may have been convinced by the recurring conflicts over religious issues that there could be no reassurance for the Jewish people and their faith while the Romans controlled their land and destiny. Evidence could be found at every turn. The fundamental ideological differences that consistently widened the gap between the Jews on one side and the Romans and the supportive Gentile populations on the other extended even into basic elements in both communal and private spheres. Ultimate conflict was virtually inevitable.

Aversion to Imagery Art

Gods and humans were commonly portrayed in the sculptures, frescoes, mosaics, vessels, and coins of the Greek, Hellenistic, and Roman realms. Personified images of elements of nature and abstract virtues were also often depicted. Statues and profiles on coins supported political systems by projecting to the public the flattering and regulated images of leaders and their affiliates and by propagating their achievements (Nodelman 1975: 19). As discussed above, statues of the emperor and of female personifications of Rome were ritually venerated throughout the empire, along with the images of local gods. Syncretism between local and Roman gods was also common and found its expression in imagery.[12] Yet, in all matters concerning figurative art, first-century Jews followed a very different direction.

The Jewish aversion to polytheism and its associated figurative representations has its origins in the First and Second Commandments (Exodus 20:2–6; Deuteronomy 5:6–10), although its application varied periodically. While monumental statuary is missing in the pre-exilic archaeological record of Israel and Judah, modest figurines are occasionally found in domestic settings (Dever 1990: 157; Mazar 1990: 498–507; Zevit 2001: 267–74, 651).[13] Conversely, by the later Hellenistic and early Roman periods interpretations of the biblical commandments became particularly strict, and, other than a few isolated exceptions (see Chapter 10), human and animal representations disappear from material contexts. Some scholars (Vermeule and Anderson 1981: 8; Eliav 2002: 415) claim that figurative imagery, being so dominant in the Helleno-Roman cultural landscape, must have also penetrated Jewish urban environments in some form. However, despite numismatic testimony to pagan temples in predominantly Jewish Sepphoris (Ne'eman 1993: 280–303) and Tiberias

(Meshorer 1985: 34–35), extensive excavations brought to light only two fragments of statues in the former, while none have surfaced in the latter (Weiss 1998: 244–45). A comparison to the abundance of statues in Helleno-Roman cites like Scythopolis, Askalon, Sebastia, Ptolemais, and Caesarea (Mazor 1988: 11; Foerster and Tsafrir 1988: 22: Foerster 2000; Aviam 2004: 36–40; Vermeule and Anderson 1981) emphasizes the ideological divergence between Jewish and non-Jewish populations over this issue.

Figure 26 Two palms and a rosette engraved on a fallen basalt lintel block in Gamla. Plant and geometric motifs are characteristic of first-century Jewish art, where animal and human images are virtually missing (courtesy of D. Syon/Gamla excavations).

Some Graeco-Roman observers were mystified by this uncompromising aversion to imagery art. Tacitus, for example, baselessly informs his readers in one place (*Histories* 5:4) that the statue of a donkey is revered at the Temple of Jerusalem. In other records, the same author more accurately states that Jews keep "no images in their cities, much less in their temples" (5:5) and accounts that as Pompey entered the Temple, he saw "no image of a god, but an empty place" (*Histories* 5:9). One might even detect some grudging respect in his summarized theological explanation:

> The Jews have no notion of any more than one divine Being; and that known only by the mind. They esteem such to be profane who frame images of gods out of perishable matter, and in the shape of men; that this Being is supreme and eternal, immutable and imperishable, is their doctrine (Histories 5.26–27).

The eighteenth-century British historian Edward Gibbon remarked that "the devout and even scrupulous attachment to the Mosaic religion, so conspicuous among the Jews who lived under the second temple, becomes even more surprising, if it is compared with the stubborn incredulity of their forefathers."[14] In fact, at least in its negative attitude towards figurative art, Late Second Temple Judaism exceeded even Genuine Jewish ritual observance during other periods of antiquity. Forth-century-BCE coins of the autonomous Persian province of Judea (*Yehud*) depict human and animal images inspired by Athenian and Persian religious motifs (Meshorer 1967: 37–40; 1998: 40–43). On mosaic floors in numerous synagogues of the Late Roman and Byzantine periods (third to seventh centuries CE) pagan deities, zodiacs, and mythological figures appear next to scenes and heroes from the Bible (Avi-Yonah 1981: 275, 283ff., 396–97; Levine 1981; Foerster 1987). Sarcophagi adorned with mythological images were also found in the Late Roman catacombs of Beth She'arim, a renowned center of Jewish religious learning in Galilee.[15] Jews in those periods clearly distinguished ritual meanings from merely decorative representations, where even blunt pagan motifs were no longer considered a threat (Avi-Yonah 1981: 268, 384; Schäfer 2002: 346; Schwartz 1998: 213; Weiss 1996b: 360). This openness, however, generally shunned statues, which remained extremely rare in Jewish contexts throughout late antiquity.

The later liberal attitude toward human and animal depictions represents a meaningful departure from first-century ideology, which considered human and animal representations as taboo. The ban remained in effect while the Temple stood and during the period that immediately followed its destruction, a time when hope for future liberation was still sustained. It was a formidable aspect of Jewish cultural identity, inspired by a religious ideology of neither precedent nor pursuing in its severity. This absolute devotion met its ultimate challenge with the catastrophic failure of the First Revolt, as the very cultural and religious existence of the Jews was placed in jeopardy.

Reactions to the Catastrophe

The devastation in the aftermath of the First Revolt was the worst the Jews had experienced since the destruction of the Kingdom of Judah by the Babylonians over six hundred years earlier. There was massive loss of life and property. The capital lay in ruins. Regional towns were razed to the ground. The traditional leadership was wiped out and entire social classes were decimated. Worst of all, the Temple of Jerusalem, venerated heart of the Jewish religion, was reduced to cinders and ashes. The fall of the Temple stunned and agonized Jews everywhere. A rabbinical source states that in its demise, "an iron wall intervened between Israel and its Father in Heaven" (*Berakhot* 32b). Josephus, who had spoken loudly about the military futility of revolt, turned to theological rationalization to make sense of the loss of the shrine (*War* 6.310–14). The surviving rebels were faced with a reality they had seemingly believed God would never permit, one that threatened the deepest foundations of their ideological convictions (see *War* 4.127, 6.98). Many would have found it nearly impossible to admit that it had all been in vain and to come to terms with what seemed to be God's indifference to their plight. Price (1992: 138) argues that some rebels may have interpreted the sequential disasters in positive apocalyptic terms as "encouraging signs of the rapid approach of the promised victory in the end." If so, their resolve to fight on regardless of the hopeless odds even after the fall of Jerusalem would have only stiffened.[16]

Some of the more extreme factions, notably the Sicarii, dealt with the downfall of Judea by devoting themselves to the sanctification of the Lord through ultimate self-sacrifice.[17] They proved their unbending ideological commitment through their suicide pact at the fortress of Masada by the Dead Sea, the last Jewish bastion of the First Revolt that refused to surrender even as Jerusalem lay three years in its debris.

During the same period, other Sicarii refugees attempted to incite the Jews in Egypt against Rome until the local Jewish leadership, alarmed at the potential repercussions, had the rebels seized and extradited to the authorities. That betrayal and the subsequent torture and executions did not break their spirit. Even Josephus, a bitter enemy of the Sicarii, could not hide his admiration for their courage:

> For when all sorts of torments and vexations of their bodies that could be devised were made use of to them, [the Romans] could not get anyone of them to comply so far as to confess, or sem to confess, that Caesar was their lord…as if they received these torments and the fire itself with bodies insensitive of pain, and with a soul that in a manner rejoiced under them. But what was the most astonishing to the beholders was the courage of the children; for not one of those children was so far overcome by these torments as to name Caesar for their lord…So far does the strength of the courage prevail over the weakness of the body (*War* 7.418–19).

Major Jewish insurgency was to challenge the legions of Rome twice again in the course of the following seven decades. Between the years 115–117 CE, during the reign of Trajan, a series of Jewish attacks on Gentile populations and Roman garrisons rocked provinces in the southern and eastern Mediterranean. Cassius Dio (68.32) and others report intense violence, widespread damage, and substantial loss of life on both sides in Egypt, Cyrene, and Cyprus, before the Romans were finally able to suppress the uprisings. There was more to come. In 132 CE, the Jews in Judea attempted once more to gain freedom from Rome under the capable leadership of Simon ben Kosiba, popularly known as Bar-Kochba ("Son of Star"), and the distinguished rabbi Aqiba ben Joseph.[18] It took three years and heavy losses, including the probable obliteration of an entire legion (the Twenty-Second *Deiotariana*), for the forces sent by Emperor Hadrian to overcome the rebels.[19] As in the previous revolts, the Jews suffered calamitous devastation. The intense religious ideological background of this revolt is reflected in the literary records pointing out the messianic pretensions of Simon ben Kosiba. It has also been confirmed by the religious contents of coins, including the depiction of what seems to be the Temple's façade (Meshorer 1967: 136, 151; Kindler 1980; Zissu and Eshel 2001), and in the defacing, in accordance with specific rabbinical regulations, of human figures on copper vessels that were taken from the Romans[20] and found in rebel hideaways in the Judean desert (Yadin 1963: 44–45, pls. 17, 20; 1971: 102–5) and in the Judean lowlands (Kloner and Tepper 1987: 342, 355; Zissu and Ganor 2003: 147).[21]

The catastrophic defeats finally convinced most Jews that military insurrections, heroic as they may have been, were against the Divine Will. Had God desired, the powerful legions and all of their works would have been crushed against the towns of Judea. Yet he decided differently, and it was for the Jews to figure out why. Unless sensible explanations could be devised, the immense despair, disorientation, and ideological crisis in the aftermath of the wars might have had dangerous repercussions to the very existence of Judaism.[22] The search for explanations, the attempts of recuperation, and the continuous struggle in its various forms were all based on religious interpretations and logic.

Figure 27 Façade of the Jerusalem Temple on a Bar Kochba coin (courtesy of D. Ariel, Israel Antiquities Authority). Note: Coin figures are presented in this book for their symbolic content and are not displayed in actual size.

Jewish sources reveal generations of intense post-war soul-searching that merged realistic analysis with theological reasoning (Stone 1981; Saldarini 2002: 222, 229). Before all else, God's decision had to be unreservedly accepted, justified, and upheld. "Writers lament, weep, cry out their pain over this calamity," observes Michael Stone (1981: 200), "yet the righteousness of God's action is not questioned." The vast military superiority of the Romans is virtually ignored, since it would have been irrelevant had God chosen to side with the rebels. The concept of sin provided a more theologically sound explanation. It is supported by numerous biblical precedents, as well as by Deuteronomy 28, where fifty-four bleak verses (15–69) describe the horrors that God would inflict on the People of Israel if they failed to follow his ways.

Yet, what could possibly have been the momentous sins that the devout Jews of late Second Temple days must have committed to deserve such terrible retribution? Rabbinical sources focused on the misconduct of the Jews as individuals and as a society before and during the war. The message was essentially that chronic disunity, violent civil strife, improper utilization of wealth, and other social injustices committed even as the capital struggled under siege persuaded God to abandon the people and dispose of the Temple. A similar but broader perspective explained the disaster as punishment for the sins of all Israel over a longer span of time (Stone 1981: 196; Goodman 1987: 85; Mendels 1992: 368; Price 1992: 176; Saldarini 2002: 232). Josephus underscored the rebellion itself as the principal offense. Following his logic, God decreed that the Romans would rule the world, and in rebelling the Jews unforgivably defied and defiled God's universal program. It was therefore only proper that the Romans acted as God's instrument of stern justice, just as he had used the Egyptians, Arameans, Assyrians, and Babylonians before (*War* 4.323, 6.110). This historical analogy is obviously imperfect. First-century Jews were not guilty of the idolatry and corruption of their biblical ancestors. The revolt itself, even if foolhardy, was fought in good faith and out of true devotion.

More complex sin-oriented explanations suggested a divine program beyond human understanding, in which sin is not circumscribed in time and place, and judgment does not respond to specific actions (Stone 1981: 200–204; Price 1992: 176). Embedded in Creation, sin cannot be avoided, and retribution preserves the cosmic balance between good and evil, beyond particular and immediate human considerations of fairness. Theological differences notwithstanding, all sin-focused explanations had a single aim in common and carried the same potential: they could help the Jews absorb the catastrophe while preserving their fundamental faith in divine justice, which was conditional for the survival of their religion.

Explanation was a crucial but only preliminary step towards Jewish recuperation. The devastation of the Judean political, social, and economic infrastructure during the war and the loss of the capital and shrine demanded a profound redefinition and reorganization of Jewish life beyond theological accommodations. Rome was victorious but sullen, suspicious, and vindictive. It showed it through the imposition of ruthless new demands, such as the deeply offensive *fiscus Iudaicus*, a special tax for the Temple of Jupiter that the Jews alone were forced to pay instead of their annual donation to the Temple of Jerusalem (*War* 7.218; Suetonius, *Lives* 8.3.12). Religion, which provided the main incentive for the uprising, now awarded many Jews with the ability for patient endurance. Others, however, it provisioned with stamina to carry on the flame of dissension, which was to flare in Judea once again before subsiding into embers and finally dying out for many centuries to come.

Without the Temple, profound adaptations in Jewish religion became inevitable to ensure communal and religious survival (Safrai 1975: 336–37). Already after the First Revolt, but to a wider extent following the failure of Bar-Kochba, rabbinical authorities aimed to contrive new religious guidelines, in both the conceptual and ritual aspects, to replace the Temple in spiritual life and also to make existence under Roman rule possible. A contemporaneous wave of emigration had to be forestalled (Avi-Yonah 1976: 25ff.; Alon 1980b: 96ff.; *contra* Schwartz 2001), and remnants of rebellious motivation had to be checked.[23] The reconstruction of the Temple was left to God and His agent, the Messiah (Avi-Yonah 1976: 69, 131, 197). The yearning for the Messiah dominated Jewish aspirations, but theological understandings did not set any specific time for his advent, leaving it to God's decree.

The desire for a restoration of the old glory did not diminish even when the means to achieve this goal had changed from sword to prayer. Key concepts, such as the sacredness of the Temple's former ground and the reestablishment of the monarchy under the Davidic royal dynasty, were never abandoned and featured in writings and prayer codes for centuries to come, surviving in essence to this day (Goodblatt 2006: 205). Religious intensity in this case was forced to shed its militant manifestations, but much of it metamorphosed into spiritual forms, while adopting some inevitable pragmatism along the way. The Jewish core approach that was eventually to emerge out of the ashes and chaos of the first two centuries of Roman occupation can be summed in the simple words of the Jewish philosopher and scholar Maimonides, uttered a thousand years later: "I believe in the coming of the Messiah, and even though he is late in coming, despite of all, I believe".[24]

A Religious-Ideological Model for the First Revolt

The repercussions of the First Revolt were terrible for the Jews but hardly surprising. Their historical experience as well as that of others who had dared to defy Rome would have made the overwhelming odds of calamitous failure clear from the onset. Why then take such risk? What could have given the rebels the hope or illusion that success was ever possible?

It is difficult to see how economic stress and class tensions could have been the major cause for the uprising. Both the poor and the rich took part in the common effort of war and shared its common burdens. Peasants, merchants, priests, and princes faced the legions from the walls. Heavy taxes were indeed imposed on Judea, but other peoples endured similar financial yokes and did not repeatedly rise against Caesar. Frustration over the tyranny, corruption, incompetence, and insensitivity of the later Roman governors undoubtedly helped trigger the revolt, but such pressures could have been sustained and indeed had been in many places for generations, including Judea itself. The troubled relations between Helleno-Roman populations and their Jewish neighbors inside and near the cities ignited occasional riots, but these were usually local and could be contained with no lasting effect. Finally, there is no evidence whatsoever for a major conspiracy that included Judea with the intention of coordinating some inter-provincial uprising against Rome.

THE SACRED CONTRACT   121

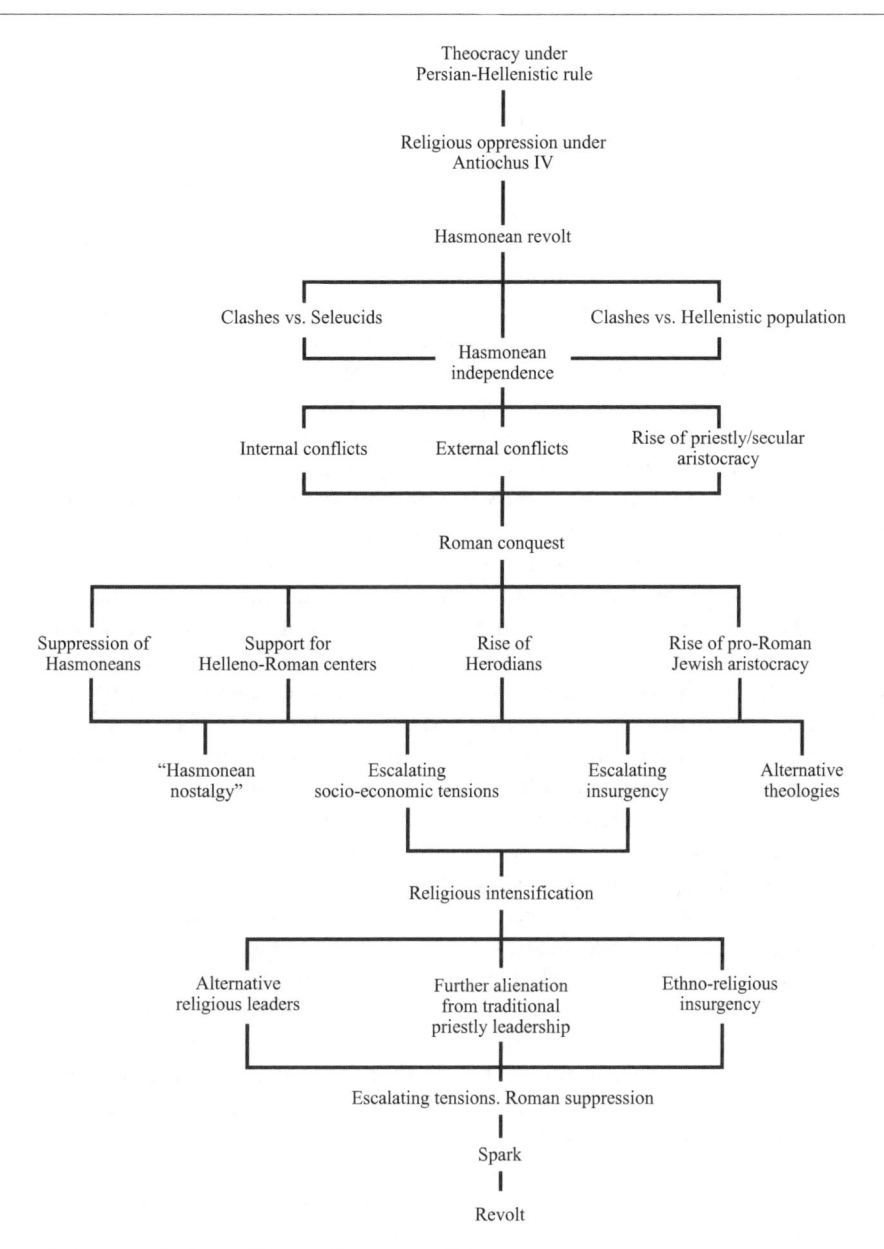

```
                    Theocracy under
                  Persian-Hellenistic rule
                            |
                   Religious oppression under
                         Antiochus IV
                            |
                      Hasmonean revolt
         ┌──────────────────┼──────────────────┐
   Clashes vs. Seleucids    |    Clashes vs. Hellenistic population
         └──────────── Hasmonean ───────────────┘
                       independence
         ┌──────────────────┼──────────────────┐
   Internal conflicts   External conflicts   Rise of priestly/secular
                                                 aristocracy
         └──────────────────┼──────────────────┘
                      Roman conquest
    ┌──────────────┬────────┴────────┬──────────────┐
 Suppression of  Support for      Rise of       Rise of pro-Roman
  Hasmoneans   Helleno-Roman     Herodians      Jewish aristocracy
                  centers
    └───────┬──────────┬─────────────┬──────────────┘
      "Hasmonean    Escalating    Escalating      Alternative
       nostalgy"  socio-economic  insurgency      theologies
                    tensions
              └──────────┴─────────────┘
                Religious intensification
         ┌──────────────────┼──────────────────┐
     Alternative      Further alienation    Ethno-religious
  religious leaders    from traditional       insurgency
                      priestly leadership
         └──────────────────┼──────────────────┘
            Escalating tensions. Roman suppression
                            |
                          Spark
                            |
                          Revolt
```

Figure 28   Religious-ideological Intensification model.

Intense religious ideological convictions remain the only viable explanation to the uprising, shedding light on both the developments that led to it and on the determined Jewish resistance during its course. The revolt was not intended as a suicide mission. The rebels apparently truly believed that they alone could overcome the empire. Considering their patchwork military organization, limited resources, and lack of unified leadership and administrative infrastructure such presumptuousness can only be justified through intense religious faith. Utter confidence in divine intervention would make the vastly uneven practical odds virtually irrelevant to the final outcome.

This was no minor expectation. The Jews must have realized that the Romans were far more powerful in every way than the Canaanites or Seleucids of old. God obviously could humble

Rome before Judea, but what made them believe that He would? Even strictly religious people may recognize the constraints of reality and forge creative compromises out of their dogmas. Freedom, for example, can remain a religious duty, but the time and form of its attainment may be left flexibly vague. Such ideological pragmatism can save societies from honorable but suicidal adventures. Josephus and Philo were certainly not the only believers in its necessity in their own time and circumstances. By 66 CE, the Roman occupation of Judea was 129 years old and, while unrest and skirmishes with the Romans and their allies occasionally happened, no major uprising had taken place. Partly influenced by socio-economic stress and other factors, religious ideology in Judea must have evolved to a state in which pragmatic compromises were no longer possible and, as a consequence, Roman occupation could no longer be tolerated.

This conclusion was by no means in consensus, but consensus would not have been necessary. War does not depend on the consent of all people, only on the determination of some and the passivity of others. There was certainly much theological and political diversity in first-century Judea. Yet, if enough people could be convinced that Roman occupation of the Promised Land was a religious abomination to be opposed by all means, there was no stopping the uprising. If previous generations had failed to repulse the original Roman advance or to eject the legions later, their allegedly imperfect religious commitment could be held responsible. On the other hand, the spectacular victory over Gallus could be seen as proof that the Jews of the present generation, unlike their ancestors, had rendered themselves worthy of God's assistance. An extension of this reasoning would dictate that the mounting ordeals of the war were not only obligatory sacrifices for the atonement of sins but also tests of faith. Those who could endure Job's tribulations and remain committed to God, as he had done, should be ultimately rewarded as he had been. Joshua, Hezekiah, and Judas Maccabeus all suffered painful setbacks, but all eventually triumphed. It would not be far-fetched to assume that the rebels against Rome entertained hopes of a similar conclusion to their own daring venture. Such perspective would explain their seemingly senseless perseverance. Besides, admission of defeat equaled recognition that religious ideals revered for generations, even the fundamental "sacred contract," may have been deceptive and that the terrible sacrifices made on their behalf had all been in vain. Desperate Jewish resistance at Machaerus and Masada after the fall of Jerusalem and its temple, the fervent attempts of Sicarii refugees to stir trouble in Egypt and Cyrene, and the later insurrections abroad and in Judea all reflect the refusal to come to terms with this excruciating understanding.

Each of the three major Jewish revolts took place under different political, social, and economic circumstances. Still, all three involved large numbers of people, demanded significant Roman mobilization, and lasted several years each, despite agonizing defeats and devastation. All three occurred within a relatively short period. Religious symbolism was extensively used in all three. Non-religious explanations based on specific historical conditions depend on the unlikely notion that these similarities are coincidental or unimportant, but they are not. The circumstantial nuances of each case and the ideological disparities between the rebels leave the basic argument for religious supremacy among the causes of the revolts unscathed. Bitter ideological disputes reflect fervent ideological commitment. Such commitment, more than any physical grievance, had led the Jews to face time and again the invincible imperial armies. Only the combined and accumulated effect of the disastrous three wars would eventually prove the futility of military rebellion and set Judaism on a different interpretation of its place in God's program.

The reasoning behind the decision to revolt against Rome is embedded in the highly religious atmosphere prevalent in Judea during the first century and in the anti-Roman directions in which it led. Data that sheds light on this atmosphere can be deduced from textual testimonies, but archaeology provides evidence from the actual homes of ordinary first-century Judean Jews. This data is independent from the subjective perspective of authors such as Josephus, a fact that makes it invaluable for the understanding of the revolt. To that intriguing class of evidence we turn in the following and last chapter of this study.

10 Unearthing Religious Intensity

Religion is one of the most researched aspects of antiquity, with archaeology contributing invaluable information about its various material indicators. Based upon Colin Renfrew's (1985: 2; 1994: 47, 51–52) analysis, markers of religion in archaeological contexts can be summarized into two main classes:

1. Special buildings, set aside from the rest, equipped with unusual, attention-focusing features and adorned with repeatedly-used symbols that may be associated with the deity or with ideological principles.

2. Unordinary objects, such as pools or basins, that may imply rites of purification and invested artifacts, including irregularly shaped or decorated receptacles, knives, and other probable ritual paraphernalia.

Spells of religious intensification would leave behind similar indicators but exceed them in frequency, density, proportion, and variety. Evidence is mostly circumstantial but must be rooted in the cultural scene and form a coherent pattern. Four general discernible types of markers can be proposed:

Messages

Innovative ideological messages, slogans, and propaganda may be inserted in inscriptions, coins, documents, and letters. Messages can be straightforward or insinuative. Previously absent religious contents may be used in administrative documents and other correspondence. Written materials may also show a sudden surge in ideological anachronism, which can be defined as the symbolic reutilization of otherwise obsolete themes associated with revered ancestors. The reappearance of archaic script, vocabulary, and artistic styles all fit into this relatively rare but highly indicative class of evidence.

Symbols

An accentuation of indigenous ideological symbols while symbols of foreign origins are avoided suggests isolationist cultural attitudes. Such symbols can often be found as decoration in the architecture of administrative buildings, monuments, and funerary contexts, as well as on domestic vessels, weapons, and furniture.

Separatism

Ideological separatism may also be alluded to by a sharp increase in the appearance of ethnic markers, such as the use of distinct culturally-associated shapes, styles, and materials in structures, vessels, and tools. At the same time, foreign imports and influences would be rejected or abandoned. Mingling with other people and cultures is a cross-cultural human tendency. It appeals to our natural curiosity and has obvious social, commercial, and defensive potential. Efforts to construct impenetrable ethno-cultural boundaries are therefore difficult to explain outside ideological contexts.

Names

Statistical analysis may expose a disproportionate frequency of personal names associated with meaningful historical and religious contexts. The phenomenon may indicate a strive for an ideal existence identified with previous generations, who presumably lived along its lines.

The individual and random appearance of these indicators can be explained in non-ideological terms. Yet, their combined emergence within the archaeological record of a circumscribed period demands a more comprehensive model, and religious intensification may convincingly provide one. If these material testimonies correlate with major historical events, we have an attractive opportunity to exploit the resources of both fields to construct a broad theoretical model. The First Jewish Revolt against Rome provides such opportunity. A combined analysis of the historical circumstances as well as the archaeological remains from first-century Judea suggests unprecedented religious intensity, which may have been a major and probably crucial contribution to the major effort to eject Rome from Jerusalem. The following survey focuses on the archaeological part of this model and provides a detailed observation of ideology-related artifacts and architecture that point to the ideology of the First Revolt and are distinct to the period.

Coinage

Jewish rebel issues are unique in Roman history for their messages of religious dedication, commitment to freedom, and separatist determination (Meshorer 1982: 99: 109–10; McLaren 2003: 144–45).[1] Symbols and slogans on First Revolt coinage are invaluable to our understanding of the visions, perspectives, and aims of the rebels. They are primary testimony, untainted by the bias and retrospect of Josephus and other ancient historians. It should be noted that despite changing circumstances, the messages on this currency are comparable to those of the later Bar-Kochba uprising and have some general aspects in common with coins minted by the Hasmoneans.

With a few exceptions, coins of all three administrations feature the ancient Hebrew ("Phoenician") script in inscriptions, rather than the "square" Aramaic letters that dominated daily and official use since the reinstitution of the Jewish political entity under Persian sanction in the late sixth century BCE (Naveh and Greenfield 1984). Cecil Roth (1962: 40) sensibly suggests that that the former script was considered more "patriotic," probably denoting the bond and continuity between the biblical kingdoms of Judah and Israel and the reestablished Jewish homeland.[2] Similar reasoning is suggested by Eshel (2002) to explain the use of the Hebrew language on Jewish coins throughout the Second Temple period, as well as in documents from both Jewish revolts in a time when Aramaic dominated daily speech and communication.[3]

Changes in the symbolic depictions on coins reflect a pattern of religious intensification over the centuries. Imagery representations of humans and animals can be found on some of the Jewish coins of the Persian period. None, not even royal portraits, appear in Hasmonean mints, as such images became anathema under the far more severe interpretations of the Second Commandment common during that time (Meshorer 1996: 437). Instead, Hasmonean coins exhibit motifs of strong ritual significance. Some of these are originally Jewish, such as the rare depiction of the seven-branch candelabra on a coin of the last Hasmonean king Mattathias Antigonus. Other coins display Hellenistic symbols re-adapted to represent Jewish themes (Meshorer 1976; 1997: 106–13), such as the anchor[4] and the cornucopia[5]. Even though the Hasmonean princes were autocratic political rulers, inscriptions on the majority of their coins proclaim their priestly rather than royal titles.[6] They may have been wary of the negative public sentiment that an official proclamation of kingship could arouse, as the Jewish royal throne was traditionally and religiously reserved for the House of David.

Herodian monarchs generally applied similar caution against human representations on coinage, at least within their Jewish domains (Schürer 1961: 143–44; Kasher 1983a: 65, Rappaport 1984: 247).[7] Even the Roman governors of Judea, including those notorious for their anti-Jewish attitudes, were careful to omit imperial images on their issues.

No human or animal images appear on the coins of either Jewish revolt. Instead, most issues display vessels and artifacts affiliated with the Temple of Jerusalem, such as the chalice representing the libation cup used in the Temple service (Roth 1962: 42) or the vessel that contained the *omer*, a ritual offering of choice grain (Meshorer 1997: 106–7). The ornate amphora was used for storing water, oil, or wine, all of which were ritually poured or drunk in various Temple rituals (Meshorer 1982: 110–11; 1997: 109). Similar vessels appear on post-revolt oil lamps (Sussman 1972: 98) and on the coins of the Bar Kochba War (Kindler 1980: 162–63; Meshorer 1997: 125). The branch with three pomegranates may have represented the ritual offering of prime agricultural products (Roth 1962: 42; Meshorer 1982: 108–9; 1997: 107). The Four Species – citron, palm twig, myrtle, and willow – relate to the Festival of Tabernacles (*sukkoth*), which, like Passover, commemorates the liberation from bondage in Egypt, with self-evident connotations to the revolt against Rome. The palm was widely used as a decorative element at the Temple. The vine leaf and grapes may have recalled the wine used in ritual ceremonies or the golden vine that stood at the Temple's entrance (*Antiquities* 15.395; Mishna *Midot* 3.8).[8]

Figure 29 Human and animal figurative representations on a Judean coin of the Persian period (courtesy of D. Ariel, Israel Antiquities Authority).

Figure 30 Coin of Hasmonean ruler John Hyrcanus. Obverse: inscription describing John as High Priest. Reverse: The cornucopia (courtesy of D. Syon/Gamla excavations).

Prior to the revolt, Jews were compelled to use the Tyrian silver shekel for the annual tribute to the Temple, despite its offensive figurative images.[9] Reflecting the exhilaration of the early days of the revolt, the pagan images on some Tyrian silver were disfigured (Eshel and Broshi 2003). More importantly, they were replaced by new shekels minted in Jerusalem, which matched their silver content and surpassed other imperial silver equivalents (McLaren 2003: 137). These prestigious new coins projected Jewish religious images and slogans, symbolically re-adapting the contents of their Tyrian predecessors (Roth 1962: 36; Meshorer 1982: 104–5; McLaren 2003: 139). The inscription "Tyre, Holy, City of Asylum" was replaced with "Holy Jerusalem." The date count of Tyre's autonomy was substituted with the number of years since the liberation of Judea. As evidence to their importance as ritual tributes and possibly also to the encouraging effect they may have had on the rebels and the general population of Jerusalem (Roth 1962: 45–46; Meshorer 1982: 123), silver shekels were still being struck during the last months of the revolt, even as the city struggled and suffered under Roman siege and resources grew alarmingly scarce.

The coins of the First Revolt were not a haphazard products of fanatic zealots tragically oblivious of the military, political, and economic realities of their time. The precision in silver weight, the systematic dating, and the planning reflected in the slogans, script, and symbols project a relatively stable and orderly administration. Those responsible for the minting belonged to the higher social and priestly echelons in Jerusalem (McLaren 2003: 149), people proficient in the business of government who contrived an efficient bureaucratic system, part of which their less experienced and more militant successors were able to preserve.[10]

Figure 31 Tyrian silver shekel (courtesy of D. Syon/Gamla excavations).

Figure 32 Silver shekels of the First Revolt showing a chalice. Left: Year one. Center: Year Two. Right: Year 3 (courtesy of D. Ariel, Israel Antiquities Authority).

The Gamla Coins

Seven unusual bronze coins of the First Revolt were recovered at the site of Gamla (Eidlin 1985: 146–47; Gutman 1994: 148–49; Syon and Yavor 2001: 31–32; 2002: 4; Syon 2002: 146).[11] A chalice is depicted on the obverse, surrounded by large archaic Hebrew letters. The writing proceeds on the opposite side, unaccompanied by images. The message has been provisionally read as LG'LT YRŠLM Q[DŠA] (to the salvation of holy Jerusalem).[12] Both the designed image and the inscription indicate that the Gamla coin is a modest local reproduction designed after the silver shekels of Jerusalem.[13]

Figure 33 The Gamla coin (courtesy of D. Syon/Gamla excavations).

The coarse workmanship, cluttered style, and crude calligraphy of the coins of Gamla reflect the work of unskilled individuals, yet their true value must have exceeded both their external appearance and their commercial transaction. Shmarya Gutman (1994: 149) sees them as a "national-political message and a statement of defiance." According to Danny Syon and Zvi Yavor (2001: 32), the inscription demonstrates that "even in the most difficult conditions…the defenders of Gamla remembered the original objective of the revolt: the liberation of the land, foremost Jerusalem, from the Roman yoke." A similar view is expressed by Meshorer (1986: 225):

> [the people of Gamla] were impressed by the nationalistic inscriptions and designs depicted on the [Jerusalem shekels] and they appreciated the political impact made by the issues. Minting of coins was often a symbol of political independence, but during the harsh siege of Gamala (*sic*), the minting of those coins was also a token of national pride to encourage the warriors on the walls.

The Gamla coin, as all rebel issues, answered to a genuine economic demand for cash currency in a period of emergency, but also served as an influential symbol aimed at both the rebels themselves and the general Jewish population of Judea (Arbel 2007).[14] While the determination for political liberty is represented by the independent minting of coins during the revolt, every written slogan and depicted image reflected the profound religious ideological motivation behind it, whether coins were professionally produced at the capital, or haphazardly improvised in remote provincial settlements.

Funerary Contexts

Numerous limestone-cut Jewish burial caves from the Early Roman period have been found and excavated since the early twentieth century, many in and around Jerusalem, and more are being regularly discovered (Sukenik 1928; Avigad 1962a; Hachlili 1979; Edelstein 2002; Wolff 1996; Greenhut 1996; Gershuny and Zissu 1996; Avni and Greenhut 1996; Badhi and Torgë 2000; Gorzalczany 2000; Abu Raya 2000a, b; Zissu 2001: 240–41; Zissu et al. 2000; Zissu and Re'em 2002; Zissu and Ganor 2002: 21; Kloner 1996; 2000; 2003; Batz 2003; Haddad 2007). Bodies were placed in sepulchral niches or burial troughs, with the bones later collected into ossuaries. Apparently, the interior of caves was often decorated, but painted adornments were compromised by grave robbing and subsequent exposure. Surviving frescoes in burial caves in Jerusalem (Avni and Greenhut 1996), Giv'at Seled (Kloner 1991), and Abud (Conder and Kitchener 1882: 362–63) show geometric and floral motifs. Rare representations of birds among vines were found in a cave in Jericho (Hachlili and Killebrew 1983: 113).

Examples from 'Ein Gedi (Avigad 1962b; Hadas 1994) and Jericho (Hachlili 1999) prove the occasional use of wooden coffins.[15] Stone sarcophagi were also used, mainly by some members of the Jewish aristocracy (see below), but the secondary deposit of bones in ossuaries was the more common practice (Rahmani 1994; Shadmi 1996; Fritz and Deines 1999; for Talmudic references see *Pessahim* 8.8; *Masechet Semahot* 12.9, 13.1). Ossuary use ranges from the late first century BCE to the second and, rarely, third century CE, although post-first century frequency shows a rapid decline (Rahmani 1994: 21–25). It should be noted that while the custom itself is far more ancient and known from various cultures (Figueras 1983: 2–3; Mazar 1992: 84–85), in first century Judea it was by and large exclusive to the Jewish population.[16]

Some rare clay or wood vessels are known (Rahmani 1994: 3), but the vast majority of surviving ossuaries were made of soft limestone, often produced in their original quarries (Gibson 1983; Amit et al. 2000; 2001; Hachlili 1997). Investment in surface and symmetry vary, yet fine workmanship is ordinary. Ossuaries were either plain or decorated with architectural elements, geometric forms, and floral motifs incised or painted over the walls or the lid.

The names of the deceased were occasionally chiseled or painted over the surfaces or lids. Calligraphy tends to be rudimentary. Writers used Hebrew, Aramaic, Greek, and rarely Latin.

Figure 34 Scene inside a Jewish burial cave in Jerusalem: Ossuary decorated with rosettes in sepulchral niche (courtesy of G. Avni / Israel Antiquities Authority).

Significantly, ossuaries carrying the names of dignitaries, such as Nicanor (Avigad 1967a), Simon "the Temple Builder" (Tzaferis 1969), and Caiaphas (Greenhut 1992: Reich 1992; Zias 1992), retain the characteristic austerity.[17] If those indeed belonged to the more affluent residents of Jerusalem, we are reminded of the rabbinical warning against wasteful funerary investment (*Semahot* 9.23).[18] Other members of the Jewish elite waived humility and prepared sumptuous rock-cut tombs in Jerusalem. These tombs featured elaborate façades and imposing memorial monuments, housing full-sized stone sarcophagi within their chambers (Avigad 1950–51; Avi-Yonah 1981: 133; Barag 2003).[19] As is the case with ossuaries, and contrary to high-class Helleno-Roman tradition, floral and geometric shapes were preferred over human and animal representations in both cave façades and sarcophagi (Kloner and Zissu 2003b: 16–22; Kloner 1994: and compare with Burckhardt 1998: 342–43; Veyne 1987: 8, 18, 164–65, 184).[20]

It has been proposed that the floral decorative motifs represent beliefs in the afterlife (Goodenough 1953: 110–39; Figueras 1983: 86–87), but the frequency of identical motifs in non-funerary architectural and artifactual Jewish contexts implies either a wider symbolic reasoning or simply fashionable preferences. Be the case what it may, almost without exception both architectural and artifactual decorative traditions among the first-century-BCE–first-century-CE Jewish population of Judea maintain the strictest interpretative guidelines of the Second Commandment.

Utilitarian Domestic Objects

Referring to attempts to distinguish ethnic identities in archaeological scenes, Siân Jones (1997: 128–29) calls for caution:

> There is rarely a one-to-one relationship between representations of ethnicity and the entire range of cultural practices and social conditions associated with a particular ethnic group. On the contrary, the resulting pattern will be one of overlapping ethnic boundaries produced by context-specific representations of cultural difference, which are at once transient, but also subject to reproduction and transformation in the ongoing process of social life.

Still, intentional projection of ethnic identities onto material objects in mixed or neighboring societies has been recorded (Stevenson 1989). Especially where circumstantial corroboration through historical sources is feasible, as in first-century Judea, we might be able to identify ethnic differences as well as ideological currents in the types, shapes, and materials of various vessels.

Using both textual and archaeological data, several studies ascertained and delineated the geographical boundaries that divided between predominantly Jewish and Gentile regions of Judea in that period, such as Galilee (Frankel and Finkelstein 1983; Frankel et al. 2001; Aviam 2004). Excavations at sites on both sides of those boundaries show that while first-century Jewish and Helleno-Roman populations lived in close proximity and depended on similar means of subsistence, their choices of clay vessels and metal objects for daily use differed to a degree that defies any option of coincidence. The mutual hostility between these neighboring but ideologically polarized communities from which would have derived a desire for complete cultural severance, offers a sensible explanation to such distinctions, which cannot be explained by either economic or other practical considerations.

Storage and Serving Receptacles

Ethnically based distinctions in ceramic containers between Jews and Gentiles existed already in the Hellenistic period. Jews refrained from using the Greek storage jars in which wine was imported, a type commonly found in non-Jewish Hellenistic contexts (Finkielsztejn 1998: 39). Jews seem to also have shunned Galilean Coarse Ware (GCW) vessels (Aviam 2004: 46). This group, which

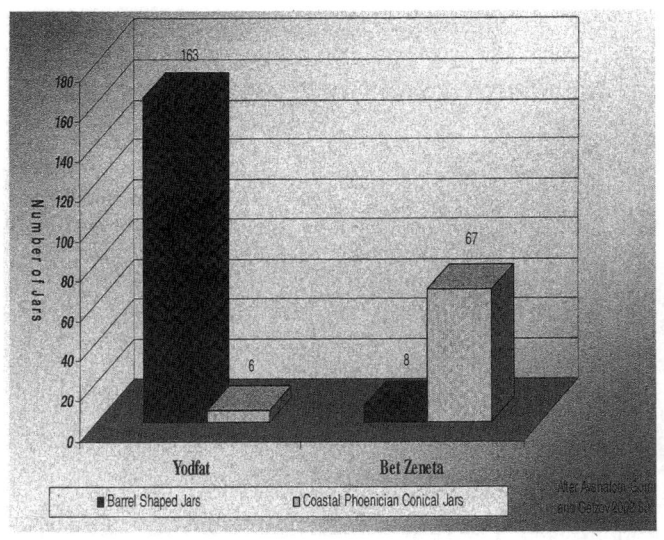

Figure 35 Percentages of coastal Phoenician conical jars and barrel-shaped jars at Yodfat and Bet Zeneta in the early Roman period.

Figure 36 Barrel-shaped jar from Jaffa (photograph: G. Pierce, University of California, Los Angeles).

also consists mostly of storage jars, abounds in strata containing Hellenistic coins and ritual figurines. GCW vessels disappear from the archeological record after the Hasmonean takeover. This development is indicated by an influx of Hasmonean coins in layers superimposing scenes of violent destruction. Mordechai Aviam (2004: 48) concludes that "the GCW could be an identifying feature of pagan residences," clearly distinct from the Jewish habitation in the Galilee.

Recent examinations prove that preferences of specific types of vessels along ethnic lines continued during the Early Roman period (Berlin 2002; Avshalom-Gorni and Getzov 2002). The process of distinction was gradual. During the first century BCE, several types of cooking, serving, storage, and other utility vessels were used across ethnic lines throughout the region. Variation crystallizes in the following century, in correlation with the growing animosity between Jewish and non-Jewish communities.

Let us stay with storage jars. The Galilean Jewish town of Yodfat and the Helleno-Roman settlement of Bet Zeneta stood only a few kilometers apart but display different ceramic traditions. Residents of Bet Zeneta used mostly conical storage vessels affiliated with the Phoenician coast, while Yodfat's barrel-shaped jars are generally associated with Jewish industry centers (Avshalom-Gorni and Getzov 2002: 78). Barrel-shaped jars are also common in other widely excavated northern Jewish sites, such as Gamla (Berlin 2006: 18–19, 48), and in Jewish assemblages elsewhere in the land.

Red-slipped Eastern Terra Sigillata pottery offers another example of this ideological tendency to material distinction. During the first century BCE, the handsome Eastern Terra Sigillata serving vessels were popular among Jews and non-Jews alike. However, in sites from the following century where historical sources and other material evidence, such as ritual baths and soft limestone vessels (see below), confirm predominantly Jewish populations, Eastern Terra Sigillata types are substituted by plain and strictly utilitarian wares (Berlin 2002: 59–61; 2006: 14).[21] Production and frequency of Eastern Terra Sigillata vessels in contemporaneous strata in Gentile and mixed settlements remains undisturbed.

Figure 37 Eastern Terra Sigillata jug from Jaffa (photograph: G. Pierce, University of California, Los Angeles).

Figure 38 Knife-pared oil lamps from Jaffa (photograph: G. Pierce, University of California, Los Angeles).

It should be noted that the apparent Jewish ban on vessels of non-Jewish origins was not limited to the Galilee. Zissu and Ganor (2002: 21) report thousands of ceramic shards at the early Roman Jewish site of Horvat 'Ethri in western Judea, with not a single imported ware among them. As explanation, they propose either purity considerations or rural modesty. Yet rural modesty did not prevent Jewish villagers of the Roman and Byzantine periods from erecting stylishly invested synagogues in their settlements, and prestigious objects are occasionally found even in modest countryside dwellings. The ideological reasoning, therefore, seems more realistic.

Oil Lamps

The high frequency and the rapidly changing forms and decoration styles of oil lamps offer invaluable inputs on chronology, artistic fashions, cultural understandings, and, in some cases, ideological beliefs in antiquity. Lamps were commonly adorned, owing to the moderate investment required in the preparation of the minute clay molds and probably also to their symbolic meaning as the carriers of light.[22] A wide range of human and animal motifs, both ritual and secular, graced first-century lamps throughout the Roman Empire. The knife-pared lamps that circulated among the Jews of Judea during that period were a striking exception to the popular custom, being either plain or carrying only simple geometric incisions.[23] Once again, we face a symbolic material expression of intensifying Jewish ideological self-seclusion.

Knife-pared lamps, which derive their name from their splayed nozzles, were produced between the end of the first century BCE and the first part of the second century CE, reaching their peak distribution during the last decades prior to the First Revolt (Smith 1966; Hershkovitz 1987b; 1992; Barag and Hershkovitz 1994: 43–58).[24] Hardly any other types are met in first-century Jewish contexts.[25] The typological pattern of lamps in the Galilee resembles that of the other ceramic forms mentioned above. Mold-made lamps, previously used by all, practically disappear during the first century CE from Jewish sites such as Yodfat, Gamla, Capernaum, and Bethsaida, being replaced by knife-pared variations (Berlin 2002: 60–61). The distinction is most acute at Gamla, owing to changes in the habitation zones within the city between the first century BCE and the first century CE. While molded lamps dominate first-century BCE assemblages, knife-pared lamps comprise ninety-nine percent of the lamp record in the parts of the city inhabited during the first century CE (Syon and Yavor 2001: 23). It should be noted that a small number of knife-pared lamps has also been found in Helleno-Roman urban centers.[26] Still, the general statistical disparity in lamp types between Jewish and Gentile or mixed settlements is too accentuated to be upset by these random artifacts. Interestingly, nearly forty knife-pared lamps were discovered in Samaria (Crowfoot 1957: 368). It would be plausible to assume that the Samaritans would have favored this type of lamp for the same religion-based reasons as the Jews. Variations of this reasoning would eventually entice many among both peoples to rise against the occupation power whose symbolic expressions were so diametrically opposed to their own.

Jerusalemite Painted Pottery

An unusual group of vessels was discovered in Jerusalem, Jericho, and sites in the Judean desert within strata dating from the late first century BCE to the destruction of the Temple (Amiran and Eitan 1973: pl. 43; Avigad 1983: 117–18; Hayes 1985: fig. 20:36; Bar-Nathan 1981: 62–63; De Vaux 1959: 241; Hershkovitz 2003a: 34). The group, known as Jerusalemite Painted Pottery, includes bowls, jugs, juglets, and kraters. Artists used brown, reddish-brown, and black paint to depict botanical motifs such as flower petals, wreaths, and rosettes. The style is believed to be of Nabatean origin, though the later vessels were manufactured in Jerusalem, including a specimen found at Nabatean Oboda (Perlman et al. 1986: 78, 81–82). The distribution of the vessels correlates with the general Jewish habitation zones of the period. As noted by Hershkovitz (2003a: 33), the themes painted on those vessels and the strict avoidance of human and animal representations abide to the rules of first-century Jewish art.

Metals

Following Matthew Ponting (2000; 2002a, b), the analysis of metal artifacts from Jewish and non-Jewish first-century sites in Judea indicates ideological preferences for particular metals and metal objects. Brass (an alloy of zinc and copper) was widely used by the Roman army during the first century CE (Ponting and Segal 1998). Roman occupation forces were responsible for the introduction of brass metalworking to the Western European and British provinces (Bayley 1990: 7; Dungworth 1997). Brass is also found in Roman military contexts in Judea; yet, unlike civilian environments elsewhere in the empire, this metal is entirely missing from Jewish metal assemblages. No traces were found in secure Jewish contexts at Masada, Gamla, Yodfat, and Ramat Hanadiv (Ponting and Segal 1998; Ponting 2000; 2002a: 561; 2002b: 4). This absence cannot be explained merely by lack of skill on the part of Jewish smiths; had they been interested in brass but unfamiliar with the technology, they could have recycled Roman objects. The fact that zinc is virtually missing from Jewish copper assemblages indicates that Jews intentionally avoided brass, with effort invested in the procurement of zinc-free copper alloys.

Bronze artifacts from Jewish and non-Jewish sites show significant differences in the percentage of lead being used. The addition of lead reached levels of twenty percent or more in late Hellenistic and Roman bronzes. Yet, while a significant lead content is present in the metals from the Helleno-Roman site of Tel Anafa, objects from Gamla and Yodfat show considerably lower lead inclusion (Ponting 2002b: 4). Distinctions are also evident in certain metal objects. Elbow fibulae were in common use in the Early Roman period in both civilian and military dress, yet fail to appear in hundreds of Jewish burial contexts. Although bronze fibulae have been found in both Masada and Gamla, these contain negligible amounts of cobalt and arsenic. On the other hand, a relatively high concentration of both elements was noted in bronze pins and cosmetic tools, clearly civilian artifacts affiliated with the Jewish civilian population (Ponting 2002b: 4–5). This clear

Table 10.1 Metal distinctions in Jewish and Gentile sites in first-century Judea (after Ponting 2002a, b).

	Brass	Lead addition	Cobalt, arsenic
Jewish contexts	Absent	Low	High
Helleno-Roman Contexts	Frequent	High	Insignificant

distinction suggests separate metalworking traditions. It would therefore not be far-fetched to attribute the fibulae found at Gamla and Masada to the many Roman soldiers known to have fallen in the battle for the former and to those reported to have been stationed at the latter following its conquest (Ponting 2002a: 561; and see *War* 4.25–29, 36, 7.407).

Sometimes the simplest explanation is the one most correct. The concept of fashion is hardly a modern innovation. Predatory capitalism and mass communication may well have sped periodical style changes in myriad cultural products to an irrational pace, but fashions have been altering for thousands of years. Still, changing fashions and tastes, devoid of ideological reasoning, cannot be responsible for the discrepancies in regular ceramics and metals between Jews and non-Jews in first-century Judea. The rustic inhabitants of the Jewish countryside can hardly be credited with an eagerness for dynamic style changes that surpassed that of the far more cosmopolitan people of the vibrant Helleno-Roman urban centers. Yet, the changes are evident in the assemblages of the former, while the latter remain loyal to extant traditions. Furthermore, changes in styles seem to crystallize precisely at the period of escalating tensions between the two populations.

Berlin (2006: 151) sees the abrupt disappearance of Phoenician imports from first-century-CE Jewish assemblages at Gamla as part of a shift to more austere dining customs that distinguished the Jews from their Helleno-Roman and Phoenician neighbors. She further suggests that the ban increased the antagonism of the shunned neighbors towards the Jews, substantiating the vicious cycle of growing mutual hostility. Dina Avshalom-Gorni and Nimrod Getzov (2002: 81), who suggest ritual purity as the original reason behind Jewish vessel choices, also identify a broader ideological-political perspective with a strong link to the First Revolt:

> In the first century AD, the Jewish population seems to have developed a growing adherence to religious dictates and commandments, which in turn caused them to become more insular and closed in…. This separatist spirit is part of the background to, and perhaps for, the Jewish rebellion.

There can be many non-ideological reasons for people's choice of materials and objects in daily use. However, within the wider historical context of first-century Judea, religious ideology becomes the most viable explanation for the multiple distinctions in both ceramic and metal assemblages. Through their preference of local material traditions, the Jews of Judea were making, in the words of Berlin (2002:69), "a political statement of solidarity and affiliation with a traditional, simple, unadorned, Jewish lifestyle."[27] The dismissal of Romanization implied a rejection of the occupation.

Soft Limestone Vessels

Several rabbinical passages refer to stone vessels being ritually utilized by the Jews in Second Temple days. The New Testament also mentions "six stone water jars, the kind used by the Jews for ceremonial washing" at the wedding in Kana (John 2:6). The importance of these vessels lay in the apparently strong religious view that stone containers were less susceptible to impurity than their ceramic equivalents.[28] Indeed, hand-made or lathe-turned soft limestone mugs, bowls, cups, lids,

UNEARTHING RELIGIOUS INTENSITY

stoppers, trays, kraters, and platters, as well as jars and even inkwells are commonly found in domestic contexts of first-century Jewish sites.

Production of soft limestone vessels began in the second half of the first century BCE and peaked during the century that followed. The vessels are particularly common in strata from the last decades prior to the First Revolt and in corresponding destruction layers (Cahill 1992; Magen 2002; Kloner 2003: 35; Gibson 2003: 302; Berlin 2006: 19). At least some workshops, which also produced ossuaries made of the same type of stone, were located in the quarries where the raw material was extracted. Several such quarries were discovered in Jerusalem and the Galilee.[29] Yitzhak Magen (2002) lists 84 sites in Israel and three additional sites in Jordan where soft limestone vessels were found. Many more were discovered during recent excavations at rural sites on the inner coastal plain in the Lod (ancient Lydda) area (Yekutieli et al. 2001: 35–39; Zissu 2001: 238; Torgë 2002: 46; Zissu and Ganor 2002: 21; Haddad, personal communication). Their frequency generally correlates with Jewish habitation regions in first-century Judea. Fragments of considerably fewer vessels were found in Helleno-Roman cities, where they may have belonged to Jewish residents or, as with the knife-pared lamps, were used by non-Jews to whom the peculiar objects might have appealed regardless of their religious connotation (Magen 2002: 162; Gibson 2003: 300).

Figure 39 Soft limestone vessel from Jaffa (photograph: G. Pierce, University of California, Los Angeles).

These relatively fragile vessels were probably more expensive than their ceramic equivalents, but as they appear across different socio-economic settings in first-century Jewish contexts (Gibson 2003: 302), their religious role evidently overruled cost and value considerations. Their commonness not only signifies the rigidity of Jewish religious devotion during this period but also the gradual intensification of faith that led to the violent conflict with Rome. Such vessels are still found in underground hiding systems dated to the early-second-century-CE Bar Kochba Revolt, but they disappear from the archaeological record later during the same century (Kloner and Tepper 1987: 355; Magen 2002: 162; Kloner 2003: 35; Gibson 2003: 302). The death or captivity of craftsmen during the two revolts and the loss of the Jerusalem quarries and workshops were probably the immediate reasons for cessation of production. Their failure to reappear later, as tensions with Rome subsided, is explained by the profound and long-term effects of both catastrophes on Jewish religious thought and ritual practice.

Domestic Decoration

Fashionable Roman-style painted panels (*fresco*), molded plaster (*stucco*), and mosaic floors were popular in first-century Judea with the Jewish elites who could afford the luxury (Yadin 1966: 42–52, 119–29; Beebe 1975: 99–100; Foerster 1976: 976, 985; 1995; Avigad 1983: 99, 102–4, 113–15; Ben-Dov and Rappel 1987: 36; Netzer 1975; 1981; Rozenberg 1981: 71–74; 2003; Gutman 1994: 126, 128; Tsafrir and Magen 1984: 30–32). Yet, contrary to the residences of upper-class Gentiles throughout the empire, where lavish imagery art was standard (Beebe 1975: 99–100; Veyne 1987: 6, 32, 38, 70, 152, 203; MacDonald 1982), human and animal images are almost completely absent

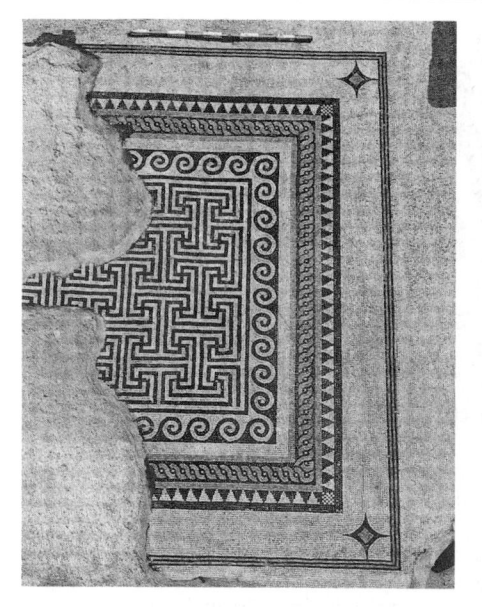

Figure 40 Geometric mosaic floor from an aristocratic residence in Jerusalem (Source: Avigad 1983).

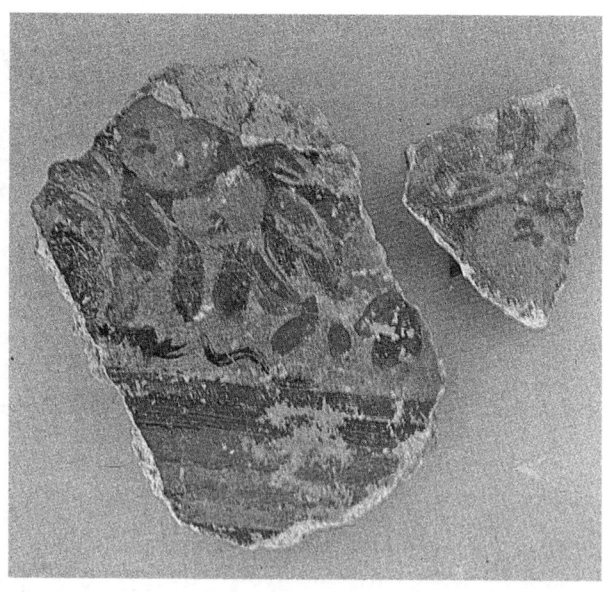

Figure 41 Fresco fragment depicting a pomegranate branch from an aristocratic residence in Jerusalem (Source: Avigad 1983).

from mansions of the Jewish aristocracy, in compliance with the religious ban on figurative representations. With rare exceptions, painted, molded, and arranged decoration in luxurious residences of Jerusalem's Upper City, home of the wealthiest and most cosmopolitan members of the Jewish society of the period, was restricted to botanical and geometric motifs. Existing evidence indicates that the same principle was rigorously followed in the periphery. No imagery art appears on the remains of fresco panels discovered in Gamla's wealthier homes (Gutman 1994: 128, 146; Syon and Yavor 2001: 14), and none is reported from other sites in the Galilee. The owners of the mansions in both the capital and the periphery probably owed at least part of their wealth to short- and long-distance trade, but their exposure to foreign arts and cultures did not entail the adoption of aspects that violated Jewish religious taboos.

The few existing examples of figurative art in Jewish residences only serve to emphasize the otherwise broad avoidance of such adornment. Notably, even King Herod, a staunch supporter of Rome and avid sponsor of Helleno-Roman art and architecture, displayed no human and animal images in his palaces (Rozenberg 2000; Foerster 1995), with the only known exception of a small sculpted head, possibly of the god Silenus, on a fragment of an imported marble washing basin found at Herodium (Netzer 2001: 114–15). Josephus tells of forbidden painted images in the palace of Herod's son Antipas in Tiberias, which were so resented by the local Jewish masses that one of the first actions of the Galilean rebels was to burn this building to the ground (*Life* 65–66). Rare fresco fragments depicting antelopes, rabbits, boars, and birds were found in Jerusalem among an abundance of strictly geometric and floral examples (Broshi 1972: 106, pl.7; Foerster 1976: 98; Ben-Dov 1982: 150–51; Rozenberg 2003). This alleged violation of the strict code of the period apparently derives from the tendency to allow people certain harmless indulgences within their private domains. Nevertheless, three-dimensional sculptures, which were commonplace in the homes of the non-Jewish upper class of that time but explicit anathema to the Second Commandment, are completely absent from the archaeological record of Jewish mansions, with very rare exceptions of animal figures fitted into parts of ornate furniture.[30]

Goodman (1987: 15–16) attributes the extraordinary examples of first-century Jewish imagery art to the variety of Jewish religious attitudes prevailing during Second Temple times, a variety that tends to be overlooked by scholars. Relating to the foreign literary sources on the period, which stress the "exotic" Jewish taboo (see previous chapter), he wonders whether the Romans, intrigued or annoyed by such barbarian eccentricities, took it more seriously than many of the Jews themselves. Yet, the remarkable irregularity of the phenomenon and the fact that figurative images can be clearly isolated in the artistic contexts of first-century Judea marks them as exceptions that merely highlight the pattern of strict rigidity in ritual interpretations which were far more characteristic of contemporaneous Jewish society, dominating both the public and private spheres.

Ritual Baths

Ritual baths are among the most reliable ethnic markers of Jewish presence at sites from the classical and Byzantine periods in Israel. These baths first appear in strata associated with the Hasmonean conquests of the late second to early first centuries BCE (Reich 1981).[31] By the late first century BCE and the first century CE, ritual baths had become a standard element of Jewish architecture.[32] The degree to which they are identified with Jewish habitation during this period is illustrated at the Galilean fort of Qeren Naftali. Josephus reports that the site had been conquered from Hasmonean supporters by King Herod's Roman legionaries and foreign mercenaries in 38 BCE (*War* 1.314–16). A ritual bath found there contained refuse that included pig bones, as well as oil lamps decorated with human and animal figures (Aviam 2004: 70–72). These objects clearly associate the filling-in phase with the guard units posted at the site after its conquest (*War* 1.329). Thus, at Qeren Naftali, ritual baths prove Jewish occupation, and their dereliction attests to its cessation.

Ritual bodily purification has its origins in biblical law (Leviticus 22:1–8). By the late Second Temple period, the original designations of impurity had been expanded through interpretation, and strict regulations had been designated for the process of cleansing (Wright 1997; Neusner 1994). The details should not concern us beyond a general outline. Certain diseases, sexual relations, contact with cadavers, carcasses, excrement, and unclean animals, as well as menstruation and childbirth were all believed to incur impurity. As exposure could not be avoided in the normal course of life, impurity itself was not regarded sinful (Magness 2002: 135), but any engagement in ritual service before appropriate cleansing, in particular at the Temple, was considered a serious religious offense. Therefore, in addition to the ritual baths that were installed in the private domain, public baths were built by the entrance of synagogues (Gutman 1985: 57–58), on pilgrim routes,[33] near cemeteries[34] (Zissu 2001: 235–36; Kloner and Zissu 2003b: 16; Kloner 2003: 32), and within industrial oil presses to serve workers as well as to purify tools and vessels involved in the production process (Kloner and Tepper 1987: 116; Gutman 1994: 130–33; Zissu 2001: 115; Aviam and Amitai 2002; Gershuny 2006: 167–68).

Figure 42 Entrance to a ritual bath at the Jewish rural site of Ben Shemen (courtesy of Y. Zelinger, Israel Antiquities Authority).

The distinct architectural plan of baths, dictated by specific religious principles, facilitates their archaeological recognition.[35] A ritual bath (*miqveh*) was to be hewn into the bedrock or dug into the soil (rather than built) in designated measures, and its inner frames had to be plastered over. Steps, of which the lowest was usually wider, were fitted inside. Rainwater was to flow in through natural gravity, though to meet the semi-arid climate of Judea, a clause allowed importation of water pending on its merging with some rainwater kept for that purpose in special containers (*otsar*). In some baths there were partitions that allowed cleansed persons to depart while avoiding accidental contamination through physical contact with incomers. People could also ritually cleanse themselves in natural bodies of flowing water, such as the sea, rivers, and springs (Wright 1997: 213).

Still, as Reich (1990) sensibly points out, it would be difficult to explain in other than ritual terms the hundreds of small plastered pools in the archaeological record of sites known to have been populated by Jews, and whose unusual plan corresponds to the strict rabbinical regulations that remained in effect for centuries.

Benjamin Wright (1997: 213) remarks that "despite the diversities that are evident in Second Temple Judaism, the fact that different Jews in different places all agreed…that immersion of one's body was the efficient means of removing impurity shows a somewhat surprising degree of unanimity." Indeed, similarly to other religious customs, ritual bathing was practiced by Jews regardless of social status or ideological faction, as it continued to be through later generations up to present-day Orthodox communities. Yet, as already mentioned, in the Early Roman period ritual baths make their first extensive appearance, providing yet another example from that time and place of the sacred realm reaching from the Temple compound into the profane realm of daily life. The very bodies of first-century Judean Jews, as well as the production of their basic foodstuffs, were kept under stern religious regulation, as practically every other aspect of their lives was. As an individual phenomenon, ritual baths may admittedly indicate religious faith, not necessarily religious intensification. Yet, the surge in their occurrence during the first centuries BCE and CE and the variety of social contexts in which they appear correlates with the image of unusually rigorous religious observance in the Jewish society of that time, as reflected by a broad assortment of other material data.

Personal Names

People's names carried considerable meaning in Jewish tradition since biblical antiquity. Already Adam, we are told, was symbolically named by God Himself, and he in turn chose symbolic names for his wife and sons (Genesis 3:20; 4:1, 25). All three patriarchs bore names deriving of their direct relationship with God or emblematically related to the peculiar circumstances of their birth (Genesis 17:5; 21:4, 6; 25:26). Jacob's second name, Israel, was also symbolically designated by God, and became the name of the nation Jacob would father (32:28). The names of the founders of the twelve tribes of Israel reflect their symbolically consequential circumstances of birth, as well as the future of their descendants (Genesis 29:32–35; 30:6–13, 18–20, 23–24; 35:18; 49:3–27). Towering figures like Moses and Samuel were named after events that related to the divine sponsorship they had enjoyed since infancy (Exodus 2:10; Samuel I, 1:20). Name symbolism was used by later prophets to substantiate and even personify their divinely inspired religious and moral messages (Isaiah 7:14; Hosea 1:4, 6). Thus, in the Hebrew language – ancient and modern – the word "name" (*shem*) also means "reputation."[36]

A form of this primordial tradition was still observed during the Early Roman period. Hence the symbolic change of the name of Simon, Jesus' chief disciple, to Peter (Matthew 16:17–18) and the more obscure renaming of James and John (Mark 3:17).

The symbolism in the name of Jesus himself is probably no coincidence; its original version, "Yeshua," stems from the same Hebrew root as the word "salvation." Jewish yearning for deliverance from occupation during that time and the hope to revive old glory receives additional circumstantial evidence from the results of separate statistical studies by Rachel Hachlili (1983) and Tal Ilan (1987; 1989). Both researchers worked with a corpus of Jewish names from the classical and Byzantine periods assembled from the Old and New Testament, the apocrypha, rabbinical literature, ancient histories, as well as archaeological sources, such as tombs, ossuaries, coins, letters, documents, ostraca, inscriptions, and graffiti. Hachlili and Ilan detect a disproportionate preference of Hasmonean names among Jews during the first century BCE to first century CE.

Sixty-three percent of male names in Hachlili's survey (1983: 189) match those of the first Hasmoneans (Mattathias, Simon, Jonathan, Judas, John, Eleazar) in their original forms or close variations. No less than eighty-six percent of women answered to the Hebrew names Miriam and Salome (Shlomzion) or to associated forms. These, by no coincidence, were the names of two famed Hasmonean queens.[37] Ilan (1987: 238) reached a lower but still substantial percentage of male Hasmonean names in the general population. Out of the 1,986 Jewish males in her sample, 612 (over 30 %) carried the name of one of the original Hasmoneans (1987: 240).[38] Of the 247 female names, no less than 119 (48 %) were variations of Miriam and Salome (Ilan 1989: 191–92). The proportions become even more impressive considering that only 145 of the total sample of names are Hebrew.

These figures cannot simply be credited to chance. The popularity of the independent Jewish dynasty that met its demise in the hands of Herod and the Romans obviously enjoyed a renaissance in late Second Temple days. Hachlili (1979; 1983: 192) proposes the customs of paponymy (naming after the grandfather) and patronymy (naming after the father), both common in Judea at that time, as at least partly responsible for the disproportionate rate of Hasmonean names. Farmer (1958: VIII) proposes a more ideological connotation but believes that it was limited to the active rebel factions. As evidence, he points out the high proportion of Hasmonean names among the rebels and their rarity amid collaborators with the Romans. Relying on evidence from burials, Ilan (1987: 239) counters the ancestral naming explanation by showing that in many cases sons were given Hasmonean names that were previously absent in their families; she also challenges Farmer's proposal by emphasizing the intricacies in the classification of rebels vs. collaborators, as exemplified in the case of Josephus. Ilan's conclusion (1987: 240; 1989: 199), as that of Williams (1995: 109), is that identification with the Hasmoneans could be found throughout Jewish society during the early Roman period. The constant conflicts with the Romans and the hostile Gentile population may have blurred the Hasmoneans' shortcomings in popular memory, turning the dynasty into a source of yearning and inspiration (Goodman 1987: 121). First-century Jewish children would receive their names as a form of ideological enculturation, a potent symbolic expression of the hope that liberty and dignity would be restored and of the determination to act towards that goal.

This hypothesis cannot be proven unequivocally, but it addresses the realities of the time. It should also be noted that in the later centuries of Roman occupation, when Jewish rebellious tendencies had long faded, the proportional rate of Hasmonean names decreased considerably. Following Hachlili (1983: 194), the frequency of Hasmonean names stands at around thirty-five percent of the male population from the late second to the forth centuries CE. This is still a substantial quantity, even compared with her previous figures, but the marked decrease cannot be ignored. In this more stable period, unlike during the tumultuous first century, paponymy and patronymy are more likely to explain the statistics. The change is also apparent in females (Hachlili 1983: 191). Out of the six female names from the third and forth centuries CE that appear repeatedly in the Jewish cemetery of Beth She'arim, Miriam is still the second most popular, yet family circulation must again be considered, as well as the fact that this was also the name of the revered biblical sister of Moses. Had the militant ideological factor still been dominant, one would expect a similar occurrence of the Hasmonean name Salome. This name, however, is altogether missing.

Finally, both researchers note the high rate in the appearance of the name Joshua, which has no known Hasmonean associations, among first-century Jewish males. Joshua comprises nine percent of Hachlili's Second Temple sample (1983:189) and three and a half percent of Ilan's (1987: 238). This name may have drawn its attraction from a similar source as the Hasmoneans.' Biblical Joshua Bin Nun led Israel's forces in their conquest of the Promised Land, overcoming the far better trained and equipped Canaanite coalitions. In addition to his strategic skill, Joshua also enjoyed divine assistance, which occasionally materialized in the form of miracles on Israel's behalf (Joshua 6:20; 10:11; 11:6). Like the Hasmoneans, Joshua would have symbolized the combination of prowess and piety that had led to victories against stronger foes in the past and could some day achieve the same against the Romans.

A Third Level of Archaeological Investigation of Religion

An archaeological analysis of religious intensification should involve three levels of interpretation. First, the religious identity of artifacts or structures must be ascertained. Second, conjectures should be made about their symbolic meanings. The final level demands comparative analysis between cultural scenes during the period under investigation and other periods and circumstances in the history of the relevant society. Patterns that suggest irregular focus on religion, such as a marked increase in the quantity and diversity of ritual artifacts and buildings, should be isolated. Such combined study of material evidence and textual sources might allow the formation of strong models, constructed of interpretations that are both imaginative and dependable.

When contextualized within the specific circumstances of each place and time, the same principles may be applied cross-culturally and cross-temporally. Caution and scrutiny must be employed in the use of archaeological evidence for this interdisciplinary design, as there will always be several ways in which the silent testimony may be understood. If material proof seems to contradict vital details provided in original texts, the possibility of the misinterpretation of finds must be explored, as well as the option of textual bias and misinformation. Where no written records exist, archaeological ideas and observations must be thoroughly examined before they are used as foundations for theoretical models.

The introduction to this chapter offers several guidelines for the archaeological detection of the process of ideological intensification in antiquity. These guidelines could all be tested against archaeological evidence from Jewish Judea during the first century CE. The religious severity characteristic of this society impacted on nearly every aspect of the daily lives of its members, setting it apart not only from contemporaneous Diaspora Jewry but also from earlier and later Jewish societies in antiquity. During the late first century BCE and the first century CE, figurative art becomes nearly obsolete in Jewish contexts, ritual baths are found in virtually every Jewish settlement, extra-pure soft limestone containers are commonplace, and unwritten ethno-religious rules dictate even the shapes and materials of ceramic receptacles and metal tools used daily.[39] Strong political-religious connotations are insinuated in the disproportionate percentage of Hasmonean personal names. When the Jews eventually rose against Rome, they chose indisputably religious themes to be depicted and stated on their currency. Another related issue not yet mentioned here concerns the institution of the Jewish synagogue. While the origins of the synagogue remain under debate, one of its principal functions was the public reading of the scriptures.[40] Following Goodblatt (2006: 40), "only regular reading of the Bible…could fill the role of a mass medium needed to disseminate a socially constructed national identity among the people. And our sources do not clearly attest such a practice before the first century." Indeed, the earliest confirmed buildings of public Jewish worship other than the Temple were built in the very late parts of the first century BCE and during the century that followed.[41]

The analysis of the evidence from first-century Judea demonstrates the unprecedented dominance of religion among the Jewish society on the eve of the First Revolt. While Romanization could not be wholly avoided, first-century Judaism employed the most effective ideological coun-

Table 10.2 Material reflection of ideological separatism: Imagery representations.

	On coins	On architecture	In funerary contexts	On oil lamps
Jews (late 1st cent. BCE–early 2nd cent. CE)	None	Extremely rare	Extremely rare	None
Jews (3rd–early 1st cent. BCE)	Rare (3rd cent. only)	Rare	Extremely rare	None
Jews (late 2nd–7th cent. CE)	NA	Mainly on mosaics	Occasional	None
Helleno-Romans	Common	Common	Common	Common

Table 10.3 Material reflection of ideological separatism: Artifacts and structures.

	Soft Limestone Vessels	Ceramics	Metals	Ritual Baths	Synagogues
Jews (1st cent. BCE –early 2nd cent. CE)	Widespread	Distinction from Helleno-Romans	Some distinction from Helleno-Romans	Common	First appearance
Jews (3rd–early 1st cent. BCE)	Only 1st cent.	Some distinction from Helleno-Romans	No known distinction	In sites from the 2nd and 1st cent. BCE	None (one possibly in Jericho)
Jews (late 2nd–7th cent. CE)	Only 2nd cent.	Little or no distinction	No known distinction	Common	Common
Helleno-Romans	N/A	Some distinction from Jews	Some distinction from Jews	N/A	N/A

termeasures to be found anywhere in the empire. Judean Judaism was thus destined to become the most formidable adversary of Helleno-Roman influence. Multitudes of passionate adherents of the former became determined to challenge the latter, limit its spread in their land, and oppose – even by force of arms – the Roman administration that endorsed it.

Raising swords against so superior a foe would have been an irresponsible folly, unless God Himself could be counted upon for help. Many Jews seem to have had full confidence that such help was forthcoming. In first-century Judea there was constant alertness to God's most minute demands from both the individual and the community. Such high commitment to God's commandments would have created a sense of intimacy with divinity. If so, this was as dangerous a conviction as the Tower of Babel had been an ambition, because both questioned God's foremost attribute: His fundamental inaccessibility to the human mind. Many first-century Jews may have come to believe that they had deciphered the means to anticipate divine logic and thus ensure the nature of divine action. In essence, they had ventured to make a deal with God, perceiving Him as a kind of Jewish Caesar, whose ultimate protection and support could be expected in return for the ultimate devotion of his subjects/disciples.

Such perceptions help explain the decision of the Jews to fight Rome and their determination and resilience while doing so. But these were the forces and this was the army that in the past had humbled the brave and pious ancestors of the Jewish rebels and overcome the sturdy and tested armies of their proud Hasmonean kings. These were also the centurions and legionnaires who had defeated foreign peoples more powerful than the Jews, whose own desperate struggles to keep Rome out of their borders had fared no better. Social, economic, political, and ethnic tensions supplied much of the emotion and some of the motivation for the First Revolt, but religion built the determination, provided the hope, set the priorities, and triggered the action. Strict monotheistic religious faith, which had been evolving in Judea through the centuries since the return of the Jews from the Babylonian exile, ripened into an ideological framework incapable of sustaining foreign occupation by an alien, pagan culture. War with Rome was as inevitable as its odds of success were bleak.

Yet, despite the crushing defeats and horrendous repercussions, a broader historical scope suggests that the futile uprisings were essential for the long-term survival of Judaism as a religion, culture, and ethnic definer. In the aftermath of the disasters, it underwent meaningful reforms, gaining the ideological elasticity necessary in order to prevail under the changing conditions. This is the paradox of religious intensity: while potentially an engineer of crisis, suffering, and destruction, the devastation that it generates may free an ideological terrain previously cluttered with derelict principles that have outlived their historical relevance. All archaeologists encounter the phenomenon of secondary utilization of fallen building stones in the construction new houses. Likewise, in time, the debris of fallen ideologies can provide the essential materials for the construction of a new social condition that allows adaptation, recuperation, and a more viable future.

11 Conclusions – Between Rome and Jericho

> Yet, O Lord God of Truth, is any man pleasing to thee because he knows these things? No, for surely that man is unhappy who knows these things and does not know thee. And that man is happy, who knows thee even though he does not know these things. He who knows both thee and these things is not the more blessed for his learning, for thou only art his blessing.
>
> St Augustine, *Confessions* 5.IV.7[1]

The "things" the highly-educated St Augustine refers to are the non-theological fields of knowledge he had studied for years, but which seemed of no use to him after his conversion to Christianity. The knowledge of divinity was now sufficient, and Augustine fully endorsed his mentor St. Ambrose's ironclad rule: "the letter kills but the spirit gives life." This is the sum of religious intensity: a complete and total switch of both mind and action to a single spiritual direction – the ultimate, unrelenting devotion.

Religious intensity takes to extreme a concept that from a practical perspective is useless and often detrimental to basic human needs, even in its moderate and less compromising forms. Worship and prayer demand time that could be invested in production, rest, or recreation. Sacrifices and alms extract funds with no material compensation to the provider. Taboos eliminate dietary, sexual, and behavioral options. Yet, religious people would see it differently. To them, faith and its rituals are in fact most cost efficient, because there can be no success in any walk of life – personal, professional, financial, or psychological – without the consent and the blessing of divinity. Moreover, religion protects society; like political states, it dictates rules aimed at the common good, but the rewards it offers for adherence and the sanctions against abusers exceed anything a state might have in store.

The more devout believers become, the less they tend to observe the lines that separate religious practice and daily conduct. Extreme religious intensity blurs these lines altogether. Under the persuasion and pressure of charismatic preachers, members of extreme and millenarian religious movements embrace a singular and total faith in a forthcoming "advent," after which all concerns of temporal existence will be obsolete. As all aspects of daily conduct and all inter-personal associations are given ritual significance, they are subjected to stringent codes of behavior that often defy the understandings and even the taboos of the outside world. An alternative reality is thus formed, where simple but explicit rules guide every step on the way to salvation. Believers welcome this relief from the preoccupations and frustrations of an individual existence, in which many of them are convinced they have failed (Fromm 1943: 134; Lewis 1998: 35). To them, this is one of the key attractions of the membership. This point is vital for the comprehension of the emergence, spread, and perseverance of millenarian religious movements in particular.

Non-millenarian religious intensity shares many features with its millenarian counterpart, but there are also some important distinctions. In the former case, the process of intensification is slower, the religious tenets are not as sharply defined, and daily conduct is not as holistically affect-

CONCLUSIONS

Table 11.1 Recurring patterns of religious intensity: Case studies presented.

	People's Crusade (Europe, 11th century)	Pueblo Revolt (Spanish North America, 16th cent.)
SOCIO-ECONOMIC, POLITICAL STRESS	Widespread poverty and feudal oppression.	Constant exploitation by Spanish authorities.
ENVIRONMENTAL STRESS	Plagues, droughts, food shortages.	Disease spells, crop failure, droughts.
AIMS	Redeeming the Holy Sepulchre from the Muslims; social and financial advancement.	Liberation from Spanish rule, reclaiming ancestral lands, expulsion of Christian Church, reinstatement of traditional life modes.
OPTION OF SUPERNATURAL INTERVENTION	Expectations for divine assistance in battle and compensation in the afterlife. No clear indication for expectations of physical divine intervention.	Expectations for divine assistance in battle. No clear indication for expectations of physical divine intervention.
IMMEDIATE OUTCOME	Defeat, massacre, dispersion.	Successful military campaign followed by gradual disintegration.
LONG-TERM OUTCOME	Possible inspiration for other medieval popular religious movements.	Significant concessions from Spanish authorities, integration of the Pueblos into the new political, administrative, and religious establishments.

	Cattle Killing (S. Africa, mid-19th cent.)	Mahdi's Revolt (Sudan, late 19th century)	First Revolt (Judea, 1st century CE)
SOCIO-ECONOMIC, POLITICAL STRESS	Loss of ancestral lands due to expanding White farms and confiscation.	Constant exploitation by corrupt Egyptian administration.	Escalating crisis due to land confiscation and heavy Roman taxation, oppression by Jewish elites, clashes with Helleno-Roman population.
ENVIRONMENTAL STRESS	Spells of lethal cattle lung disease, droughts.	Harsh climate, animal and human disease, spells of famine.	Recurrent droughts.
AIM	Liberation from British rule, reinstatement of traditional life modes.	Liberation from British-sponsored Egyptian rule, instatement of *sharia* law.	Liberation from Roman occupation, reinstatement of Jewish state.
OPTION OF SUPERNATURAL INTERVENTION	Anticipation for the active participation of ancestor armies against British forces.	Expectation for divine assistance in battle, some expectation for super-natural participation. Sightings of angel-warriors and bullet immunity.	Expectation for divine assistance in battle, no clear indication to expectation of physical divine participation.
IMMEDIATE OUTCOME	Physical catastrophe, mass starvation of dozens of thousands of people.	Military success, expulsion of foreign forces, establishment of Islamic state. Gradual disintegration and British-Egyptian reconquest. Substantial loss of life.	Military defeat, general destruction and massacres. Ruin of Jerusalem and the Temple. Substantial loss of life.
LONG-TERM OUTCOME	Penetration and spread of Christianity, Prolonged social and economic crisis, deep demoralisation, cultural disintegration.	Several failed messianic follow-ups eliminate the intense religious option. Political activities and organization facilitating ultimate Sudanese independence.	Beginning of post-Temple religious re-adaptation. Rebelliousness fades but re-flares in the Bar-Kochba revolt.

ed. Such movements are certainly based on severe religious interpretations, and divine participation and support is expected if the goals of the movement are to be met, but contrary to messianic movements an apocalypse is not necessarily the expectation. The Pueblo Revolt is one example of such a movement. The First Jewish Revolt is another. The Jewish rebels would have certainly welcomed a miraculous intervention by angels as in Hezekiah's day, but there is no real indication that this was their actual anticipation. Apparently, they simply wanted God to help them defeat the oppressors of Israel in battle, as he had done for Joshua, the Judges, the righteous kings of old, and the early Hasmoneans. In this book, both varieties of intense religious movements have been addressed. Despite the differences, a general model can be built that includes the main factors in the historical career of intense religious movements.

The Recurring Pattern of Religious Intensity

Ten stages in the rise and fall of intense religious movements can be defined:

1. Socio-economic, socio-political, and environmental crises evolve. In small-scale cases, especially in western societies, the crisis affects individual and psychological levels.
2. Traditional responses are proven unsuccessful.
3. Distress reaches intolerable levels.
4. Official institutions fail to provide relief, and their prestige and authority are severely compromised.
5. Alternative and more extreme religious directions introduced by informal or deviant preachers are met with enthusiastic response.
6. Irrational and self-destructive measures are taken under uncompromising religious directives.
7. Initial failure and confusion.
8. Rejection of failure revitalizes self-destructive action.
9. Final failure occurs, entailing cultural, social, and psychological breakdown within the movement.
10. In large-scale cases, fundamental socio-cultural understandings and political institutions irreversibly alter.

(Stages 7–8 may repeat several times)

Table 11.1 applies the process to the main historical cases discussed in this study. A recognizable pattern emerges, despite local variation and the absence of one or two stages in some cases.

The Dominant Role of Religious Intensity

Two determinants are at the base of the model of religious intensity proposed in this book:

A. While other factors were responsible for the mounting stress that led to mass action, when action took place it was generated and motivated by intense religious faith. Charismatic preachers outside the religious establishment organized and directed the moves.

B. The movements' activities significantly influenced the historical trajectory of the peoples involved. While manifestations vary according to local circumstances, the actual impact cannot be doubted.

As the lasting repercussions in each case are discussed in the previous chapters and summed up in Table 11.1, there is no need to reiterate them here, but the first determinant merits some elaboration. A number of points indicate dominant religious motivation in all cases discussed:

- The movements ignored what were by any logical estimation non-existent odds of success. Action was either purely ritual or ritual-militant. Leaders and followers openly disclosed their reliance on divine assistance against enemies superior by all physical and military measures. Initial military successes, as in the cases of the Pueblo and Mahdi's revolts, and the Jewish crushing of the Gallus expedition were credited to divinity.

- Significant numbers of people refused to recognize failure, despite overwhelming evidence to the contrary. Such irrational reaction is characteristic of disciples of messianic movements, reflecting their total investment in the movement and their dismay at the prospect of having been deceived by false promises.

- Aggressive religious argumentation featured in the ideological platforms of the movements, confirming sincere commitment rather than mere façades for social, economic, or political grievances.

- The prominent monotheistic traits that appear even in the theological platforms of nativistic movements adverse to European influence indicate a dynamic religious-ideological scene.

- Mounting environmental, social, economic, and political stress afflicted all discussed cases. Such stress is historically proven to generate religious explanations and responses.

- Most movements bluntly defied religious and political establishments, risking assertive and potentially violent suppression. Cynical pseudo-religious manipulators would not have gone to such lengths, as this might have jeopardized the movement as a whole and placed their own lives at risk. The preachers apparently believed their own visions, and the disciples shared their convictions.

I am not suggesting that non-ideological factors were immaterial to the emergence of the movements, but the actual response crystallized through intensified faith. This explains the vital common factor mentioned several times before: the striking disregard for the odds of success, exceptional even in the wider scene of religiously-inspired action. Let us return for a moment to the adversaries the movements challenged. What chances did disorganized hordes of European peasants have against the battalions of skillful mounted archers of the Seljuk sultanate? How could the Pueblos equal Spain during the peak of its political and military power? The prospects of Jewish farmers fighting professional Roman legionnaires and Sudanese spear-men facing square formations of disciplined British infantry may be similarly questioned. While the developments in each case differed and in some cases the underdogs initially prevailed, even the rebels themselves knew that they were facing forces against which no amount of bravery, determination, and self-sacrifice would suffice in the long run. The one thing that could have changed the odds would have been the interference of a heavenly force superior to all armies.

Religion, far from merely being a complementary factor, was the chief element in generating action and assumed the combined role of motivator, planner, trigger, and executor. We may justly wonder at the Jewish zealots braving Caesar's legions, the Christian peasants battling Muslim horsemen, the Native Americans burning Spanish farms, and the Sudanese tribesmen hurling themselves, the Mahdi's flag in one hand and the sword in the other, against the solid British lines of fire. Yet, in essence, all of these courageous warriors were doing no more than the passive Xhosa who, once having disposed of all their food resources, sat by the door of their homes and stared into the rising sun, searching the heavens for traces of their saviour-ancestors whose imminent arrival Nongqawuze had promised. They all experienced similar adventures, born of similar hopes, carried out in similar faith, to face similar failure. Circumstances change, but the hopes, faith, adventures, and failures of religious intensity seem to follow strikingly reminiscent historical paths.

The Case for Comparison

Anthropologists and social scientists have questioned the advantage of comparative analysis between societies distant in place, time, and culture (Boas 1940 [1896]: 274–76; Hobart 1987). Still, it is difficult to see how guidelines to human behaviour can be detected at all if groups are inspected in virtual isolation. Thomas Gregor and Donald Tuzin (2001: 7–8) rightly comment that "we cannot describe one society without having others in mind…[comparison] stimulates and provokes new perspectives on findings from particular cultures; and it allows us to search for general principles." As cultural anthropologists, Gregor and Tuzin relay to their own discipline, but there is just so much resemblance in the attitudes and responses of different groups in different places and periods that historians and archaeologists cannot afford to dismiss this information. The diffusion of ideas and their exchange cannot be responsible for similarities noted between societies that have never interacted. As far as we know, ceramic production and metalworking appeared in different parts of the world independently, as did the bow and arrow, funerary practices, art, music, and personal adornment. We must also accept the possibility that separate peoples might adopt markedly similar modes of reaction regardless of environmental and cultural variance. Religious intensification as a response to communal or individual crisis offers instructive examples worldwide.

An important criterion in choosing the case studies for this book has been the lack of cultural, geographical, circumstantial, and chronological association between the societies involved.[2] Such distance is a precondition for the construction of true cross-cultural and cross-temporal models. Naturally, models will always be imperfect. Religious intensification among societies under foreign political, economic, and cultural pressure differs substantially from that found among isolated small-scale groups in free and affluent states, such as the peculiar millenarian groups that tend to crop up in the United States. Islamic fundamentalism occurs in both environments and shows aspects of both types of intensity but can be fully related to neither. Religious intensification also manifests itself in various outlines, and the fundamental tenets of some may diametrically contradict the moral understandings of others. Thus, extreme Jainism opposes even the killing of pests, while the Xhosa's plan for salvation flowed in streams of livestock blood. Native American millenarianism urged the revival of ancestral traditions, while south Pacific Cargo Cults incited for their annihilation. Sexual promiscuity is literally prescribed by several American millenarian prophets, while Mahmoud Ahmadinejad, President of Iran, boasts an Islamic society so sexually distilled that – if we are to take this gentleman's assertions at face value – not a single homosexual can be found among his seventy million compatriots.[3]

Yet, the ten-stage pattern delineated above proves valid even against this vast variation in the objective circumstances, theological tenets, and ritual behaviour of each group. Not all ten stages can be detected in all cases, but the major steps are always present. Plains Indian Ghost Dancers, Xhosa Cattle Killers, South Pacific Cargo iconoclasts, warriors of the Mahdi, American Millerite believers, Jonestown suicides, medieval Christian messianic enthusiasts, Jewish anti-Roman zealots, their descendants who followed Sabbatai Zevi, and countless others all followed similar paths. As the more extreme and dangerous, yet simultaneously most attractive and compelling intense religious movements rise, confusion, fury, frustration, and more than all, an overwhelming common desire for change can almost always be found at the background. People do not intensify their faith because they are Christians, Jews, Muslims, or believers of native religions. They do not recruit their God to fight the particular burdens of British, Spanish, or Roman occupation, nor only those of a troubled and unhappy personal existence. The circumstances of any specific

CONCLUSIONS

timeframe are not responsible for such exceptional communal upsurges either. The particular identities of place, time, or people involved are of little consequence to the overall model, which virtually all cases of extreme religious intensification address. Therefore, beyond the necessary meticulous analysis of individual cases, religious intensification must also be studied as a pan-human phenomenon. Comparison is not an academic indulgence but an actual precondition for the understanding of this phenomenon, which has changed countless lives in the past, and is yet to affect many more in the future.

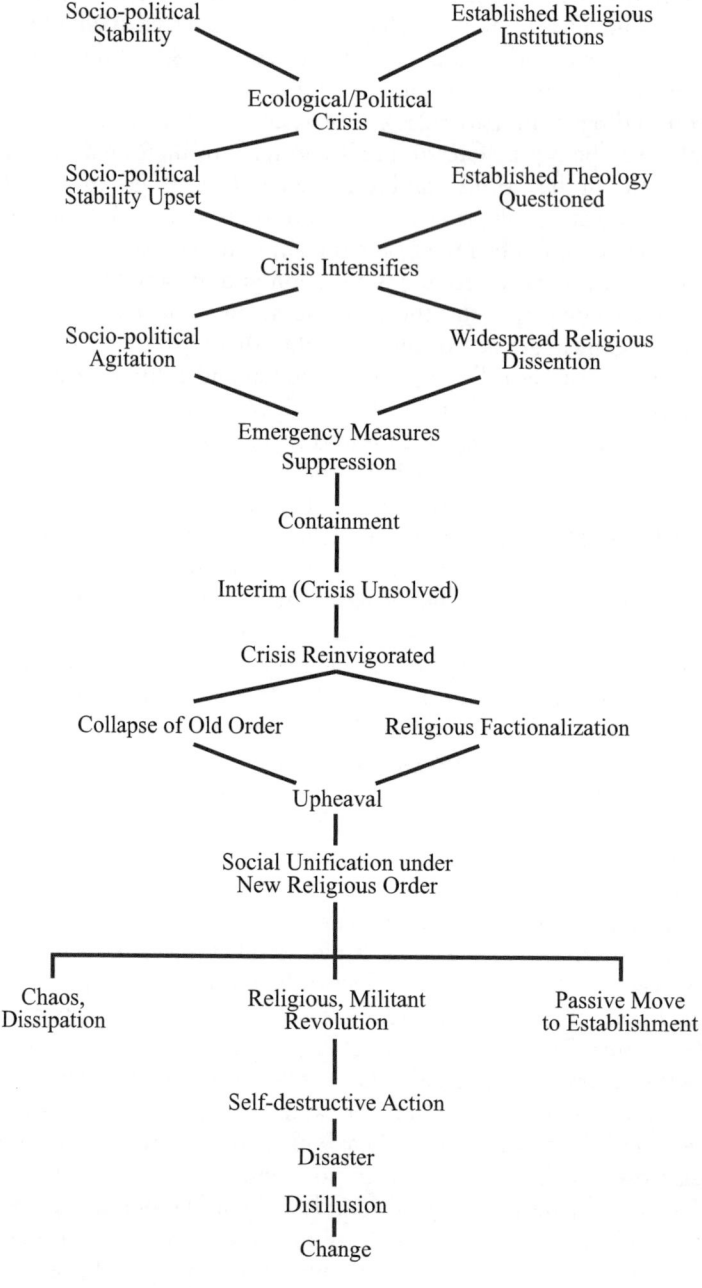

```
       Socio-political                    Established Religious
         Stability                            Institutions
                   \                      /
                    Ecological/Political
                           Crisis
                    /                 \
       Socio-political                    Established Theology
       Stability Upset                        Questioned
                    \                 /
                       Crisis Intensifies
                    /                 \
       Socio-political                    Widespread Religious
          Agitation                          Dissention
                    \                 /
                    Emergency Measures
                       Suppression
                            |
                        Containment
                            |
                    Interim (Crisis Unsolved)
                            |
                    Crisis Reinvigorated
                    /                 \
       Collapse of Old Order      Religious Factionalization
                    \                 /
                         Upheaval
                            |
                  Social Unification under
                     New Religious Order
          ┌─────────────────┼─────────────────┐
        Chaos,         Religious, Militant    Passive Move
      Dissipation         Revolution         to Establishment
                            |
                    Self-destructive Action
                            |
                         Disaster
                            |
                        Disillusion
                            |
                          Change
```

Figure 43 Religious intensity and historical impact.

Key Points in the Archaeology of Religious Intensity

The feasibility of tracing testimony for religious intensity in archaeological materials has been discussed in the last chapter. Yet, several factors limiting the use of archaeology in this field of research must be recognized and taken into consideration before looking into such evidence:

- The reconstruction of an ancient ideological process through material remains requires substantial interpretation. The general features listed in chapter 8 must be applied cautiously and with constant attention to the actual conditions at the historical locale.

- The listed features may not necessarily reveal the volume of popular support for the ideologically-inspired action and participation in it. For example, evidence suggests that ritual bathing, possession of soft limestone vessels, and a ban on figurative art were commonplace in first-century Judea. Still, many observant Jews seem to have considered the correlation between religious piety and revolt against Rome preposterous.

- In assessing the status and circulation of religious intensity, the loss of related perishable artifacts and the transparence of others must be taken into account.

- The growth and spread of intense religious movements often depends on the charisma and rhetoric skill of their leaders. However, unless documented in writing, charisma and oral eloquence do not leave retrievable traces.

- The discovery of documents that can be associated with an otherwise unknown non-institutional religious group raises the possibility that other such groups existed and influenced the ideological, political, and social scenes while remaining obscure to us. There is only so much we can assume lacking the actual evidence, but that possibility must not be ignored.

- Material and literary testimony will never relay to us the full meaning of the movements in their societies, nor the substance of their intellectual and ideological impact.

By keeping these issues in mind, researchers can reduce the odds of rushing into far-fetched and even fanciful conclusions attractive to the ear, mind, and imagination but of questionable relevance to the studied culture.

There are six key indicators that investigators should search for during the actual analysis of material evidence for marks of religious intensity. The absence of one or more of these indicators does not rule out religious intensity but leaves the door open to other, less spiritual explanations based on function, styles, fashions, availability of materials, or simply taste.

1. *Variety*: Several types of finds assumed to be of ritual purpose must be present.
2. *Frequency*: Ritual artifacts and/or structures must be found in a regularity that clearly surpasses their number in other places or periods and minimizes the odds of coincidence.
3. *Distribution*: Relevant ritual artifacts and/or structures should be found in more than one site.
4. *Oddity*: Ritual artifacts and/or structures must stand out against local and regional traditional forms, materials, and architectural styles.
5. *Ideological affiliation*: Basic associations must be present between the ritual artifacts and/or structures presumably related to intense ideological currents and the standard local religion.
6. *Literary corroboration (optional)*: Original documents can be invaluable for the identification and classification of ritual artifacts and/or structures, although correlation between finds and historically known movements, attractive as it might be, must be thoroughly and critically examined.

Each of these points could be applied to Judea during the first century CE. Prominent classes of Jewish ritual artifacts and structures are unique to that time, appear in wide distribution, and can be aligned with religious regulations and traditions articulated in extensive ancient literature. The same model could apply to less extensively documented cases, pending on the attention and perception of excavators and their familiarity with comparative data.

The Gates of Rome and the Walls of Jericho

The story of intense religious movements oddly resembles the career of a successful theater play. Generations of actors on stage, altering sets in the background, but a plot that remains basically the same. Caught in the rhetoric of self-proclaimed charismatic preachers, desperate people across the globe join intense religious movements hoping to solve the wrongs on Earth with the help of Heaven. Engulfed by the fanfare promises of their capricious leaders they ignore delicate existential balances upon which generations of their ancestors depended and through which countless predicaments were outlived. Instead, extreme modes of action are eagerly espoused and blindly followed. Formerly rational people undergo a remarkable metamorphosis, engaging in behavior bizarre at best and suicidal at worst and mistaking it for ultimate piety, worthy of divine intervention on behalf of their cause. As the prophetic promises fail to materialize, they face devastating disappointment, frustration, and bewilderment. After an arduous process of disenchantment, some recuperate, though into a life irreversibly changed. Others, ignoring the evidence, refuse to acknowledge the failure. Some even challenge the confirmed death of their leader and for a while sustain the group's illusion, until its inevitable final dispersion.

Intense religious movements stir tremendous energies, but their ideological structures are often vague, sometimes confused, and occasionally erratic. Disciples with little in common in their background and ideals join together into a heterogeneous aggregation of characters, worldviews, and expectations. As articulated by Martin Buber, foreign observers of intense religious movements face a bewildering spectacle:

> We frequently find, at one and the same time, the most exalted concept of the Messianic ideal next to the vulgar notions of future comforts. Hence, the Messianic movements are a mixture of the most holy and most profane, of a future oriented purpose and lack of restraint, of love of God and avid curiosity. Here, too, the people's bents resist spiritualization, and tarnish the purity of fulfillment.[4]

The disciples of intense religious movements cannot be blamed for expecting nothing less than everything out of what has been assured to be a special relationship with divinity. But organizations that promise anything to anyone tend to end up giving nothing to everyone. There is a limit beyond which leaders, however skilled and charismatic, are no longer capable of controlling their disciples and patching together their diverse yet passionate individual aspirations. These same passionate aspirations, which once were the original construction blocks of the movement, may now act as its self-destruction devices.

It seems that intense religious movements invariably find their way to turmoil, heartbreak, and disintegration. Must it always be so? Will the intense religious choice constantly be a negative projection of human despair, a senseless exchange of earthly disillusion for delusions of heaven? Actually, not always. Born Again Christians, Jews who revert to ancestral orthodoxy, Muslims who devote themselves to reciting the Koran, meditating dwellers in the monasteries of Buddha – to many of these people the intensification of faith is nothing less than a genuine blessing, giving them confidence, inner peace, happiness, direction, and, foremost, hope where previously little could be found. The curse of religious intensity strikes as the sin of impatience. There is nothing wrong with passionate faith in God. The problem begins when the devout, under stress by the predicaments of reality, try to modify God's journal and instruct Him on what He is to do, when He is to do it, and to whom.

In dark times of trouble violence beckons temptingly, because it offers immediate solutions and even ultimate salvation to believers. But salvation can be perceived in many forms, some of them not militant at all. Here is Buber's vision of the Savior:

> When I was a child I read an old Jewish tale I could not understand. It said no more than this: "Outside the gates of Rome there sits a leprous beggar, waiting. He is the Messiah. Then I came upon an old man whom I asked: 'what is he waiting for?' And the old man gave me an answer I did not understand at the time, an answer I learned to understand only much later. He said: 'He waits for you.'" [5]

Buber's messiah is humble but confident and at peace. Eventually, he will be recognized and assume the role he has been assigned by divinity. In the meantime, he ignominiously sits upon the bare earth by the gates of the great city, abused as leprous beggars are and enduring as they must; he waits for eyes to open, one believer at a time. This imagery of patient determination is as powerful as that of any wondrous warlord of native millenarianism, but to people locked into extreme duress it rarely suffices. The Jews themselves, who spent millennia of suffering by taking comfort in the prospect of redemption undetermined in time, lost their patience on occasion. Some of them then grasped at the hollow promises of the Sabbatai-Zevi-variety of false messiahs, who always were present to reap in the fields of despair. They, as so many others in history, eventually found out that there are no shortcuts to salvation. Nonetheless, there are many impulsive religious agents ready to lead the hopeful and unsuspecting onto winding trails through menacing forests, with neither maps, compasses, nor knowledge, but only wild instincts to guide them. Why have so many people followed them? Buber was a young boy when he read the enigmatic tale, a boy curious enough to wonder, confident enough to ask, rational enough not to understand, and wise enough to wait years before comprehending the message. But curiosity, confidence, rationality, and wisdom all depend to some degree on patience and endurance, and those living in strenuous realities and in dire need for relief may have little patience in store and endurance may seem to have reached its outermost limits. That is where the visionaries of intense religious movements, with their flowing rhetoric, force of character, and captivating charisma, step in to offer hope and direction.

Buber's silent beggar-messiah by the dusty Roman gate has substituted the desert-born chieftains who stormed the fallen walls of Jericho and the ruthless warlords who fought to free their Jewish homeland from bondage to an empire. This exchange reflects the fluctuations of Jewish history. As vulnerable minorities in the Diaspora, the Jews were compelled to replace their ancient ploughs and swords with iron-willed endurance and principled humility in order to survive. The transformation drew inspiration from their ancient traditions, in which greatness sprouting from modesty is not an alien concept. In fact, the Hebrew Bible abounds with examples: the wandering, tent-dwelling patriarchs; the reluctant, stuttering Moses; the brigand-outcast Jephthah; the shepherd-fugitive David; the bitter Jeremiah, languishing in a prison pit and hated by all; the compliant Hosea, who exposes himself to ridicule by marrying a prostitute upon God's command; the suffering, righteous Job, left with nothing but a potshard to scratch at his wounds and his steadfast faith in his creator. Christianity adopted the model wholeheartedly. Its savior emerged from a provincial carpenter's workshop and was executed as a common criminal. His original disciples were former fishermen, tax collectors, and women who had lived in sin. His admiring audience comprised the poor and the destitute. He pledged the Earth to the meek and denied the proud their place in Heaven. The principle is less pronounced in Islam but nevertheless exists, with Koranic passages assuring believers that earthly wealth and power means nothing if its owners lack virtue and faith.[6]

Millenarian figures are often of modest ancestry and birth but tend to forget this as they predict the Advent the way meteorologists forecast rain for the next morning. It is rare indeed to find among them a follower of Moses, who, appalled by the prospect of becoming the leader and rescuer of his people, pleaded with God to "please send someone else" (Exodus 4:13). Very few of them seem to identify with the courage and humility of Jesus, who accepted his ghastly fate with the simple words "thy will be done" (Matthew 26:42). The typical millenarian leader better relates to amended versions of these famous statements, something along the lines of "send *only* me" and "*my* will be done, and everyone else's be damned."

Monotheism views divinity as being, by its very nature, beyond human control or full understanding. Many people find this a disturbing prospect, a symbol and reflection of human frailty and powerlessness. Religion supplies two ways for confronting this problem. It offers explanation; the urge to reconcile what one sees and experiences with one's understanding is embedded in the human psyche, and religion provides vital explanations of the origins, course, and aftermath of life, from the emergence and nature of the universe to the existence of each individual. That is why virtually all human groups developed creation myths and observe some form of funerary rites. It also offers control control, the partial fulfillment of the yearning of men and women for some power over their own destinies. People will do anything to maintain at least a semblance of such control, as the repercussions of its loss are terrifying. Standard religion teaches that prayer, rituals, good deeds, and sacrifice (of animals, property, others, or self) is to be rewarded, but the reward is rarely delivered at once and selsom answers to the particular needs of the hour. This is the source from which religious intensity draws its vibrancy, vitality, and appeal. Its associated movements are simply much better equipped to promise the transformation of these most human desires for control, justice, and retribution from amorphous and timeless to tangible and immediate. Tragically, as proven countless times by past historical experience and likely to be proven again in the future, they are also the least capable of delivering.

Notes

Chapter 1

1   Cited from *The Middle Ages, Volume I: Sources of Medieval History*, ed. B. Tierny, New York: Knopf, 1970. Source translated by M. E. McGinty.
2   All biblical quotations in this book are cited from *The New Oxford Annotated Bible*, New York: Oxford University, 2001.

Chapter 2

1   *What is the Purpose of Life?*, pp. 18–19.
2   *Isaiah's Prophecies: Light for All Mankind*, Watch Tower Bible and Tract Society of Pennsylvania, p. 414.
3   For example, a booklet titled "Awake!" (handed to the author in San Diego by a street distributor in 2001) includes articles on issues as diverse as fake fossils, polluted mountain lakes, styles of graves, lead in jewelry, natural habitats in Zambia, communication with children, disappearing languages, urban problems in Mexico City, the beauty of the Canadian Northwest, and senior citizens leading a good life. The religious message is subtle but certainly there: God is everywhere and involved in everything – and the Jehovah's Witnesses have the best road map to His care and attention.
4   Cited from *The Middle Ages, Sources of Medieval History*. Volume I. Ed. B. Tierny. New York: Knopf, 1970, p. 21.
5   This phenomenon can be found in numerous cultures. See, for example, Pharaonic Egypt (Kemp 1989: 198–99; Baines and Yoffe 1998: 206), the Roman Empire (Zanker 1988: 316–17), Inca Peru (Bauer 1996: 333), and possibly even biblical Judah (Propp 1999: 546).
6   Spanish colonial authorities demanded tributes in basic foodstuffs, such as maize, which had to be paid from the surpluses that local populations traditionally stored against the not uncommon event of drought. Some colonial officials also instigated clashes between Pueblo peoples and nomadic Apaches in order to capitalize on the enslavement of war captives (Knaut 1995: 59ff., 159–60).
7   All rulers of Muslim countries must exhibit a basic commitment to Islam, and so did Saddam Hussein who, despite public prayer sessions, the declarative slogan on the national flag, and lip service statements of devotion to the Faith, was as secular as a Muslim leader can be. Saddam was one of the latest in a very long and colorful list of despots who had ruled Islamic lands and empires over the ages. Theological tolerance towards these powerful and less than pious rulers rests on the notion of deference and respect for Muslim leadership in general that is rooted in some of the earliest teachings of Islam. The Koran itself calls upon the faithful to "obey God and obey the Apostle, and those among you invested with authority" (4:63). The purpose is the preservation of Islamic unity against the ever-present hazards of internal discord (Lewis 1986), which has nevertheless plagued the political history of that religion almost since its genesis.
8   "Dividing Jerusalem risks invoking God's wrath, Pat Robertson says," *The Jerusalem Post*, October 17, 2007, p.3.
9   "Evangelicals raise $8.5 million for Jewish state," *The Jerusalem Post*, October 18, 2007. p.7
10 Under the influence of extreme ideological incitement, words tend to lead some people to action. Unsurprisingly, in such cases European legalistic logic often proves to be an asset to Islamic terrorists. As an example, evidence painstakingly collected by Spanish police and security services in connection to the Madrid train bombings of March 11, 2004, was found sufficient by a Spanish court to hand maximum prison sentences to only three of the twenty-eight defendants in the case. Seven were acquitted altogether, including one Rabei Osman, an Egyptian national who was wiretapped boastingly taking credit for the idea of the bombings. Spanish Prime minister Jose Luis Rodriguez Zapatero,

however, saw no fault with the outcome of the trial. His reaction to the incredibly light verdicts on the massacres that left 191 people dead and over 1800 wounded was that "Justice was rendered today" ("21 guilty in Madrid train bombing trial," *The Jerusalem Post,* November 1, 2007, p. 8).

Chapter 3

1. It should be noted that ritual cleansing is also known in North American indigenous traditions (La Barre 1969: 61). Still, within the ideological context of the Pueblo Revolt, this primary concept of Christianity may have had an independent impact.

2. Judaism will be referred to in the later chapters of this book, in the detailed discussion of first-century Judea and the revolt against Rome.

3. The discrepancy between the actual conduct of higher Church echelons and the principles of social justice at the base of the Christian faith is held to be one of the motives behind the French Revolution. Having mentioned the immense wealth accumulated by Catholic institutions until the revolution and the liberal tax exemptions they had enjoyed from the Court, Winston Churchill (1957: 270) comments that "most of the rank and file [clergy] were devout, self-denying, and upright, but a crust of politically covetous, worldly, and cynical prelates had weakened and degraded the dignity and influence of organized Christianity." Indeed, the Church and its institutions were the targets the revolutionaries vehemently sought, and scars of that persecution can still be seen in churches and cathedrals in France.

4. Cited from *The Epic of Gilgamesh*. Translated by N. K. Sandars. London: Penguin, 1972, p. 108.

5. Koranic citations in this book: *The Koran,* Translated by J. M. Rodwell. New York: Bantam Dell, 2004 (with minor adaptations).

6. Albert Camus, *The Plague*. Translated by S. Gilbert. London: Penguin, 1960, pp. 90–91.

7. *Germania,* cited from Tierney 1970: 37–38.

8. From the sermon of Pope Urban II at the Council of Clermont. Accounted by Fulcher of Chartres, *Chronicle of the First Crusade*, trans. M. E. McGinty (Philadelphia: University of Pennsylvania, 1941). Cited from *The Middle Ages, Vol.1: Sources of Medieval History*, ed. B. Tierny (New York: Knopf, 1970).

9. It has been argued that this notable literary and theological passage and several other famous teachings of the gospels were drawn from Jewish sources. It would have been natural for the earthly Jesus in his capacity as a Jewish rabbi and teacher. According to this view, Paul's projection of Jesus as a religious reformer does not agree with the nature of Jesus' teachings, which are all rooted deep in Jewish scripture and tradition. See S. Boteach, "Jesus was Jewish," *The Jerusalem Post,* October 22, 2007.

10. Modern Athlit on the northern Israeli coastal plain.

11. Historically, accusations of perversion, immorality, and criminality were common weapons of the official clergy against alarmingly popular religious challengers (Brown 1971: 84). It should be noted that some modern millenarian movements did encourage promiscuous sexual behavior among their disciples (Bromley and Silver 1995: 154–56; Lewis 1998: 86–87, 75).

12. "On the right to change one's religion," *Common Ground News Service*. Cited from *The Jerusalem Post,* October 25, 2007, p.16.

13. Mike Seid, "Jerusalem Mufti: Western Wall was never part of Jewish temple," *The Jerusalem Post,* October 25, 2007, p. 7. Moslems, of course, are not alone in attempting to intercept appeals to the One God made in Jerusalem through other religious venues. In the very same Jerusalem Post issue appears another story about the arson of a Baptist church in that city, in all likelihood by Jewish extremists (Etgar Lefkovitz, "Arsonists torch Jerusalem church," p. 5).

14. There is more than a fraction of sanctimoniousness in the common motto that states that "one's terrorist is another one's freedom fighter." Terrorists may profess high ideological goals, but they will ever differ from guerilla or freedom fighters by their deliberate choice of victims or their indifference to the latter's identity. Guerillas attack enemy soldiers and government officials. Terrorists intentionally target uninvolved civilians or readily consider their deaths or maiming as collateral damage. Incidentally,

branding the bombing of civilian populations in time of war as "terrorism by a state" would only dilute the severity of the criminal aspect of real terrorism, because it spreads the net to practically no end. Transgressions committed by the military and civilian officials of a state in time of war must be judged under war crime acts, distinct from atrocities by irregular groups and factions acting on their own accord. Whether taking the law into one's own hands is better or worse than evil-doing under the umbrella of a formal legislation is up to individual judgment, but the distinction between the two should be recognized.

15 The literature on this multi-faceted subject is extensive. For comprehensive overviews and bibliographies see Lewis 1974; 1993; 1995.

16 Hamas is an acronym for "The Islamic Resistance Movement" (*Harakat Al-Muqawama Al-Islamia*), originally a self-professed Palestine branch of the Egyptian founded Muslim Brotherhood movement. For an up-to-date survey, see http://www.globalsecurity.org/military/world/para/hamas.htm

17 Anton La Guardia, Said Ghazzali, Ohad Gozani, and Sean O'Neill, "British bombers posed as peace activists," http://www.telegraph.co.uk, May 4, 2003. "Details of April 30, 2003 Tel Aviv suicide bombing," http://www.mfa.gov.il, June 3, 2003. David Rudge, "Bomb horror hits Tel Aviv disco," http://info.jpost.com, June 4, 2001. "Tel-Aviv suicide bombing at the Dolphin disco - June 1, 2001," http://www.mfa.gov.il, June 3, 2003. For background information about the bomber see Pape 2006: 231–34.

18 Osama Bin Laden, *Declaration of War against the Americans Occupying the Land of the Two Holy Places*. Cited in Pape 2006: 124.

19 Ayman el-Zawahiri, *Knights Under the Banner of the Prophet*. Cited in Pape 2006: 122.

20 K. H. Pollack, "The Crisis of Islam: Faith and Terrorism in the Muslim World," *New York Times Book Review*, April 6, 2003.

21 From a *Mojahedin* official publication: *Pasokh be etehamat-e akhir-e rezhim* ("Answer to the regime's latest insults"), 1973, pp. 10–13. Cited in Abrahamian 1989: 102.

22 Unfortunately, there is a clear discrepancy between official positions and the reality in the streets, as would be evident to anyone placing a casual Web search on the burning of churches in the West Bank and Gaza, and on the fear that is part of the life of the diminishing Christian communities there.

Chapter 4

1 David Goodblatt (2006: 16) notes that the biblical perspective is that while the God of Israel is the only true god, other nations are free to worship their own deities until at some undetermined stage in the future the unique status of Yahweh is universally recognized. Even then, the universal submission to the God of Israel will not compromise ethnic and cultural distinctions.

2 Hence, for example, the Aramean king Hazael is chosen to humiliate the sinful kingdom of Israel on the battlefield (Kings II 8:12–13), and the Persian King Cyrus, who allowed the return of the Jews to their homeland, is referred to as "the anointed," or messiah, of the Lord (Isaiah 45:1).

3 Such hopes had firm foundations in the Scriptures. See for example Deuteronomy 32:43.

4 To mention one aspect in several that illustrates the variance: while peasants worldwide are renowned for their revolutionary fervor (Wolf 1966: 103; Mousnier 1970), urban twentieh-century populations in Germany, Iran, Nicaragua, and Northern Ireland have proven themselves just as potentially volatile (Peukert 1987: 93–100; Mühlberger 1991: 119, 160–62; Pool 1997: 28, 49–50; Kamrava 1990: 34; Moaddel 1993: 98–99, 107–8, 113–14; Martin 2000: 64ff., 201; Rolston 1991; Santino 1999).

5 According to Dispensational theological doctrines the period between the crucifixion and the Second Coming is missing in the biblical narrative – the 'sacred history.' Believers must constantly scan for signs of the resumption of scriptural testimony, according to prophecies in Revelation. These signs are, essentially, interpretations of unfolding dramatic developments. This ambiguity permits millenarian expectations, but only of the 'everyday' variety, since the exact schedule remains obscure (after Robbins 2001: 543–44).

6   The literal translation is "with God's assistance," but "consent" better represents the original intention. As nothing happens against God's Will, his accord is a form of assistance in itself.

7   Each sura of the Koran opens with this declaration.

8   The influence of Catholicism on Pueblo ideology cannot be disputed, but neither should the fundamental determination of the rebels to revive their original religions. Tainted as it was with monotheistic markers, it was an essentially polytheistic religious framework, with its foundations and general structure based on pre-contact traditions that were remembered by most locals and still practiced by many.

Chapter 5

1   The exact number of fatalities is unknown and estimations vary considerable. Meintjes (1971: 259) counts "nearly 100,000." Millin (1954: 45) writes that 70,000 perished, while Peires (1989: 242) states the more conservative figure of 40,000 dead.

2   Some diseases, including the lung disease that precluded the Cattle Killing, were unwittingly transported to the region on European ships (Peires 1989: 70).

3   G. W. Steevens, for example, was rather unimpressed with the north of the country: "…a God-accursed wilderness, an empty limbo of torment for ever and ever" (From Steevens, G. W. 1899. *With Kitchener to Khartoum*. New York: Dodd, Mead & Co). E. S. Grogan's view of the south was even less flattering: "For God-forsaken, dry-sucked, fly-blown wilderness, commend me to the Upper Nile; a desolation of desolations, an infernal region, a howling waste of weed, mosquitoes, flies and fever, backed by a groaning waste of thorns and stones – waterless and waterlogged. I have passed through it and have now no fear for the hereafter" (From Grogan, E. S., and Sharp, A. H. 1900. *From the Cape to Cairo*. London: Hurst and Blacket). Local Sudanese had no illusions about their land either. Following a local adage, "when Allah made Sudan he laughed" (Farwell 1967:xxii).

4   This Arabic term (هجرة) literally translates to "emigration." It became a key concept in the history of Islam when the prophet Mohammed, threatened by the pagans of Mecca, was forced to relocate to Medina. There, his new religion gained the momentum it needed to take over Arabia, including Mecca itself. The Mahdi's use of the term *hijra* to designate his own adventure may seem pretentious, but unfolding developments show striking similarities to the early career of the Prophet, a fact that did not escape the attention of his many enthusiastic supporters in Sudan.

5   Nonetheless, in the last period of his life the Mahdi himself immersed himself in carnal indulgences. European witnesses describe him as an enormously fat man who spent much of his time in the company of the numerous women he had received as political gifts (Farwell 1967: 24). In living thus, he not only contradicted his own teachings but neglected the instructions of the Koran itself, on which they were presumably based. Sura 18:27, for instance, warns: "Be patient with those who call upon their Lord at morn and even, seeking His face: and let not thine eyes be turned away from them in quest of the pomp of this life; neither obey him whose heart We have made careless of the remembrance of Us, and who followeth his own lusts, and whose ways are unbridled."

6   Wahhabism, a variance of Salafism, is named after its founder Muhammad Ibn Abd al Wahhab (1703–92). Its followers strive to strictly emulate the Prophet and his Companions, while dismissing later interpretations. The official religious ideology of Saudi Arabia, this is also the form of Islam in which Osama bin Laden was educated (Pape 2006: 106–7).

7   The idea of supernatural Mahdism dates back to the early decades of Islam. The first recorded case is the Mukhtār Revolt in Kūfa, which took place in 685–87 CE (Lewis 1993: 74–75).

8   Charles Dickens, *The Chimes*. In "The Christmas Books," Penguin Popular Classics, London 1994, p. 133.

9   Some Cargo Cults went further than that and held that attractive goods were actually not European at all, but that the spirits had produced them for the local peoples. The Europeans, it was explained, merely intercepted them at sea (Burridge 1969: 78).

Chapter 6

1. The revolt is known by different names. The term used by Josephus, "Jewish War" (*Bellum Iudaicum*), follows the Roman custom of calling foreign wars after the peoples involved. Hence, Julius Caesar's work on the wars in Gaul, *Comentarii de Bello Gallico*, and Appianus' *Bella Illyrica, Bella Macedonica, Bella Syriaca, Bella Punica, Bella Celtica,* and *Bella Iberica*. Modern authors favor the names Great Revolt or First Revolt. The term "Great" highlights its exceptional scale, surpassing a series of more limited violence. The title "First" distinguishes it from the second large-scale Jewish uprising against Rome, better known as the Bar-Kochba War (132–135 CE), after the name of its leader. Similar logic is behind the terms Great War or First World War. The idiom First Revolt will be used through this book.

2. Some authors seem to take the very existence of departments of archaeology in universities as a personal offense. Archaeologists have been branded with being trained "not to lift their eyes above their trenches and sorting tables" (Starr 1992: 4), belittled as mere "potsherd collectors" (Ogden 1997: 4), and caustically reminded that "it has been said that the spade cannot lie but it owes this merit to the fact that it cannot even speak" (Grierson 1959: 129). Witty observations, no doubt, but somehow counterproductive to the prospects of dialogue.

3. The term refers to a disproportionate and uncritical reliance on the attractive but subjective and inevitably biased testimony of historical texts.

4. Even respectable historians such as Thucydides and Josephus exaggerate the historical magnitude of the wars of which they write. According to Thucydides, the Peloponnesian War was "the greatest disturbance in the history of the Hellenes, affecting also a large part of the non-Hellenic world, and indeed, I might almost say, the whole of mankind" (*The Peloponnesian War*, 1). Josephus, probably influenced by the renowned Athenian, refers to the Jewish revolt against Rome as the "greatest of all those [wars], not only that have been in our times, but in a manner, of those that ever were heard of" (Preface to *Jewish War*, 1). Both must have known better, but were probably lured by a patriotic desire to glorify the histories of their respective peoples. The Roman Titus Livius (Livy) openly professed such intention in the introduction to his *History of Rome*.

5. Suetonius concludes his famous and sharply critical biography of the Julio-Claudian and Flavian Caesars with generous compliments dedicated to the imperial line of Hadrian, under whom he had worked (*Lives of the Emperors* 8.3,23). For the example of Josephus, see below.

6. Several examples are discussed in this book, placed within the cultural context of the Eastern Mediterranean in Roman imperial days. Others can be found in various other historical locales. Referring to Aztec human sacrifice, the Spanish chronicler José de Acosta comments that "in the number of men they sacrificed and in the horrible way [the Aztecs] did it they surpassed the people of Piru (*sic*) and indeed all the nations of the world." He goes on to lament "the state of blind misfortune in which the devil kept these people" (*Natural and Moral History of the Indies,* published in 1590. Cited in Gruzinski 1992: 156). Acosta, like other Spanish authors who were understandably distressed by the excessive religious customs of the peoples of the New World, were citizens of a state and members of a Church that enthusiastically sanctioned and implemented the horrors of the Inquisition, but they were oblivious to the irony.

7. Mocking of man-made deities and their limited powers abounds in the Hebrew Bible and the Koran, but as one example of the monotheistic attitude among many let us observe a Christian account. In 384 CE, Symmachus, the prefect of the city of Rome, petitioned against the removal of the pagan statue of Victory from the senate house by the relatively new, and correspondingly zealous, imperial Christian authorities. In his response, St. Ambrose, then Bishop of Milan, paid little heed to common courtesy: "…Your sacrifice is a rite of being sprinkled with the blood of beasts. Why do you seek the voice of God in dead animals?… You worship the works of your own hands, we think it an offense that anything which can be made should be esteemed by God. God wills not that He should be worshipped in stones…" (*Letters of St. Ambrose*. Cited from Tierney 1970: 25).

8   For example, in his *Refutation of All Heresies*, Hyppolitus, a leading third-century Christian theologian, offers interesting details regarding the beliefs of the Jewish-Christian movement known as the Ebionites, yet he does so in an argumentative form that is blatantly hostile to his subject. Thus, among various detailed descriptions of Ebionite faith, we also read of its "outrageous absurdity" and "impious doctrine" and are duly notified that "the name of Ebionites hints at the poverty of their intelligence, for this is the way in which a poor man was referred to by the Hebrews" (Cited from Hultgren and Haggmark 1996: 119–20).

9   Millenarianism is a very early Christian phenomenon. The Montanist movement in Phrygia, Anatolia, for example, dates as early as 156 CE.

10   Ethnographic studies show that Bedouin domestic or burial structures became places of ritual once a Bedouin group had left its original territory (Yekutieli and Gabai 1995: 50–51).

11   Mark Leone (1984; 1988) proposes that the precise geometry and perfect perspectives of William Paca's garden in Annapolis, MD, were planned to project an illusion of rightful stability, wealth, and power, thus supporting the privileged few in a period of dynamic sociopolitical changes. That may be so, but the core ideas of such conclusions seem to be influenced by Marxist ideology, the relevance of which to the realities of the 18th century may be questioned. Yet, Leone's thinking does follow an analytical outline that merits consideration. The ideological zealotry of some other modern researchers penetrates the realms of absurdity. I was once told of a male student who had dared to ask a question during a public meeting of feminist archaeologists in Germany. The student was brusquely silenced and reprimanded for his interference in a forum where no male participation was welcome. Feminist archaeology does highlight some worthy issues previously barely attended to, but its scientific merit might be somewhat compromised if its proponents adopt rather irrational approaches.

12   An interesting example is a statue of Queen Boudicca, who revolted against the Roman occupation of her kingdom in southern Britain in the mid-first century CE. The statue was erected in 1902 by the London County Council near Westminster Bridge in central London. The inscription on the imposing stone platform, upon which the heroic figure is depicted riding her war chariot, is dedicated to "Boudicca, Queen of the Iceni who died A.D. 61 after leading her people against the Roman invader." It is of course no coincidence that the memorial for this proud tribal princess was placed at the heart of the imperial British capital, adjacent to its government buildings and symbols of power. The genetic links (to say nothing of the cultural affiliations) between the people of Victorian England and the Iceni are probably slimmer than those that bind the English to the Vikings, Normans, and the large numbers of Roman troops and settlers who had settled permanently in Boudicca's land. This fact was not lost on some other Victorians, even such souls no less romantic than Thomas Thornycroft who sculpted the statue. Rudyard Kipling's poem *The Roman Centurion's Song* is a fine illustration to that effect.

13   *San Diego Union Tribune*, October 27, 2004.

14   An example from the Israeli site of Masada shows that impartial investigation remains a viable possibility even where the interference of modern cultural-political ideologies is indisputable. In 73 CE, nearly a thousand Jewish rebels and their families committed suicide at the desert fortress of Masada rather than sustain the hardships and humiliation of enslavement in Roman captivity (*Jewish War* 7.275–406). Masada became a national Israeli symbol, was excavated as such in the early 1960's, and was subsequently developed into a major tourist attraction and an educational lighthouse for Israeli students and soldiers. Nevertheless, the results of the excavations have been scientifically published (Aviram et al. 1994/1995) and various aspects of the research stimulated vibrant scholarly debates that have nothing to do with contemporary ideology (Cohen 1982; Cotton and Price 1990; Geva 1996; Hershkovitz 1996; Zias et al. 1994; Zias 1998; Eshel 1999; Ben Yehuda 1995; Ponting and Segal 1998).

15   Original *Annales* historians suggested that the traditional emphasis on great persons and dramatic events should be drastically reduced and that a broad view at the environmental and social processes at the background of the historical developments should be favored instead (Braudel 1972; Febvre 1973; Stoianovitch 1976).

16   "New" or "Processual" archaeology advocates a substantial increase in the utilization of methods from the natural sciences and statistics in the explanation of archaeological scenes (Binford 1977; Clarke 1978: 11).

Chapter 7

1   The term Judea covered different geographical regions in different times, following both ethnic and political fluctuations. For a survey of the subject see Goodblatt 2006: 140ff.

2   Jewish opposition to Hellenism was never monolithic. There were some, in particular among the rising Jewish aristocracy, that readily adopted Hellenistic cultural fashions at the expense of Jewish orthodoxy. As an example, carved representations of lions, oxen, and eagles were discovered at the mansion of the Tobias family at 'Araq el Amir, Jordan (Glueck 1939: 154–56; Lapp 1983; and see direct reference by Josephus in *Antiquities* 12.230). The Hellenized Tobiads thus violated the ban on imagery art, which was strictly observed during that period.

3   Destruction layers related to the Hasmonean conquest and an influx of Hasmonean coins reflect the transition from Seleucid to Hasmonean rule. Corresponding replacement of pagans by Jews is attested to at the important Galilean center of Yodfat (Adan-Bayewitz and Aviam 1997: 161).

4   The issue has been extensively researched. For some references see Bar-Kochva 1989: 45, 374; Sievers 1990: 68–79, 98–99.

5   The term Helleno-Roman relates here to Greek-speaking populations of mixed origins who comprised the majority of citizens in the large urban centers of the Eastern Mediterranean. They shared pseudo-Hellenistic religious and cultural affiliations, and most of them saw themselves as part of the Roman political and cultural sphere.

6   The Fifth Legion (*Macedonica*), the Tenth Legion (*Fretensis*), the Fifteenth Legion (*Apollinaris*), and the survivors of the Twelfth Legion (*Fulminata*).

7   According to Suetonius (*Lives* 8.1,1), Vespasian's father had been a tax collector and money-lender.

8   The inscriptions on the arch boast that Titus "subdued the Jewish people and destroyed the city of Jerusalem, which all generals, kings, and peoples before him had either attacked without success or left entirely unassailed" (Lewis and Reinhold 1990: 15). Two earlier conquests of the city by Pompey and Sossius (63 BCE and 37 BCE, respectively) were conveniently ignored.

9   Numerous underground systems were excavated in Judea and the Galilee, but most lack distinct archaeological strata. Based on Roman and rabbinic records (see below) and finds from mostly unsealed layers, many of those systems are dated to the Bar Kochba War (Tepper and Shahar 1987: 324), the second major Jewish revolt against Rome (132–135 CE). The underground spaces or tunnels reported by Josephus to have been used during the First Revolt (*War* 4.9, 5.104, 330, 6.429–33) were assumed to be water systems, ditches, escape routes, cisterns, or natural or artificial caves (Tepper and Shahar 1987: 323–24; Kloner 1987: 363). Recently, the dating of underground systems has been re-considered, based on the discovery of systems in Galilean sites that Josephus claims to have fortified and on mid-first-century finds in some of these systems (Kloner and Zissu 2003a: 187–89; Zissu and Ganor 2002: 21; Aviam 2004: 124–25, 126–27, 129, 132). The issue remains under debate.

10   The exact battlegrounds remain unknown – a common problem in the archaeology of warfare. Ancient battle sites tend to be indistinguishable in open terrain, even where cultivation or urban expansion has not altered the scene altogether, as is often the case (Bartel 1985: 22). Most archaeologically investigated battlefields are relatively recent. Nineteenth-century examples include the Zulu-British battle site at Isandlwana, South Africa (J. Roberts, personal communication, 2001), and the American sites of Little Bighorn (Scott et al. 1989) and Palo Alto (Haecker 1996). Still later examples are World War I trenches in Europe (Saunders 2002). A famous ancient battlefield that has been detected and is archaeologically investigated is the site of the Roman defeat in the Teutoburg Forest, Germany, where three legions were wiped out by the Germans under Arminius in 9 CE (Schlüter 1999; Harnecker 2004: 42–47).

158 NOTES

11 A destruction scene related to the First Revolt was also exposed in Ashdod (Dothan and Freedman 1967: 32), although, since most of the population of this coastal town was probably not Jewish, the exact circumstances of the event remain unclear.

12 Tombstones of Roman soldiers from the first and second centuries CE usually belong to troops and officers who died during their service in non-combat circumstances (Hope 2003: 85).

13 Violence, as well as some types of disease, tends to leave detectable traces on bones (Mays 1998: 163ff.; Thorpe 2003: 152–59). Warfare offers a more feasible explanation to signs of trauma found on a high percentage of skeletons in a single context than do individual accidents, confrontations, crimes, and executions. This principle applies in particular where historical and archaeological data attests to military confrontations in the relevant period, as in the case of the Jewish revolt (Brayne and Roberts 2003: 171–73; Thorpe 2003: 150–51; Fiorato et al. 2000).

Chapter 8

1 Many of the estate owners lived in Jerusalem. Sumptuous mansions unearthed at the site of the Upper City, in the present-day Jewish Quarter in the Old City of Jerusalem, allowed their aristocratic inhabitants a standard of living comparable to that of their counterparts elsewhere in the empire. At the same time, their strict religious observance is reflected in the frequency of ritual baths in the houses, the almost complete avoidance of imagery art, and the absence of pig bones in the faunal record (Avigad 1983: 95ff.).

2 Large estates dating to the first century CE were discovered at Qawarat Beni Hassan, near Nablus (Dar 1986), Kalandia, north of Jerusalem (Magen 1984; 2004), and Ramat HaNadiv, by the southern slopes of the Carmel ridge (Hirschfeld 2000). Several of Jesus' parables vividly portray daily life, interpersonal relationships, and domestic tensions at first-century estates (Mark 12:1–12; Luke 15:11–31, 16:1–9).

3 References to first-century Jewish attitudes towards Roman taxes can be found in the New Testament. Hence the attempt by the Pharisees to trap Jesus by enticing him to condemn Roman taxation (Matthew 22:21). Spite towards Jewish tax collectors is reflected in Matthew 6:46, 9:9-11, Mark 2:16–17, and Luke 5:27–30, 19:1–9.

4 In addition to economic grievances, the popular animosity towards the aristocracy also likely fed on the aristocracy's history of collaboration with foreign occupiers. The Jewish masses resented the support of some aristocrats for Seleucid policies of forced religious-cultural assimilation, the nomination of corrupt lackeys to the high priesthood by Herod, and the assistance rendered by high level priests and officials to Roman governors in the persecution of dissidents. The ineffectiveness of the Jewish leadership in challenging exploitative Roman policies must have added to the alienation. Unsurprisingly, once the revolt finally erupted the upper classes were virtually decimated by the rebels.

5 Similar examples in Roman history are known from Thrace, North Africa, Spain (Millar 1967: 228–29; Dyson 1975: 145, 147–48), and even Italy (Cassius Dio 77,10).

6 Coponius (6–9 CE), Ambibulus (9–12 CE), Rufus (12–15 CE), and Gratus (15–26 CE).

7 As an example, unlike other governors, Pilate had offensive Graeco-Roman cultic imagery depicted on some of his coins (Kindler 1974: 94, 102–3; Rappaport 1983: 135), although even he avoided human representations.

8 Fadus (44–46 CE), Tiberius Alexander (46–48), Cumanus (48–52), Felix (52–60), Festus (60–62), Albinus (62–64), and Florus (64–66).

9 *Annals* 12. Felix also scandalized the Jews by marrying the Jewish princess Drusilla, sister of the Herodian king Agrippa II (*Antiquities* 20.141–43).

10 Archaeological evidence confirms a reduced rural Jewish settlement in Galilee towards the middle of the first century CE (Aviam 2004: 14).

11 In the conflicts under Cumanus no mention is made of the ethnic origins of the offending soldiers, but the contempt for Jewish religious sensitivities and precise knowledge of how to offend them the most smacks of the vicious intimacy of neighborly spite.

NOTES

12 At the same time, Samaritans and Jews seem to have held a common resentment of Roman rule, which led to a brief Samaritan uprising during the Jewish Revolt and perhaps to occasional cooperation between Samaritans and Jews (Alon 1980a: 33). A scroll of probable Samaritan origins was discovered at Masada, implying that Samaritans took shelter on the mountain along with the Jewish rebels (Cotton and Price 1990).

13 Other sources on the views of the historical Rabbi Judah cast some doubts on the accuracy of this story (Ben-Shalom 1984).

14 Rabbinical authorities were deeply perturbed by the tendency of many Jews to learn Greek, visit theaters and amphitheaters, and even participate in the performances (Lieberman 1980: 3; Rajak 1995: 8; Weiss 1996a: 444–45).

15 A theater was also built in Tiberias. Its location is known, some of its architecture visible, but only full exposure may determine the period of its construction.

16 Hence the "faces which spout out water in towns" (*Tosefta Avodah Zarah* 6.6), as rabbinical literature calls the images that adorned public fountains (*nymphaea*).

17 The phenomenon of prophetic figures prompting the Jews into uprising is discussed in the next chapter.

18 Mid-first-century-CE earthworks possibly associated with John's fortifications were discovered at that site (Aviam 2004: 107).

19 Several examples of proselytes whose conversion is indicated in their names are known from the early Roman period (Hachlili 1983: 198).

20 An extreme anti-Roman Jewish faction, named after the short dagger (*sica*) with which they used to assassin political rivals among the Jewish leadership (*War* 2.254–55). Hundreds of Sicarii, under Eleazar ben Yair, fled to Masada with their families in the early days of the revolt after their leader, Menachem, was lynched by a mob in Jerusalem (*War* 2.441–47).

21 Further reading of the passage implies that John's reasoning was logical rather than religious, but in a later and more serious situation (*War* 6.98) John plainly denies the possibility that God would allow the fall of Jerusalem.

22 Monobazus and Kenedeus, convert princes from the Northern Mesopotamian kingdom of Adiabene, fought bravely on the Jewish side (*War* 2.520), but whether they arrived in Judea before or during the revolt is not clear. Silas, an early commander of the revolt (*War* 2.520, 3.11), was also of Babylonian origin, but, having previously served under Agrippa II, he must have been a long-time resident in Judea by then.

Chapter 9

1 A late-second-century-BCE layer containing arrowheads and evidence for destruction has been unearthed during yet unpublished excavations at the Lower City gate of Marissa (Maresha) in 1992. The date is consistent with the conquest by John Hyrcanus I.

2 The Assyrian version, narrated on the Prism of Sennacherib (Pritchard 1973: 200–201), emphasizes conquests elsewhere in Judea and gloats over locking Hezekiah in his capital "like a bird in a cage," but fails to mention the circumstances of the withdrawal.

3 According to traditions related in *Avoth de Rabbi Nathan* A, chapter 4, this rabbi, who was among the leading spiritual authorities of the period, was smuggled by his students out of besieged Jerusalem in a coffin. He then received Vespasian's permission to establish a new center of Jewish religious scholarship at Yavneh, a town west of Jerusalem. For elaboration on Rabbi Yohanan and his motives, with various other references, see Tropper 2005.

4 Ya'akov Meshorer (1986) lists other instances in the history of Jerusalem in which coins have been used for encouragement under siege: Herod's siege of the Hasmoneans (37 BCE), the Persian siege of the Byzantine city (614 CE), and Saladin's siege of the Crusaders (1187 CE).

5 The court (*temenos*) within which the temple stood measured 480 x 475 x 315 x 280 meters. Retaining walls reaching 30 meters in height separated the court from the avenues below, with corner towers

rising nearly 35 meters. Fine cut stones of outstanding dimensions can still be seen in surviving compound walls. The largest stone measures 13.7 x 3.5 m. Ground-penetrating radar tests calculated a wall width of 4.2–4.9 m. Its estimated weight is over 550 tons (Source: Bahat 1994:181).

6 The widespread bitterness is illustrated in a poem preserved in the rabbinical literature, which warns against both the words and the truncheons that the aristocratic priestly families employed against common Jews (*Tosefta Menahot* 13.21). The disillusioned masses placed their confidence in the priests of the lower ranks, who shared many of their tribulations and were considered more loyal to the moral responsibilities of their position (see *Antiquities* 20.181).

7 Assuming that the essentials of Titus' speech are truthfully recorded, he was not the only leader in history that nurtured a curious indignation at the thanklessness of indigenous people whose homeland had been occupied by an ostensibly enlightened foreign power. Referring to the fierce Spanish uprising against Napoleon, Winston Churchill (1957: 318) notes that the French emperor "could not understand a people who preferred misgovernment of their own making to rational rule imposed from without."

8 The common appearance of motifs related to the freedom festivals of Passover and Tabernacles on revolt coinage (Meshorer 1997: 112–13, 226; see next chapter) raises the possibility that some in the aristocratic government were more enthusiastic about the revolt than Josephus would have his readers believe (see also *War* 4.175, 246).

9 The Persian, Ptolemaic, and early Seleucid occupations were not devoid of incidents, yet few are historically familiar and none is known to have escalated into anything on the scale of the Hasmonean and anti-Roman uprisings. A confrontation that apparently took place during the reign of the Persian king Artaxerxes III (358–338 BCE) is explained by Josephus as the outcome of political power struggles between candidates for the high priesthood in Jerusalem (*Antiquities* 11.297–301). This incident was aggressively resolved by the senior Persian commander Bagoses, who imposed a punitive tax over Judea and, while at it, also desecrated the Temple. Judea was apparently part of the general unrest in the region during that period, and the Persians had some Jews deported and may have also reduced the territory of the autonomous province. Echoes of these incidents can be found in the writings of Eusebius and other later Christian chroniclers. Evidence for friction during the reign of Ptolemy Philadelphos (285–246 BCE) is reported in the Zeno papyri, but the dispute is over taxes, not ideology (Stern 1980: 248). According to Josephus (*Antiquities* 12.156–74), financial discord was also the cause of conflict between the High Priest Onias II and the Ptolemaic court, although the historicity of this episode has been challenged (Gera 1990: 35–38). Some tensions originating in the Ptolemaic period seethed into early Seleucid rule, as hinted at in several harsh verses in chapter 36 of the book of Ben Sira (Sirach), written before 180 BCE.

10 For a discussion and references on the complex issue of national identity in antiquity, see Goodblatt 2006, chapter 1, pp. 1ff.

11 Julius Caesar was deified before Augustus but was nominally never an emperor.

12 Tacitus even speculates about an identification of the Jewish God with the Roman gods Saturn and Bacchus (*Histories* 5.4–5).

13 The complex and widely researched subject of pre-exilic Israelite religion exceeds the scope of this book. See Zevit 2001 for an extensive coverage and related bibliography.

14 Edward Gibbon, *The History of the Decline and Fall of the Roman Empire*. Penguin Books, London, 2000, p. 124.

15 While important as such, pictorial representations were not the general practice in Beth She'arim; they appear in only 8 out of 33 burial caves, and in 12 of the 83 halls within the caves (Weiss 1996b: 360).

16 Even captivity did not always mean the end of struggle. According to Cassius Dio (61, 5.3), Jewish prisoners committed acts of sabotage in the camps where they were being held and ambushed Roman soldiers.

17 For the possible priestly origins of the sanctification of God through one's own death see Goodblatt 1995: 28.

18 The available data on the Bar-Kochba revolt consists of a patchwork of brief Roman, Christian, and Samaritan summaries, rabbinical tales, and archaeological discoveries. The most detailed Roman account can be found in Cassius Dio's third-century-CE *Roman History* (59.11–15), preserved in a summarized version by the eleventh-century monk Xiphilinus.

19 The widely accepted assumption that the Twenty-Second Legion was lost during the Bar-Kochba war is based on its ascertained participation in the revolt and its subsequent disappearance from the records. More direct evidence is lacking. A similar problem relates to the fate of the Ninth Legion *Hispana*, which disappeared roughly during the same period and is presumed to have been destroyed, yet the location, circumstances, and even the specific conflict are debated (Frere 1978: 161–62; *contra* Shotter 1996: 58–59).

20 "How is an idol desecrated? If a Gentile cut off the tip of its ear, or the end of its nose, or the tip of its finger, or battered it even though naught was broken off, he has desecrated it" (*Mishnah, Avodah Zarah* 4.5).

21 Found at the sites of Horvat Midras and Moran 1. Ceramic vessels, mainly oil lamps, decorated with Roman-style human and animal figures were also occasionally defaced during the same period. Lamps with mutilated images were found, for example, in possibly Jewish tombs dated to the late first or early second century CE at Horbat Zikhrin, in the lowland region between the coast and Samaria, near modern Rosh Ha'Ain (Haddad 2007: 49).

22 Hanan Eshel (1999: 232–33) suggests that Josephus chose the dramatic fall of Masada to conclude his *Jewish War* because at the time of writing he may have believed that the Jewish people could not survive without the temple. Eshel detects the morbid pessimism of the author in the resignation of Masada's Sicarii commander Eleazar ben Yair to God's "decree against the whole Jewish nation, that we are to be deprived of this life" (*War* 7.359).

23 Some aspirations for an immediate and physical reestablishment of the old glory survived through at least another two centuries. Brief mentioning of otherwise unknown conflicts with the Jews later in the second century appear in the *Historia Augusta* (Antoninus Pius 5.4–5). Limited information is available on a Jewish uprising in Galilee, known as the Gallus Revolt, against Byzantine rule (351 CE). Led by the otherwise unknown Patricius, it centered around Sepphoris (Diocaesarea). This revolt was apparently put down without widespread destruction (Aurelius Victor, *Liber de Caesaribus* 42:9–12; Socrates, *Historia Ecclesiastica* II, 33). A decade later, hope was rekindled from unexpected quarters. As part of his political and cultural struggle against Christianity and the Christian establishment, the Roman emperor Julian permitted the reconstruction of the Temple in Jerusalem (Browning 1975: 176; Bowersock 1978: 88–90). Many Jews responded enthusiastically, but those plans were frustrated by Julian's death in Mesopotamia during a campaign against the Persians (June 26, 363 CE).

24 Maimonides, *The Twelfth Article of Faith*.

Chapter 10

1 Examples of rebel coinage in Roman history are rare. Julius Vindex and Clodius Macer, who separately attempted to put an end to the rule of Nero in 68 CE, minted their own coins (Millar 1967: 172; Sutherland and Carson 1984: 188–96, 198–201, 206–9; Mildenberg 1990: 62–66; Foss 1990: 69–72), as did Zenobia, a third-century-CE queen of Palmyra, Syria (Mildenberg 1990: 67–70). Yet, Vindex and Macer never meant to disengage from Rome, and Zenobia, while clearly aspiring for preeminence in her region, still displayed affiliation with the empire by choosing Roman symbols, language, and titles on her coins. These cases clearly differ from the rebel issues of Judea.

2 A similar phenomenon has been noted in Phoenicia, although not in rebel contexts. Slogans on some Tyrian, Sidonian, and other Phoenician coins from the Hellenistic up to the early Roman period boast archaic Phoenician letters beside the standard Greek (Millar 1983).

3 The complex issue of a possibly ideological background to the use of Hebrew in Judea during the Hasmonean and Early Roman period has been addressed by various scholars. For a recent summary, discussion, and references, see Goodblatt 2006, ch. 3, "Constructing Jewish Nationalism: The Hebrew Language."

4   The anchor, originally a Seleucid symbol of hope and safe harbor, was probably used by the Hasmoneans as a commemorative reminder of their coastal conquests.

5   In the Graeco-Roman world, the cornucopia was an attribute of the goddess Demeter. On Judea's coins it is depicted crowned with a pomegranate, one of the Seven Species with which the Land of Israel has been blessed (Deuteronomy 8:8) and a fruit laden with Jewish symbolism. Pomegranates represented majesty, fortune, and fertility and were appropriately sculpted on the two monumental pillars flanking the front of Solomon's Temple (Kings I, 7:42). Miniature pomegranate figurines were part of the High Priest's vestments (Exodus 28:33). The fruit also appears on Hasmonean coins (Meshorer 1997: 37), Jewish ossuaries, sarcophagi (Avigad 1962a), oil lamps (Sussman 1972: 45), elegant furniture (Avigad 1983: 106–7, 125, 136, 173), and on mosaics and frescoes of synagogues and private mansions throughout the Roman-Byzantine period (Sukenik 1934; Yadin 1966; Avi-Yonah 1981: 274; Avigad 1983: 99–103, 111, 113–15, 154–60). Beneath such a powerful emblem, even Demeter's attribute could have been effectively "converted."

6   Alexander Jannaeus (103–76 BCE), a king for all practical purposes and addressed as such by Josephus (*Antiquities* 13.320) and Strabo (*Geography* 16:2,40), boasted the title on his coins mostly in Greek (ΑΛΕΞΑΝΔΡΟΥ ΒΑΣΙΛΕΩΣ) and Aramaic (מלכא אלכסנדר; Goodblatt 2006: 150). The title in Hebrew appears only on very few known specimens (Rappaport 1984: 136). Mattathias Antigonus struck coins with royal Greek inscriptions (ΑΝΤΙΓΟΝΟΥ ΒΑΣΙΛΕΩΣ), while the Hebrew version on the reverse side states his other title of "high priest."

7   The later Herodian rulers Agrippa I and Agrippa II did have portraits on their coins, but only on those struck in non-Jewish regions.

8   The vine or bunches of grapes also appear on Herodian coins and on the coins of Bar Kochba (Porton 1976: 174; Avi-Yonah 1981: 142–43), as well as in monumental funerary art (Hachlili and Killebrew 1983: 113).

9   The ritual demanded the use of silver, yet the Romans refused the Jews the right of minting silver currency.

10 It should be noted that severe post-war Roman sanctions were imposed against those caught in possession of rebel currency. This rule is probably behind the rabbinical expression *Ma'ot shel Sakanah* – "coins of danger" (*Ma'asser Sheni* 1.2). Even though their monetary value was obsolete and despite the risks involved, it seems that enough Jews had preserved coins of the revolts to cause discomfort to the Roman authorities. The ideological attraction of the coins and their symbols apparently outlived the tragic outcome of the war in the service of which they had been produced.

11 An additional coin was found at the site of Sartaba-Alexandrion in the Jordan Valley (Syon and Yavor 2001: 33) and is assumed to have been brought there by a refugee or traveler from Gamla. A ninth coin surfaced in 1992 in the antiquities market in Zürich (Syon, personal communication).

12 In an intriguing article, Yoav Farhi (2006) proposes to read the name of Gamla itself on the coin. For a critical analysis of Farhi's proposal, see Syon 2007.

13 No Jerusalem silver shekels were among the over 6200 coins discovered at Gamla, but it should be remembered that Jerusalem issues are generally rare in Galilee. Only 39 are presently known, many of them not from controlled scientific excavations (Syon, personal communication). None, for example, were found during the extensive excavations at Yodfat (Adan-Bayewitz and Aviam 1997: 157, note 30), although one is reported from an earlier survey at the site (Berman 1962: 42–43).

14 A more concise version of the same idea within a wider body of publications focused on Gamla will be published by this author as part of the third volume of the final report of the excavations: D. Syon ed., *Gamla* III. *The Shmarya Gutmann Excavations 1976–1989. Finds and Studies* (IAA Reports, forthcoming).

15 Wood fragments found in caves at Qumran have also been interpreted as remains of such coffins (De Vaux 1973: 46–47).

16 Early Christians, or Judeo-Christians, may also have practiced secondary burial in ossuaries (Figueras 1983: 10–11). First-century Jewish ossuaries have also been found in later Christian contexts in secondary use as reliquaries (Shapira 2003).

17 Nicanor was a renowned magnate who, according to several rabbinical traditions, ordered immense ornate bronze doors to be produced in Alexandria and imported to the Temple of Jerusalem *(*Examples: *Mishnah Yoma 3,10; Sheqalim 6,3; Palestinian Talmud, Yoma III 41a; Babylonian Talmud, Yoma 38a)*. It is unclear whether this Simon donated memorable sums for the building of the Temple or was a senior architect with a major role in the stages of planning or construction. Whatever the exact nature of his involvement, he must have been a man of some stature to earn his undoubtedly highly honorable byname or title. Caiaphas was a high priest best known from the trial of Jesus as described in the New Testament (Matthew 26:57; John 11:49).

18 Jewish funeral customs generally remain modest to the present day. Unless requested otherwise in life, Israeli leaders are buried in a designated plot on Mt Herzl, Jerusalem, within a serene and meticulously tended garden, meters away from a large military cemetery. The founder of the Zionist movement, Theodor Herzl, Prime Ministers Golda Meir and Yitzhak Rabin, and other notables were all laid to rest there. The founder of the nation and its first Prime Minister, David Ben Gurion, is interred near Kibbutz Sde Boker in the Negev Desert and the famous Defense Minister Moshe Dayan lies in the small cemetery in the northern village of Nahalal. All of these gravesites are strikingly simple, often not more remarkable than those of regular citizens.

19 Those luxurious complexes, rather than the modest ossuaries, are the more truthful representations of the hierarchical Jewish society of the first centuries BCE–CE. In their discussion of the egalitarian shift in American funerary architecture since the nineteenth century, Peter Metcalf and Richard Huntington (1991: 16) dryly note that "it is hard to posit an equivalent narrowing of inequalities of wealth and power." The observation would have been as appropriate in first-century Judea.

20 A rare exception is the second-century-BCE "Jason's Tomb," located in the modern neighborhood of Rehavia in western Jerusalem. Animals and humans, the latter involved in what seem to be a sea battle, are sketched on the walls, but these are likely to be casual graffiti post-dating the original use of the structure (Avigad 1967b; Benoit 1967; Avi-Yonah 1975: 252; Kloner 2003: 31).

21 It should be noted that the more cosmopolitan members of the Jewish aristocracy were less willing to give up the high fashions of the period. Eastern Terra Sigillata vessels are found in the Upper City of Jerusalem in layers dated to the destruction in 70 CE, indicating sub-distinctions *within* Jewish society (Berlin 2006: 152).

22 Nearly all pagan religions nominate one of its deities to be the giver or guardian of light or of the sun as its source. Monotheistic faiths followed in the tradition. The Hebrew Bible tells that light was the very first of God's creations (Genesis 1:3–5).
Conversely, Darkness was the ninth plague inflicted on Egypt as Pharaoh refused to let the People of Israel go (Exodus 10:21–23).
Jesus announces that he himself is "the light of the world," promises that his followers "will never walk in darkness but will have the light of life" (John 8:12), and elsewhere teaches that "Your eye is the lamp of your body. If your eye is healthy, your whole body is full of light" (Luke 11:34). The day he died on the cross, "darkness came over the whole land" (Mark 15:33).
Sura 24:35 of the Koran states that "God is the light of the heavens and of the earth. His light is like a niche in which is a lamp – the lamp encased in glass – the glass…a glistening star. From a blessed tree it is lighted, the olive neither of the East nor of the West, whose oil would well nigh shine out, even though fire touched it not."

23 Rare lamps carrying what Hershkovitz (1985) interprets as schematic human faces were discovered in pre-destruction levels in the Jewish Quarter in Jerusalem, where knife-pared lamps or ornate types with no figurative art are otherwise standard (Rosenthal-Heginbottom 2003: 204–5). Hershkovitz suggests that when kept away from public view at private quarters, the unusual lamps would have been less offensive. She uses the same argument in explaining the animal representations on fresco

panels, furniture, and gemstones from the same site (Hershkovitz 2003b: 296–301). A figurine and gemstones showing animal and human depictions were also found at Gamla (Gutman 1994: 48, 54, 138; Syon and Yavor 2001: 22).

24 Knife-pared lamps are commonly discovered in pre-70-CE Jerusalem, in associated tombs, and in surrounding settlements (Rosenthal-Heginbottom 2003: 219, pls. 6.8:4–5, 6.9:43–44, 6.10:21; Wolff 1996: 27; Ben-Arieh and Coen Uzzieli 1996: 83; Greenhut 1996: 44–45; Mazor 1996: 53–54; Gershuny and Zissu 1996: 46, 51; Abu Raya 2000a, b; Nahshoni et al. 2002; Kloner and Zissu 2003b: 59–60). Fragments of nearly 1200 lamps were found at Gamla, almost all knife-pared (Gutman 1994: 142–44; Syon and Yavor 2001: 23). 150 out of 160 lamp shards unearthed at Yodfat were of that type (Adan-Bayewitz and Aviam 1997: 165), as were over 800 of the 1160 lamps and lamp fragments discovered at Masada (Barag and Hershkovitz 1994: 3). They were also standard at other sites associated with Jewish populations, such as Gischala (Meyers et al. 1990: 128, lamp pl. A; Aviam 2004: 108, fig. 10.3:14, 15), Bethany (Saller 1957: 167, pl. 110.a4–5), Senir (Stepansky 2004: 1), Meiron (Meyers et al. 1981: 227, pls. 9.14, 9.15), Khirbet el-Hamam/Narbata (Zertal 1984: 52), Kalandia (Magen 1984: 69; 2004: 114–17), Ramat HaNadiv (Calderon 2000: 101–2; Silberstein 2000: 448–52), Herodium (Bar-Nathan 1981: 65), Macherus (Loffreda 1996: 108–11, 134), and several recently excavated Jewish villages in the Lod region between Jerusalem and Jaffa (Avisar and Shabo 1998; Shmueli and Yannai 1998; Yekutieli et al. 2001: 35–39). This is only a partial list, intended to illustrate the frequency of this class of objects also found in numerous other places.

25 Far less frequent than knife-pared lamps, but also present in some first-century-CE Jewish sites, is the type known as "Gray Molded Lamps" (Amiran and Eitan 1973: pl. 43:1; Hershkovitz 1992: pl. 7:7; Barag and Hershkovitz 1994: 59–71, figs. 18–20). While Gray Molded Lamps were probably influenced by Roman Imperial lamps (Barag and Hershkovitz 1994: 64, 67), human and animal representations are avoided and botanical themes, such as stylized flowers, twigs of olive and myrtle, oak leaves, acorn, plantain, caper, and mallow, are used for decoration instead.

26 Some knife-pared lamps were found in Scythopolis-Beth Shean (Hadad 2002: 13–15), Dor (Rosenthal-Heginbottom 1995: 244, fig. 5.21), Caesarea (Sussman 1996: 351), Pella (Smith and McNicoll 1992: 127, pl. 87.4), Gadara (Kerner 1997), and Philadelphia (Harding 1946: 60, pl. XX:2; 1951: 30, pl. IX.3). They may have belonged to Jews, whose presence in some of these cities is attested by Josephus, although not necessarily (Barag and Hershkovitz 1994: 46–47). Several knife-pared lamps were found at Nabatean sites in northern Sinai (Hershkovitz 1987b: 319), probably having arrived through commerce.

27 Berlin's own previous research (1997) shows that cultural identification through the symbolic preference of utilitarian vessels was not an exclusively Jewish strategy. She perceives the import of coastal ceramic vessels by Phoenician hinterland populations, even though similar vessels were locally available, as a reaction to growing Hasmonean pressure during the second and first centuries BCE.

28 For a full cover of the issue and a survey of rabbinical sources, see Magen 2002: 138–47.

29 Quarrying and production sites in Jerusalem were found at Hizma, Tell el-Full, Jebel Mukabar, and Mt. Scopus (Magen 1985; 2002; Gibson 1983; 2003: 288–90; Amit et al. 2000; 2001; Kloner 2003: 36). The Galilean site is located at Reina (Gal 1991: 25–26).

30 An ornate stone table discovered in Jerusalem carried the relief of a fish (Avigad 1983: 169). A lion's head on a piece of furniture was found at the Jewish estate in Ramat HaNadiv (Hirschfeld 2003).

31 Examples include Gamla in the Golan (Syon and Yavor 2001: 8), Qeren Naftali in the Upper Galilee (Aviam 2004: fig. 7.11), Gezer (Reich 1981: fig.1), and possibly Maresha (Bliss and Macalister 1902: 56; Finkielsztejn 1998: 47–48), the latter both in the Shephela.

32 Numerous units were discovered in and around Jerusalem, in Judea, the coastal hinterland, and the Galilee (Reich 1984; 1990; Greenhut 1997; Zissu 2001: 169; Adan-Bayewitz and Aviam 1997: 164; Aviam 2002: 121; Hirschfeld 2000; Syon and Yavor 2001: 11; Syon 2002: 135; Zissu and Ganor 2002: 20).

33 Ritual baths in Jewish settlements on the roads to Jerusalem probably served pilgrims to the city, as may have done the baths discovered at almost each of the houses adjacent to the Temple Mount (Amit 1999; Reich 1984; Magen 1984; Ben-Dov 1982: 150–53; Kloner 2003: 46).

34 This specific facet of the custom is still maintained at present, though in a more modest form; taps and sinks for ritual cleansing can be found near the entrances of modern Jewish cemeteries.

35 For a comprehensive survey of the architectural characteristics and rabbinic sources of ritual baths, see Reich 1990.

36 Proverbs 22:1 states that a "good name is to be chosen rather than great riches," and in similar spirit Ecclesiastes 7:1 instructs that "a good name is better than precious ointment." In the Hebrew spoken in modern Israel, *shem tov* (a "good name") usually means a good reputation, be it in personal morals or the conduct of business, although, as elsewhere in the world, it might also be a compliment over a name chosen for a newborn. All personal names used in modern Israel derive from common terms, be it a personal quality, geographical feature, religious intent, precious stone, or even a handsome animal, although a name might be chosen for its lyrical quality as much as for its actual meaning. Either way, the meanings of the vast majority of names is understood by all, with the exception of ancient names whose significance is debated even by scholars.

37 The Hebrew name Shlomzion means literally "Peace of Zion," and it has been suggested that its popularity implies an identification with Jerusalem and/or the Temple, rather than with the Hasmonean queen (Barrois 1962: 960). However, as noted by Goodblatt (2006: 182), there is no evidence in the period's literature to suggest that Zion represented anything of importance, while the statistical frequency of the name Miriam and male Hasmonean names supports the Hasmonean explanation. See Goodblatt 2006: 167ff. for a detailed analysis of the meaning of the name Zion in the late Second Temple period and on the coins of the First Revolt.

38 Ilan (1987: 240) remarks that with the addition of the names Joseph and Hannaniah, the Hasmonean share reaches 41% of the sample (total of 817). Maccabees II 8:22 does mention an otherwise obscure Joseph as one of the brothers of the original Hasmonean family. That list omits John, and the two names may somehow refer to the same person. Joseph is the second most common name after Simon, and its frequency is comparable to that of other Hasmonean male names. In at least one of the Hasmonean branches, that of Josephus, the name was inherited (*Life* 5). Hannaniah is an adaptation of John (Yehohanan), and both names share the same meaning.

39 Analysis of glass assemblages from several Jewish sites of the late first and second centuries CE raises the possibility that certain glass types from the general vessel repertoire of the period were more in demand among the Jews of Judea. There were no "Jewish types" as such, and the vast majority of vessels from Judea could also be found elsewhere in the empire. Yet, a markedly denser distribution of some types has been noted, while others were apparently far less popular or shunned altogether, as were, not surprisingly, vessels carrying human and animal imagery. At the same time, the option of ethno-ideological reasoning for the preference of some undecorated types over others demands considerable caution.
As a material, glass may have also been popular among the Jews because unlike ceramics, glass could be purged of ritual impurity through immersion in a ritual bath (see Amit 1999: 82 for glass vessels discovered in a ritual bath at Alon Shevut, note 4 *ibid.* for rabbinical references, and Gorin-Rosen 1999 for a specification of the vessels). Still, any attempt to attach ideological interpretations to choices of glass vessels would demand the isolation of the ideological element from alternative explanations involving style, fashion, and commercial availability. At present, these non-ideological options cannot be overruled.
It should also be stressed that the observations were made at sites dating to the period between the First Revolt and the Bar Kochba uprising, such as the recently excavated Shuaffat, north of Jerusalem (Bar Nathan and Sklar-Parnes 2007), rather than at sites predating the First Revolt, as in the case of ceramic and metal distinctions discussed in this chapter. As the systematic research into this point is in an early stage, there are few related publications. See Katsnelson 2007 for a brief discussion and references.

40 The subject is extensively discussed in scholarly literature (see Alon 1980b: 46; Safrai 1991; Levine 1981: 1; 1987: 7; 2000: 35ff.; Riesner 1995; Flesher 1995; Binder 1999). For a recent deliberation of the issue of public reading of scriptures and an extensive bibliography, see Goodblatt 2006, ch.1, "Constructing Jewish Nationalism: The Role of Scripture."

41 In addition to the famous examples from Herodium, Gamla, and Masada (Foerster 1977; Gutman 1981), first-century synagogues have been recently discovered at Kiryat Sefer (Magen et al. 1999; 2004) and Khirbet Umm el-'Amdan (Weksler et al. 2003: 72–77). Possible synagogues were also identified at Horvat 'Ethri (Zissu and Ganor 2002: 23–27) and Jericho, where the Hasmonean origin suggested by the excavator raised much debate (Netzer 1999; 2000; 2003; Netzer et al. 1999; *contra* Ma'oz 1999 and Rapuano 2001).

Chapter 11

1 St Augustine, *Confessions*. Translated by A. C. Oulter. Library of Christian Classics, Vol. VII, Westminster Press, 1955.

2 The one important aspect in common is the impact of monotheistic faiths but each society responded to religion and related to it through its own cultural tools and was unaffected, as far as it can be determined, by any of the others.

3 "Ahmadinejad speaks, outrage and controversy follow," CNN.com, September 24, 2007. "No gays in Iran? CNN's Jeanne Moos looks at Iranian President Mahmoud Ahmadinejad's gay gaffe," CNN, September 25, 2007.

4 "Renewal of Judaism." *The Early Addresses, 1909–1918*. In: *On Judaism* (Ed. N. N. Glatzer), New York, Schocken, p. 51.

5 "Judaism and the Jews." *Ibid*, p. 21.

6 See for example, Sura 36, 4:9:75–79, 86.

References

Aberle, D. F.
1962   A Note on Relative Deprivation Theory as Applied to Millenarian and Other Cult Movements. Pp. 209–14 in *Millenarian Dreams in Action,* ed. S. Thrupp. The Hague: Mouton.

Abrahamian, E.
1989   *Radical Islam. The Iranian Mojahedin.* London: I.B. Tauris.

Abu Raya, R.
2000a   Jerusalem, Issawiya. *ESI* 111: 64–65.
2000b   Jerusalem, Rockefeller Museum. *ESI* 111: 67–68.

Adams, B.
1943   *The Law of Civilization and Decay.* New York: Knopf.

Adams, R. M.
1966   *The Evolution of Urban Society.* Chicago: Aldine.

Adan-Bayewitz, D. and M. Aviam
1997   Iotapata, Josephus and the Siege of 67: Preliminary Report on the 1992–94 Seasons. *JRA* 10: 131–65.

Aldred, C.
1988   *Akhenaten.* New York: Thames and Hudson.

Alon, G.
1980a   The Bar Kochba War. Pp. 23–25 in *The Bar Kochba Revolt*, ed. A. Oppenheimer. Jerusalem: The Zalman Shazar Center, The Israeli Historical Society (Hebrew).
1980b   *The Jews in their Land in the Talmudic Age.* Jerusalem: Magness, Hebrew University.

Amiran, R. and A. Eitan
1973   Excavations in the Citadel, Jerusalem, 1968–1969 (Preliminary Report). *EI* 11: 213–18 (Hebrew with English summary).

Amit, D.
1999   A Miqve Complex Near Alon Shevut. *'Atiqot* 38: 75–84.

Amit, D., J. Seligman, and I. Zilberbrod
2000   Jerusalem, Mount Scopus (East). *ESI* 111: 65–66.
2001   A Quarry and Workshop for the Production of Stone Vessels on the Eastern Slope of Mount Scopus. *Qadmoniot* 122: 102–10 (Hebrew).

Amit, M.
2003   *A History of the Roman Empire.* Jerusalem: Hebrew University, Magness Press.

Ammerman, N.
1991   North American Protestant Fundamentalism. Pp. 1–65 in *Fundamentalists Observed,* ed. M. E. Marty and R. S. Appleby. Chicago: University of Chicago.

Amorosi, T., P. Buckland, A. Dugmore, J. H. Ingimundarson, and T. H. McGovern,
1997   Reading the Landscape: Human Ecology in the Scandinavian North Atlantic. *Human Ecology* 25.3: 491–518.

Anderson, B.
1983   *Imagined Communities: Reflections on the Origins and Spread of Nationalism.* London: Verso.

REFERENCES

Applebaum, S.
1975 The Peasant Land Struggle and the Great Revolt. *EI* 12: 125–28.

Arbel, Y.
2007 The Gamla Coin: A New Perspective on the Circumstances and Date of its Minting. Pp. 257–75 in *Milk and Honey: Essays on Ancient Israel and the Bible in Appreciation of the Judaic Studies Program at the University of California, San Diego*, eds. S. Malena and D. Miano. Winona Lake, IN: Eisenbrauns.

Arnold, C.
1986 Archaeology and History: The Shades of Confrontation and Cooperation. Pp. 32–39 in *Archaeology at the Interface: Studies in Archaeology's Relationships with History, Geography, Biology and Physical Science*, eds. J. Bintliff and C. Gaffney. BAR International Series 300. Oxford: BAR.

Aviam, M.
1993 Galilee. *NEAEHL* 1993: 453–58.
2002 Yodefat/Jotapata: The Archaeology of the First Battle. Pp. 121–33 in *The First Jewish Revolt: Archaeology, History and Ideology*, eds. A. M. Berlin and J.A. Overman. London: Routledge.
2004 *Jews, Pagans and Christians in the Galilee*. Land of Galilee 1. Rochester, NY: University of Rochester Press).

Aviam, A. and A. Amitai
2002 Excavations at Khirbet esh-Shuhara. Pp. 119–33 in *Eretz Zafon: Studies in Galilean Archaeology*, ed. Z. Gal. Jerusalem: Israel Antiquities Authority (Hebrew).

Avigad, N.
1950–51 The Rock-carved Façades of the Jerusalem Necropolis. *IEJ* 1: 96–106.
1962a A Depository of Inscribed Ossuaries in the Kidron Valley. *IEJ* 12: 1–12.
1962b Expedition A – The Burial Caves in Nahal David. *IEJ* 12: 169–83.
1967a Jewish Rock-Cut Tombs in Jerusalem and the Judean Hill Country. *EI* 8: 119–42 (Hebrew, with English Summaries).
1967b Aramaic Inscriptions on the Tomb of Jason. *IEJ* 17: 101–11.
1983 *Discovering Jerusalem*. Nashville, TN: Nelson.

Aviram J., G. Foerster, and E. Netzer (eds.)
1994 *Masada: The Yigael Yadin Excavations 1963–1965, Final Report*. Jerusalem: Hebrew University.

Avisar, M. and E. Shabo
1998 Kula. *HA*108: 74–76 (Hebrew).

Avi-Yonah, M.
1975 Jewish Art and Architecture in the Hasmonean and Herodian Periods. Pp. 250–81 in *The World History of the Jewish People, The Herodian Period*, ed. M. Avi-Yonah. New Brunswick, NJ: Rutgers University.
1976 *The Jews of Palestine: A Political History from the Bar Kokhba War to the Arab Conquest*. Oxford: Blackwell.
1981 *Art in Ancient Palestine, Selected Studies*. Collected and prepared for publication by H. Katzenstein and Y. Tsafrir. Jerusalem: Magness.

Avni, G. and Z. Greenhut
1996 Architecture, Burial Customs and Chronology. Pp. 1–39 in *The Akeldama Tombs: Three Burial Caves in the Kidron Valley, Jerusalem*, eds. G. Avni and Z. Greenhut. IAA Reports 1. Jerusalem: Israel Antiquities Authority.

Avshalom-Gorni D. and N. Getzov
2002 Phoenicians and Jews - A Ceramic Case-Study. Pp. 74–83 in *The First Jewish Revolt: Archaeology, History and Ideology*, eds. A. M. Berlin and J. A. Overman. London: Routledge.

Badhi, R. and H. Torgë
2000   Shoham (East: B). *ESI* III: 45–46.

Bahat, D.
1994   The Western Wall Tunnels. Pp. 177–90 in *Ancient Jerusalem Revealed*, ed. H. Geva. Jerusalem: Israel Exploration Society).

Baines, J. and N. Yoffe
1998   Order, Legitimacy and Wealth in Ancient Egypt and Mesopotamia. Pp. 199–260 in *Archaic States*, eds. G. M. Feinman and J. Marcus. Santa Fe, NM: School of American Research.

Balikci, A.
1970   *The Netsilik Eskimo.* Prospect Heights, IL: Waveland.

Barag, D.
1992–93 New Evidence on the Foreign Policy of John Hyrcanus. *INJ* 12: 1–12.

Barag, D. and M. Hershkovitz
1994   The Lamps from Masada. pp. 1–78 in *Masada IV: The Yigael Yadin Excavations 1963–1965, Final Report,* eds. J. Aviram, G. Foerster and E. Netzer. Jerusalem: Hebrew University.

Barber, R. K.
1932   *Indian Labor in the Spanish Colonies.* Historical Society of New Mexico, Publications in History 6. Albuquerque, NM: University of New Mexico.

Bar-Kochva, B.
1974   Notes on the Fortresses of Josephus in Galilee. *IEJ* 24: 108–16.
1989   *Judas Maccabaeus, The Jewish Struggle Against the Seleucids.* Cambridge: Cambridge University.
2000   The First Greek Account Concerning the Jews: Theophrastus' Anthropological Theory and Jewish Sacrificial Practices. Pp. 43–69 in *Jerusalem and Eretz Israel, Arie Kindler Volume,* eds. J. Schwartz, Z. Amar and I. Ziffer. Tel Aviv: Eretz Israel Museum (Hebrew with English abstract).

Bar Nathan, R.
1981   The Finds at Lower Herodium. Pp. 54–70 in *Greater Herodium,* ed. E. Netzer. Qedem 13. Jerusalem: Hebrew University.

Bar Nathan, R. and A. Sklar-Parnes
2007   A Jewish Settlement in Orine Between the Two Revolts. Pp. 57–74 in *New Studies in the Archaeology of Jerusalem and its Region, Collected Papers,* eds. J. Patrich and D. Amit. Jerusalem: Israel Antiquities Authority and Hebrew University (Hebrew).

Barrois, G. A.
1962   Zion. *Interpreters' Dictionary of the Bible* IV: 959–60.

Bartel, B.
1985   *Comparative Historical Archaeology and Archaeological Theory.* BAR International Series 233. Oxford: BAR.

Bartlett, W. B.
2001   *The Assassins: The Story of Medieval Islam's Secret Sect.* Stroud, Gloucester: Sutton.

Batz, S.
2003   A Second Temple Period Cemetery at Horvat Beit Sila. Pp. 111–22 in *One Land – Many Cultures, Archaeological Studies in Honour of S. Loffreda,* eds. G. C. Bottini, L. Di Segni and L. D. Chrupcala. Studium Biblicum Franciscanum Collection Maior 41. Jerusalem: Franciscan.

Bauer, B. S.
1996   Legitimization of the State in Inca Myth and Ritual. *AA* 98: 327–37.
1998   *The Sacred Landscape of the Inca: The Cusco Ceque System.* Austin: University of Texas.

REFERENCES

Bayley, J.
1990   The Production of Brass in Antiquity with Particular Reference to Roman Britain. Pp. 7–27 in *2000 Years of Zinc and Brass,* ed. P. T. Craddock British Museum Occasional Papers 50. London: British Museum.

Beard, M., J. North, and S. Price
1998   *Religions of Rome.* Cambridge: Cambridge University.

Beattie, J.
1960   *Bunyoro, An African Kingdom.* New York: Holt, Rinehart and Winston.

Beebe, H. K.
1975   Domestic Architecture and the New Testament. *BA* 38, Vol. 3-4: 89–104.

Bell, C.
1992   *Ritual Theory, Ritual Practice.* New York: Oxford University.

Bellah, R. N.
1985   *Tokugawa Religion: The Cultural Roots of Modern Japan.* New York: Free.

Ben-Arieh, R. and T. Coen Uzzieli
1996   The Pottery. Pp. 73–94 in *The Akeldama Tombs: Three Burial Caves in the Kidron Valley, Jerusalem,* eds. G. Avni and Z. Greenhut. Jerusalem: Israel Antiquities Authority.

Ben-Arieh, S. and E. Netzer
1974   Excavations along the 'Third Wall' of Jerusalem, 1972–1974. *IEJ* 24: 97–107.

Ben-Dov, M.
1982   *In the Shadow of the Temple: The Discovery of Ancient Jerusalem.* New York: Harper and Row.

Ben-Dov, M. and Y. Rappel
1987   *Mosaics of the Holy Land.* New York: Adama.

Benedict, R.
1989   *The Chrysanthemum and the Sword: Patterns of Japanese Culture.* Boston: Houghton Mifflin.

Benoit, P.
1967   L'inscription Grecque du Tombeau de Jason. *IEJ* 17: 112–13.

Ben-Shalom, I.
1984   Rabbi Judah B. Ilai's Attitude Towards Rome. *Zion* 49: 4–24 (Hebrew).

Ben-Yehuda, N.
1995   *The Masada Myth: Collective Memory and Mythmaking in Israel.* Madison, WI: University of Wisconsin.

Berger, P. L.
1969   *A Rumor of Angels: Modern Society and the Rediscovery of the Supernatural.* Garden City, NY: Doubleday.

Bergman, J.
1995   The Adventist and Jehovah's Witnesses Branch of Protestantism. Pp. 33–46 in *America's Alternative Religions,* ed. T. Miller. Albany, NY: State University of New York.

Berlin A. M.
1997   From Monarchy to Markets: The Phoenicians in Hellenistic Palestine. *BASOR* 306: 75–88.
2002   Romanization and Anti-Romanization in Pre-Revolt Galilee. Pp. 57–73 in *The First Jewish Revolt: Archaeology, History and Ideology,* eds. A. M. Berlin and J. A. Overman. London: Routledge.
2006   *Gamla I: The Pottery of the Second Temple Period.* IAA Reports. Jerusalem: Israel Antiquities Authority.

REFERENCES

Berman, A.
1962   Seker Numismati be-Yodefat. *Yediot Numismatiot be-Yisrael* 2: 42–43, (Hebrew).

Bianchi, S. and F. Faggella
1993   The Resumption of the Archaeological Investigation at Qal'at El-Mishnaqa, 1992 Excavation: A Preliminary Report. *ADAJ* 37: 407–16.

Bilde, P.
1979   The Causes of the Jewish War According to Josephus. *JSJ* 10: 179–202.

Binder, D.
1999   *Into the Temple Courts. The Place of the Synagogue in the Second Temple Period.* Atlanta: Society of Biblical Literature.

Binford, L. R.
1972   *An Archaeological Perspective*. New York: Seminar.
1977   General Introduction. Pp. 1–10 in *For Theory Building in Archaeology – Essays on Faunal Remains, Aquatic Resources, Spatial Analysis and Systemic Modeling*, ed. L. R. Binford. New York: Academic.

Bintliff, J.
1991   The Contribution of the Annaliste/Structural History Approach to Archaeology. Pp. 1–33 in *The Annales School and Archaeology*, ed. J. Bintliff. London: Leicester University.

Birley, A. R.
1998   *Hadrian, The Restless Emperor.* London: Routledge.

Bix, H. P.
2001   *Hirohito and the Making of Modern Japan.* New York: Perennial.

Blanton, R. E., G. M. Feinman, S. A. Kowalewski, and P. N. Peregrine
1996   A Dual-Processual Theory for the Evolution of Mesoamerican Civilization. *CA* 37.1: 1–14.

Bliss, F. J. and R. A. S. Macalister
1902   *Excavations in Palestine during the Years 1898–1900.* London: Palestine Exploration Fund.

Boas, F.
1940   The Limitations of the Comparative Method of Anthropology. Pp. 271–304 in *Race, Language and*
[1896]   *Culture.* New York: Macmillan.

Bohak, G.
2003   The Ibis and the Jewish Question. Ancient "Anti-Semitism" in Historical Context. Pp. 27–43 in *Jews and Gentiles in the Holy Land in the Days of the Second Temple, the Mishnah and the Talmud*, eds. M. Mor, A. Oppenheimer, J. Pastor and D. R. Schwartz. Jerusalem: Yad Ben-Zvi.

Bottéro, J.
1992   *Mesopotamia: Writing, Reasoning, and the Gods.* Chicago: University of Chicago.

Bowersock, G. W.
1978   *Julian the Apostate.* Cambridge, MA: Harvard University.

Brandon, S. G. F.
1967   *Jesus and the Zealots.* Manchester: Manchester University.

Braudel, F.
1972   *The Mediterranean and the Mediterranean World in the Age of Phillip II*, vol. I. New York: Harper & Row.

Brayne, K. and J. A. Roberts
2003   Human Skeletal Remains 1993–2001. Pp. XX in *Amorium Reports II: Research and Technical Studies*, ed. C. S. Lightfoot. BAR International Series 1170. Oxford: BAR.

Breglia, L.
1968   *Roman Imperial Coins.* New York: Praeger).

Brewster, A. B.
1922   *The Hill Tribes of Fiji.* Philadelphia: Lippincott.

Bridge, A.
1980   *The Crusades.* London: Granada.

Brockelmann, C.
1980   *History of the Islamic Peoples.* London: Routledge & Kegan Paul.

Bromley, D. and E. D. Silver
1995   The Branch Davidians: A Social Profile and Organizational History. Pp. 149–58 in *America's Alternative Religions,* ed. T. Miller. Albany, NY: State University of New York.

Broshi, M.
1972   Excavations in the House of Caiaphas, Mount Zion. *Qadmoniot* 19–20: 104–7 (Hebrew).

Brown, P.
1971   The Rise and Function of the Holy Man in Late Antiquity. *JRS* 61: 80–101.

Browning, R.
1975   *The Emperor Julian.* London: Weidenfeld & Nicolson.

Bruce, S.
1996   *Religion in the Modern World: From Cathedrals to Cults.* Oxford: Oxford University.

Burckhardt, J.
1998   *The Greeks and Greek Civilization.* New York: St. Martin's.

Burgat, F.
2003   *Face to Face with Political Islam.* London: I.B. Tauris.

Burridge, K.
1969   *New Haven, New Earth.* New York: Schocken.

Butzer, K.
1976   *Early Hydraulic Civilization in Egypt.* Chicago: University of Chicago.

Cahill, J. M.
1992   The Chalk Assemblages of the Persian/Hellenistic and Early Roman Periods. Pp. 190–274 in *Excavations at the City of David, 1978–1985 Directed by Yigal Shiloh III,* eds. A. De Groot and D. T. Ariel. Qedem 33. Jerusalem: Hebrew University.

Calderon, R.
2000   Roman and Byzantine Pottery. Pp. 91–165 in *Ramat HaNadiv Excavations, Final Report of the 1984–1998 Seasons,* ed. Y. Hirschfeld. Jerusalem: Israel Exploration Society.

Canaan, T.
1927   *Mohammedan Saints and Sanctuaries in Palestine.* London: Palestine Exploration Society.

Canseco, M. R. D.
1999   *History of the Inca Realm.* Cambridge: Cambridge University.

Cary, M.
1962   *A History of Rome Down to the Reign of Constantine.* New York: St Martin's.

Castells, M.
1997a   The Power of Identity. *The Information Age: Economy, Society and Culture,* Vol. II. Oxford: Blackwell.

1997b   The Rise of Network Society. *The Information Age: Economy, Society and Culture,* Vol. I. Oxford: Blackwell.

Champion, T.
1990   Medieval Archaeology and the Tyranny of the Historical Record. Pp. 79–95 in *From the Baltic to the Black Sea: Studies in Medieval Archaeology,* eds. D. Austin and L. Alcock. London: Unwin Hyman.

Chazan, R.
1996   *In The Year 1096: The First Crusade and the Jews.* Philadelphia: Jewish Publication Society.

Childe, V. G.
1956   *A Short Introduction to Archaeology.* London: Muller

Churchill, W. S.
1943   *My Early Life.* London: Macmillan.
1957   *A History of the English Speaking Peoples: The Age of Revolution.* New York: Dodd.

Clairmont, C.
1954/55   Greek Pottery From the Near East. *Berytus* 11: 85–141.

Clarke, D. L.
1978   *Analytical Archaeology.* London: Meuthen.

Clauss, M.
2000   *The Roman Cult of Mithras.* Edinburgh: Edinburgh Univeristy.

Coe, M. D.
1984   *Mexico.* London: Thames and Hudson.

Cohen, S. J. D.
1982   Masada: Literary Tradition, Archaeological Remains and the Credibility of Josephus. *JJS* 33: 385–405.

Cohn, N.
1962   Medieval Millenarianism: Its Bearing on the Comparative Study of Millenarian Movements. Pp. 31–43 in *Millenarian Dreams in Action,* ed. S. Thrupp. The Hague: Mouton.
1970   *The Pursuit of the Millennium.* New York: Oxford University.

Coleman, W. S. E.
2000   *Voices of Wounded Knee.* Lincoln, NE: University of Nebraska.

Comaroff, J.
1985   *Body of Power, Spirit of Resistance: The Culture and History of a South African People.* Chicago: University of Chicago.

Conder, C. R and H. H. Kitchener
1882   *Survey of Western Palestine, II: Samaria.* London: Palestine Exploration Fund.

Conrad, G. and A. Demarest
1984   *Religion and Empire: The Dynamics of Aztec and Inca Expansionism.* Cambridge: Cambridge University.

Corbo, V.
1969   L'Herodion di Giabal Fureidis. *LA* 17: 65–121.

Cotton, H. M. and J. Price
1990   Who Conquered Masada in 66 CE and Who Lived There Until the Fortress Fell? *Zion* 55: 449–54.

Crocombe, R. G.
1961   A Modern Polynesian Cargo Cult. *Man* 28: 40–41.

Cross, F. M.
1958   *The Ancient Library of Qumran and Modern Biblical Studies.* Garden City, NY: Doubleday.

REFERENCES

Crowfoot, G. M.
1957 Lamps and an Early Stone Lamp Holder. Pp. 365–78 in *The Objects from Samaria*, eds. J. W. Crowfoot, G. M. Crowfoot and K. M. Kenyon. London: Palestine Exploration Fund.

Crummy, P.
1997 *City of Victory: The Story of Colchester – Britain's First Roman Town*. Colchester: Colchester Archaeological Trust.

Dar, S.
1986 *Landscape and Pattern: An Archaeological Survey of Samaria 800 BCE–636 CE*. BAR International Series 308. Oxford: BAR.

De Vaux, R.
1959 Fouilles de Feshkha. *RB* 55: 225–55.
1973 *Archaeology and the Dead Sea Scrolls*. London: Oxford Univeristy.

Dever, W. G.
1990 Recent Archaeological Discoveries and Biblical Research. Seattle: University of Washington.
1996 Archaeology and the Current Crisis in Israelite Historiography. *EI* 25: 18–27.

Dickson, G.
2000 *Religious Enthusiasm in the Medieval West*. Aldershot: Ashgate/Valorium.

Dothan, M. and D. N. Freedman
1967 Ashdod I, The First season of Excavations. *'Atiqot* 7.

Douglas, M.
1973 *Natural Symbols*. New York: Vintage.

Drucker, P., R. F. Heizer, and J. J. Squier
1959 *Excavations at La Venta, Tabasco, 1955*. Bureau of American Ethnology Bulletin 170. Washington, DC: Bureau of American Ethnology.

Dungworth, D.
1997 Roman Copper Alloys: Analysis of Artifacts from Roman Britain. *JAS* 24: 901–10.

Dunne, P. M.
1968 *Black Robes in Lower California*. Berkeley, CA: University of California.

Durkheim, E.
1915 *The Elementary Forms of Religious Life*. London: Allen and Unwin.

Dvorjetski, E.
1999 Social and Cultural Aspects of Medicinal Baths in Israel. Pp. 117–30 in *Roman Baths and Bathing – Proceedings of the First International Conference on Roman Baths held at Bath, England, 30 March-4 April 1992*, eds. J. DeLaine and D. E. Johnston. Journal of Roman Archaeology Supplement 37. Portsmouth, RI: Journal of Roman Archaeology.

Dyson, S. L.
1971 Native Revolts in the Roman Empire. *Historia* 20: 239–74.
1975 Native Revolts Patterns in the Roman Empire. *Aufstieg und Niedergang der Römischen Welt* II, Vol. 3. Berlin: De Gruyter.

Earle, T. K.
1997 *How Chiefs Come to Power*. Stanford, CA: Stanford University.

Edelstein, G.
2002 Two Roman-Period Burial Caves near Tel Qedesh. *'Atiqot* 43: 99–105 (Hebrew with English summary).

Eidlin, D.
1985 The Numismatic Finds in the Excavations of Gamla. Pp. 138–47 in *Gamla - A Summary of Eight Excavation Seasons*, ed. S. Gutman. Tel Aviv: Hakibbutz Hame'uhad (Hebrew).

Eliav, Y. Z.
2002 Viewing the Sculptural Environment: Shaping the Second Commandment. Pp. 411–33 in *The Talmud Yerushalmi and Graeco-Roman Culture*, Vol. III, ed. P. Schäfer. Tübingen: Mohr Siebeck).

Ellis, P. B.
1990 *The Celtic Empire: The First Millenium of Celtic History, 1000 BC – 51 AD*. London: Constable).
1994 *The Druids*. London: Constable.

Eshel, H.
1999 Josephus' View on Judaism without the Temple in Light of the Discoveries at Masada and Murabba'at. Pp. 229–38 in *Community without Temple*, eds. B. Ego, A. Lange and P. Pilofer. Tübingen: Mohr Siebeck.
2002 Documents of the First Jewish Revolt from the Judean Desert. Pp. 157–63 in *The First Jewish Revolt: Archaeology, History and Ideology*, eds. A. M. Berlin and J. A. Overman. London: Routledge.
2003 Qumran and the Scrolls – Response to the Article by Yizhar Hirschfeld. *Cathedra* 109: 51–62 (Hebrew).

Eshel, H. and M. Broshi
2003 Excavations at Qumran, Summer of 2001. *IEJ* 53.1: 61–73.

Evans, R. J.
1990 *Proletarians and Politics: Socialism, Protest and the Working Class in Germany before the First World War*. London: Harvester Wheatsheaf.

Evans-Pritchard, E. E.
1948 *The Divine Kingship of the Shilluk of the Nilotic Sudan*. Cambridge: Cambridge University.

Fadiman, A.
1997 *The Spirit Catches You and You Fall Down: A Hmong Child, Her American Doctors and the Collision of Two Cultures*. New York: Noonday.

Farhi Y.
2006 The Bronze Coins Minted at Gamla Reconsidered. *INJ* 15: 69–76.

Farmer, W. R.
1958 *Maccabees, Zealots and Josephus*. New York: Columbia University.

Farwell, B.
1967 *Prisoners of the Mahdi*. London: Longmans.

Febvre, L.
1973 *A New Kind of History: From the Writings of Lucien Febvre*, ed. P. Burke. London: Routledge & Kegan Paul.

Festinger, L.
1957 *A Theory of Cognitive Dissonance*. Emerson, IL: Peterson.

Festinger, L., H. W. Riecken, and S. Schachter
1956 *When Prophesy Fails*. Minneapolis, MN: University of Minnesota.

Figueras, P.
1983 *Decorated Jewish Ossuaries*. Leiden: Brill.

Fiensy, D. A.
1991 *The Social History of Palestine During the Herodian Period: The Land is Mine*. Studies in the Bible and Early Christianity 20. Lewiston, NY: Mellen.

Finkelstein, I.
1998 The Great Transformation: The 'Conquest' of the Highlands Frontier and the Rise of Territorial States. Pp. 349–65 in *The Archaeology of Society of the Holy Land*, ed. T. E. Levy. London: Leicester University.
2005 A Low Chronology Update: Archaeology, History and the Bible. Pp. 31–42 in *The Bible and Radiocarbon Dating: Archaeology, Text and Science*, edis. T. E. Levy and T. Higham. London: Equinox.

Finkelstein, I. and N. A. Silberman
2001 *The Bible Unearthed: Archaeology's New Vision of Ancient Israel and the Origin of its Sacred Texts*. New York: Touchstone.

Finkielsztejn, G.
1998 More Evidence on John Hyrcanus I's Conquests: Lead Weights and Rhodian Amphora Stamps. *Bulletin of the Anglo-Israel Archaeological Society* 16: 33–63.

Fiorato, V., A. Boylston, and C. Knüsel
2000 *Blood Red Roses: The Archaeology of a Mass Grave from the Battle of Towton, AD 1461*. Oxford: Oxbow.

Fishwick, D.
2004 *The Imperial Cult in the Latin West*, Vol. III: Provincial Cult, Part 3 The Provincial Centre; Provincial Cult. Leiden: Brill.

Flannery, K. V.
1994 The Ground Plans of Archaic States. Pp. 15–57 in *The Ancient Mind*, eds. C. Renfrew and E. B. W. Zubrow. Cambridge: Cambridge University.

Flesher, P. V. M.
1995 Palestinian Synagogues Before 70 CE, a Review of the Evidence. Pp. 27–39 in *Ancient Synagogues, Historical Analysis and Archaeological Discovery*, eds. D. Urman and P. V. M. Flesher. Leiden: Brill.

Foerster, G.
1976 Art and Architecture in Palestine. Pp. 971–1006 in *Compedia Rerum Iudaicarum ad Novum Testamentum – The Jewish people in the First Century*, Vol. 2, eds. S. Safrai and M. Stern. Assen: Van Gorcum.
1977 The Synagogues at Masada and Herodion. *Journal of Jewish Art* 3–4: 1–10.
1983 The Great War Against the Romans and the Archaeological Finds. pp. 139–52 in *The Jewish Revolts*, ed. U. Rappaport. The History of the People of Israel, eds. M. Avi-Yonah and A. Schalit. Jerusalem: Am Oved (Hebrew).
1987 The Zodiac in Ancient Synagogues and its Place in Jewish Thought and Practice. *EI* 19: 225–34 (Hebrew with English summary).
1995 Art and Architecture. Pp. 347–65 in *Masada IV: The Yigael Yadin Excavations 1963-1965, Final Report*, eds. J. Aviram, G. Foerster and E. Netzer. Jerusalem: Hebrew University.
2000 A Statue of Dionysus from Bet-Shean (Nysa-Scythopolis). Pp. 135– 141 in *Agathos Daimon: Mythes et Cultes, Études d' Iconographie en l' honneur de Lilly Kahil*. Bulletin de Correspondence Hellenique Supplement 38. Athens: École française d'Athènes.

Foerster, G. and Y. Tsafrir
1986 Nysa-Scythopolis – A New Inscription and the Titles of the City on its Coins. *INJ* 9: 53–58.
1988 The Beth She'an Excavations Project. Excavations in the Amphitheater and its Surroundings. *HA* 91: 15–31 (Hebrew).

Foss, C.
1990 *Roman Historical Coins*. London: Seaby.

Foss, M.
1997 *People of the First Crusade*. New York: Arcade.

France, J.
1997   Patronage and the Appeal of the First Crusade. Pp. 5–20 in *The First Crusade, Origins and Impact*, ed. J. Phillips. Manchester: Manchester University.

Frankel, R. and I. Finkelstein
1983   The Northwest Corner of Eretz-Israel in the Baraita Boundaries of Eretz-Israel. *Cathedra* 27: 39–46.

Frankel, R., N. Getzov, M. Aviam, and A. Degani
2001   *Settlement Dynamics and Regional Diversity in Ancient Upper Galilee*. IAA Reports 14. Jerusalem: Israel Antiquities Authority.

Franzius, E.
1969   *History of the Order of Assassins*. New York: Funk and Wagnalls.

Frere, S.
1978   *Britannia, A History of Roman Britain*. London: Routledge & Kegan Paul.

Freud, S.
1959   *Group Psychology and the Analysis of the Ego*. New York: Norton.

Freyne, S.
2002   The Revolt from a Regional Perspective. Pp. 43–56 in *The First Jewish Revolt: Archaeology, History and Ideology*, eds. A. M. Berlin and J. A. Overman. London: Routledge.

Friedheim, E.
2002   Raban Gamaliel and the Bathhouse of Aphrodite in Akko: A Study of Eretz-Israel Realia in the 2nd and 3rd Centuries CE. *Cathedra* 105: 7–32.

Friedman, T. L.
1995   *From Beirut to Jerusalem*. New York: Anchor.

Fritz, V. and R. Deines
1999   Catalogue of the Jewish Ossuaries in the German Protestant Institute of Archaeology. *IEJ* 49: 222–41.

Fromm, E.
1943   *The Fear of Freedom*. London: Kegan Paul.

Fuks, G.
1982   The Jews of Hellenistic and Roman Scythopolis. *JJS* 33: 407–16.
1989   Some Remarks on Simon Bar Giora. *SCI* 8–9: 106–19.

Gabba, E.
1990   The Finances of King Herod. Pp. 160–68 in *Greece and Rome in Eretz Israel*, eds. A. Kasher, U. Rappaport and G. Fuks. Jerusalem: Israel Exploration Society.

Gager, J. G.
1975   *Kingdom and Community: The Social World of Early Christianity*. Englewood Cliffs, NJ: Prentice-Hall.
1998   Messiahs and their Followers. Pp. 37–46 in *Toward the Millenium: Messianic Expectations from the Bible to Waco*, eds. P. Schäfer and M. Cohen. Leiden: Brill.

Gal, Y.
1991   A Stone-Vessel Manufacturing Site in the Lower Galilee. *'Atiqot* 20: 25–26 (Hebrew with English summary).

Geertz, C.
1968   *Islam Observed: Religious Development in Morocco*. New Haven, CT: Yale University.

Geiger, J.
2004 The Ruler Cult in Ancient Palestine. *Cathedra* 111: 5–14 (Hebrew).

Gera, D.
1990 On the Credibility of the History of the Tobiads. Pp. 21–38 in *Greece and Rome in Eretz Israel*, eds. A. Kasher, U. Rappaport and G. Fuks. Jerusalem: Israel Exploration Society.

Gershuny, L.
2006 Excavations at Khirbat Marmita. *'Atiqot* 53: 139–78.

Gershuny, L. and B. Zissu
1996 Tombs of the Second Temple Period at Giv'at Shapira, Jerusalem. *'Atiqot* 30: 45–59 (Hebrew).

Geva, H.
1996 The Siege Ramp Laid by the Romans to Conquer the Northern Palace at Masada. *EI* 25: 297–306 (Hebrew with English summary).
2000 (ed.) *Jewish Quarter Excavations in the Old City of Jerusalem, Final Report*, Vol. I. Jerusalem: Israel Exploration Society.

Gibbon, E.
2000 *The History of the Decline and Fall of the Roman Empire*. Abridged Edition of the 1776 original, edi. D. Womersley. London: Penguin.

Gibson, S.
1983 The Stone Vessel Industry at Hizma. *IEJ* 33: 176–88.
2003 Stone Vessels of the Early Roman Period from Jerusalem and Palestine. A Reassessment. Pp. 287–308 in *One Land – Many Cultures, Archaeological Studies in Honour of S. Loffreda*, eds. G.C. Bottini, L. Di Segni and L.D. Chrupcala. Studium Biblicum Franciscanum Collection Maior 41. Jerusalem: Franciscan.

Glueck, N.
1939 *Explorations in Eastern Palestine,* III. AASOR 19. New Haven, CT: American Schools of Oriental Research).

Golani, A. and V. Zbenovitch
2001 Modi'in. *ESI* 103: 60–70.

Gorin-Rosen, Y.
1999 The Glass Vessels from the *Miqveh* Near Alon Shevut. *'Atiqot* 38: 85–90.

Goodblatt, D.
1995 Suicide in the Sanctuary: Traditions on Priestly Martyrdom. *JJS* 46: 10–29.
1996 Priestly Ideologies of the Judean Resistance. *JSQ* 3.3: 225–49.
1998 From Judeans to Israel: Names of Jewish States in Antiquity. *JSJ* 29: 1–36.
2001 *Ancient Zionism? The Zion Coins of the First Revolt and Their Background*. International Rennert Guest Lecture Series 8. Ramat Gan: Bar Ilan University.
2006 *Elements of Ancient Jewish Nationalism*. New York: Cambridge University.

Goodenough, E. R.
1953 *Jewish Symbols in the Graeco-Roman Period,* Vol I. New York: Pantheon.

Goodman, M.
1987 *The Ruling Class of Judaea*. Cambridge: Cambridge University.
1990 The Origins of the Great Revolt: A Conflict of Status Criteria. Pp. 39–53 in *Greece and Rome in Eretz Israel*, eds. A. Kasher, U. Rappaport and G. Fuks. Jerusalem: Israel Exploration Society.
1998 Jews, Greeks and Romans. Pp. 3–14 in *Jews in the Graeco-Roman World*, ed. M. Goodman. Oxford: Clarendon.

Goren-Inbar, N.
1986   A Figurine from the Acheulian Site of Berekhat Ram. *Mi'Tekufat Ha'Even* 19: 7–12.

Gorzalczany, A.
2000   Shoham (East: C). *ESI* 111: 46–47.

Grant, M.
1974   *The Army of the Caesars*. New York: Scribner's.
1993   *The Emperor Constantine*. London: Weidenfeld & Nicolson.

Gray, R.
1993   *Prophetic Figures in Late Second Temple Jewish Palestine*. New York: Oxford University.

Graziano, F.
1999   *The Millennial New World*. New York: Oxford University.

Greenhut, Z.
1992   The 'Caiaphas' Tomb in North Talpiyot, Jerusalem. *'Atiqot* 21: 63–71.
1996   Two Burial Caves of the Second Temple Period in Rehavia, Jerusalem. *'Atiqot* 29: 41–46 (Hebrew).
1997   The Rural Settlement in the Jerusalem Region From the Early Roman to the Byzantine Periods. Pp. 147–59 in *The Village in Ancient Israel*, eds. S. Dar and Z. Safrai. Tel Aviv: Eretz (Hebrew).

Gregor, T. A. and D. Tuzin
2001   Comparing Gender in Amazonia and Melanesia, A Theoretical Orientation. Pp. 1–16 in *Gender in Amazonia and Melanesia*, eds. T. A. Gregor and D. Tuzin. Berkeley, CA: University of California.

Grierson, P.
1959   Commerce in the Dark Ages: A Critique of the Evidence. *Transactions of the Royal Historical Society* 9: 123–40.

Grossman, D.
1995   *On Killing: The Psychology and Cost of Learning to Kill in War and Society*. Boston: Little Brown.

Gruen, E. S.
2002   Roman Perspectives on the Jews in the Age of the Great Revolt. Pp. 27–42 in *The First Jewish Revolt: Archaeology, History and Ideology*, eds. A. M. Berlin and J. A. Overman. London: Routledge.

Gruzinski, S.
1992   *The Aztecs: Rise and Fall of an Empire*. New York: Abrams.

Gutman, S.
1981   The Synagogue at Gamla. Pp. 30–34 in *Ancient Synagogues Revealed*, ed. L. I. Levine. Jerusalem: Israel Exploration Society.
1985   *Gamla - A Summary of Eight Excavation Seasons*. Tel Aviv: Hakibbutz Hame'uhad) (Hebrew).
1994   *Gamla, A City in Rebellion*. Tel Aviv: Ministry of Defense (Hebrew).

Haas, J.
1982   *The Evolution of Prehistoric Societies*. New York: Columbia University.

Hachlili, R.
1979   The Goliath Family in Jericho: Funerary Inscription from a First Century A.D. Jewish Monumental Tomb. *BASOR* 235: 31–66.
1983   Names and Nicknames of Jews in Second Temple Times. *EI* 17: 188–211.
1997   A Jericho Ossuary and a Jerusalem Workshop. *IEJ* 47: 238–47.
1999   The Finds. Pp. 60–92 in *Jericho, The Jewish Cemetery of the Second Temple Period*, eds. R. Hachlili and A. E. Killebrew. IAA Reports 7. Jerusalem: Israel Antiquities Authority.

Hachlili, R. and A. Killebrew
1983 Jewish Funerary Customs During the Second Temple Period in Light of the Excavations at the Jericho Necropolis. *PEQ* 115: 109–39.

Hackett, C. W. and C. C, Shelby (eds.)
1942a *Revolt of the Pueblo Indians of New Mexico, and Otermin's Attempted Reconquest, 1680–1682,* Vol. 1. Albuquerque, NM: University of New Mexico.
1942b *Revolt of the Pueblo Indians of New Mexico, and Otermin's Attempted Reconquest, 1680–1682,* Vol. 2. Albuquerque, NM: University of New Mexico.

Hadad, S.
2002 The Oil Lamps from the Hebrew University Excavations at Bet Shean. Pp. XX–XX in *Excavations at Bet Shean,* Vol. 1, eds. G. Foerster and Y. Tsafrir. Qedem 4. Jerusalem: Hebrew University / Israel Exploration Society.

Haddad, E.
2007 A Burial Cave from the First–Second Centuries CE and Double-*Arcosolia* Tombs from the Forth–Fifth Centuries CE on the Fringes of Horbat Zikhrin. *'Atiqot* 56: 25–57 (Hebrew with English summary).

Hadas, G.
1994 Nine Tombs of the Second Temple Period at 'En Gedi. *'Atiqot* 24: XX–XX (Hebrew with English summary).

Haecker, C. M.
1996 The Guns of Palo Alto. *Archaeology* 49.3: 48–53.

Halpern, B.
1997 Text and Artifact: Two Monologues? Pp. 311–41 in *The Archaeology of Israel: Constructing the Past, Interpreting the Present,* eds. N. A. Silberman and D. Small. Journal for the Study of the Old Testament, Supplement Series 237. Sheffield: Sheffield Academic.
2005 David Did It, Others Did Not: The Creation of Ancient Israel. Pp. 423–38 in *The Bible and Radiocarbon Dating: Archaeology, Text and Science,* eds. T. E. Levy and T. Higham. London: Equinox.

Hamel, G.
1989 *Poverty and Charity in Roman Palestine, First Three Centuries.* Berkeley, CA: University of California.

Hanson, R. S.
1980 *Tyrian Influence in the Upper Galilee, Meiron Excavation Project No.2.* Cambridge, MA: American Schools of Oriental Research.

Harding, G. L.
1946 A Nabataean Tomb in Amman. *QDAP* 12: 58–62.
1951 A Roman Tomb in Amman. *ADAJ* 1: 30–33.

Harnecker, J.
2004 *Arminius, Varus and the Battlefield at Kalkriese.* Bramsche, Germany: Rasch.

Harris, M.
1985 *The Sacred Cow and Abominable Pig: Riddles of Food and Culture.* New York: Simon & Schuster.

Harris, S.
2005 *The End of Faith: Religion, Terror and the Future of Reason.* London: Free.

Hart, P.
1999 *The I.R.A. and its Enemies: Violence and Community in Cork, 1916–1923.* New York: Clarendon.

Hartal, M.
1987 The History of the Golan during the Second Temple Period. *Ariel* 50–51: 69–76 (Hebrew).

Hawkes, C.
1954 Archaeological Theory and Method: Some Suggestions from the Old World. *AA* 56: 155–68.

Hayes, J. W.
1985 Hellenistic to Byzantine Fine Wares and Deriatives in the Jerusalem Corpus. Pp. 189–94 in *Excavations in Jerusalem 1961–1967*, Vol. I, ed. A. D. Tushingham. Toronto: Royal Toronto Museum.

Hengel, M.
1989 *The Zealots: Investigations into the Jewish Freedom Movement in the Period from Herod I until 70 A.D.* Edinburgh: Clark.

Hershkovitz, M.
1985 More on Lamps: Schematic Faces on Jewish Lamps of Herodian (Second Temple) Period. *EI* 18: 43–45 (Hebrew with English summary).
1987a Aroer during the Late Second Temple Period. P. 21 in *The Thirteenth Archaeological Congress in Israel, 16–18 February 1987*. Beer Sheva: Ben-Gurion University.
1987b The Pottery of the First and Second Centuries CE from Giv'at Ram. *EI* 19: 314–25 (Hebrew with English summary).
1992 Aro'er at the End of the Second Temple Period. *EI* 23: 309–19 (Hebrew with English summary).
1996 Roman Medical Instruments on Masada: Possible Evidence of a Roman Infirmary. *EI* 25: 351–55 (Hebrew with English summary).
2003a Jerusalemite Painted Pottery from the Late Second Temple Period. Pp. 31–34 in *Nabateans in the Negev*, ed. R. Rosenthal-Heginbottom. Haifa: Hecht Museum, University of Haifa.
2003b Gemstones. Pp. 296–301 in *Jewish Quarter Excavations in the Old City of Jerusalem, Final Report*, Vol. II, ed. H. Geva. Jerusalem: Israel Exploration Society.

Hirschfeld, Y.
1995a Tiberias. *HA* 104: 34–36.
1995 *The Palestinian Dwelling in the Roman-Byzantine Period*. Jerusalem: Franciscan.
2000 *Ramat HaNadiv Excavations, Final Report of the 1984-1998 Seasons*. Jerusalem: Israel Exploration Society.
2002 A Lion's Head from the Herodian Palace at Ramat HaNadiv. *Israel Museum Studies in Archaeology* 2: 11–16.
2004 Excavations at 'Ein Feshkha, 2001: Final Report. *IEJ* 54.1: 37–74.

Hittman, M.
1997 *Wovoka and the Ghost Dance*. Lincoln, NE: University of Nebraska.

Hobart, M.
1987 Summer's Day and Salad Day. The Coming of Age of Anthropology? Pp. 22–51 in *Comparative Anthropology*, ed. L. Holy. Oxford: Blackwell).

Hobsbawm, E. J.
1985 *Bandits*. Harmondsworth, UK: Penguin.

Hodder, I.
1999 *The Archaeological Process*. Oxford: Blackwell.

Hodgson, J.
1982 *The God of the Xhosa*. Cape Town: Oxford University.

Hoffer, E.
1951 *The True Believer*. New York: Harper and Row.

Holland, T. A.
1977   A Study of Palestinian Iron Age Baked Clay Figurines, with Special Reference to Jerusalem: Cave 1. *Levant* 9: 121–55.

Holley, A. E.
1994   The Ballista Balls from Masada. Pp. 347–65 in *Masada IV: The Yigael Yadin Excavations 1963–1965, Final Report*, eds. J. Aviram, G. Foerster and E. Netzer. Jerusalem: Hebrew University.

Holum, K. G.
1998   Identity and the Late Antique City: The Case of Ceasarea. Pp. 157–77 in *Religious and Ethnic Communities in Later Roman Palestine*, ed. H. Lapin. Bethesda, MD: University of Maryland.

Holt, P. M.
1961   *A Modern History of the Sudan*. New York: Praeger.

Hope, V. M.
2003   Trophies and Tombstones: Commemorating the Roman Soldier. *World Archaeology* 35: 79–97.

Horsley, R. A.
1979   Josephus and the Bandits. *JSJ* 20: 37–63.
1987   *Jesus and the Spiral of Violence: Popular Jewish Resistance in Roman Palestine*. San Francisco: Harper and Row.
1995   *Galilee. History, Politics, People*. Valley Forge, PA: Trinity.
2002   Power Vacuum and Power Struggle in 66–7 C.E. Pp. 87–109 in *The First Jewish Revolt: Archaeology, History and Ideology*, eds. A. M. Berlin and J. A. Overman. London: Routledge.

Hourani, A.
1991   *A History of the Arab Peoples*. New York: Warner.

Howitt, A. W.
1904   *The Native Tribes of Southeast Australia*. London: Macmillan).

Hultgren, A. J. and S. A. Haggmark (eds.)
1996   *The Earliest Christian Heretics: Readings from Their Opponents*. Minneapolis, MN: Fortress.

Humbert, J.-B. and A. Chambon
1994   *Fouilles de Khirbet Qumran et de 'Ain Feshkha*. Novum Testamentum et Orbis Antiquus Series Archaeologica 1 (Göttingen: Vandenhoeck & Ruprecht).

Hunter, F.
2002   Roman Coin Hoards Discovered in Northern Scotland. *Minerva* 13.3: 54–56.

Ibrahim, H. A.
2004   *Sayyid 'Abd al-Rahman Al-Mahdi: A Study of Neo-Mahdism in the Sudan, 1889–1956*. Leiden: Brill.

Ilan, T.
1987   The Names of the Hasmoneans in the Second Temple Period. *EI* 19: 238–41 (Hebrew, English summary).
1989   Notes on the Distribution of Jewish Women's Names in Palestine in the Second Temple and Mishnaic Period. *JJS* 40.2: 186–200.

Ilan, Z. and E. Damati
1987   *Meroth, The Ancient Jewish Village*. Tel Aviv: Society for the Protection of Nature in Israel (Hebrew).

Ilan, Z. and A. Izdarechet
1988   *Arbel*. Tel Aviv: HaKibbutz Hameuhad (Hebrew).

Iritani, T.
1991   *Group Psychology of the Japanese in Wartime*. London: Kegan Paul.

REFERENCES

Johnson, K. O.
1994 *Why do Catholics Do That? A Guide to the Teachings and Practices of the Catholic Church.* New York: Ballantine.

Johnson, M. A.
2000 Self-Made Men and the Staging of Agency. Pp. 213–31 in *Agency in Archaeology*, eds. M-A. Dobres and J. Robb. London: Routledge).

Johnson, A. W. and T. Earle
1987 *The Evolution of Human Societies.* Stanford, CA: Stanford University.

Jones, A. H. M.
1986 *The Later Roman Empire, 284–602*, Vol.1. Baltimore, MD: Johns Hopkins University.

Jones, S.
1997 *The Archaeology of Ethnicity.* London: Routledge.

Joyce, A. A. and M. Winter
1996 Ideology, Power, and Urban Society in Pre-Hispanic Oaxaca. *CA* 37: 33–47.

Judah, T.
1997 *The Serbs, History, Myth and the Destruction of Yugoslavia.* New Haven, CT: Yale University.

Kalyvas, S. N.
2001 "New" and "Old" Civil Wars: A Valid Distinction? *World Politics* 54: 99–118.

Kamrava, M.
1990 *Revolution in Iran: The Roots of Turmoil.* London: Routledge.

Kanael, B.
1953 The Historical Background of the Coins 'Year Four…of the Redemption of Zion. *BASOR* 129: 18–20.

Kaplan, Y.
1993 Jaffa. *NEAEHL* 1993: 656–59.

Kasher, A.
1983a Introduction: The Circumstances and Causes to the Jewish War Against the Romans. Pp. 9–92 in *The Great Jewish Revolt: Factors and Circumstances Leading to its Outbreak*, ed. A. Kasher. Jerusalem: Zalman Shazar Center.
1983b Foreword. Pp. 7–8 in *The Great Jewish Revolt: Factors and Circumstances Leading to its Outbreak*, ed. A. Kasher. Jerusalem: Zalman Shazar Center (Hebrew).
1988 *Jews, Idumaeans and Ancient Arabs.* Tübingen: Mohr.

Katsnelson, N.
2007 Early Roman Glass Vessels from Judea – Locally Produced Glass? Preliminary Report. Pp. 5–11 in *New Studies in the Archaeology of Jerusalem and its Region, Collected Papers*, eds. J. Patrich and D. Amit. Jerusalem: Israel Antiquities Authority / Hebrew University.

Kemp, B.
1989 *Ancient Egypt: The Anatomy of a Civilization.* London: Routledge.

Kenyon, K.
1974 *Digging up Jerusalem.* New York: Praeger.

Kerner, S.
1997 Umm Qays-Gadara: A Preliminary Report, 1993–1995. *ADAJ* 41: 283–302.

Kindler, A.
1974 *Coins of the Land of Israel.* Jerusalem: Keter.

1980   The Coins of the Bar-Kochva War. Pp. 159–77 in *The Bar-Kochva Revolt*, ed. A Oppenheimer. Jerusalem: Historical Society of Israel (Hebrew).

King, A.
1990   *Roman Gaul and Germany.* London: British Museum.

Kloner, A.
1987   The Dating of the Hiding Systems. Pp. 361–65 in *The Hiding Complexes in the Judean Shephela*, eds. A. Kloner and Y. Tepper. Tel Aviv: Hakibbutz Hameuchad (Hebrew).
1991   A Burial Cave from the Early Roman Period at Giv'at Seled in the Judean Shephelah. *'Atiqot* 20: 159–63.
1994   Burial Caves With Wall Paintings from the First Century CE in Jerusalem and Judea. Pp. 165–72 in *Graves and Burial Practices in Israel in the Ancient Period*, ed. I. Singer. Jerusalem: Israel Exploration Society (Hebrew).
1996   A Tomb with Inscribed Ossuaries in East Talpiyot, Jerusalem. *'Atiqot* 29: 15–22.
2000   *Survey of Jerusalem, The Southern Sector.* Jerusalem: Israel Antiquities Authority.
2003   *Survey of Jerusalem, The Northwestern Sector.* Jerusalem: Israel Antiquities Authority.

Kloner, A. and Y. Arbel
1996   Maresha – Area 61 (Underground System). *HA* 105: 146–51 (Hebrew).

Kloner, A., G. Finkielsztejn, and Y. Arbel
1996   Maresha – Area 100. *HA* 105: 146–51 (Hebrew).

Kloner, A. and Y. Tepper
1987   *The Hiding Complexes in the Judean Shephela.* Tel Aviv: Hakibbutz Hameuchad (Hebrew).

Kloner, A. and B. Zissu
2003a Hiding Complexes in Judea: An Archaeological and Geographical Update on the Area of the Bar Kochba Revolt. Pp. 181–216 in *The Bar Kochba War Reconsidered*, ed. P. Schäfer. Tübingen: Mohr Siebeck.
2003b *The Necropolis of Jerusalem in the Second Temple Period.* Jerusalem: Yad Ben-Zvi / Israel Exploration Society (Hebrew).

Knaut, A. L.
1995   *The Pueblo Revolt of 1680.* Norman, OK: University of Oklahoma.

Knight, V. J., Jr.
1986   The Institutional Organization of Mississippi Religion. *American Antiquity* 51: 675–87.

Krader, L.
1968   *Formation of the State.* Foundations of Modern Anthropology Series, ed. M. D. Sahlins. Englewood Cliffs, NJ: Prentice Hall.

La Barre, W.
1969   *The Peyote Cult.* New York: Schocken.
1970   *The Ghost Dance.* Garden City, NY: Doubleday.

Lapp, N. L.
1983   *The Excavations at Araq el-Emir 1.* AASOR 47. Cambridge, MA: American Schools of Oriental Research.

Leone, M. P.
1984   Interpreting Ideology in Historical Archaeology: Using the Rules of Perspective in the William Paca Garden in Annapolis, Maryland. Pp. 25–35 in *Ideology, Power and Prehistory*, eds. D. Miller and C. Tilley. Cambridge: Cambridge University.
1988   The Relationship Between Archaeological Data and the Documentary Record: 18th Century Gardens in Annapolis, Maryland. *Historical Archaeology* 22.1: 29–35.

Leslie, C. M.
1960   Now We are Civilized: A Study of the World View of the Zapata Indians of Malta, Oaxaca. Detroit: Wayne State University.

Levine, L. I.
1981   Ancient Synagogues, A Historical Introduction. Pp. 1–10 in *Ancient Synagogues Revealed*, ed. L. I. Levine. Jerusalem: Israel Exploration Society.
1987   The Second Temple Synagogue: The Formative Years. Pp. 7–32 in *The Synagogue in Late Antiquity*, ed. L..I. Levine. Philadelphia: American Society of Oriental Research.

Levy, T. E. (ed.)
2005   *Archaeology, Anthropology and Cult: The Sanctuary at Gilat*. London: Equinox.

Lewis, B.
1968   *The Assassins: A Radical Sect in Islam*. New York: Basic.
1976 (ed.) *Islam: From The Prophet Muhammad To The Capture of Constantinople*. New York: Walker.
1986   On the Quietist and Activist Traditions in Islamic Political Writing. *Bulletin of the School of Oriental and African Studies, University of London*, 49.1: 141–47.
1993   *The Arabs in History*. Oxford: Oxford University
1995   *The Middle East: A Brief History Of The Last 2,000 Years*. New York: Scribner.
2003   *The Crisis of Islam: Holy War and Unholy Terror*. New York: Modern Library.

Lewis, C. S.
1991   *The Great Divorce*. London: Fount.

Lewis, J. R.
1998   *Cults in America*. Santa Barbara, CA: ABC-Clio.

Lewis, N. and M. Reinhold
1990   *Roman Civilization*, II, 3rd edition. New York: Columbia University.

Lieberman, S.
1980   'So it Was and So it Will Be' – The Jews in The Land of Israel and in the Diaspora During the Mishnaic and Talmudic Period. *Cathedra* 17: 3–10 (Hebrew).

Lindholm, C.
2002   Culture, Charisma, and Consciousness: The Case of the Rajneeshee. *Ethos* 30.4: 357–75.

Lipset, S. M. and E. Raab
1970   *The Politics of Unreason: Right Wing Extremism in America, 1790–1970*. New York: Harper and Row.

Loffreda, S.
1981   Preliminary Report on the Second Season of Excavations at Qal'at El-Mishnaqa Machaerus. *ADAJ* 25: 85–94.
1996   *La Ceramica di Macheronte e dell'Herodion (90a.C. – 135 d.C.)*. Jerusalem: Franciscan.

MacDonald, W. L.
1982   *The Architecture of the Roman Empire*, Vol.1. New Haven, CT: Yale University.

Magen, Y.
1984   Kalandia – A Vineyard Farm and Winery of Second Temple Times. *Qadmoniot* 66–67: 61–71 (Hebrew).
1985   Jerusalem as the Center of the Stone Vessel Industry in the Time of Herod. *Qadmoniot* 68: 124–27 (Hebrew).
1993   Mount Gerizim and the Samaritans. Pp. 91–148 in *Early Christianity in Context*, eds. F. Manns and E. Alliata. Jerusalem: Franciscan.
2002   *The Stone Vessel Industry in the Second Temple Period*. JSP 1. Jerusalem: Israel Exploration Society.
2004   Qalandiya – A Second Temple Period Viticulture and Wine-manufacturing Agricultural Settlement. Pp. 29–144 in *The Land of Benjamin*, eds. Y. Magen, D. T. Ariel, G. Bijovsky, Y. Tzionit and O. Sirkis. JSP 3. Jerusalem: Israel Antiquities Authority.

Magen, Y., Y. Zionit, and E. Sirkis
1999 A Jewish Village and Synagogue of the Second Temple Period. *Qadmoniot* 117: 25–32 (Hebrew).
2004 Khirbet Badd 'Isa –Qiriat Sefer. Pp. 179–241 in *The Land of Benjamin,* eds. Y. Magen, D. T. Ariel, G. Bijovsky, Y. Tzionit and O. Sirkis. JSP 3. Jerusalem: Israel AntiquitiesAuthority.

Magness, J.
2002 *The Archaeology of Qumran and the Dead Sea Scrolls.* Grand Rapids, MI: Eerdmans.

Malina, B. J.
1981 *The New Testament World: Insights from Cultural Anthropology.* Atlanta: Knox.

Mann, M.
1986 *The Sources of Social Power, Volume 1: A History of Power from the Beginning to A.D. 1760.* Cambridge: Cambridge University.

Ma'oz, Z. U.
1987 The Golan from the Second Temple Period to the Roman-Byzantine Period in the Light of Archaeological Research. *Ariel* 50–51: 60–68 (Hebrew).
1999 The Synagogue that Never Existed in the Hasmonean Palace at Jericho: Remarks Concerning an Article by E. Netzer, Y. Kalman and R. Laureys [Qadmoniot 32 (117) 1999, pp. 17–24]. *Qadmoniot* 118: 120–21 (Hebrew).

Marcus, J. and K. V. Flannery
1994 Ancient Zapotec Ritual and Religion: an Application of the Direct Historical Approach. Pp. 55–74 in *The Ancient Mind*, eds. C. Renfrew and E. B. W. Zubrow. Cambridge: Cambridge University.

Marcuse, H.
1968 *Negations: Essays in Critical Theory.* London: Penguin.

Martin, V.
2000 *Creating an Islamic State: Khomeini and the Making of a New Iran.* London: I.B. Tauris.

Matthews, J. S.
1975 The Naming, Opening and Dedication of Stanley Park. *Vancouver Historical Journal* 2.

Mauss, M.
1990 *The Gift. The Form and Reason for Exchange in Archaic Societies.* London: Norton.

Mays, S.
1998 *The Archaeology of Human Bones.* London: Routledge.

Mazar, A.
1990 *Archaeology of the Land of the Bible, 10,000–580 BCE.* New York: Doubleday.

Mazor, G.
1988 The Beth She'an Excavations Project. Excavations in the Amphitheater and its Surroundings. *HA* 91: 15–31 (Hebrew).
1996 A Columbarium Cave at Ras Esh-Sheikh 'Anbar, East of Jerusalem. *'Atiqot* 29: 51–55 (Hebrew).

Mazor, G. and R. Bar-Nathan
1998 The Beth She'an Excavation Project 1992–1994, Antiquities Authority Expedition. *ESI* 17: 7–35.

McAteer, W.
1991 *Rivals in Eden: A History of the French Settlement and British Conquest of the Seychelles Islands, 1742–1818.* Lewes, Sussex: Book Guild.

McGovern, T. H.
1991 Climate Correlation, and Causation in Norse Greenland. *Arctic Anthropology* 28.2: 77–100.

McLaren, J. C.
2003 The Coinage of the First Year as a Point Reference for the Jewish Revolt (66–70 CE). *SCI* 27: 135–52.

McNicoll, A. W.
1992 The Hellenistic Period. Pp. 103–18 in *Pella in Jordan 2: The Second Interim Report of the Joint University of Sydney and College of Wooster Excavations at Pella 1982–1985*, eds. A. W. McNicoll, P. C. Edwards, J. Hanbury-Tenison, J. B. Hennessy, T. F. Potts, A. Walmsley, and P. W. Watson. Sydney: Mediterranean Archaeology.

Mead, M.
1963 *Sex and Temperament in Primitive Societies*. New York: Morrow Quill.

Meintjes, J.
1971 *Sandile: The Fall of the Xhosa Nation*. Cape Town: Bulpin.

Mendels, D.
1992 *The Rise and Fall of Jewish Nationalism*. New York: Doubleday.

Mertus, J. A.
1999 *Kosovo: How Myths and Truths Started a War*. Berkeley, CA: University of California.

Meshorer, Y.
1967 *Jewish Coins of the Second Temple Period*. Tel Aviv: Am Hassefer.
1976 The Double Cornucopiae as a Jewish Symbol. *Judaica Post* 4.2: 282–85.
1982 *Ancient Jewish Coinage*, Vol. II. New York: Amphora.
1985 *City Coins of Eretz-Israel and the Decapolis in the Roman Period*. Jerusalem: Israel Museum.
1986 Siege Coins of Judea. Pp. XX–XX in *Proceedings of the 10th International Congress of Numismatics, London, September 1986*, ed. I. Carradice. IAPN Publications 11. London: IAPN.
1996 The Ear of Yahweh on a Yehud Coin. *EI* 25: 435–37.
1997 *A Treasury of Jewish Coins from the Persian Period to Bar Kochba*. Jerusalem: Yad Ben-Zvi (Hebrew).
1998 *Ancient Means of Exchange, Weighs and Coins*. Haifa: University of Haifa.

Metcalf, P. and R. Huntington
1991 *Celebrations of Death: The Anthropology of Mortuary Ritual*. Cambridge: Cambridge University.

Meyers, E. M.
1998 The Early Roman Period at Sepphoris: Chronological, Archaeological, Literary and Social Considerations. Pp. 343–55 in *Hesed ve-Emet, Studies in Honor of Ernest S. Frerichs*, eds. J. Magness and S. Gitin. Atlanta: Scholars.
2002 Sepphoris: City of Peace. Pp. 110–19 in *The First Jewish Revolt: Archaeology, History and Ideology*, eds. A. M. Berlin and J. A. Overman. London: Routledge.

Meyers, E. M., C. L. Meyers, and J. F. Strange
1990 *Excavations at the Ancient Synagogue of Gush Halav*. Meiron Excavations Project 5. Winona Lake, IN: American Schools of Oriental Research.

Meyers, E. M., J. F. Strange, and D. E. Groh
1978 The Meiron Excavations Project: Archaeological Survey in Galilee and Golan, 1976. *BASOR* 230: 1–24.

Meyers, E. M., J. F. Strange, and C. L. Meyers
1981 *Excavations at Ancient Meiron, Upper Galilee, Israel, 1971–72, 1974–75, 1977*. Cambridge, MA: American School of Oriental Research.

Mildenberg, L.
1990 Rebel Coinage in the Roman Empire. Pp. 62–74 in *Greece and Rome in Eretz Israel*, eds. A. Kasher, U. Rappaport and G. Fuks. Jerusalem: Israel Exploration Society.

Millar, F.
1967   *The Roman Empire and its Neighbors*. London: Weidenfeld & Nicolson.
1983   The Phoenician Cities: A Case-Study in Hellenization. *Proceedings of the Cambridge Philosophical Society* 209: 55–71.
1993   *The Roman Near East 31 BC–AD 337*. Cambridge, MA: Harvard University.

Miller, D. and C. Tilley (eds.)
1984   *Ideology, Power and Prehistory*. Cambridge: Cambridge University.

Millin, S. G.
1954   *The People of South Africa*. New York: Knopf.

Mithen, S.
1996   *The Prehistory of the Mind: The Cognitive Origins of Art, Religion and Science*. London: Thames and Hudson.

Moaddel, M.
1993   *Class, Politics and Ideology in the Iranian Revolution*. New York: Columbia University.

Modrzejewski, J. M.
2003   "*Filios suos tantum*" – Roman Law and Jewish Identity in Historical Context. Pp. 108–36 in *Jews and Gentiles in the Holy Land in the Days of the Second Temple, the Mishnah and the Talmud*, eds. M. Mor, A. Oppenheimer, J. Pastor and D. R. Schwartz. Jerusalem: Yad Ben-Zvi.

Moreland, J.
2001   *Archaeology and Text*. London: Duckworth.

Mousnier, R.
1970   *Peasant Uprisings in Seventeenth-Century France, Russia, and China*. New York: Harper and Row.

Mühlberger, D.
1991   *Hitler's Followers: Studies in the Sociology of the Nazi Movement*. London: Routledge.

Nahshoni, P., B. Zissu, N. Sarig, A. Ganor, and A. Avganim
2002   A Rock-Cut Burial Cave from the Second Temple Period at Horbat Zefiyya, Judean Shephelah. *'Atiqot* 43: 49–71.

Naveh, J. and J. Greenfield
1984   Hebrew and Aramaic in the Persian Period. Pp. 115–29 in *The Cambridge History of Judaism*, eds. W. D. Davies and L. Finkelstein. New York: Cambridge University.

Ne'eman, Y.
1993   *Sepphoris in the Period of the Second Temple, the Mishna and the Talmud*. Jerusalem: Shem (Hebrew).

Netzer, E.
1975   The Hasmonean and Herodian Winter Palaces of Jericho. *IEJ* 25: 89–100.
1981   *Greater Herodium*. Qedem 13. Jerusalem: Hebrew University.
1999   A Synagogue from the Hasmonean Period Recently Exposed in the Western Plain of Jericho. *IEJ* 49: 203–21.
2000   The Synagogue in Jericho – Did it Exist or Not? A Response to U. Z. Ma'oz's Remarks in *Qadmoniot* 32 (1999). *Qadmoniot* 120: 69–70 (Hebrew).
2001   *The Palaces of the Hasmoneans and Herod the Great*. Jerusalem: Yad Ben-Zvi.
2003   The Synagogues from the Second Temple Period According to Archaeological Finds and in Light of the Literary Sources. Pp. 277–86 in *One Land – Many Cultures: Archaeological Studies in Honour of S. Loffreda*, eds. G. C. Bottini, L. Di Segni and L. D. Chrupcala. Studium Biblicum Franciscanum Collection Maior 41. Jerusalem: Franciscan.

REFERENCES 189

Netzer, E., Y. Kalman, and R. Loris
1999   A Hasmonean Period Synagogue at Jericho. *Qadmoniot* 117: 17–24 (Hebrew).

Netzer, E. and Weiss, Z.
1994   *Zippori*. Jerusalem: Israel Exploration Society.

Neusner, J.
1994   *Introduction to Rabbinic Literature*. New York: Doubleday..

Nichol, F. D.
1944   *The Midnight Cry*. Washington, DC: Review and Herald.

Nodelman, S.
1975   How to Read a Roman Portrait. *Art in America* 63: 26–33.

Odahl, C. M.
2004   *Constantine and the Christian Empire*. London: Routledge.

Ofer, A.
1986   Tell Rumeideh (Hebron) – 1985. *ESI* 5: 92–93.
1993a   Hebron. *NEAEHL* 1993: 606–9.
1993b   Judean Hills Survey. *NEAEHL* 1993: 815–16.

Ogden, D.
1997   *The Crooked Kings of Ancient Greece*. London: Duckworth.

Overman, J. A.
2002   The first Revolt and Flavian Politics. Pp. 213–20 in *The First Jewish Revolt: Archaeology, History and Ideology*, eds. A. M. Berlin and J. A. Overman. London: Routledge.

Pagels, E.
1979   *The Gnostic Gospels*. New York: Random House
1995   *The Origins of Satan*. New York: Vintage.

Papadopoulos, J. K.
1999   Archaeology, Myth-History and the Tyranny of the Text: Chalkidike, Torone and Thucydides. *Oxford Journal of Archaeology* 18.4: 377–94.

Pape, R. A.
2003   The Strategic Logic of Suicide Terrorism. *American Political Science Review* 97.3: 20–32.
2006   *Dying to Win. The Strategic Logic of Suicide Terrorism*. New York: Random House.

Paynter, R.
1990   Afro-Americans in the Massachusetts Historical Landscape. Pp. 49–62 in *The Politics of the Past*, eds. P. Gathercole and P. Lowenthal. One World Archaeology 12. London: Unwin Hyman.

Parapetti, R.
1983–84 Architectural and Urban Space in Roman Gerasa. *Mesopotamia* 18: 37–74.

Peires, J. B.
1989   *The Dead Will Arise: Nongqawuse and the Great Xhosa Cattle Killing Movement of 1856–7*. Bloomington, IN: Indiana University.

Perlman, I., J. Gunneweg, and J. Yellin
1986   Pseudo-Nabataean Ware and Pottery of Jerusalem. *BASOR* 262: 77–82.

Peters, E. (ed.)
1998   *The First Crusade: The Chronicle of Fulcher of Chartres and Other Source Materials*. Philadelphia: University of Pennsylvania.

Peukert, D. J. K.
1987   *Inside Nazi Germany: Comformity, Opposition and Racism in Everyday Life.* London: Batsford.

Philbrick, N.
2006   *Mayflower.* New York: Penguin.

Piggot, S.
1975   *The Druids.* New York: Praeger.

Pollock, S.
1999   *Ancient Mesopotamia.* Cambridge: Cambridge University.

Ponting, M. J.
2000   The Chemical Analysis of a Selection of the Copper-Alloy Metalwork from the Early Roman Fortified Complex. Pp. 504–10 in *Ramat HaNadiv Excavations, Final Report of the 1984–1998 Seasons,* ed. Y. Hirschfeld. Jerusalem: Israel Exploration Society.
2002a   Roman Military Copper-Alloy Artefacts from Israel: Questions of Organization and Ethnicity. *Archaeometry* 44.4: 555–71.
2002b   Keeping up with the Romans? Romanization and Copper Alloys in First Revolt Palestine. *Journal of the Institute of Archaeometallurgical Studies* 22: 3–6.

Ponting, M. J. and I. Segal
1998   ICP-AES Analyses of Roman Military Copper-Alloy Artefacts from the Excavations of Masada, Israel. *Archaeometry* 40: 109–23.

Pool, J.
1997   *Hitler and his Secret Partners: Contributions, Loot and Rewards, 1933–1945.* New York: Pocket.

Porath, Y.
1998   The Caesarea Excavations Project, March 1992 – June 1994, Expedition of The Antiquities Authority. *ESI* 17: 39–49.

Porton, G. G.
1976   The Grape Cluster in Jewish Literature and Art of Late Antiquity. *JJS* 27: 159–76.

Postgate, J. N.
1992   *Early Mesopotamia: Society and Economy at the Dawn of History.* London: Routledge.

Preucel, R. E.
2000   Making Pueblo Communities: Architectural Discourse at Kotyiti, New Mexico. Pp. 58–77 in *The Archaeology of Communities,* eds. M. A. Canuto and J. Yaeger. New York: Routledge).

Price, B. J.
1978   Secondary State Formation: An Explanatory Model. Pp. 161–86 in *Origins of the State: The Anthropology of Political Evolution,* eds. R. Cohen and E. R. Service. Philadelphia: Institute for the Study of Human Issues.

Price, J. J.
1992   *Jerusalem Under Siege: The Collapse of the Jewish State 66–70 CE.* Leiden: Brill.

Pritchard, J. B. (ed.)
1973   *The Ancient Near East,* Volume I: An Anthology of Texts and Pictures. Princeton, NJ: Princeton University.

Propp, W. H. C.
1999   Monotheism and "Moses." The Problem of Early Israelite Religion. Ugarit-Forschungen 31, eds. M. Dietrich and O. Loretz. Münster: Ugarit.

Prunier, G.
1995   *The Rwanda Crisis: History of a Genocide.* New York: Columbia University.

REFERENCES

Rahmani, L. Y.
1994   *A Catalogue of Jewish Ossuaries in the Collections of the State of Israel.* Jerusalem: Israel Antiquities Authority.

Rajak, T.
1983   *Josephus: The Historian and His Society.* London: Duckworth.
1995   The Location of Cultures in Second Temple Palestine: The Evidence of Josephus. Pp. 1–14 in *The Book of Acts in its First Century Setting*, Vol. 4, ed. R. Bauckham. Carlisle: Paternoster.
2002   Jewish Millenarian Expectations. Pp. 164–88 in *The First Jewish Revolt: Archaeology, History and Ideology*, eds. A. M. Berlin and J. A. Overman. London: Routledge.

Rappaport, R.
1999   *Ritual and Religion in the Making of Humanity.* Cambridge: Cambridge University.

Rappaport, U.
1982   John of Giscala: From Galilee to Jerusalem. *JJS* 33: 479–93.
1983   The Coins in Judea and Rome. Pp. 129–37 in *Judea and Rome: The Jewish Revolts*, ed. U. Rappaport. Jerusalem: Am Oved (Hebrew).
1984   *A History of Israel in the Period of the Second Temple*, 3rd edition. Tel Aviv: Amihai (Hebrew).

Rapuano, Y.
2001   The Hasmonean Period 'Synagogue' at Jericho and the 'Council Chamber' Building at Qumran. *IEJ* 51: 48–56.

Rashad, A. J.
1993   Hamas: The History of the Islamic Opposition Movement in Palestine. *Washington Report on Middle East Affairs*. Http://www.wrmea.com/backissues/0393/9303037.htm.

Reich, R.
1981   Archaeological Evidence of the Jewish Population in Hasmonean Gezer. *IEJ* 31: 48–52.
1984   A Miqweh at 'Isawiya near Jerusalem. *IEJ* 34: 220–23.
1990   *Miqva'ot (Jewish Ritual Baths) in the Second Temple Period and in the Period of the Mishna and Talmud.* Unpublished Ph.D. dissertation, The Hebrew University, Jerusalem (Hebrew, with an English abstract).
1992   Ossuary Inscriptions from the 'Caiaphas' Tomb. *'Atiqot* 21: 72–77.

Reich, R. and Y. Billig
1999   Excavations near the Temple Mount and Robinson's Arch, 1994–1996. *Qadmoniot* 117: 33–40 (Hebrew).
2000   A Group of Theatre Seats Discovered Near the South-Western Corner of the Temple Mount. *IEJ* 50: 175–84.
2001   A Group of Theatre Seats from Jerusalem. *Qadmoniot* 122: 93–95 (Hebrew).

Renfrew, C.
1985   *The Archaeology of Cult: The Sanctuary at Phylakopi.* London: Thames and Hudson.
1994   The Archaeology of Religion. Pp. 47–54 in *The Ancient Mind*, eds. C. Renfrew and E. B. W. Zubrow. Cambridge: Cambridge University.

Rex, J.
2002   Islam in the United Kingdom. Pp. 51–76 in *Islam, Europe's Second Religion*, ed. S. T. Hunter. Westport, CT: Praeger.

Richards, I. A.
1993   Introduction. Pp. 5–26 in *The Iliad of Homer.* New York: Norton.

Riesner, R.
1995   Synagogues in Jerusalem. Pp. 179–211 in *The Book of Acts in its First Century Setting*, Vol. 4: *The Book of Acts in its Palestinian Setting*, ed. R. Bauckham. Carlisle: Paternoster.

Riley-Smith, J.
1984   The First Crusade and the Persecution of the Jews. *Studies in Church History* 21: 51–72.
1985   *The First Crusade and the Idea of Crusading.* Philadelphia: University of Pennsylvania.

Rippin, A.
2001   *Muslims: Their Religious Beliefs and Practices.* London: Routledge.

Robbins, J.
2001   Secrecy and the Sense of an Ending: Narrative, Time and Everyday Millenarianism in Papua New Guinea and in Christian Fundamentalism. *Comparative Studies in Society and History* 43: 525–51.

Robins, S. and J. M. Post
1997   *Political Paranoia: The Psychopolitics of Hatred.* New Haven, CT: Yale University.

Robinson, J. M. (ed.)
1977   *The Nag Hammadi Library in English.* New York: Harper.

Rokeah, D.
1990   Tacitus and the God of Israel. *Zion* 55: 265–68 (Hebrew).

Rolston, B.
1991   *Politics and Painting: Murals and Conflict in Northern Ireland.* London: Associate University.

Rose, G.
1978   *The Melancholy Science: An Introduction to the Thought of Theodor W. Adorno.* London: Macmillan.

Rosenthal-Heginbottom, R.
1995   Imported Hellenistic and Roman Pottery. Pp. 183–288 in *Excavations at Dor, Final Report,* Volume IB: *Areas A and C: The Finds,* ed. E. Stern. Qedem 2. Jerusalem: Hebrew University.
2003   Hellenistic and Early Roman Fine Ware and Lamps from Area A. Pp. 192–223 in *Jewish Quarter Excavations in the Old City of Jerusalem, Final Report,* Vol. II, ed. H. Geva. Jerusalem: Israel Exploration Society.

Ross, A.
1970   *Everyday Life of the Pagan Celt.* London: Batsford.

Roth, C.
1960   Simon Bar Giora, Ancient Jewish Hero. *Commentary* 25: 52–58.
1962   The Historical Implications of the Jewish Coinage of the First Revolt. *IEJ* 12.1: 33–46.

Roy, O.
1998   Has Islamism a Future in Afghanistan? Pp. 199–211 in *Fundamentalism Reborn: Afghanistan and the Taliban,* ed. W. Maley. New York: New York University.

Rozenberg, S.
1981   Frescoes and Stucco. Pp. 71–74 in *Greater Herodium,* ed. E. Netzer. Qedem 13. Jerusalem: Hebrew University.
2000   Wall Paintings in Herod's Palace at Jericho. *Michmanim* 14: 16–17 (Hebrew with English abstract.
2003   Wall painting Fragments from Area A. Pp. 302–28 in *Jewish Quarter Excavations in the Old City of Jerusalem, Final Report,* Vol. II, ed. H. Geva. Jerusalem: Israel Exploration Society.

Rudich, U.
1993   *Political Dissidence Under Nero: The Price of Dissimulation.* New York: Routledge.

Runciman, S.
1954   *A History of The Crusades.* Cambridge: Cambridge University.

Sabloff, J.
1990   *The New Archaeology and the Ancient Maya.* New York: Scientific American Library.

Saddington, D. B.
1982   *The Development of the Roman Auxiliari Forces from Caesar to Vespasian (49 B.C.–A.D.79*. Harare: University of Zimbabwe.

Safrai, S.
1991   The Synagogue. Pp. 169–96 in *The Jewish Diaspora in the Hellenistic-Roman Period*. Jerusalem: Zalman Shazar Center (Hebrew).

Safrai, Z.
1975   The Temple and the Divine Service. Pp. 282–337 in *The World History of the Jewish People: The Herodian Period*, ed. M. Avi-Yonah. New Brunswick, NJ: Rutgers University.

Sahlins, M.
1985   *Islands of History*. Chicago: University of Chicago.

Saldarini, A. J.
2002   Good from Evil: The Rabbinic Response. Pp. 221–36 in *The First Jewish Revolt: Archaeology, History and Ideology*, eds. A. M. Berlin and J. A. Overman. London: Routledge.

Saller, S. J.
1957   *Excavations at Bethany (1949–1953*. Jerusalem: Franciscan.

Salway, P.
1981   *Roman Britain*. Oxford: Clarendon.

Sandars, N. K.
1972   Introduction. Pp. 7–58 in *The Epic of Gilgamesh*. London: Penguin.

Sanderson, G. N.
1974   The European Partition of Africa: Coincidence or Conjecture? *Journal of Imperial and Commonwealth History* 3.1: 154.

Santino, J.
1999   Public Protest and Popular Style: Resistance from the Right in Northern Ireland and in South Boston. *AA* 101: 515–28.

Saunders, N. J.
2002   Excavating Memories: Archaeology and the Great War, 1914–2001. *Antiquity* 76 (291): 101–8.

Schäfer, P.
1995   *The History of the Jews in Antiquity*. Luxembourg: Harwood Academic.
1996   The Exodus Tradition in Pagan Greco-Roman Literature. Pp. 9–38 in *The Jews in the Hellenistic-Roman World, Studies in Memory of Menachem Stern*, eds. I. M. Gafni, A. Oppenheimer and D. R. Schwartz. Jerusalem: Zalman Shazar Center for Jewish History.
2002   Jews and Gentiles in Yerushalmi Avodah Zarah. Pp. 335–52 in *The Talmud Yerushalmi and Graeco-Roman Culture*, Vol. III, ed. P. Schäfer. Tübingen: Mohr Siebeck.

Schlüter, W.
1999   The Battle of the Teutoburg Forest: Archaeological Research at Kalkriese Near Osnabrück. Pp. 125–59 in *Roman Germany. Studies in Cultural Interaction*, eds. J. D. Creighton and R. J. A. Wilson. Journal of Roman Archaeology, Supplementary Series 32. Portsmouth, RI: JRA.

Schnapp, A.
1994   Are Images animated: the Psychology of Statues in Ancient Greece? Pp. 40–44 in *The Ancient Mind*, eds. C. Renfrew and E. B. W. Zubrow. Cambridge: Cambridge University.

Schürer, E.
1961   *A History of the Jewish People in the Time of Jesus*. New York: Schocken.

REFERENCES

Schwartz, S.
1998 Gamaliel in Aphrodite's Bath: Palestinian Judaism and Urban Culture in the Third and Fourth Centuries. Pp. 203–17 in *The Talmud Yerushalmi and Graeco-Roman Culture*, Vol. I, ed. P. Schäfer. Tübingen: Mohr Siebeck.
2000 Herod, Friend of the Jews. Pp. 67–76 in *Jerusalem and Eretz Israel, Arie Kindler Volume*, eds. J. Schwartz, Z. Amar and I. Ziffer. Tel Aviv: Eretz Israel Museum.

Scott, D. D., M. A. Connor, M. A. and D. Harmon
1989 *Archaeological Perspectives on the Battle of the Little Bighorn*. Norman, OK: University of Oklahoma.

Sells, M. A.
2002 Islam in Serbian Religious Mythology. Pp. 56–85 in *Islam and Bosnia, Conflict Resolution and Foreign Policy in Multi-Ethnic States*, ed. M. Shatzmiller. Montreal: McGill–Queen's University.

Service, E. R.
1962 *Primitive Social Organization*. New York: Random House.
1975 *Origins of the State and Civilizations: the Process of Cultural Evolution*. New York: Norton.

Seyrig, H.
1950 Irenopolis-Neronias-Sepphoris. *Numismatic Chronicle* 10: 284–99.

Shadmi, T.
1996 The Ossuaries and the Sarcophagus. Pp. 41–55 in *The Akeldama Tombs: Three Burial Caves in the Kidron Valley, Jerusalem*, eds. G. Avni and Z. Greenhut, IAA Reports 1. Jerusalem: Israel Antiquities Authority.

Shanks, M. and C. Tilley
1987 *Re-constructing Archaeology: Theory and Practice*. Cambridge: Cambridge University.

Shapira, L.
2003 A Second Temple Period Ossuary from the Large Byzantine Structure in Area XV. Pp. 129–32 in *The Temple Mount Excavations in Jerusalem 1968-1978, Directed by Benjamin Mazar*, ed. E. Mazar. Qedem 43. Jerusalem: Hebrew University.

Shaw, B. D.
1979 Rural Periodic Markets in Roman North Africa. Pp. 91–117 in *Research in Economic Anthropology*, ed. G. Dalton. Greenwich, CT: JAI.

Shmueli, O. and E. Yannay
1998 Ben Shemen. *HA* 108: 85–86 (Hebrew).

Shotter, D.
1996 *The Roman Frontier in Britain: Hadrian's Wall, The Antonine Wall and Roman Policy in the North*. Preston, UK: Carnegie.

Shupe, A. and D. G. Bromley
1995 The Evolution of Modern American Anticult Ideology: A Case Study in Frame Extension. Pp. 411–16 in *America's Alternative Religions*, ed. T. Miller. Albany, NY: State University of New York.

Sievers, J.
1990 *The Hasmoneans and their Supporters from Mattathias to the Death of John Hyrcanus I*. Atlanta: Scholars.

Silberstein, N.
2000 Hellenistic and Roman Pottery. Pp. 448–52 in *Ramat HaNadiv Excavations, Final Report of the 1984–1998 Seasons*, ed. Y. Hirschfeld. Jerusalem: Israel Exploration Society.

Sinopoli, C. M. and K. D. Morrison
1995 Dimensions of Imperial Control: The Vijayanagara Capital. *AA* 97: 83–96.

REFERENCES

Sinnigen, W. G. and A. E. R. Boak
1977 *A History of Rome to A.D. 565.* New York: MacMillan.

Smallwood, E. M.
1976 *The Jews under Roman Rule.* Leiden: Brill.

Smith, R. H.
1966 The Household Lamps of Palestine in the New Testament Times. *BA* 29: 2–27.

Smith, R. H. and A. W. McNicoll
1992 The Roman Period. Pp. 119–44 in *Pella in Jordan 2: The Second Interim Report of the Joint University of Sydney and College of Wooster Excavations at Pella 1982–1985,* eds. A. W. McNicoll, P. C. Edwards, J. Hanbury-Tenison, J. B. Hennessy, T. F. Potts, R. H. Smith, A. Walmsley, and P. Watson. Sydney: Mediterranean Archaeology.

Sperber, D.
1998 *The City in Roman Palestine.* New York: Oxford University.

Starr, C. G.
1992 History and Archaeology in the Early First Millennium B.C. Pp. 1–6 in *Greece Between East and West: 10th-9th Centuries B.C. Papers of the Meeting at the Institute of Fine Arts, New York University, March 15th-16th,* eds. G. Kopcke and I. Tokumaro. Mainz: von Zabern.

Stegemann, E. W and W. Stegemann
1999 *The Jesus Movement: A Social History of its First Century.* Edinburgh: Clark.

Steinbauer, F.
1979 *Melanesian Cargo Cults: New Salvation Movements in the South Pacific.* St. Lucia: University of Queensland.

Stepansky, Y.
2004 Senir. *ESI* 116: 1–2.

Stephenson, C. and B. Lyon
1951 *Mediaeval History.* New York: Harper and Row.

Stern, E. (ed.)
1993 *New Encyclopedia of Archaeological Excavations in the Holy Land.* New York: Simon and Schuster.

Stern, M.
1980 The Hellenistic Period. Pp. 223–54 in *History of the Land of Israel,* ed. Y. Rappel. Tel Aviv: Ministry of Defense (Hebrew).
1979 The Expulsion of Jews from Rome in Antiquity. *Zion* 44: 1–27 (Hebrew).
1982 Josephus and the Roman Empire. Pp. 237–45 in *Josephus Flavius, Historian of Eretz-Israel in the Hellenistic-Roman Period,* ed. U. Rappaport. Jerusalem: Yad Izhak Ben Zvi (Hebrew).
1991 The Jews in Roman Historiography. Pp. 465–77 in *Studies in Jewish History: The Second Temple Period,* eds. M. Amit, I. Gafni and M. D. Herr. Jerusalem: Yad Izhak Ben-Zvi) (Hebrew).

Stevenson, M. G.
1989 Sourdoughs and Cheechakos: The Formation of Identity-Signaling Social Groups. *JAA* 8: 270–312.

Stoianovitch, T.
1976 *French Historical Method: The Annals Paradigm.* Ithaca, NY: Cornell University.

Stone, M. E.
1981 Reactions to the Destruction of the Second Temple. *JSJ* 12: 195–204.

Strange, J. F.
1992 Six Campaigns at Sepphoris: The University of South Florida Excavations, 1983–1989. Pp. 344–51 in *The Galilee in Late Antiquity.* New York: Jewish Theological Seminar.

Strobel, A.
1974 Observations about the Roman Installations at Mukawer. *ADAJ* 19: 101–27.

Sukenik, E. L.
1928 A Jewish Hypogeum near Jerusalem. *The Journal of the Palestine Oriental Society* 8: 113–21.
1934 *Ancient Synagogues in Palestine.* London: Milford.

Sukenik, E. L. and L. A. Mayer
1931 *The Excavations of the Third Wall of Ancient Jerusalem.* Jerusalem: Hebrew University.

Sussman, V.
1972 *Ornamented Jewish Oil Lamps, from the Fall of the Second Temple to the Revolt of Bar Kochba.* Jerusalem: Bialik Institute / Israel Exploration Society) (Hebrew).
1996 Caesarea Illuminated by Its Lamps. Pp. 346–58 in *Caesarea Maritima, A Retrospect after Two Millenia,* eds. A. Raban and K. G. Holum. Leiden: Brill.

Sutherland, C. H. V.
1974 *Roman Coins.* London: Barrie and Jenkins.

Sutherland, C. H. V. and R. A. G Carson
1984 *Roman Imperial Coinage,* Vol. I. London: Spink.

Sutton, J. E. G.
1998 Ntusi and Bigo: Farmers, Cattle-herders and rulers in Western Uganda, AD 1000–1500. *Azania* 33: 39–72.

Syon, D.
2002 Gamla: City of Refuge. Pp. 134–53 in *The First Jewish Revolt: Archaeology, History and Ideology,* eds. A. M. Berlin and J. A. Overman. London: Routledge.
2007 Yet Again on the Bronze Coins Minted at Gamla. *Israel Numismatic* Research 2: 117–22.

Syon, D. and Z. Yavor
2001 Gamla – Old and New. *Qadmoniot* 121: 2–33 (Hebrew).
2002 Gamla 1997–2000. *ESI* 114: 2–4.

Tabor, J. D.
1998 Patterns of the End: Textual Weaving from Qumran to Waco. Pp. 409–30 in *Toward the Millenium: Messianic Expectations from the Bible to Waco,* eds. P. Schäfer and M. Cohen. Leiden: Brill.

Tal, O., Y. Tepper, and A Fantalkin
2000 Josephus' Fortifications at Beersheba (Galilee). Pp. 155–63 in *Jerusalem and Eretz Israel, Arie Kindler Volume,* eds. J. Schwartz, Z. Amar and I. Ziffer. Tel Aviv: Eretz Israel Museum (Hebrew with English abstract).

Tapper, R.
1984 Holier than Thou: Islam in Three Tribal Societies. Pp. 244–65 in *Islam in Tribal Societies,* eds. A. S. Ahmed and D. M. Hart. London: Routledge & Kegan Paul).

Tepper, Y. and Y. Shahar
1987 Hiding Complexes in the Galilee, Pp. 279–326 in *The Hiding Complexes in the Judean Shephela,* eds. A. Kloner and Y. Tepper. Tel Aviv: Hakibbutz Hameuchad (Hebrew).

Thorpe, I. J. N.
2003 Anthropology, Archaeology, and the Origin of Warfare. *World Archaeology* 35: 145–65.

Tierney, B. (ed.)
1970 *The Middle Ages,* Vol.I: *Sources of Medieval History.* New York: Knopf.

Todd, M.
1999 *Roman Britain.* Oxford: Blackwell.

REFERENCES

Todorov, T.
1984 *The Conquest of America: The Question of the Other.* New York: Harper Perennial

Torgë, H.
2002 Khirbet Burnat (West). *ESI* 114: 46–47.

Trigger, B. G.
1989 *A History of Archaeological Thought.* Cambridge: Cambridge University.

Tropper, A.
2005 Yohanan ben Zakkai, *Amicus Caesaris*: A Jewish Hero in Rabbinic Eyes. *Jewish Studies, an Internet Journal* (Bar Ilan University) 4: 133–49.

Tsafrir, Y. and Y. Magen
1984 Two Seasons of Excavations at the Sartaba/Alexandrium Fortress. *Qadmoniot* 65: 26–32 (Hebrew).

Turner, V. W.
1967 *The Forest of Symbols.* Ithaca, NY: Cornell University.
1969 *The Ritual Process.* Chicago: Aldine.

Tuzin, D.
1997 *The Cassowary's Revenge: The Life and Death of Masculinity in a New Guinea Society.* Chicago: University of Chicago.

Tzaferis, V.
1969 The Burial of Simon the Temple Builder. *Qadmoniot* 1: 137–38 (Hebrew).

Van Henten, J. W.
2003 2 Maccabees as a History of Liberation. Pp. 63–86 in *Jews and Gentiles in the Holy Land in the Days of the Second Temple, the Mishnah and the Talmud,* eds. M. Mor, A. Oppenheimer, J. Pastor and D. R. Schwartz. Jerusalem: Yad Ben-Zvi.

Van Zandt, D. E.
1995 The Children of God. Pp. 127–32 in *America's Alternative Religions,* ed. T. Miller. Albany, NY: State University of New York.

Vardaman, J.
1969 *Preliminary Report on the Results of the 1968 Excavations at Machaerus.* A Study presented to the New Testament Graduate Colloquium (New Testament 530b), March 13, 1969. Louisville, KY: Southern Baptist Theological Seminary.

Vermeule, E.
1996 Archaeology and Philology: The Dirt and the Word. *Transactions of the American Philological Association* 126: 1–10.

Vermeule, C. and K. Anderson
1981 Greek and Roman Sculpture in the Holy Land. *The Burlington Magazine*: 7–19.

Veyne, P.
1987 *The Roman Empire.* Cambridge, MA: Belknap.

Volkan, V. D.
2002 Bosnia-Herzegovina: Chosen Trauma and Transgenerational Transmission. Pp. 86–97 in *Islam and Bosnia: Conflict Resolution and Foreign Policy in Multi-Ethnic States,* ed. M. Shatzmiller. Montreal: McGill–Queen's University.

Vucinich, W. S. and T. A. Emmet (eds.)
1991 *Kosovo, Legacy of a Medieval Battle.* Minneapolis, MN: University of Minnesota.

Wallace, A. F. C.
1966   *Religion, an Anthropological View.* New York: Random House.

Waters, F.
1977 [1963] *Book of the Hopi.* New York: Penguin.

Weber. D. J.
1992   *The Spanish Frontier in North America.* New Haven, CT: Yale University.

Weber, M.
1947   *The Theory of Social and Economic Organization.* New York: Free.
1958   *The Protestant Ethic and the Spirit of Capitalism.* New York: Scribner.

Webster, D.
1993   The Study of Maya Warfare: What it Tells Us About the Maya and About Maya Archaeology. Pp. 415–44 in *Lowland Maya Civilization in the Eighth Century A.D*, eds. J. A. Sabloff and J. S. Henderson. Washington, DC: Dumbarton Oaks.

Webster, G.
1969   *The Roman Imperial Army of the First and Second Centuries A.D.* London: Adam and Charles.
1993   *Boudica: The British Revolt Against Rome A.D.60.* London: Routledge.

Weinberg, G. D.
1970   Hellenistic Glass from Tel Anafa in Upper Galilee. *Journal of Glass Studies* 12: 17–27.

Weinberg, S. S.
1971   Tel Anafa, The Hellenistic Town. *IEJ* 21: 86–109.

Weiss, Z.
1996a   The Jews and the Games in Roman Caesarea. Pp. 443–53 in *Caesarea Maritima, Retrospect after Two Millennia,* eds. A. Raban and K. G. Holum. Leiden: Brill.
1996b   Hellenistic Influences on Jewish Burial Customs in the Galilee during the Mishnaic and Talmudic Period. *EI* 25: 356–64 (Hebrew).
1998   Greco-Roman Influences on the Art and Architecture of the Jewish City in Roman Palestine. Pp. 219–46 in *Religious and Ethnic Communities in Later Roman Palestine*, ed. H. Lapin. Bethesda, MD: University of Maryland.

Weksler-Bdolah, S., A. Onn and Y. Rapuano
2003   Identifying the Hasmonean Village of Modi'in. *Cathedra* 109: 69–86 (Hebrew).

Wetzler, P.
1998   *Hirohito and War: Imperial Tradition and Military Decision-Making in Prewar Japan.* Honolulu, HI: University of Hawaii.

White, L.
1959   *The Evolution of Culture: Civilization to the Fall of Rome.* New York: McGraw-Hill.

Wicke, C. R.
1971   *Olmec: An Early Art Style of Precolumbian Mexico.* Tucson, AZ: University of Arizona.

Williams, F. E.
1978   *The Vailala Madness and the Destruction of Native Ceremonies in the Gulf Division.* New York: AMS.

Williams, M. H.
1995   Palestinian Jewish Personal Names in Acts. Pp. 79–113 in *The Book of Acts in its First Century Setting,* Vol. 4, ed. R. Bauckham. Carlisle: Paternoster.

Witt, R. E.
1971   *Isis in the Graeco-Roman World.* London: Thames and Hudson.

REFERENCES

Wolf, E. R.
1966   *Peasants.* Englewood Cliffs, NJ: Prentice Hall.

Wolff, S.
1996   A Second Temple Period Tomb on the Shu'afaat Ridge, North Jerusalem. *'Atiqot* 29: 23–28.

Woolf, G.
1998   *Becoming Roman: The Origins of Provincial Civilization in Gaul.* Cambridge: Cambridge University.

Worsley, P.
1968   *The Trumpet Shall Sound: A Study in 'Cargo' Cults in Melanesia.* 2nd edition. New York: Schocken.

Wright, B. G.
1997   Jewish Ritual Baths – Interpreting the Digs and the Texts: Some Issues in the Social History of Second Temple Judaism. Pp. 190–214 in *The Archaeology of Israel: Constructing the Past, Interpreting the Present,* eds. N. A. Silberman and D. B. Small. Journal for the Study of the Old Testament, Supplement Series 237. Sheffield: Sheffield Academic.

Wuthnow, R. and M. P. Lawson
1994   Sources of Christian Fundamentalism in the United States. Pp. 18–56 in *Accounting for Fundamentalism: The Dynamic Character of Movements,* eds. M. E. Marty and R. S. Appleby. Chicago: University of Chicago.

Yadin, Y.
1963   *The Finds from the Bar Kochba Period at the Cave of Letters.* Jerusalem: Israel Exploration Society.
1966   *Masada: Herod's Fortress and the Zealots' Last Stand.* New York: Random House.

Yahya, A. H.
2005   Archaeology and Nationalism in the Holy Land. Pp. 66–77 in *Archaeologies of the Middle East: Critical Perspectives,* eds. S. Pollock and R. Bernbeck. Oxford: Blackwell.

Yavetz, Z.
1993   Judeophobia in Classical Antiquity: A Different Approach. *JJS* 44: 1–22.

Yekutieli, Y, Y. Ben Yishay, T. Harpak, and S. Talis
1998   Ben Shemen (East: A). *HA* 108: 86 (Hebrew).
2001   *Salvage Excavations at Site 77 on the Course of the Cross Israel Highway.* Unpublished summary in preparation for final report, Dept. of Bible and Ancient Near East. Beer Sheva: Ben Gurion University (Hebrew).

Yekutieli, Y, and M. Gabai
1995   Survey of Bedouin Structures in the Nothern Negev in the 1940's – A Test Study of the Archaeology of Nomads (First Report). *Archaeologya* 4: 43–57.

Zaharoni, I.
1982   A Survey Along the Wall from the Great Revolt. *Qardom* 20: 79–80 (Hebrew).

Zanker, P.
1988   *The Power of Images in the Age of Augustus.* Ann Arbor, MI: University of Michigan.

Zelinger, Y.
2004   Ben Shemen Junction. *Excavations and Surveys in Israel.* Http://www.hadashot-esi.org.il/.

Zertal, A.
1981   The Roman Siege System at Khirbet el-Hammam (Narbata) in Samaria. *Qadmoniot* 3–4 (55–56): 112–18 (Hebrew).
1984   Khirbet el-Hammam, 1982. *IEJ* 34: 52.
1993   The Mount Manasseh (Northern Samaria Hills) Survey. *NEAEHL* 1993: 1311–12.

Zevit, Z.
2001 *The Religions of Ancient Israel: A Synthesis of Parallactic Approaches.* London: Continuum.

Zias, J.
1992 Human Skeletal Remains form the 'Caiaphas' Tomb. *'Atiqot* 21: 79–80.
1998 Questioning Masada: Whose Bones? *BAR* 24.4: 40–45, 64–66.

Zias, J., A. Segal, and I. Carmi
1994 The Human Skeletal Remains from the Northern Cave at Masada – A Second Look. Pp. 366–67 in *Masada IV: The Yigael Yadin Excavations 1963–1965, Final Report*, eds. J. Aviram, G. Foerster and E. Netzer. Jerusalem: Hebrew University.

Zissu, B.
2001 *Rural Settlement in the Judean Hills and Foothills from the Late Second Temple Period to the Bar Kochba Revolt.* Unpublished Ph.D. dissertation. The Hebrew University, Jerusalem (Hebrew with English abstract).

Zissu, B. and H. Eshel
2001 The Geographic Distribution of the Bar-Kokhba Coins. Pp. 17–40 in *New Studies on the Bar Kochba Revolt*, eds. H. Eshel and B. Zissu. Proceedings of the 21st Annual Conference of the Martin (Szusz) Department of the Land of Israel Studies, March 13th 2001. Ramat Gan: Bar-Ilan University (Hebrew).

Zissu, B. and A. Ganor
2001 Horbat 'Etri. *ESI* 113: 101–4.
2002 Horbat 'Etri – A Jewish Village from the Second Temple Period in the Shephelah of Judea. *Qadmoniot* 123: 18–27 (Hebrew).
2003 New Finds from the Period of the Bar-Kokhba Revolt in the Southern Shephelah of Judaea. *Judea and Samaria Research Studies* 12: 139–56 (Hebrew).

Zissu, B., S. Gibson, and J. Tavor
2000 Jerusalem, Ben Hinnom Valley. *ESI* 111: 70–72.

Zissu, B. and A. Re'em
2002 Jerusalem, Mount Scopus (B). *ESI* 114: 74–75.

Index

A

Aaron (biblical) 107
Abdul Hamid II (Sultan) 55
Abdullah ibn Sayed Mohammad el Taaisha (Caliph) 55–57
Abyssinia, Abyssinian 55
Adam 136
Adiabene 84, 159
Acre (Ptolemais) 115, 117
Afterlife 10, 128, 142
Akhenathen 12
Albinus (Roman governor) 86–87, 109, 158
Alexander (Hasmonean prince) 106
Alexander Jannaeus (King) 71, 105, 162
Alexander of Macedon 71
Alexandria, Alexandrians 115, 163
Alexius I Comnenus 29
Al-Zawahiri, Ayman 35–36
Ambibulus 158
America, American 2, 10, 14–15, 20, 22, 31, 37–38, 47, 49, 58, 61, 142, 152, 157, 163
Amphitheater 92, 159
Anafa, Tel 131
Ananus 112, 114
Anatolia (Asia Minor) 29–30, 43, 156
Anglesey (Wales) 102
Anglican 53
Antigonus, Matthatias 101, 106, 124, 162
Antiochus IV Epiphanes 71, 112, 114, 121
Apion 92, 115
Apocalypse, apocalyptic 30, 41, 43–45, 47–49, 51–53, 57, 59, 61, 93, 95, 118, 143
Apocrypha 137
Aqiba (rabbi) 118
Arab, Arabs, Arabia 31, 33, 35, 90–91, 154
Aramean, Arameans 119, 153
'Araq el-Amir 157
Arch of Titus 73
Archelaus 73, 113
Armenia 97, 99, 102
'Aroer 77
Ashdod 158
Askalon 117
Assassins. *See* Isma'ili
Assyrian, Assyrians 41, 110, 119, 159
Athenian 117, 155
Athronges 84
Atta, Mohammed 37
Augustus 66, 87, 92, 98, 115, 160

B

Babylon, Babylonian 13, 24, 27, 71, 87, 91, 101, 111, 118–20, 159
Bandits, Banditry 29, 60, 84–85, 87, 94–95, 97–98, 149
Bar Kochba Revolt 81, 93, 98, 118–20, 124–25, 133, 142, 155, 157, 161, 165
Bassus, Lucillius 73
Bathhouses 92
Ben Gurion, David 163
Ben Shemen 135
Berber, Berbers 12, 111
Berg, David Brandt 47–48
Beth Shean (Scythopolis) 92, 106, 117, 164
Beth She'arim 117, 137, 160
Bethany 164
Bethsaida 130
Bet Zeneta 129
Bhagavad-Gita 109
Bible. *See* Old Testament; New Testament.
Bin Laden, Osama 35–38, 153–54
Boudicca 87, 98, 156
Branch Davidians 45
Britain (Roman) 72, 87, 98, 102, 115, 131, 156
Britain, British 2, 12, 34, 53–60, 67, 102, 117, 142, 144–45, 153, 156–57
Buber, Martin 92, 148–49
Burial caves 126–27, 131, 137, 156, 160, 163
Byzantium, Byzantines 2, 29, 91–92, 117, 130, 135, 137, 159, 161–62.

C

Caesar, Julius 66, 102–3, 155, 160
Caesarea 73, 90–92, 113, 115, 117, 164
Caesarea Philippi (Paneas) 115
Caesars (Roman emperors) 43, 68, 83, 110, 114–15, 118, 120, 144, 155
Caiaphas 128, 163
Caligula 73, 101, 114–15
Camus, Albert 26
Canaan, Canaanites 66, 121, 138
Cape Colony 52
Capernaum 130
Cargo Cults 22, 59, 61–62, 145, 154
Cassius Dio 99, 111, 118, 160–61.
Catholics, Catholicism 2, 15–16, 22–23, 29–30, 42, 50–51, 152, 154
Cattle Killing (cult) 52–54, 58–61, 142, 154
Celtic, Celts 23, 103, 155

Charisma, charismatic figures 11, 14, 29, 31, 45–46, 48, 51, 60, 86, 94, 96, 105, 108–9, 141, 143, 147–49.
Christianity, Christians 10–17, 20, 22–25, 27–31, 33, 36–39, 41–44, 47, 49–50, 53–56, 58, 60, 62–65, 70, 102–3, 112, 141–42, 144–45, 148–49, 152–53, 155–56, 160–61, 163.
Churchill, Winston S. 23, 56, 58, 152, 160
Cicero 91–92
Civilis, Julius 97
Classicus, Julius 97
Claudius 115
Clodius Macer 161
Cognitive dissonance 57–58
Coinage, coins 57, 76, 93, 95–96, 98, 106, 111, 113, 116–19, 123–26, 129, 137, 139, 157–62, 165
"Coins of Danger" 162
Colchester (Camulodunum) 98
Colonial, colonialism
  Belgian 56
  British 53
  French 56
  Spanish 15–16, 51, 61, 151
Constantine 12–14
Cook Islands 59
Coponius 73, 158
Corruption 17, 30, 54, 86, 112, 142, 158
Crop failure 15, 52, 142
Crucifixion 30, 42–43, 60, 87, 153
Crusades, Crusaders 1, 22, 28–31, 35, 38–39, 47, 61, 70, 142, 159
Cumanus 73, 86, 89, 113, 158
Cyprus 118
Cyrene 109, 118, 122

D

Dacia, Dacians 97
David (King) 13, 95, 110, 149
Davidic dynasty 13, 120
Dead Sea 73–74, 118
Dead Sea Scrolls 64
Demeter 162
Destruction layers 71, 106, 133, 157
Deuteronomy 13, 110, 116, 119, 153, 162
Diaspora 112, 138, 149
Disease 15, 29, 52–54, 135, 142, 154, 158
Divine Assistance 8, 51, 60, 96, 106, 110, 138, 142, 144
Divitiacus 102
Domitian 74, 97–99
Domitius Marsus 101
Dor (Dora) 115, 126
Dortus 84
Drought 15, 28, 53–54, 74, 86, 142, 151
Druids, Druidism 23, 97, 102–3

Dumnorix 102

E

Eagle Standard 75, 97
Economy 4–5, 19, 29, 35, 37, 46, 52, 56, 61–62, 70–73, 83–86, 88, 90, 93–94, 96, 100, 105–6, 114, 120–22, 125–26, 128, 133, 140, 142–45, 158
Egypt, Egyptians 12–14, 18, 24, 28, 33, 43, 54–57, 66, 71, 91–92, 101, 109, 111, 115, 118–19, 122, 125, 142, 151, 153, 163
'Ein Feshkha 78
'Ein Gedi 127
Eleazar (Hasmonean) 137
Eleazar ben Dineus 84, 91
Eleazar ben Simon 93, 95
Eleazar ben Yair 114, 159, 161
Elijah 107
Emperor Cult 114–15
England, English. *See* Britain, British.
Environment, environmental 3–4, 7, 16, 24, 27, 31, 44, 48–49, 53, 57, 84–85, 88, 90, 94, 142–45
Eritrea 56
Eschatology 30, 57, 110
Estates 12, 83–84, 86, 95, 158, 164
Ethnic markers, 123 135
Europe, European 11, 15, 17, 20, 28–31, 39, 47, 53, 55–56, 60–62, 65, 96, 99, 101, 103, 131, 142, 144, 151, 154, 157
Eusebius 160

F

Fadus 109, 158
Farmers 15, 23, 61, 84, 144
Felix 86, 109, 158
Festivals 9, 14, 65, 106, 113, 125, 160
Festus 73, 109, 158
Feudal system 12, 30–31, 61, 142
Figurines 65, 116, 129, 162, 164
Fiji Islands 60
First Commandment 116
First Jewish Revolt 5, 63, 68, 70, 73, 76–81, 83, 92–93, 96, 99, 106–7, 110–11, 113, 117–18, 120, 124–26, 130, 132–33, 138, 140, 142–43, 155, 157–58, 165
Fiscus Iudaicus 120
Floods 24, 28
Florus, Gessius 72–73, 87, 158
Fortifications 55, 71–72, 74–78, 80, 83, 93, 98, 157, 159
Frescoes 116, 127, 133–34, 162–63
Funerary contexts 123, 126, 128, 139, 145, 150, 162–63

G

Gabinius 89, 112
Gadara 164

INDEX

Gager, John 106
Galilee 16, 72–73, 76–77, 80, 84, 93–95, 105–6, 113, 117, 128–30, 133–35, 157–58, 161–62, 164
Galilean Coarse Ware 128–29
Gallus, Cestius 72, 75, 77, 87, 95, 110, 122, 144
Gallus Revolt 161
Gamla 75–77, 79–81, 117, 125–26, 129–32, 134, 162, 164, 166
Gaul (Gallia) 86–87, 97, 102, 108, 115, 155
Germany (modern) 38, 153, 156
Germany (Roman) 28, 72, 87, 97–98, 157
Ghost Dance 22, 61, 145
Gischala 77, 93, 164
Gladstone, William 55
Golan Heights 80, 105–6, 164
Gordon, Charles George 55–56
Gratus 158
Greece, Greeks 24–25, 27, 43, 75, 89, 91–92, 108–9, 116, 127–28, 157, 159, 161–62
Greenland (Norse settlement) 27

H

Hadrian 98, 118, 155
Hagee, John 20
Hamas 32–34, 36, 38, 153
Hasmoneans 71–72, 75–76, 89, 101, 105–7, 110, 112, 121, 124–25, 129, 135, 137–38, 140, 143, 157, 159–62, 164–66
Hebrew Bible 3, 12, 19, 23, 91, 109, 149, 155, 163
Hebron 77
Hellenism, Hellenistic 41, 71, 106, 116, 121, 124, 128–29, 131, 157, 161
Helleno-Roman cities 72–74, 84, 86, 88–93, 106, 110, 113, 115–17, 120–21, 128–29, 131–34, 139, 142, 157
Herod I 71–73, 92, 100–101, 105, 111, 113, 115–16, 134–35, 137, 158–59
Herod Agrippa I 89, 100–101, 162
Herod Agrippa II 96–99, 105, 108, 158–59, 162
Herod Antipas 134
Herodium 73, 134, 164, 166
Hezbollah 33, 38
Hezekiah 96, 110, 122, 143, 159
Hicks, William 55
High Priest, High Priesthood 1, 13, 105, 112–14, 125, 158, 162–63
Hijra 55, 154
Hizma 164
Holy Sepulcher 8, 28–30, 42, 59
Horvat 'Ethri 77, 130, 166

I

Iconoclasm 7, 13–14, 19–20, 62, 145
Idolatry 10, 19, 25–27, 42, 89, 119
Idumeans 106, 114
Iliad 27, 109
Imagery art 116–17, 133–35, 157
Imperium Galliarum 97
Insurgency 75, 85, 88, 94, 97, 103, 118, 121
Islam, Muslims 5, 14–15, 17, 20, 22–23, 28–29, 31–39, 50, 54–57, 59, 61–63, 65, 70, 142, 144–45, 148–49, 151, 153–54
Islamic fundamentalism 5, 20, 37, 145
Islamic Jihad 33
Isma'ili (sect) 14, 35, 45
Israel (biblical) 3, 12–14, 19, 23, 26–27, 41, 65, 106–8, 110, 112, 116, 124, 136, 138, 143, 153, 160, 162–63
Israel (state) 17, 20, 32–34, 38, 65, 70, 76, 133, 135, 153, 156, 163, 165
Italy, Italian 56, 158
Itureans 106

J

Jaffa 34, 77, 129–30, 133, 164
Jehovah's Witnesses 10–11, 18, 151
Jephthah 149
Jeremiah 25, 149
Jericho 127, 131, 139, 141, 148–49, 166
Jerusalem 1, 8, 13, 20, 25, 28, 30–32, 35, 41–42, 59, 68, 70–73, 75–81, 86–87, 89, 91–93, 95–96, 101, 106, 109–12, 114–20, 124–28, 131, 133–34, 142, 151–52, 157–65
Jesus 16, 23–25, 30, 41–43, 47, 49–50, 53–54, 59–60, 62, 90, 109, 112–13, 136, 150, 152, 158, 163
Jewish Quarter 81, 158, 163
Jewish, Jews 5, 16–17, 20, 23, 25, 29–30, 32–33, 39, 41–43, 50, 55, 62–64, 68, 70–75, 78–93, 99–166
Jihad 35–36, 39, 55
John (apostle) 136
John (Hasmonean) 137, 165
John Hyrcanus I 105, 159
John Hyrcanus II 112, 125
John of Gischala 93–96, 111, 159
Jonathan (Hasmonean) 137
Jonathan the Sicarius 109
Jones, James Warren ("Jim"), Jonestown 46, 145
Jordan (Kingdom) 70, 76, 133, 157
Jordan River 77, 109
Jordan Valley 162
Josephus 64, 68, 70, 72, 75–77, 80–81, 83–87, 89, 91–96, 99, 101–2, 105, 107–8, 110, 112–15, 118–19, 122, 124, 134–35, 137, 155, 157, 160–62, 164–65
Joshua bin Nun 109, 122, 137–38, 143
Joshua ben Gamala 114
Josiah 13–14
Judah (biblical kingdom) 13, 116, 118, 124, 151
Judah (rabbi) 91, 159
Judaism 31, 43, 56, 62, 64, 84, 91–92, 113, 117, 119, 122, 136, 138–40, 152

INDEX

Judas Aristobulus I 105
Judas Aristobulus II 106
Judas Maccabeus 105, 110, 122, 137
Judas the Galilean 73, 113
Judea 5, 62, 68–92, 96, 98–142, 147–48, 152, 157, 159–61, 163–65.
Judean desert 119, 131
Judges (biblical) 13, 26, 108, 143
Julian 12, 161

K

Kalandia 158, 164
Kana 132
Kenedeus 159
Khartoum 55
Khirbet Umm el-'Amdan 166
Kiriat Sefer 166
Kitchener, Horatio Herbert 56
Knights Templar 31
Koran 32, 35–36, 39, 47, 50, 56, 148, 151, 154–55, 163
Kosovo 17, 66

L

Latin 97, 127
Liberation Tigers of Tamil Eelam (LTTE) 38
Liberty, liberation 17, 42, 61, 81–82, 84–85, 95–96, 108, 113–14, 117, 125–26, 137, 142, 152
Little Bighorn 157
Lod (Lydda) 80–81, 133, 164
London 33, 98, 156

M

Maccabees, Maccabean 89, 96, 106–8, 110
Machaerus 73–74, 77–78, 81, 122
Mahdi, Mahdi Revolt 5, 52, 54–57, 59, 61, 70, 142, 144–45, 154
Mahmud II 56
Maresha (Marissa) 106, 159, 164
Mariccus 97
Maronites (Lebanon) 17
Marullus 73
Mary 16
Masada 73, 77–79, 81, 95, 114, 118, 122, 131–32, 156, 159, 161, 164, 166
Matthatias 107, 137
Matthias ben Margalothus 116
Mecca 154
Melanesia 22
Menachem ben Yair 159
Meroth 77
Messiah, Messianic 29, 43, 52, 60, 95, 105, 109, 118, 120, 142–45, 148–49, 153
Mesopotamia 18, 84, 101, 159, 161

Mhlakaza (Wilhelm Goliath) 52-53
Millennium, Millenarianism 4–5, 14, 22, 30–31, 40–54, 56–62, 64, 84, 101, 145, 149–50, 152–53, 156
Millerite movement 58, 145
Milošević, Slobodan 17
Mission, missionaries 4, 15–16, 51, 53–54, 62
Miriam (Hasmonean) 137, 165
Mithras 92
Mlanjeni 53
Modi'in 71, 80
Mohammed (Prophet) 47, 54–57, 154
Mohammed Ali 56
Mohammed Tawfiq (Khedive) 55
Monobazus 159
Montanist movement 156
Mosaics 116–17, 133–34, 139, 162
Moses 96, 106–7, 109, 136–37, 149–50
Mt Arbel 77
Mt Gedir 55
Mt Gerizim 106
Mt Sinai 3
Mt Scopus 164
Mt Tabor 76–77
Mythology, myths 1, 17, 23, 55, 105–6, 117, 150

N

Narbata (Khirbet el-Hamam) 77–78, 81, 164
Naram-Sin 12
Ndungumoi 60
Negev desert 163
Nero 72, 93, 96–99, 102, 161
New England 102
New Testament 113, 132, 137, 158, 163
Nicanor 128, 163
Nile 24, 55, 154
Nomad, nomadic 23, 65, 99, 151
Nongqawuze 52–54, 58, 60, 145
North Africa 12, 96, 98, 109, 158
Nxele 53, 60

O

Oglala Sioux 61
Oea 99
Oil lamps 125, 130, 135, 139, 161–62
Old Testament 12, 19, 26, 91
Oil Press 79, 135
Omdurman 55–58
Ossuaries 127–28, 133, 137, 162–63

P

Pacorus 101
Pagans, Paganism 13, 26, 65, 89, 109, 112, 114, 116–17, 125, 129, 140, 154–55, 157, 163

INDEX

Palo Alto 157
Papua New Guinea 7, 28, 49, 62
Parthia, Parthians 75, 96–97, 99–102
Passover 13, 93, 113, 125, 160
Paul (apostle) 25, 43, 47, 62, 152
Paulinus, Suetonius 102
Pax Deorum 114
Peasants 18, 24, 29, 31, 60, 65, 84, 86, 120, 144, 153
Pella 106, 164
People's Crusade 22, 28–31, 38–39, 61, 70, 142
Persia, Persian 71, 92, 114, 117, 121, 124–25, 153, 159–61.
Peter (apostle) 43, 136
Peter the Hermit 29
Petronius 101, 115
Pharisees 25, 43, 158
Philadelphia (Transjordan) 164
Phineas (biblical priest) 106–8
Philo of Alexandria 73, 122
Phoenician 124, 129, 132, 161, 164
Pilate, Pontius 73, 86, 116, 158
Pilgrimages, Pilgrims 1, 8, 30, 73, 84, 93–94, 111–13, 135, 164
Plagues 26, 79, 107, 142, 163
Plains Indians 61, 145
Pliny the Elder 91
Pliny the Younger 43
Pompey 71, 112–13, 117, 157
Popé 50
Propaganda 17, 32, 64, 73, 115, 123
Prophets, prophecy 4, 19, 24–26, 30, 32, 41–42, 45–48, 50, 52–61, 72, 93–94, 97, 105, 107–9, 112, 136, 145, 148, 153–54, 159
Ptolemaic kingdom, Ptolemids 71, 114, 160
Ptolemais (Acre) 115, 117
Pueblos, Pueblo Revolt 15–16, 22, 50–51, 61, 70, 142, 144, 151–52, 154

Q

Qawarat Beni Hassan 158
Qeren Naftali 135, 164
Quarries 127, 133, 164
Qumran 78, 162

R

Rajneesh, Bhagwan Shree 45, 48
Ramat HaNadiv 131, 158, 164
Red Sea 41
Regional abandonment 80
Religion 1–3, 5–7, 9–13, 15–16, 18–19, 22–23, 25, 27, 32, 35–36, 38–39, 41–43, 50, 56–57, 61, 64–65, 71, 87, 91–92, 102–3, 114, 117–18, 120, 123, 131, 138, 140–41, 144, 150–52, 154, 160, 166

Resurrection 22, 41, 53
Rio Grande 15–16, 50
Ritual baths 129, 135–36, 138–39, 147, 158, 164–65
Roman Empire 12, 75, 97, 99, 111, 130, 151
Roman legions
    Fifth 97, 157
    Ninth 161
    Tenth 157
    Twelfth 72, 157
    Fifteenth 157
    Seventeenth 87
    Eighteenth 87
    Nineteenth 87
    Twenty-Second 118, 161
Romanization 102–3, 132, 138
Rome 5, 63, 66, 68, 70–75, 82–84, 86–87, 91–93, 95–97, 99–103, 105–11, 113–16, 118, 120–22, 124–25, 133–34, 138–41, 147–49, 152, 155, 157, 161
Rufus 158

S

Sabbath 71, 92
Saladin 159
Samaria 71, 92, 106, 131, 161
Samaritans 73, 84, 90, 106, 131, 159, 161
Sarcophagi 117, 127–28, 162
Sardinia 87
Sarhili 53
Sartaba (Alexandrion) 162
Saturn 60
Saudi Arabia 33, 38, 154
Scotland, Scots 98, 111
Scythopolis 92, 106, 117, 164. See also Beth Shean
Sebastia 115, 117
Second Coming 41, 50, 153
Second Commandment 116, 124, 128, 134
Selame 77
Seleucid, Seleucids 71, 89, 105, 107, 110, 114, 121, 157–58, 160, 162
Seljuk, Seljuks 29, 144
Sennacherib 41, 109
Sepphoris 83, 92–93, 116, 161
Serb, Serbia 17
Seychelles Islands 2
Shari'a (Islamic Law) 31–32, 57
Shlomzion (Salome) 105, 137, 165
Shekel
    Jerusalem 126, 162
    Tyrian 125–26
Shi'a 38, 56
Sicarii 64, 95, 118, 159, 161
Silva, Flavius 73
Simon (Hasmonean)

INDEX

Simon bar Giora 86, 93–96, 114
Simon bar Yochai 91
Simon ben Cathalas 114
Simon Ben Kosiba (Bar Kochba) 93, 118–20, 162
Simon "The Temple Builder" 128, 163
Simon "The Zealot" (disciple) 42
Sin 26, 28, 40, 109, 148–49
Soft limestone vessels 127, 129, 132–33, 138–39, 147
Solomon 19, 66, 71, 162
South Africa 11, 18, 22, 52, 61, 157
Spain 15, 61, 87, 98, 144, 158
Sri Lanka 33, 38
St Albans (Verulamium) 98
Stephen (martyr) 112
Strabo 92, 162
Sudan, Sudanese 2, 5, 52, 54–58, 61, 142, 144, 154
Suetonius 87, 155
Suicide bombing. See Terror, terrorism.
Sunni 38, 56
Symbolism 2, 7, 9, 11, 14, 17, 19–20, 25, 48, 54–55, 65, 72, 79, 102–3, 107, 111–12, 116, 119, 122–26, 128, 130–31, 136–38, 150, 156, 161–62
Symbolism on Jewish coins
    Amphora 125
    Anchor 124, 162
    Candelabra 124
    Cornucopia 124–25, 162
    Four Species 125
    Libations Cup 125
    Palm 117, 125
    Pomegranate 124–25, 162
    Rosette 117, 127, 131
    Vine 125, 162
Synagogues 79, 115, 117, 130, 135, 138–39, 162, 166
Syncretism 92, 116
Syria, Syrians 71, 73, 87, 89, 93, 101, 108, 115, 161

T

Tabernacles 125, 160
Taboos 7, 25, 47, 61, 84, 114, 117, 134–35, 141
Tacitus 28, 86–87, 91–92, 102–3, 117, 160
Tambaran 7, 62
Taxation, taxes 15, 19, 22, 53, 57, 71–72, 80, 83–87, 90–91, 94, 96, 100, 120, 157–58, 160
Temple, temples 12, 18–19, 22, 27, 32, 65, 68, 71, 74, 89, 115, 116, 120
Temple of Jerusalem 13, 25, 32, 68, 72–73, 79, 86–87, 93, 95, 107, 109, 111–13, 115–20, 122, 124–25, 128, 131–32, 135–38, 142, 152, 159, 161, 163–65
Temple of Solomon 65, 71, 162
Terror, terrorism 5, 22, 31–39, 151–52
Teutoburg Forest 87, 157
Theater 89, 92, 159

"The Egyptian" (Jewish rebel) 109
Theudas 109
Tiberias 83, 92, 101, 116, 134, 159
Tiberius (emperoro 116
Tiberius Alexander 158
Tiridates, King of Armenia 102
Titus 68, 72–74, 93, 95–96, 99, 105, 111, 114, 157, 160
Tobias, Tobiads 157
Trade, traders 9, 71, 79, 93, 98, 134
Trajan (emperor) 97, 118
Transjordan 72, 74, 77, 89, 105–6
Tuka Revival 60
Tutor, Julius 97

U

Underground hiding systems 133
United States 12, 22, 28, 45, 50, 58, 145
Upper City (Jerusalem) 79, 81, 134, 158, 163
Urban II 28–30, 152

V

Vailala Madness 62
Varus, Quinctilius 73, 87
Vespasian 68, 72, 74, 77, 91, 95, 97, 99, 111, 157, 159
Victoria, Queen 55
Victorian, Victorians 2, 54, 67, 103, 156
Vindex, Julius 97, 161
Vitellius 116

W

Warfare 57, 62–63, 72, 70–81, 93, 103, 157–58
Western Wall 32, 79, 152
Witchcraft 4, 53
World War I 157
World War II 14, 33

X

Xhosa 52–54, 58, 60–61, 70, 144–45
Xiphilinus 161

Y

Yodfat (Jotapata) 72, 76–79, 81, 113, 129–31, 157, 162, 164

Z

Zealotry, zealots 1, 3, 5, 14–15, 17, 28, 30–31, 35–36, 44, 95, 125, 156
Zealots (Jewish rebel movement) 64, 93, 95, 106–7, 144–45
Zenobia 161
Zodiac 117
Zulu 157